D0148880

# Colonial and Revolutionary America

## TEXT AND DOCUMENTS

Alan Gallay

*The Ohio State University*

**Prentice Hall**

Boston   Columbus   Indianapolis   New York   San Francisco   Upper Saddle River   Amsterdam
Cape Town   Dubai   London   Madrid   Milan   Munich   Paris   Montreal   Toronto   Delhi
Mexico City   São Paulo   Sydney   Hong Kong   Seoul   Singapore   Taipei   Tokyo

Editorial Director: Craig Campanella
Publisher: Charlyce Jones Owen
Editorial Assistant: Maureen Diana
Director of Marketing: Brandy Dawson
Senior Marketing Manager: Maureen Prado Roberts
Production Manager: Fran Russello
Art Director: Jayne Conte
Cover Designer: Suzanne Behnke
Cover Art: "Painting of the Pilgrim Signing of the Mayflower Compact by Jean Leon Gerome Ferris";
The Bettman Collection/Corbis NY
Full-Service Project Management: Chitra Ganesan/PreMediaGlobal

Text Font: Minion

Credits and acknowledgments borrowed from other sources and reproduced, with permission, in this textbook appear on appropriate page within text.

Copyright © 2011 Pearson Education, Inc., publishing as Prentice Hall, One Lake Street, Upper Saddle River, NJ, 07458. All rights reserved. Manufactured in the United States of America. This publication is protected by Copyright, and permission should be obtained from the publisher prior to any prohibited reproduction, storage in a retrieval system, or transmission in any form or by any means, electronic, mechanical, photocopying, recording, or likewise. To obtain permission(s) to use material from this work, please submit a written request to Pearson Education, Inc., Permissions Department, Prentice Hall, One Lake Street, Upper Saddle River, NJ, 07458.

Many of the designations by manufacturers and seller to distinguish their products are claimed as trademarks. Where those designations appear in this book, and the publisher was aware of a trademark claim, the designations have been printed in initial caps or all caps.

**Library of Congress Cataloging-in-Publication Data**

Gallay, Alan.
    Colonial and Revolutionary America : text and documents / Alan Gallay.
        p. cm.
    Includes index.
    ISBN-13: 978-0-205-80969-1
    ISBN-10: 0-205-80969-3
    1. United States—History—Colonial period, ca. 1600–1775—Textbooks.   2. United States—History—Revolution, 1775–1783—Textbooks.   I. Title.
    E188.G258   2011
    973.2—dc22                                                                              2010038320

**Prentice Hall**
is an imprint of

www.pearsonhighered.com

9 10 V036 18 17 16 15

ISBN 10:      0-205-80969-3
ISBN 13: 978-0-205-80969-1

*For my friend and colleague, Leonard Helfgott*

# CONTENTS

# ABOUT THE AUTHOR

Alan Gallay holds the Warner R. Woodring Chair in Atlantic World and Early American History at The Ohio State University, where he is director of The Center for Historical Research. His books include the Bancroft Prize winning, *The Indian Slave Trade: The Rise of the English Empire in the American South, 1670–1717*, and *The Formation of a Planter Elite: Jonathan Bryan and the Southern Colonial Frontier, Voices of the Old South: Eyewitness Accounts, 1528–1861, Indian Slavery in Colonial America*, and *The Colonial Wars of North America, 1512–1763: An Encyclopedia*.

# PREFACE

The study of colonial and revolutionary America has been one of the richest areas of historical study in world history. The diversity of the subject and its importance for providing the foundation for the history of the United States have attracted generations of talented scholars, many of whom have not only revealed the nature of the key themes that shaped the American experience, but also constructed methodologies and questions that can be applied to the study of other places and times.

In the early 20th century, the historiography of early America was driven by political, institutional, and imperial questions. Much of this work, along with the class analysis that preoccupied the Progressive historians, attempted to explain how the colonial period ended with the first modern revolution against a colonial power. Historians studied colonial charters and constructed constitutional histories, the relationship between Britain and its colonies, or, alternatively, the class and self-interests that rendered apart imperial ties. Another strand of historiography also developed that focused on the religious lives of Puritans in New England, and how their particular brand of Protestantism shaped later American conceptions of being God's chosen people with a mission to set an example for the rest of the world.

By the 1960s, and particularly in the 1970s, historians began constructing cultural and social histories with less focus on the Revolution as the product of the colonial era and more upon an array of themes that had enormous impact on the lives of early American peoples, and which continued to have impact through the centuries regardless of the important political events that ordinarily served as historical markers dividing one era from another. Community formation, concepts of citizenship, and family dynamics have been studied in great depth alongside the evolution of concepts of race and racism, the distinctive nature of diverse geographic areas, the profound alterations of the environment, and the intensity of cultural interactions and exchange among an array of American Indian, African, and European peoples. Although much continued to be written about New England, with great success in reconstructing town life that connected micro to macro history, much of the historiography shifted to the history of other geographic areas, especially to the Chesapeake colonies, Pennsylvania, and New York, and then to the Lower South, the frontier, and the Spanish and French colonies. A slew of studies on various American Indian communities, and on interactions between Indians and Europeans, measured the impact of colonialism on indigenous peoples, while also revealing how cross-cultural interactions played a significant role in transforming European settlers into American colonials.

The historiographic trend of examining in detail understudied areas and peoples in early America has converged in the 21st century with a new trend that contextualizes American colonial life in an Atlantic, and even global, context. The basic themes that guided the development of colonial North America also affected colonized areas in South America, the Caribbean, Africa, and Asia. These processes included the migration of large numbers of people from one continent to another, the creation of new communities and societies, the expansion of global trade networks, the intercontinental exchange of goods, ideas, and technology, and the construction of empires that competed with one another while also attempting to assimilate and control the labor of indigenous peoples. In this regard, the experience of the American colonies was no longer unique, or exceptional, but part of larger historical trends that could be compared with other colonial adventures around the globe. Comparison and contextualization helps identify both the similarities and the uniqueness of each area where colonialism occurred. The historian must place his or her story into a larger interregional context with an eye pealed for parallel developments guided by similar historical forces at work elsewhere. Though I do not usually make these connections explicit in the text, my analysis of American colonial history is informed by a broad reading of colonialism in South America, the Caribbean, and Asia.

This book synthesizes much of the scholarship on colonial America, while adding my own particular take on which information and analysis best illustrates its history. It would be impossible to cover every thematic development and to do justice to every story. Not every colony is treated equally, nor could every group of native people receive its due. In broad terms, the larger thematic issues addressed here include the multifaceted migration of diverse European and African peoples, who settled in diverse environments and interacted with diverse American Indians. I have tried to explain the nature of many of the cross-cultural interactions that played a huge role in shaping early America. This involves unpacking the cultural baggage that colored peoples' perception of the world they lived in and how they tried to fit outsiders into their world. These cultural perceptions influenced the ways people made use of the environment and adapted to geopolitical factors that shaped opportunities and decisions on how to live and prosper. Early Americans, whether they were African, Indian, or European, made life decisions drawn from their own personal and group experiences, but also learned from the "new" cultures they encountered, as they negotiated "new" or altering landscapes, the seemingly endless migration of peoples from one place to the next, and the impact of global trade, diseases, and ever more complex diplomatic situations.

I have integrated the story and stories of American Indians in a variety of ways. In broad terms, I have presented American Indian history as being more than a before-and-after picture of contact with Europeans by emphasizing a larger continuum of time to display the dynamic evolutionary aspects of native cultures. On the other hand, European colonization had enormous impact on native life in just so many ways, and I have tried to identify some of the ways Indians adapted to the era's large historical forces. Both the Europeans and the Africans were likewise influenced not only by the large historical forces of the time, but also by the array of Indian cultures they encountered. Indian adoption and adaptation of European guns, textiles, and metal goods, European incorporation of Indian styles of warfare and African religious sensibilities and music, and African conversion to Christianity are just a few of the ways that the peoples of early America learned new things from one another. This process of learning and adaptation did not turn Europeans into Indians, for instance, though thousands of Europeans *did* become Indians, but evokes how the intimacy of interactions among early Americans, even under hostile circumstances, transformed the cultures of all.

Briefly, by way of example, I will introduce here one of the historical forces as an example of what this book intends to accomplish in its presentation of the history of early America: the impact of global trade. The desire of Europeans to obtain tropical and sub-tropical goods for both their own consumption and trade with Asia played a foundational role in drawing Europeans to the Americas, and to their importing of Africans and poor Europeans to labor to produce these commodities. American Indians were also employed to produce commodities as slaves and in other forms of bound labor, and also as free people who could exchange the products of their labor to obtain European commodities. The importance of geography was manifest in this process as environmental conditions dictated which commodities could be produced in a given area. Yet culture also played a role. Individuals and groups possessed traditions and preferences on not only *how* to produce commodities, but which commodities they should purchase, and the processes by which commodities should be exchanged. An entire book could be written documenting just the cultural aspects of exchange. Native and European peoples, for instance, held very different concepts of exchange and were forced to accommodate to one another. Alas, I have not explored the details of the exchange of goods, since so many other factors of cultural exchange, the market place, commodity production, and the history of Indians, Europeans, and Africans requires attention. Nonetheless, I do try to show how the exchange of goods entwined with other areas of life, such as political relations between groups, status within communities, and in shaping the quality of life for all.

There is risk in even listing the themes that have guided this book because it reifies them, and can undermine the nuances of the past and the ways that history is more than the sum of its parts. No historian can do complete justice to the past. Every detail cannot be included because we do not know every fact, nor if we did could the history ever be finished or comprehensible. And so we return to the eclectic nature of the historian's task: to reconstruct as best we can not only what we think happened, but what is important; to suggest how and why the pieces fit together. In many ways, mine has been a traditional approach. Distinguishing the history of one colonial region from another sheds light on the particular development of each, while the comparative perspective illuminates the larger historical processes at work. At various times, I refer to even larger comparative perspectives to help with contextualization, by referring in the early chapters to Spanish colonization in the Caribbean, Mexico, and South America, and later to English/British colonization in the West Indies. In points of comparison, I also contextualize distinctions among the Spanish, French, English, and other colonial projects in North America. Moreover, I have woven the religious lives of people into the fabric of the book. Religious views and institutions played an important role in shaping how people understood their world and interacted with one another. Moreover, religious concepts and institutions evolved as they were influenced by larger historical forces and the exposure of people to new religions and religious forms and ideas. Politics also played a substantial role in peoples' lives, whether on the imperial, colonial, or local level. Political concepts and institutions evolved as much for Indians as Europeans, and also involved the need for diplomacy and new forms of diplomacy as early Americans tried to secure themselves and attain advantageous trade relations with a variety of peoples.

Warfare, too, was a ubiquitous factor of early American life, with a huge impact on the course of empires, colonies, groups, and individual lives. From beginning to end, the colonial era saw intense military competition among European colonizers, among Indians, and in complex wars where Indians and Europeans allied together against other groups of Indians and Europeans. Inter-group violence often took the form of colonial wars that comprised but one component of larger imperial conflicts. This violence included massive invasions for conquests of entire colonies or peoples, slave rebellions, and a variety of forays to obtain booty, glory, and land; often the imperial component was secondary to local interests. Military activities shaped the course of early America as much as any other aspect of life; certainly military threats influenced security, trade, and prosperity and contributed immensely to how Europeans and Indians organized their societies. At the end of the colonial era, warfare precipitated the crisis between the British colonies and their mother country; a long war, the Revolution, then ended with the independence of those colonies and was immediately followed by further wars between the new United States and Indian peoples.

The book ends with an examination of the American Revolution. The Revolution was not an inevitable outcome of the colonial era, but a product of historical circumstances that most people in Britain and the colonies did not expect until the fissure between the two had already appeared. Even as it occurred, no one could foresee the shape that the post-colonial world would take, even as many welcomed the opportunity to build anew. The revolutionaries were colonists, shaped by their colonial lives, and Britain understood them as colonists. Many Euro-Americans in the rebellious colonies, often a majority during much of the course of the conflict, either wished to remain colonials or subscribed to various shades of neutrality. The Revolution ended the colonial status of the rebellious colonies, but there is no reason to think that the colonies could not have remained part of the empire for much longer under different historical circumstances. Nonetheless, the Revolution did occur. In this book, I try to explain the forces that converged to render apart the British empire, and also address what this rendering meant for various groups of people, such as American Indians and African Americans. The legacies of the Revolution were undoubtedly mixed. It unleashed a wave of violence against Indian communities, many of which had allied with the United States against Great Britain. For African Americans, the Revolution provided hope for liberty, actual liberty (sometimes by joining the British against the rebels), but also further entrenchment of the institution of slavery.

The Revolution also provided the dawning of a new day with profound consequences not just for American but for world history. The creation of a new nation by right of self-determination inspired revolutions and independence movements around the globe. (Ironically, Americans sometimes opposed these movements.) The survival and flourishing of a nation born of revolution, devoted to principles of equality, demonstrated the potential to construct a society both stable and dynamic, which could contend with perilous and unforeseen circumstances. Yet it would be a mistake to assume that American history begins with the Revolution—the colonial past provides the fabric of modern American society. Each generation re-tailors the cloth that has been passed down through the generations. From the Puritan quest to provide a beacon of light to the world, to the promise of equality in the Declaration of Independence; from the opportunities to better one's life that attracted to American shores the dispossessed, the persecuted, and the adventurous, to the belief that government should not interfere with the individual quest for self-fulfillment; from the sense of entitlement that fostered exploitation of humans and resources in the rich American environment with nary a thought to the consequences, to the resistance of people to exploitation and the demand to create a just and equitable society: in just so many ways, colonial and revolutionary America remains close and relevant to the present day.

# PART 1

The Impact of European Colonization on Early America

# 1

# The Regions and Peoples of North America

**Mexico to the Arctic**
**The Eastern Woodlands and the Mississippians**

## INTRODUCTION

Although it remains unclear when humans first reached the American continents, and some indigenous Americans posit that they have *always* lived in the Americas, most scholars believe that the forbearers of American Indians crossed the Bering Land Bridge from Siberia at least 11,000 years ago, and possibly much earlier. Estimates vary widely as to the number of people inhabiting North America before European contact. Mexico, one of the most densely populated areas of the continent, is believed to have had from 20 to 40 million people. Calculating population in the area north of Mexico is even more difficult, with estimates generally ranging from 5 to 15 million, with most recent scholars tending to a figure towards the high end of the spectrum. North America's population in the late 15th century was approximately half to four-fifths of Europe's, and about four-fifths of South and Central America combined.

Diversity characterized the peoples of North America. Hundreds of languages were spoken on the continent. Social systems varied from the highly organized, stratified, and literate societies of Mexico, to the relatively egalitarian decentralized bands of people of northern Canada. In places like Mexico and the American South, powerful groups forced their neighbors to pay tribute to them; in other, less densely populated regions, such as New England, neighboring peoples often shared natural resources in a noncompetitive way. Some North Americans built urban environments that remained continuously occupied for hundreds of years, relying upon agriculture augmented by hunting and gathering. Others followed the plenty of the seasons and moved from place to place, annually returning to rich hunting grounds or estuaries, and trading surplus to neighbors.

Abundance of natural resources has characterized and shaped North American life for thousands of years. Rich fertile lands created a plethora of wild foods, and supported both crops and animals, while massive forests provided excellent wood for housing and fuel in large areas across the continent. Indigenous peoples made excellent use of their environment, whether harvesting ocean resources in Alaska that could be exchanged for needed items from inland peoples or adapting to the relatively inhospitable conditions of the arid Southwest by building canals that brought water to villages and created farmlands. In many regions, American Indians consciously preserved the abundance: rotating crop fields so as not to overuse the land, moving from one hunting preserve to the next to prevent depletion of game, and burning portions of the forest, particularly underbrush, to attract game, restore the land, and create pathways to new areas. It is little wonder that the spiritual life of so many American Indians celebrated the sun, animals, and other features of the environment.

Whereas most Europeans shared a Judeo-Christian religious culture (though Islam was strong in Eastern Europe and paganism survived both within and without Christianity), American Indians possessed no comparable shared theology, nor unified view of human origins. Yet many American Indians possessed similar spiritual attributes: worship of the sun, belief in a variety of spirits that inhabited sacred places, sacredness of animals, and importance of performing religious rituals. Perhaps the most significant difference between the religious life of American Indians and Europeans lay in the holistic nature of the former. American Indians thoroughly integrated every aspect of life into their religious worldview. Success in warfare and hunting, the nature of social organization and polity, the past and the future, were all manifestations of the spiritual world. Europeans possessed a similar outlook in the Middle Ages—that all aspects of man's activities were subject to God's domain—but by the 16th century, Europeans were rapidly compartmentalizing life, separating the sacred from the profane, and drawing sharp distinctions between the material and ethereal. The point could be overstated, for early modern Christians also understood natural disasters, disease, and military victory or defeat as God-ordained. But Europeans increasingly turned to mathematics and science to explain the physical properties of the universe, and blamed the shortcomings of man for the failures of society; American Indians understood that all things possessed spiritual power, that the universe was governed by spirits, and that their own successes and failures were reflections of their spirituality and success and ability to fulfill ceremonial rites. The spirit of a slain deer, for instance, had to be thanked for its sacrifice to clothe and feed the hunter's family. Deceased humans had to be properly buried to insure rest for their spirits—failure to do so could lead to a natural disaster. Many American Indians built temples and had priests and shamans who mediated the spiritual world for the minions, much as priests did in the Catholic Church. American Indians' reverence for sacred places was akin to medieval Europeans' endowment of the shrines of saints with special properties. Europeans valued relics and charms as possessing special properties of luck and protection, much as American Indians did. The intense spirituality of American Indians (as with Europeans and Africans) was not incompatible with a pragmatic and practical lifestyle. Hunters, farmers, and warriors all had to master their crafts to survive and flourish. Religion provided a system of beliefs, a world view, that made the world understandable, and helped shape peoples' concepts of what was valuable.

## MEXICO TO THE ARCTIC

The diversity of peoples in North America largely stemmed from the ecological diversity of the vast continent. In Mexico and Central America, rich agricultural and mineral resources led to huge populations, and subsequent highly organized and stratified societies, such as the Maya and Aztec. In northern Mexico and the American Southwest, shortages of water led to the construction of elaborate aqueduct systems and much less densely populated areas. On the other hand, to the west and north, the Pacific Coast from California to British Columbia provided an abundance of food in temperate climates to support denser populations with little agricultural production. Directly above the Southwest, in the Great Basin, harsh climates and reliance on the buffalo for food and clothing led to small mobile societies that moved with the seasons. Much further north, Arctic peoples adjusted to the seasonal wealth and scarcity of animal populations by creating long trade networks to help fulfill their material needs. In all these areas, we witness adaptation to climate and environment, particularly in technological innovations for housing, hunting, food gathering, transportation, and warfare. Those American Indians who lived in the most inhospitable climates tended to be the ones who had little to no contact with Europeans for the longest period of time, as in the Arctic and Great Basin—the Europeans would have to adopt Indian technologies or create new ones to inhabit these areas.

### Mesoamerica

Located in Guatemala and southern Mexico, the Maya had great impact upon their neighbors to both the north and the south. The "Classic" Maya period extended from approximately the mid-3rd century A.D. to the 10th century, and included the subjection of many peoples, as well as the construction of numerous palaces, pyramids, and other buildings. The Maya displayed expert stone craftsmanship, sumptuous artistic displays and pageants, and greatly stressed their own history and sacred knowledge of texts. Renowned for their mathematical and astronomical knowledge, the Maya created a highly complex society that emphasized the importance of lineage, religion, trade, warfare, and alliance to the maintenance and expansion of their society.

The successor peoples to the Maya adapted and incorporated numerous aspects of Mayan civilization, from blood sacrifice to the sophisticated social organization of vast numbers of people. The decline of the Classic period saw the movement of the Maya and other peoples into and out of the region, and to new environments within Mesoamerica. One of the groups that rose to prominence were the Toltecs, who developed warrior cults, then, like the Maya, disbursed to different areas and extended their influence in a variety of ways, though many remained in central Mexico. Toltec power declined by the early 13th century as new peoples migrated to central Mexico. One of these groups was the Mixtecs, a society of highly developed decorative artists who worked in many media, including jade, gold, and crystal. As with many Mesoamerican peoples before them, the Mixtecs placed great importance upon their lineage and history, music, learning, and spirituality.

In the 13th century, another important group of people entered central Mexico, known as the Mexica, and later as the Aztecs. The Aztecs recorded in books detailed histories of their society and lineages, the purpose of which was to justify their right to rule and expound upon the meaning of their destiny. The Aztecs dominated much of Mexico from 1428 to 1521. At first they allied with other peoples in central Mexico, then they emerged as the dominant force, demanding tribute from their neighbors. Claiming ancestry from the Toltecs, the Aztecs emphasized their military prowess. They were less innovators of culture than appropriators, successfully adapting from their predecessors and neighbors to suit their needs. Marriage was the key institution for securing alliance with neighboring peoples, strengthening relations between families, and for the formation, maintenance, and extension of *calpulli*, the main social organization within Aztec society.

Service to God was expressed in many ways, including blood sacrifice. Long lines of victims, often warriors taken in battle, were marched up the pyramids to their ritualized deaths. At other times, blood sacrifice involved few victims, who met their deaths after sumptuous and elaborate ceremonies of food, music, and dance. If ritualized killings were a spectacle in 16th-century Europe, which were, to a large extent, meant to display the power of the state and the just rewards due to its victims, in Mexico the innocent victims had committed no crime, no insults to the state or priesthood. The so-honored victims died to appease deities—death was to maintain the living.

The killings were part of the sinews of America's greatest city, Tenochtitlan—today's Mexico City. Tenochtitlan floated on a large lake, its sections elaborately linked by causeways. Almost three times more populous than Seville, the largest city in Spain, it was indeed one of the most spectacular cities in the world. Tenochtitlan's population of 200,000 inhabited a planned city whose beauty and cleanliness were unparalleled. Canals and footpaths, regularly maintained and swept clear of obstructions, linked this city of temples, gardens, and courtyards. A great aqueduct system brought in water, but the city's needs grew so great that boatmen made water deliveries to houses. The elite lived in stone houses, while the common people inhabited mud dwellings. In the center city stood the great pyramids and other stately buildings, and the market that daily attracted 50,000 to 60,000 people. Most of the city's food had to be brought in from outside. Maize was the staff of life, as through much of the Americas. Although the denizens of Tenochtitlan could not produce enough food to feed themselves, they obtained what they needed through trade and tribute. The city's laborers engaged in a great variety of crafts, from weaving to sandal-making, and to more specialized crafts producing jewelry and other adornments.

## The Southwest

To the north of the Aztecs and their tributary neighbors lay the Southwest culture area. It extended from the modern-day Mexican states of Chihuahua and Sonora north to the southern reaches of Utah and Colorado. Ecologically, this region is mostly desert with some mountain ranges, its inhabitants living from a combination of sedentary agriculture and hunting and gathering. Archaeologists recognize three distinct culture areas of the Southwest. Anasazi, mostly in northern Arizona and New Mexico; Mogollon, in central Arizona and central and southern New Mexico; and Hohokan, in southern Arizona and northern Mexico. Within each area, more than one ethnic group likely resided, but each area was distinguished by its architecture, ceramics, cosmology, and lifestyle.

Southwest peoples created special places to conduct religious ceremonies. In Anasazi and Mogollon, they built Great Kivas, which were large structures containing a multiplicity of subterranean rooms. Hohokan religious ceremonies took place at oval-shaped ball courts, which were replaced by platform mounds around 1150. The ball courts and platform mounds, it is believed, also served as places where ceremonies were conducted to facilitate exchanges between peoples. Throughout North America, American Indians established an array of ceremonies for diplomatic and trade purposes—this is one of the important links between the pre–European contact and post–European contact periods.

Throughout the Southwest, masonry pithouses were the basic housing structure, particularly from A.D. 900 to 1300, but other more substantial structures, particularly pueblos, were built containing hundreds of rooms. Settlement size varied greatly. Before A.D. 900, Anasazi settlements rarely were above 40 households and 200 people, but some reached 2,000 to 5,000 people by 1150. Estimates for Hohokan settlements range from a few hundred individuals to upwards of 7,000. The largest Mogollon pueblos had over 300 rooms, with deceased inhabitants buried underneath the floors, sometimes numbering over 1,000.

Except among the Hohokan, towns were sedentary but not permanent, as people moved to follow game and other available food supplies and then returned to their towns. The Hohokan built an extensive canal system, however, which enabled them to remain in one place year-round. These were the most labor-intensive structures constructed in the Southwest and more complex than the canals built in Mexico. The movement of water to and within the Southwest remains key to the maintenance of present-day life in the region.

The cosmology of Southwest peoples possessed many similarities, even if religious ceremonies varied from one area to the next. Some of the similarities were also shared with the peoples of Mexico. The most commonly shared belief held the existence of a multitiered universe. Other connections between the regions include the association of particular colors with geographic directions, creation theories, mythological stories of spider women and warrior twins, and the practice of the fire ceremony. One important difference with Mexico was the lack of blood sacrifice in the Southwest, though a few archaeologists believe it could have existed there, though not on the grand scale evident in Mexico.

It cannot be proven whether the shared cultural concepts arrived from Mexico, or hearken back to an earlier shared ancestry in the Pleistocene era (1.8 million to 10,000 years ago). There was little contact between Mexico and the Southwest in terms of material culture. Most Mesoamerican artifacts at Southwest sites have been found in the western areas, and the aggregate number is relatively small, indicating no regular or frequent contact between the regions. What contact existed declined even more by 1350, perhaps the result of growing distance between the northernmost settlements of Mesoamerica and the southernmost Southwest settlements.

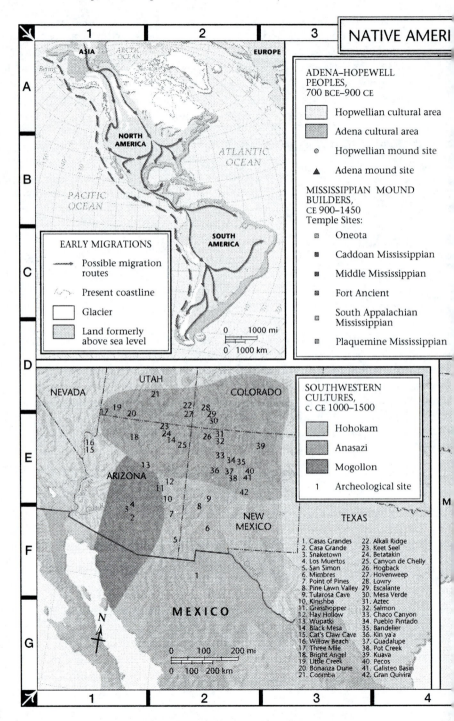

**NATIVE AMERI**

ADENA–HOPEWELL
PEOPLES,
700 BCE–900 CE

- Hopwellian cultural area
- Adena cultural area
- ⊙ Hopwellian mound site
- ▲ Adena mound site

MISSISSIPPIAN MOUND
BUILDERS,
CE 900–1450
Temple Sites:
- Oneota
- Caddoan Mississippian
- Middle Mississippian
- Fort Ancient
- South Appalachian Mississippian
- Plaquemine Mississippian

EARLY MIGRATIONS

- Possible migration routes
- Present coastline
- Glacier
- Land formerly above sea level

0    1000 mi
0    1000 km

SOUTHWESTERN
CULTURES,
c. CE 1000–1500

- Hohokam
- Anasazi
- Mogollon
- 1 Archeological site

1. Casas Grandes
2. Casa Grande
3. Snaketown
4. Los Muertos
5. San Simon
6. Mimbres
7. Point of Pines
8. Pine Lawn Valley
9. Tularosa Cave
10. Kinishba
11. Grasshopper
12. Hay Hollow
13. Wupatki
14. Black Mesa
15. Cat's Claw Cave
16. Willow Beach
17. Three Mile
18. Bright Angel
19. Little Creek
20. Bonanza Dune
21. Coomba
22. Alkali Ridge
23. Keet Seel
24. Betatakin
25. Canyon de Chelly
26. Hogback
27. Hovenweep
28. Lowry
29. Escalante
30. Mesa Verde
31. Aztec
32. Salmon
33. Chaco Canyon
34. Pueblo Pintado
35. Bandelier
36. Kin ya'a
37. Guadalupe
38. Pot Creek
39. Kuava
40. Pecos
41. Galisteo Basin
42. Gran Quivira

0    100    200 mi
0    100    200 km

**Map 1.1  Native American Peoples to 1450**

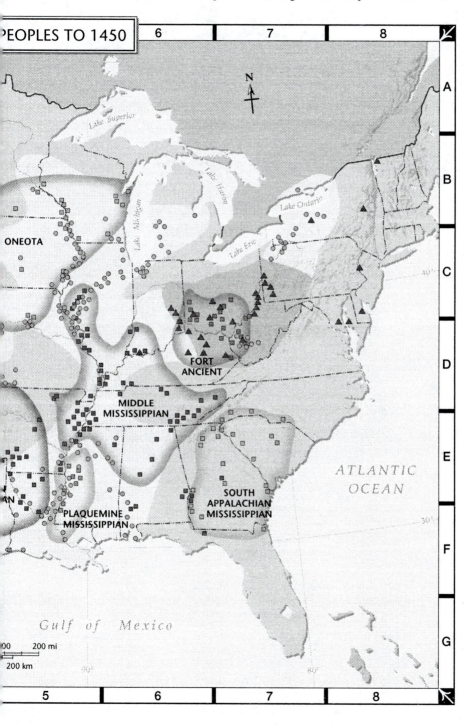

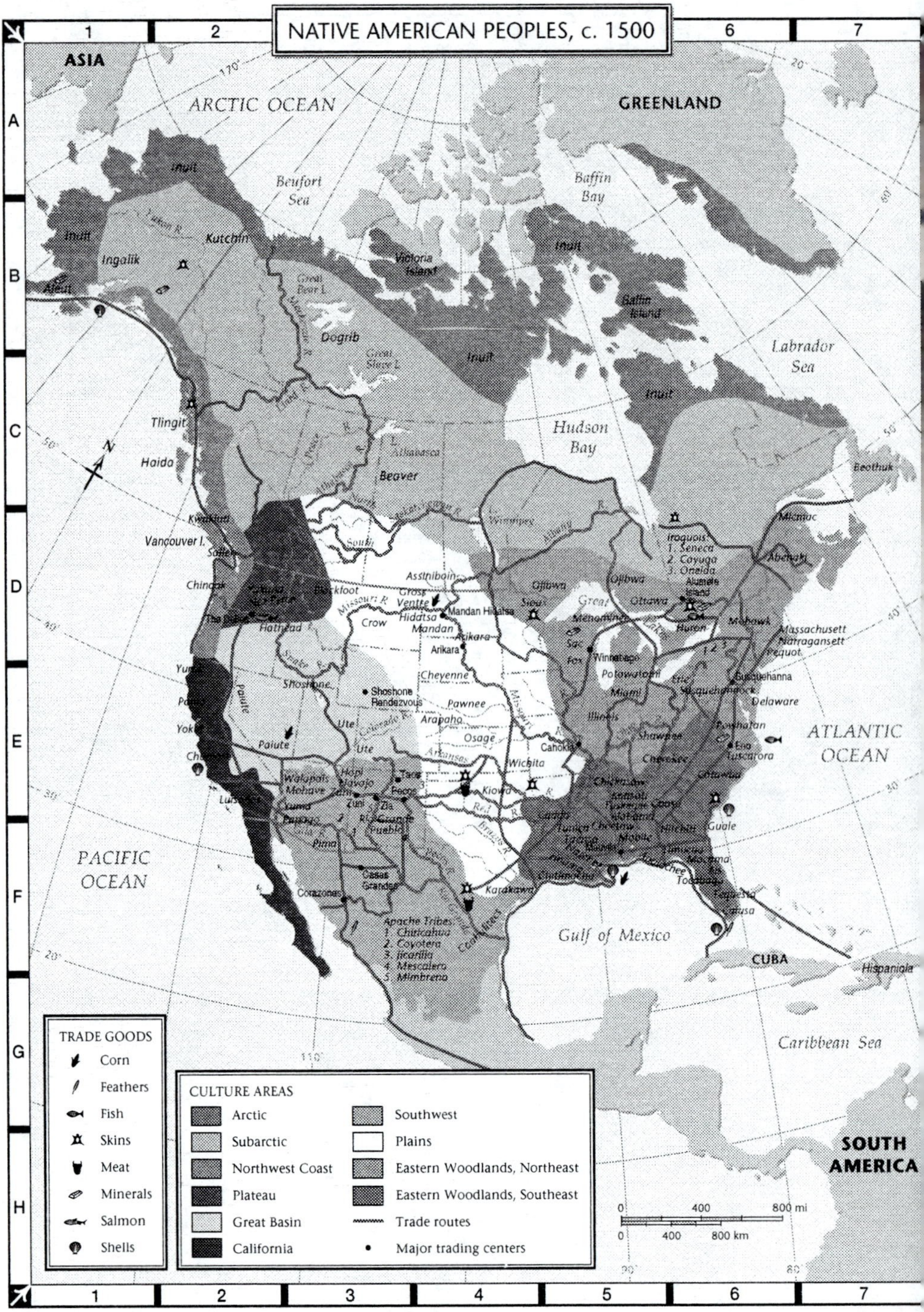

**Map 1.2 Native American Peoples, c. 1500**

The Hohokan and Mogollon cultures did not survive past the 16th century. A great flood in the Phoenix region eradicated Hohokan settlements about 1360, while to the south Paquimé, the most remarkable cosmopolitan center of Hohokan, disappeared for unknown reasons before the 16th century. As Hohokan and Mogollon disappeared, the Pueblo, who arose in the Anasazi region circa 1200–1450, expanded their population into the Mogollon region. They also expanded to places that previously lacked major agricultural settlements—including the valley of the Rio Grande, and towards the Sierra Madre in Mexico.

Despite the continuity between modern-day Pueblo and pre-contact Pueblo, little is known about some of the basic characteristics of life in the earlier period. For instance, it is still a hotly debated issue whether Southwest peoples lived in egalitarian or hierarchical societies. One reason for our lack of knowledge is the paucity of detailed written records as existed in Mexico, and the fact that the first Spanish arrivals recorded few details about Southwestern life, as they had elsewhere. Also, environmental conditions precluded a situation where archaeology could disclose material culture as it has for neighboring regions, particularly because urbanization in places such as Phoenix and Tucson destroyed many important native sites.

## The Great Basin and the Great Plains

Just above the Southwest, from the Rocky Mountains to the Sierra Nevadas, in the modern-day states of Utah, Nevada, western Wyoming, Colorado, southern Idaho, eastern California, and Oregon, is the region called the Great Basin. Its inhabitants were among the most ecologically adaptable in all North America. Sometimes living in deserts, sometimes moving to high altitudes, they formulated survival strategies and technologies to contend with the dramatic climatic changes that often beset the region. Long periods of aridity could be followed by great rainfall and the sudden appearance of lakes. Yet winters could be counted on for their severity. Great Basin peoples had to store large amounts of food each year to withstand the severe winter conditions.

In the agriculturally rich areas of the Great Basin, particularly in Utah, southern Idaho, and western Colorado, emerged the "Fremont" people. They lived largely by farming and shared many characteristics with the peoples of the Southwest, including the building of pithouses, cultivation of maize, stone construction, and similarities in pottery. Fremont origins are unknown both geographically and chronologically. We do not know whether they migrated from the Southwest or elsewhere. Moreover, trade goods entered the Great Basin from other regions but seemed to have had little impact on Fremont culture—leaving us to wonder about the sources for their cultural development and the nature of their relations with their neighbors.

Fremont culture ended in the mid-14th century, apparently due to a "Little Ice Age" that also decimated the Anasazi and other societies: maize could no longer be produced easily in the region due to climatic changes, forcing out-migration. There is no evidence that the later inhabitants of the Great Basin, such as the Shoshone and Paiute, were descendants of the Fremont peoples. They might have entered the region after the Fremont peoples left. The recent discovery of an extremely well-preserved Fremont settlement—over 12 miles long and containing hundreds, if not thousands of sites, in a remote canyon of eastern Utah, will undoubtedly shed light on these peoples' lives, their relations with neighboring regions, and perhaps give us clues as to their fate.

To the east of the Rockies, and extending from northern Texas to southern Canada, is the region known as the Great Plains. There, most of the inhabitants relied on bison hunting for thousands of years, with agriculture entering the region about A.D. 1200. Environmental conditions and bison hunting lead Plains Indians to adopt highly mobile lifestyles, though in some areas conditions supported a more sedentary social organization and lifestyle. Bison were hunted on foot with spears and bows and arrows, and were also killed as they were driven over steep cliffs. In one example of many, at Wardell, in Wyoming, the remains of over 1,000 bison, killed over a period of five centuries, have been found beneath a steep cliff. Plains people had to study bison habits to predict where the herds would be, and how best to achieve the most kills. Failure could lead to starvation—for once the herds moved from an area, hunters might not be able to reach them again until the following year. Bison remained a dietary staple on the Great Plains and were also used for clothing and blankets until the last quarter of the 19th century.

## The Far West

To the far west, in California and the Pacific Northwest, native peoples inhabited rich environments that permitted stability of settlements. The northwest coast had great forests of softwoods that could easily be transformed into houses and canoes. Craftsmen constructed an elaborate array of adornments, including the famed totem poles that celebrated lineages.

From the coastal waters of Juneau, Alaska, to the Columbia River Basin, great numbers of whales, sea lions, and other mammals, as well as numerous species of fish, including halibut that weighed up to 500 pounds, were caught. Salmon were the staple for many, as they are today, and the fish were easily stored against lean times when smoked. Gathering of fruit, acorns, and a variety of plants supplemented peoples' diets. This food abundance lead to cultural stability. Chiefdoms developed that fostered the redistribution of resources both within and without communities. Some cultures, like the modern-day Salish, can be traced to at least the early 13th century, and the archaeological record shows evidence of lively trade networks up and down the Pacific Coast.

Further south, along coastal California, can be found some of the densest populations on the North American continent. California's native peoples carefully managed food sources by burning and harvesting wild foods, while also engaging in hunting and fishing. A complex system of exchange facilitated the trade of goods, with beads serving as a primary currency among persons of all ranks. Trade drew many Indians to the area. One-fifth of the almost 500 different languages of Native North America were spoken in California in the 15th century.

Northern California groups tended to have their primary settlements along river drainage areas, seasonally moving to other camps to follow food sources. Smaller groups joined together in the autumn to catch and process fish. In southern California, settlements tended to be larger than in the north, with some containing as many as 1,000 people and having many connecting outlying villages. Houses were dome-shaped and villages stockaded and possessed sweat houses (as among the peoples along the Pacific Coast to the north). Despite not adopting agriculture, the southern California Indians formed complex social hierarchies, a result of the region's food abundance and the success of the people engaging in long-distance trade that extended far into the Southwest.

## The Far North

The indigenous peoples of the Arctic and sub-Arctic inhabited regions of extremely cold winters and short summers. With minimal green plant cover, mammals were few. Those mammals that did reside in the Arctic, most notably the caribou, became central to the needs of indigenous peoples, who also made use of the migratory birds that flocked north each summer. The tundra, too, though it had harsh winters, became a land of plenty in summer, full of mammals, birds, and plants.

Aleuts, Eskimos (in the post–European contact period called Inuits), and Athabascans are the main peoples of the Far North. Aleut life largely revolved around the sea, and exchanging the products of the sea for those produced by inland peoples. Whereas Aleut settlements along the Bering Sea tended to be permanent, since they were so close to food sources, Athabascan settlements were forced to follow the caribou and moose.

The bow and arrow first appeared in North America in the Arctic about 2000 B.C. for use against caribou and waterfowl. (It took about 2,000 years for the bow and arrow to reach southern Canada, and shortly thereafter the Southwest.) Athabascan speakers, one of the largest language families in the Far North and the Southwest, were among the first users of the bow and arrow. Athabascan culture, dating to about 4000 B.C., extended from Alaska to the western reaches of Hudson Bay. The Apache and Navajo of the Southwest, among others, are Athabascan speakers who originally hailed from the Far North. Some argue that the Algonquin language family of the Eastern Woodlands is also an offshoot of the Athabascan, but the connection remains uncertain.

The eastern Arctic was settled by migrants from the west after A.D. 1000. Within 300 years, Eskimos had reached Greenland. The people of the east followed a very similar lifestyle to those of the west—caribou and fishing were primary food sources—but they increased expertise in hunting sea mammals, particularly whales. The communal cooperation necessary to hunt whales carried over into other areas of daily life, as Eskimos became extremely efficient in developing survival skills. Great care, time, and effort were expended on harpoon production (and much less time in the decoration of other material goods). The efficiency of northern hunters also owed to three innovations that facilitated travel: dogsleds, kayaks, and large boats made of skins.

Success in whaling may have been the draw that kept westerners moving east in the 400 years before European arrival. Archaeologists believe there was much contact between east and west, as evinced by the great distances trade goods were carried, including tools of iron, bone, ivory, and copper.

Norsemen began contact with Greenland about A.D. 1000—the first Europeans to have sustained contact with the indigenous peoples of North America. This trade, however, collapsed around 1480. Contact would not be renewed until a century later, and even then only was occasional with little impact on Inuits. Not until the 1740s, with Russian entry into Alaska, and a century later, when Europeans obtained the ability to winter in the far northeast, were native peoples of the Arctic and sub-Arctic regions heavily influenced by outsiders. Because of the remoteness and harsh conditions, many Inuits continued to follow their traditional life undisturbed by outsiders well into the 20th century.

## THE EASTERN WOODLANDS AND THE MISSISSIPPIANS

The peoples of the Eastern Woodlands and the Mississippians lived in a largely forested and temperate area along the Atlantic Coast from southern Canada to the Florida peninsula, and west to the Mississippi Valley. Maize agriculture was the most significant source of calories for most peoples in the region, supplemented with the hunting of deer and other animals, as well as fishing along the Atlantic Coast, and in rivers, lakes, and ponds. Denser populations inhabited the southern half of the region where the Mississippians lived, due to the longer growing season and subsequent abundance of food. This agricultural plenty led to very different political and social organizations than in the Eastern Woodlands to the north. Northern peoples tended to reside in smaller, more egalitarian bands than in the south, where polities tended to be highly organized and stratified with class divisions. Within regions, there was also cultural variance. The Iroquoians, for instance, were patrifocal, whereas their Algonquin neighbors were matrifocal. And in the South, many of the coastal peoples lived in less-centralized polities than their inland neighbors. Our knowledge of Eastern Woodlands peoples' lives before contact with Europeans varies greatly. For much of the Eastern Woodlands, we know more about their "ancient" history than for the thousand years immediately before contact with Europeans, as little material culture for the latter era has survived in the archaeological record. We do possess oral histories for some of these people, but there also exists huge evidentiary gaps. In the South, oral history can be combined with the rich archaeological record for the 500 years before contact with Europeans, plus the accounts of Spanish explorers who criss-crossed the region and left written accounts of native peoples who had never previously encountered Europeans. These can be supplemented with paintings by the Frenchman Jacques Le Moyne in Florida, and particularly by the Englishman John White in Virginia, who in the 1580s created the most substantive visual account of native peoples above Mexico until the age of photography. Thus we have a rich array of sources for understanding the southern Indians along a broad continuum of time from about A.D. 1200 forward, with one substantial gap in information from about 1550 to 1650, except for the area along the Atlantic Coast.

### The Eastern Woodlands

Below the sub-Arctic, the Eastern Woodlands extended west from the Atlantic Ocean to the Great Plains. West of Pennsylvania, many of the people constructed massive mounds of earth. Mound building could be found as far north as Wisconsin and Michigan, though it proliferated in Ohio and among the Mississippians below the Ohio River. Some of the oldest and best studied areas of early mound building are in Ohio among the Adena (circa 1000 B.C.–100 B.C.), where hundreds of mounds have been discovered. As among the Mississippians (discussed later), natives were buried in the mounds with a variety of artifacts, their bodies sometimes painted. Sacred circles were constructed near the mounds, denoting the importance of these locations for religious ceremonies.

Adena culture was followed by Hopewell culture, the latter without many of the elaborate ceremonies of its predecessor. The Hopewell lasted until about A.D. 400. The Hopewell period witnessed the enlargement of trade networks in all directions. Marine shells from as far away as Florida, copper from the Lake Superior region, and obsidian from the Rocky Mountains can be found at Hopewell sites. Some Hopewellians lived in manufacturing areas, particularly in Illinois and southern Ohio, producing goods for inter- and intra-regional trade. The organization of trade and manufacturing indicates complex hierarchical social organizations, which is further evident from the distinctively elaborate burials of particular individuals.

After A.D. 1000, we describe the Eastern Woodlands peoples as the ancestors of the Algonquin and Iroquois. The Algonquin inhabited the lands to the west and east of the Iroquois. Their origins are unknown, but their language is believed to have been spoken in the Eastern Woodlands for 7,000 to 9,000 years. Their way of life was similar to the Iroquois, though they were not matrilineal like the Iroquois. Great variance developed among Algonquins, probably as a result of their inhabiting a variety of locations. Coastal Algonquins engaged heavily in fishing, while inland peoples hunted (particularly deer), gathered wild foods, and cultivated maize to varying extents. Those living in rich agricultural lands followed less mobile lifestyles than those who depended more on hunting and gathering.

The New England Algonquins developed only limited exchange with the Hopewellian to the west, though they earlier were influenced by Adena burial practices. The lifestyle of New England natives changed little during the last 500 years or more before contact with Europeans. Then, European fishermen began visiting the Newfoundland fisheries in the 1490s. In the 16th and early 17th centuries, some of these fishermen apparently began camping on the New England coast to dry their fish before returning to Europe. These fishermen carried microbes that spread disease among many of the coastal peoples, leading to great population decline by the time French and English began colonizing the region in the 17th century.

To the west of New England, the Iroquois lived in New York and Pennsylvania, in communities of as many as 1,500 people. They built longhouses that persisted into the historic period. These may have been organized along clan lines. As large communities exhausted timber supplies and agricultural land, they shifted to new locales. Cannibalism can be documented among the Iroquois beginning in the 14th century, but was apparently for symbolic purposes rather than subsistence. Warfare also increased, perhaps as a result of competition for resources, but more important may have been the quest for prestige.

Iroquois peoples joined together into confederacies, at least by the late 16th century, perhaps to reduce warfare and as protection against outsiders. Unity into one confederacy probably took place after the European arrival, and played a major role in the history of the region as late as the early 19th century.

## The Mississippians: Maize Culture

The Mississippian culture area largely corresponded with the American South, extending from Oklahoma east into southern Illinois, northeast to the Ohio River Valley, south to the Gulf of Mexico, and east to the Atlantic Ocean. Rituals and religious life centered on the thousands of mounds built by Mississippian peoples throughout the South—hence the name often ascribed to them: the Moundbuilders. The mounds served as burial grounds for individuals and as platforms on which to build temples and houses for chiefs. Many were multilevel and used for hundreds of years. From the mounds and surrounding village sites, archaeologists can assess stages of occupation, hierarchy, political organization, subsistence, nutrition, and patterns of trade.

The inhabitants' lives—and their culture—centered around maize production. Easily storable and highly nutritional, maize bore little resemblance to today's corn, which has a much smaller percentage of the original caloric, mineral, and vitamin values. Roasted, pounded into hominy, fried, boiled, and baked, corn was processed by southern Indians into dozens of dishes from which many people received more than half of their calories. Archaeologists are unsure whether maturing political organization led to increased maize production or, more likely, increased cultivation led to new and more sophisticated polities, but the results were the same: maize became the building block of the so-called Mississippian Cultures (circa 1000–1730), the most complex societies north of Mexico.

Maize allowed southern Indians to create permanent residences on stable farmsteads successively occupied for generations. Because of the rich soils and favorable climate, southern farmers produced two crops of maize per year: a green corn harvested in summer and a second crop in autumn. Early in the Mississippian period, maize was stored in large below-ground pits. The rise of chiefdom polities (circa 1000) led to the pooling and storage of the surplus in above-ground structures at local centers. Storage life was usually one to two years, perhaps longer. Chiefs redistributed maize to commoners during droughts and exchanged surplus for prestige items from neighboring peoples. Maize was also incorporated into religious ceremonies, some of which persisted into the historic period, notably the Green Corn ceremony still celebrated by many southern peoples.

With the rise of maize, hunting and gathering did not end, but intensive agricultural production allowed native peoples to spend less time attaining subsistence and more time in craft production, religious and leisure activities, and warfare. It also meant that some individuals did not have to engage in subsistence and could specialize as administrators, servants, artisans, and perhaps soldiers. Surplus and specialization led to multitiered societies of elites and commoners. Archaeologists agree that the chiefdom polities all shared this inegalitarian social structure, though class relations varied in each. The ethnohistorical record—the reports of the first Spanish explorers—describes chiefs of substantial kingdoms carried in litters. Chiefs had the power of life and death over their subjects, and they ritually sacrificed commoners in religious ceremonies and at the death of the highest-ranking elites. Birth defined status, and at least some chiefs claimed descent from the sun, but personal skills, such as in warfare and hunting, could elevate an individual's rank within the hierarchy.

## The Mississippians: Hierarchy and Warfare

By comparing sites throughout the South and to other regions of the world, archaeologists can furnish much information on social and political organization. In general, they divide chiefdoms into two types: simple and complex. Simple chiefdoms were characterized by two-tiered organization, whereas the complex, or paramount chiefdoms, had three or more tiers. Paramount chiefdoms collected tribute from simple chiefdoms, thus the extra tier of organization. They generally had larger populations than simple chiefdoms, were highly organized, commanded huge amounts of labor, and conducted sophisticated military campaigns. Although some survived into the historic period, the paramount chiefdoms, and the Mississippi Cultures in general, peaked in the South in the 14th century.

Chiefs established networks of power, marrying kin into nearby villages, from which they received tribute and labor. They also built and maintained power by monopolizing religious rituals—the group's ideology—which gave them and their birth lines the right to rule. Examination of burials provides the most substantial record of hierarchical organization among the chiefdoms. From skeleton remains we have learned that elites often had a better and more balanced diet than commoners. Prestige goods—items produced outside the chiefdom, badges of office, and highly specialized craft items—signify elite burials. Among these prestige goods were columella, pendants, sheet-copper hair ornaments and headdresses, robes, pearls, discoidals, and ear ornaments. Fineware ceramics and marine-shell beads were others. The complex chiefdoms had more specialization than the simple chiefdoms, and the chiefs had greater access to distant trade goods and raw materials because of their control over external relations.

Signs of warfare are evident from burial remains, the building of bastioned palisades, and the ethnohistorical evidence that records endemic warfare between neighboring peoples. The advent of the bow and arrow in the Late Woodlands era (A.D. 600–1000) led to improved fortifications. The Mississippians constructed plastered palisades and wattle-and-daub houses to protect against fire arrows. Extensive moats and bastions increased the strength of local centers. Some of the palisades were quite large and built to protect fields as well as housing and storehouses. Cahokia, the largest known Mississippian center (in Illinois across the Mississippi River from modern-day St. Louis, Missouri), used about 20,000 logs in each of its four phases of palisades construction. Cahokia was a larger city than almost all European cities of the Middle Ages. Fortification construction drew labor from outlying villagers, who would have benefited from the protection of their surplus—thus illustrating the ability of certain chiefdoms to command and organize many laborers over a fairly large area.

There is much disagreement about the causes of warfare. It is unclear whether chiefdoms pursued warfare to control natural resources, to obtain captives for labor, or for other reasons. Complex chiefdoms undoubtedly employed their military to undertake conquest and exact tribute. Raiding was more common than conquest, but the scale of warfare may have owed as much to geography and demography as to any other factors. For instance, in the South Appalachian area, where chiefdoms had both a great deal of land and buffer zones between them, warfare was largely confined to raiding, and Indians had little knowledge of the core center of neighboring chiefdoms. In contrast, in the central and lower Mississippi Valley, rival chiefdoms existed in close contact: warfare was extensive with conquest always a possibility.

Whether by raiding or conquest, if enemies reached one's mounds, then a disaster of the first magnitude occurred. Desecration of mounds by invaders undermined elites' right to rule, for those rights were based on their genealogical–religious authority. This may explain how Spanish explorers hastened the decline of many chiefdoms in the 16th century. Spanish abuse of chiefs and disrespect for sacred sites undercut the sanctity of native leaders. Moreover, Hernando de Soto's *entrada*, in particular, but others as well, brought into closer contact Indians from competing chiefdoms. These Indians traveled with the Spanish or went to meet them. They may have used their newly gained knowledge of their neighbors' core centers for attacking sacred places. It took just one successful attack on the mounds to wreak havoc and destruction on these politically unstable polities.

Mississippian chiefdoms varied in size and complexity, but they shared many characteristics. The riverine system of the Southeast encouraged the movement of goods and ideas, particularly on the Mississippi, Tombigbee, Coosa, and Savannah River watersheds, so even where extensive trade did not take place, there was enough exchange of goods and technology to create general cultural similarities. Religious iconography was similar throughout the region, particularly in the stylization of bird figures, bilobed arrows, and square-cross gorgets, which leads scholars to perceive much affinity in belief systems, though the nature of those beliefs remains elusive. A few scholars believe that resemblance between Aztecan and Mississippian symbols resulted from a network of direct exchange, but more believe that any shared morphology occurred discretely and not from direct contact.

## The Mississippians: Instability and Continuity

The chiefdoms were politically unstable. Population growth, territorial expansion, and factional competition among elites all fed instability. A chief's death always presented the potential for internal problems. The Spanish explorers recorded murders of claimants and their supporters; internal divisions also led to break-offs of villages and simple chiefdoms, usually to join other chiefdoms. Only with difficulty, and the threat of military reprisal, could paramount chiefs maintain influence and control over their more distant villages—which through new combinations could challenge a chiefdom's core. With this pattern of rise and fall, there was no linear development to a more sophisticated political structure, and it is unclear what new factors would have been necessary for the southern chiefdoms to have evolved, if at all, into states, without first having outside states organize chiefdoms into confederacies as a mode of control and taxation.

It is also unclear why so many of the major Mississippian centers disappeared by 1400. There is no archaeological evidence of severe climatic or environmental change or of epidemic disease or an increase in warfare. Likewise, the second wave of declension that occurred with the Spanish arrival in the 16th century is also difficult to document. There is little archaeological evidence of pandemic disease in the early contact period. There *is* much ethnohistorical evidence of disease in the 17th century— but we are nowhere close to making informed judgments on the impact of disease in the 16th century, when the Spanish first arrived. There may not be a link between disease and the collapse of the chiefdoms because (1) so many chiefdoms disappeared by 1400, not 1500, before Europeans brought new pathogens to the region and (2) the large waves of pandemic disease of the 17th century occurred after the collapse of the chiefdoms encountered by the Spanish in the 16th century. Moreover, the survival of the Natchez chiefdom into the early 1730s provides evidence that chiefdoms could and did exist side by side with European colonies. Chiefdoms also existed in similar form among some of the Natchez's neighbors, so it cannot be said that the European presence inherently caused the collapse of chiefdoms, either by disease or by the mere presence of a more sophisticated social and political system in the region. Disease and European expansion into the South might have contributed to some chiefdoms' disintegration, but there must have been other factors involved, because not all collapsed yet so many disappeared before European arrival.

Further disputes exist over the relationship of pre– and proto–European contact peoples to those of the historic period. In many instances, post-contact peoples did not inhabit the same exact area as their ancestors. Migration, and the creation of new towns and political identities, was quite common throughout the pre-contact and post-contact eras. Towns and groups of towns broke from one chiefdom and joined another, and remnants converged into new towns. Sometimes entire areas became nearly depopulated as large-scale out-migration occurred. The disappearance of polities and the movement of peoples do not negate the ancestry of the historic-era southern Indians to the earlier chiefdoms. They were as much the same peoples as the English were born of Saxons, Normans, Celts, Romans, and others. Southern Indians of the historic period inherited their ancestors' Moundbuilder culture, technology, and religion. They continued to rely on the bow and arrow for hunting and fighting; they still lived in palisaded towns and built bastioned fortifications; maize was their dietary staple; kinship still defined a person's place in society, even as other identities altered; canoes and piraguas persisted as the main source of transportation for many; and the ancient game of chunky, which involved throwing spears at rolling stone discs, remained a favorite pastime. Both pre-contact chiefdoms and post-contact bands were characterized by villages of small family homesteads. Warfare was endemic for both. So what changed?

Although slaves were kept in both chiefdoms and bands, they were unimportant to the band economy, whereas there is evidence of chiefdoms employing unfree labor in the fields. In bands (and probably in chiefdoms), the keeping of slaves was a mark of status and demonstrated warriors' prowess. Slaves had the further utility of demonstrating to free Indians an alternative and undesirable existence as an "other," an individual without substantive identity—and thus a reminder to all of the importance of kinship. Europeans did not introduce slavery or the notion of slaves as laborers to the American South but instead would be responsible for stimulating a vast trade in American Indians as commodities. Because of their previous history of raiding for captives, many southern Indians adapted to European slave trading practically overnight.

There were other important changes from the pre–European contact to post–European contact peoples: social stratification declined, tribute was no longer delivered to local centers, and towns entered into decentralized confederacies. Spiritual life also undoubtedly changed greatly. Except for the Mississippi River peoples who remained in chiefdoms and maintained temples, other southern Indians no longer built temples and retained a priesthood, whose work revolved in part around the temples. In spite of the loss of rituals, temples, and priestcraft, the spiritual substance largely survived. Southern native religion remained holistic: there was no separation between the sacred and the secular, as existed among Europeans. Respect for authority, the importance of kin identity, and the centrality of animals and the environment in the spiritual worldview all carried over from the Mississippian era.

## Conclusion

One of the great myths of American history posits that American Indians were destined to lose their land because they lived in inflexible Stone Age cultures unable to compete with technologically superior Europeans. This myth has no historical foundation and is based on several misconceptions of Native American societies. These misconceptions are that native peoples lived in static cultures incapable of adaptation, native peoples did not possess technology of their own, and native peoples did not have the ability to form social organizations to contend with the colonizing powers.

It is evident from the archaeological record that American Indians successfully adapted to an array of ecological conditions, and that they often shaped their environment to meet their needs. They built canals, selectively burnt forest and underbrush, and participated in long-distance trade to exchange their surplus for needed and luxury items. Social systems varied from region to region, and sometimes within regions, as people formulated strategies to contend with often rapidly changing climatic and geopolitical conditions. Some groups, like the Aztecs and the Mississippians, excelled at organizing labor and production, formed densely populated communities, and collected tribute. This enabled them to create large urbanized settlements with numerous specialized crafts and services, and an extensive ceremonial complex that required the devotion of great resources. These sophisticated societies contrast with those of the Eastern Woodlands and elsewhere, which comprised small villages that seasonally joined with other villages to hunt and fish, but otherwise lived isolated from large communities. There was no single Native American polity or social system or economy; each was as subject to evolutionary developments as societies elsewhere in the world affected by great alterations in the environment, demography, and intrusions of new cultures.

Native American pre–European contact technology was quite effective in suiting local needs, whether using spears to hunt bison, or bows and arrows that frequently were more efficient than 16th-century European guns for hunting and warfare. American Indians created the tools necessary not only to survive but to flourish. They moved vast amounts of earth to build mounds as high as ten stories, constructed pyramids and water canals, invented numerous kinds of fish weirs and trapping devices, and crafted portable housing. Other forms of technology, most notably those used for transportation, such as kayaks, canoes, piraguas, and snowshoes, would be readily adopted by Europeans upon their arrival in the New World. Rather than one culture possessing technology and the other not, Europeans and Indians had developed largely different technologies. The Europeans had numerous advantages, most notably with their ocean-going ships that could transport large numbers of people, animals, and cargo; European-forged metal tools, utensils, and pots were important labor-saving devices that Indians coveted. American Indians proved as adept as Europeans in adapting to new technologies.

Technology was not the only adaptation natives made after European arrival. Many Southeastern Indians altered their polities from chiefdoms to bands to confederacies, and successfully treated with their European neighbors for hundreds of years militarily and economically. In most areas north of Mexico and west of the Appalachian Mountains, native peoples held the preponderance of military power until the early 19th century. Europeans depended on Native American military prowess to defend their colonies and conduct offensive operations against their enemies. Moreover, natives quickly entered the global economy, using their expert skills hunting, trapping, and processing pelts to obtain European trade goods. Much of the colonial economy revolved around trade with American Indians. The question was not could American Indians adapt to living alongside and with European societies—they could and did—the issue was whether European societies would mobilize their efforts to dispossess Indians of their land, enslave them, and kill them.

The European arrival in North America presented a host of new challenges for native peoples, not the least of which were the deadly pathogens that killed tens of thousands, while also undermining social bonds. In Mexico and elsewhere, native peoples had to contend with a Spanish imperial power intent on controlling their labor and converting them to Christianity. The Southeast would also be visited by the conquistadors, but there Spanish (and later English and French) gains would be much more modest, and native peoples would control most of the region until the end of the 18th century. New England Indians faced intense European population pressures from the English in the 17th century, which spread through Algonquin and Iroquois lands in the 18th century, by the end of which, virtually all native peoples east of the Mississippi and from the Southwest to Mexico, and in southeastern Canada, the Aleutians, and parts of California were intensively involved with European settlers and/or traders, missionaries, diplomats, and soldiers. On the other hand, native groups that lived in many remote areas would be largely unaffected by the Europeans, even into the mid-19th century and later.

## Bibliography

Anderson, David G. *The Savannah River Chiefdoms: Political Change in the Late Prehistoric Southeast* (1994).

Brose, Davis S., and N'omi Greber, eds. *Hopewell Archeology* (1979).

Carlon, Roy, ed. *Indian Art Traditions of the Northwest Coast* (1983).

Clendinnen, Inga. *Aztecs: An Interpretation* (1991).

Cordell, Linda S., and George J. Gumerman, eds. *Dynamics of Southwest Prehistory* (1989).

Dumond, Don. *Eskimos and Aleuts* (1987, 2nd ed.).

Fagan, Brian M. *Ancient North America: The Archaeology of a Continent* (1991).

Frison, George. *Prehistoric Hunters of the High Plains* (1978).

Galloway, Patricia K., ed. *The Southeastern Ceremonial Complex: Artifacts and Analysis* (1990).

Mason, Ronald J. *Great Lakes Archaeology* (1981).

Maxwell, Moreau. *The Prehistory of the Eastern Arctic* (1985).

Meyer, Michael C., and William H. Beezley. *The Oxford History of Mexico* (2000).

Meyer, Michael C., William L. Sherman, and Susan M. Deeds. *The Course of Mexican History* (2003, 7th ed.).

Moratto, Michael J. *California Archaeology* (1984).

Neitzel, Jill E., ed. *Great Towns and Regional Polities in the Prehistoric American Southwest and Southeast* (1999).

Pauketat, Timothy R. *The Ascent of Chiefs: Cahokia and Mississippian Politics in Native North America* (1994).

Smith, Bruce D., ed. *The Mississippian Emergence* (1990).

Smith, Bruce D., with C. Wesley Cowan and Michael P. Hoffman. *Rivers of Change: Essays on Agriculture in Eastern North America* (1992).

Soustelle, Jacques. *Daily Life of the Aztecs: On the Eve of the Spanish Conquest* (1961).

Thornton, Russell. *American Indian Holocaust and Survival: A Population History Since 1492* (1987).

Tuck, James A. *Onondaga Iroquois Prehistory* (1971).

Webb, William S., and R. S. Baby. *The Adena People No. 2* (1957).

Webb, William S., and C. E. Snow. *The Adena People* (1945).

# 2

# Spain in America: The 16th Century

## INTRODUCTION

Ships and trade connected the world's continents. The goods of the East, particularly spices and silks, found an insatiable market in Europe. Cloves, pepper, nutmeg, cinnamon, and mace were among the dozens of Asian commodities that Europeans purchased to flavor foods and transform into cosmetics, perfumes, medicines, dyes, and cleansers. The nobility and the middle classes purchased the great bulk of imported goods to improve the material quality of their lives, but also as signs of social status—that they had access to exotic lands on other sides of the world.

From the late Middle Ages through the 15th century, most Asian goods destined for Europe were carried to Constantinople, the capital of the Ottoman Empire on the eastern end of the Mediterranean Sea. Moslem traders brought grain from the Nile River Valley and western Asia, silk from China and Persia, cinnamon from Ceylon, cloves from the Moluccas, pepper from Sumatra, gems from Burma, and calico, pepper, and teak from India. The Ottomans held monopolistic arrangements with Italians from Genoa and Venice, who provided the conduit through which these goods reached European markets. The Italians offered arms and armor in return, and other manufactured metal items from work-shops in Italy and Germany, as well as woolen textiles, olive oil, Spanish raisins, Venetian glass, wine, and cheese from southern and western Europe.

Portugal was the first European nation to effectively break open the Italian–Ottoman monopoly of Asian–European trade. Building upon their long-standing trade with North Africa, the Portuguese spread their influence and trade roots southward in the mid-15th century. After colonizing the Azores Islands off of northwest Africa, they extended into West Africa establishing trade ports and colonies. From there the Portuguese sailed around the southern tip of Africa to the Indian Ocean and established themselves in India (1498), soon making Goa their central entrepôt in Asia. Imitating the Italians, they monopolized their trade route, barring other European nations from taking in fresh water and other supplies at their ports in South Africa and elsewhere on the continent.

Ultimately, the Portuguese opened a profitable trade between China and Japan, as the two countries refused to trade with one another directly but desired each other's goods. They carried Chinese silks and porcelain to Nagasaki in exchange for silver. The Portuguese became great middlemen in Asia, and their language became a lingua franca for trade. In Asia, the Portuguese competed with Moslem and other Asian traders, but for over a century no European power successfully challenged their trade route. Widely published Portuguese travel accounts recounted the exploits and successes of that nation's adventurers, explorers, and traders, prompting jealousy among other Europeans who also wished to gain access to the riches of Asia. The Portuguese nobility and wealthy merchants placed orders for personalized goods produced in India: furniture bearing families' coats of arms, chess sets, and so on; exotic animals such as tigers and hawks were among the many items imported.

The Portuguese government collected navigation charts and maps for their ship captains to study, and then zealously guarded the information from other nations. The jealous nations of western Europe, particularly Spain, France, and England, sought access to Asian trade. Italian ship captains also desired to explore new routes to Asia, but the Italian city-states had no desire to undermine their trade monopoly with Constantinople by opening new routes to Asia. Thus, Italian sailors like Christopher Columbus sought funding in western Europe. Columbus succeeded in convincing the Spanish monarchy to authorize and fund his sailing west across the Atlantic in 1492, to open a new trade route with Asia. Columbus, of course, failed to reach Japan, but found America instead.

Columbus was not the first European to land in America. Norsemen entered North American waters much earlier, and there is reason to believe that European fishermen operated in North American waters in the 15th century, but after Columbus's landfall the Americas and Europe began sustained interaction. Columbus failed to establish trade in the valuable commodities of the land that America had to offer, but he did initiate a trade in enslaved American Indians, a harbinger of terrible things to come.

## EARLY EXPLORATION AND CONQUESTS

Only two European powers—Portugal and Spain—built overseas empires in the late 15th century. To reduce conflict between them, in the Treaty of Tordesillas (1494), the Pope drew a line dividing the world for purposes of expansion. Essentially, Portugal received Asia, and Spain the Americas, except for Brazil. The line would be revised and disputed several times, and later ignored by Protestant interlopers like the English and Dutch, as well as by Catholic France, all refusing to be left out of empire-building. But the process of making and revising such a line indicates an underlying assumption that conquest of new lands was a legitimate enterprise.

Spain's presence in America began with Hispaniola—the island of Santo Domingo, where Columbus established a permanent colony on his second voyage in 1493. Columbus believed he had reached the East Indies, and he hoped to open a direct trade with Asia, but many of his contemporaries realized he was wrong. Yet Spanish interest was piqued by finding the Native Indians in possession of gold, a precious metal highly valued in Europe and Asia, which the Spanish could and did use to finance military operations in Europe. But Columbus had "discovered" not only new lands, but people, the Arawaks. And when he did not have enough gold to send to Spain to pay for his expedition, he shipped Arawaks for sale in the slave markets of Spain, initiating a wide-scale trade in American Indian slaves. Most Arawaks, however, were forced to labor on Hispaniola, to provide the Spanish with gold and food. Within 30 years of Columbus's arrival, the island's approximately 1 million native inhabitants were reduced to about 30,000 by disease, overwork, and altered environmental conditions. Within another 20 years, the entire population was decimated.

In Europe, news of Columbus's discoveries led others to explore the new-found lands across the Atlantic. By 1497, the Italian John Cabot, sailing for the English crown, reached Northern New England, though like Columbus he thought he had reached the Far East. Cabot returned to England, and in 1498 set off again across the Atlantic with five ships full of goods in a futile search for Japan. Four of five ships disappeared in a storm and the fifth limped home unsuccessful. Another Italian, Amerigo Vespucci, had much better luck. Employed first by Spain, and then by Portugal, the Florentine made four voyages from 1497 to 1503 or 1504, exploring much of the American mainland coast. Unlike Cabot, Vespucci knew he had discovered a new continent—which was named for him by contemporary mapmakers.

Explorers and fishermen of many nations followed the Atlantic Coast northward, leading to the discovery—or rediscovery—of the rich Newfoundland fisheries. Intermittently, for over a hundred years afterwards, Europeans sought passage west through the islands and mainland of the far north in hopes of finding a route to Asia, but it was the northern fisheries that had lasting importance, feeding millions of Europeans in the coming centuries. The fisheries did not involved permanent colonization, but seasonal camps to fish and dry the fish before returning to Europe. Far to the South, however, the Spanish set the pattern for permanent European colonization in the 16th century. Spanish explorers, conquistadors, priests, and settlers established colonies in the Caribbean and on the American mainland. They exploited natural resources and native labor; built cities, towns, and missions; and sought to assimilate America's native peoples through various means into their empire. Spain's impact on colonization was indelible, and a model to be followed in some ways, and avoided in others, by later European colonizers of the New World.

## Expansion in the West Indies

Spanish settlement in the Americas remained confined to Hispaniola from 1493 to 1508. Then in quick succession, they explored and conquered several new places—affirming for many the Black Legend, which depicted the Spanish as a peculiarly cruel and bloodthirsty people. In 1508, Spain conquered Puerto Rico and Jamaica and enslaved the natives. Shortly thereafter, they ravaged the Bahamas, where they did not settle but instead captured the inhabitants for use as slaves elsewhere. Cuba fell in 1511.

The Spanish also launched expeditions onto the American mainland into northern South America. In Panama, Vlasco Nuñez de Balboa instituted an alternative model of colonization: he prevented his soldiers from abusing the native peoples and actively worked to establish good relations. But Balboa was ultimately executed on bogus charges by his enemies, and his policy of peaceful coexistence died with him.

The Spanish had sighted Florida at least by 1501. Juan Ponce de Leon, one of the richest men in the Caribbean and the conqueror and former governor of Puerto Rico, received the right to settle in Bimini in the Bahamas off the Florida coast. Leon reached Florida, just above St. Augustine in 1513. Contrary to legend, he was not seeking the Fountain of Youth—he was looking for more Indians to capture and enslave. Florida natives opposed Leon wherever he landed along the coast—the first recorded instance of Europeans being met with violence upon first contact with American Indians—but given Leon's intentions, and Spanish enslaving on the nearby Bahamas, there can be little wonder as to the reason for native hostility.

Leon later attempted to conquer the Caribbean island of Guadeloupe and was defeated there as well. He traveled to Spain and received permission to conquer the "island" of Florida—he was unaware that Florida was attached to the mainland—then returned to where he had previously landed on the peninsula only to be wounded by Calusa Indians. Leon retreated to Cuba and died from his wound.

## The Conquest of Mexico: Model for Empire-Building

Spanish conquests in the Caribbean and first steps onto the American continents did not prepare them for the riches soon to be found. Although medieval legends of cities of phenomenal wealth spurred the explorers, and they had attained riches on Hispaniola, no one could conceive of what awaited in Mexico and Peru. Discovery of incredible wealth in both places inspired the imperial ambitions of not just Spain, but also the Portuguese, French, English, and Dutch. Hernán Cortés's story, in particular, became an important model for future European conquest.

Cortés led an 11 ship expedition of over 500 men from Cuba to the Gulf Coast of Mexico in the winter of 1519. At the last minute, he received news he should not leave—Governor Velasquez of Cuba did not trust him—Cortés quickly departed anyway. When he reached Mexico, he destroyed his ships, signifying to his men that they would not leave until they had accomplished their ends. Cortés was an experienced military leader, often brilliant in his diplomatic strategies towards friends and foes alike. In Mexico, he intimidated the Cempolans, tributaries to the Aztecs, into becoming allies, and then after defeating the Tlaxcalans, also tributaries to the Aztecs, turned them into allies as well. Cortés negotiated his way into Tenochtitlan, modern-day Mexico City, the heart of the great Aztec empire. To the Spanish, it was a city of wonders, unlike any they had ever seen, with beautiful causeways, palaces, and temples signifying a wealth of riches.

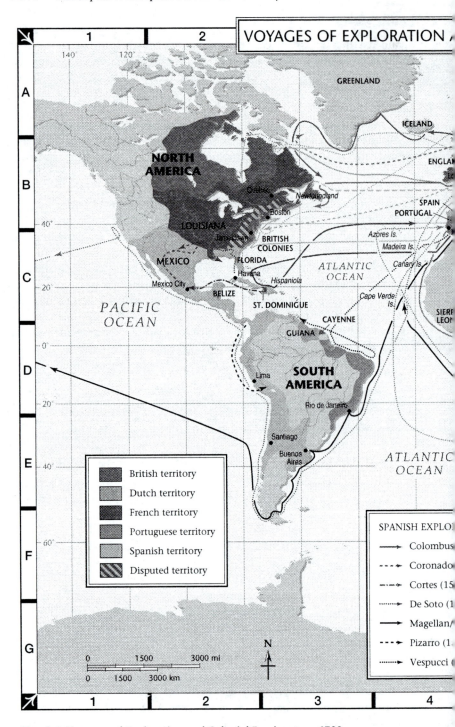

**Map 2.1  Voyages of Exploration and Colonial Empires to c. 1700**

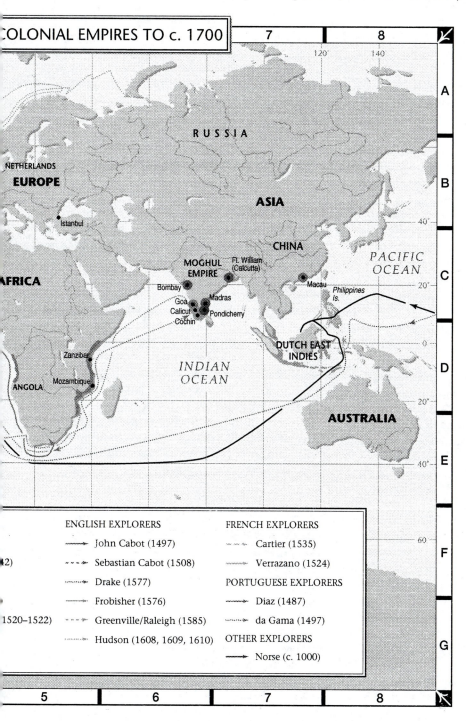

COLONIAL EMPIRES TO c. 1700

ENGLISH EXPLORERS

⟶ John Cabot (1497)

~~~⟶ Sebastian Cabot (1508)

⟶ Drake (1577)

⟶ Frobisher (1576)

~~~⟶ Greenville/Raleigh (1585)

⟶ Hudson (1608, 1609, 1610)

FRENCH EXPLORERS

~~~ Cartier (1535)

⟶ Verrazano (1524)

PORTUGUESE EXPLORERS

⟶ Diaz (1487)

⟶ da Gama (1497)

OTHER EXPLORERS

⟶ Norse (c. 1000)

The Spaniards' relations with the Aztecs were difficult at best. Montezuma, the Aztec ruler, became a hostage of the Spanish. Religious differences threatened to erupt into violence when Cortés insisted on Christianizing Aztec temples. On the other hand, Cortés and his men were in the midst of the lion's den and could be destroyed at any moment. When news arrived of a Spanish expedition from Cuba having reached the Mexican Gulf Coast in pursuit of Cortés, the conquistador left Tenochtitlan to defeat them, and he succeeded and incorporated most of the men into his expanding army. While away, he learned that the Aztecs had attacked the Spanish he had left behind in Tenochtitlan.

The Aztecs let Cortés and his men return to the city—to trap them. Cortés regained the palace, where Montezuma died in an Aztec assault. Fearing defeat, Cortés and his men fled the city with much loot in tow. Cortés lost 400 men and several thousand native allies, and it appeared that the Aztecs were on the verge of total victory.

Receiving sanctuary among his Tlaxcalan allies, Cortés recruited native followers among groups that chafed under tributary status to the Aztecs. He constructed a fleet of brigs to blockade the Aztec capital and starve it into submission. From their brigs, Spanish cannon opened fire on the Aztecs and the Spanish began to reduce the city, which was further weakened by food shortages and a small pox epidemic. By late August 1521, Cortés won his victory, and almost immediately began the subjection of the surrounding provinces.

Europeans learned many lessons from Cortés's conquest of the Aztecs. They surmised that the Americas possessed both good and bad Indians. The bad Indians (like the Aztecs) were assumed to be cannibals who would resist Christianity and oppose the Europeans' every step. The good Indians (like the Tlaxcalans) would feed, fight, and help the Europeans overcome the bad Indians. It was not necessary, Europeans believed, to outnumber natives to defeat them in battle. Future conquistadors must find the good Indians, who chafed under the oppression of bad Indians, ally with them, and lead them into battle against the bad. All one needed was to locate other rich cities like Tenochtitlan that would be worth conquering, such as El Dorado, the legendary city of gold.

## The Conquest of Peru: The Origins of the Global Economy

In 1531, the Spanish did not find El Dorado, but they did locate vast stores of incredible wealth in Peru among the Inca. In 1522, the Spanish had made an exploratory expedition south from Panama, which returned with rumors of a rich Indian empire. Two years later, Francisco Pizarro unsuccessfully sought this civilization, his expedition ending in disaster. The men suffered food shortages and defeat by the natives. Undeterred, Pizarro tried again only to be stranded on the island of Gallo. Seven months later, reinforcements arrived that had captured a large native raft filled with gold, silver, and other treasure. Despite this proof of riches, the governor of Panama refused to support a third expedition, so Pizarro returned to Spain to seek investors and more men.

When he returned, the new expedition entered the northern reaches of the lands of the Inca just as the Indians were in the midst of a great civil war, which Pizarro successfully exploited. They tricked Atahualpa, one of the Inca leaders, into a situation where the Spanish were able to capture him and kill over 1,500 Incans without losing a single man. Atahualpa's followers were hesitant to act without their leader, though they could have overwhelmed the Spanish but feared losing their chief in the battle. The

Incan king offered a ransom for his life, which the Spanish accepted. It was a phenomenal treasure. The Spanish melted down a huge store of gold and silver items created by Incan artisans—leaving them with over 13,000 pounds of 22 carat gold and twice as much silver. The Spanish divided the loot by shares—every member of the expedition was a rich man, as the lowliest infantryman received 45 pounds of gold and twice that of silver. Despite the ransom, Pizarro executed Atahualpa.

The Incans were not subdued, however, and continued their own civil war; the Spanish engaged in civil war in Peru as well. Not until 1572 were the Incans finally defeated—40 years after Pizarro had first encountered Atahualpa. The Spanish then controlled a vast domain in South America that extended from Columbia to Chile, while they expanded New Spain (Mexico) south into Central America and north into the southwest of the future United States.

The greatest benefit the Spanish reaped from the conquest of Peru was the discovery of the great silver mines of Potosí in modern-day Bolivia. Potosí silver provided Spain with the means to greatly expand trade with China, the world's foremost economy, and with other parts of Asia, such as Japan and the Spice Islands. Many historians and economists believe that Potosí silver initiated the modern world economy. The large stores of silver facilitated trade between Europe, Africa, North and South America, and Asia. The flow of silver fostered the creation of new colonies and cities engaging in international trade, directly linking Potosí in the Andes Mountains with Acapulco in Mexico, Manila in the Philippines, Nagasaki in Japan, Macao in China, and Goa in India. From these cities, further trunk lines extended to East Africa and around the Cape of Good Hope in South Africa to Europe. The economic stimulus of Potosí silver led households in China to produce silks worn by remote villagers in South America. Alongside of Potosí silver traveled American food crops on ships bound for Europe and Asia, introducing the potato to Ireland and China, where it became a dietary staple. Taken together, the Spanish ability to wrest gold and silver from Mexico and Peru prompted an increased desire by Europeans to seek riches in other parts of the Americas.

# EXPLORERS AND CONQUISTADORS IN THE AMERICAN SOUTHEAST AND SOUTHWEST

Many Spanish, including veterans from both Mexico and Peru, eyed the lands north of Mexico as the next place to find great native cities full of riches. But the impetus to explore the American Southeast and Southwest crossed paths with other desires: to colonize new lands and convert the native peoples to Christianity. Although not mutually exclusive, in each Spanish attempt, one of these ideas—riches, colonization, and conversion—predominated over the others until the Spanish crown became more determined to shape the development of its empire. Then they ended the age of the conquistador and sought to regularize colonization as a permanent process that would enlarge the empire while expanding the Catholic Church.

## Exploration of La Florida

In the 1520s, the Spanish hoped to repeat their success in Mexico in "La Florida"— the Spanish term for the American Southeast—but they considered other ways to wealth, namely, the sending of large numbers of colonists to undertake agricultural development. This was the rationale in the first real attempt to colonize the mainland of the future United States by Lucas Vázquez de Ayllón, who received the king's permission to build a colony in what is now South Carolina. A local Indian whom the Spanish captured in 1521 had convinced the Spanish Court that the region would produce wonderful agricultural products.

In 1526, Ayllón led 600 colonists to the land of Chicora, named for the Indian who so eloquently described the place to the Spanish. But the land did not reflect Chicora's stories, so the Spanish sailed further south, building the first European town in the future United States, San Miguel De Gualdape, in modern-day Georgia. They arrived too late to plant crops, and as sickness debilitated the settlers, they grew demoralized and abandoned the colony, returning to Hispaniola, many more dying along the way, so that only one-quarter survived the expedition.

The next attempt to establish a permanent presence in La Florida was even more disastrous. This was an expedition of 600 soldiers—not colonists—led by Panfilo de Narváez, a veteran of the Cortés expedition, who sailed into Tampa Bay in 1528. By then the Spanish were aware that Florida was not an island, as they had explored the coast of the Gulf of Mexico all the way from Florida to Mexico.

Narváez hoped to repeat Cortés's success in Mexico by discovering rich mines and caches of precious metals and gems. Local Indians told Narváez what he wanted to hear—there were untold riches northward—and the intrepid explorer led his men to the land of the Apalachee. Narváez made the fatal mistake of heading inland while leaving his ships to follow along the Gulf Coast.

The Spanish were no match for Apalachee military prowess. Apalachee archers' bows shot arrows that penetrated European armor. The Spanish were ill-suited to pursue their enemies in the Florida terrain. So fierce were the Apalachee against this and future Spanish *entradas* (royally sanctioned expeditions) that the Spanish named the Appalachian Mountains after them. Though the Apalachee lived hundreds of miles south of the mountains, the Spanish perceived that such a powerful people must control them as well.

After a year, the Spanish ships gave up waiting for Narváez and his men to return. The Spanish entrada had been pushed steadily to the northwest before abandoning hope and heading south to the Gulf of Mexico. By the time they reached the Gulf, most of the men had died and almost all the rest soon perished. They constructed makeshift rafts and sailed to Texas where the Karankawas enslaved them, disgusted that the Spanish had been living off the flesh of dead comrades.

## Cabeza de Vaca

Four other survivors, one an African slave, set out to find their countrymen in Mexico, an overland journey that brought their leader, Alvar Núñez Cabeza de Vaca, great fame among the Indians who believed him to be a holy man, and then in Spain as a great adventurer. De Vaca published an account of his sojourn from Florida to Mexico, which he reached in 1536, eight years after his first landing in America. De Vaca's book recounts the first stages of Spanish enslavement of the natives of the American Southwest, as raiders scoured the region for Indians to take to the mines of Mexico. The Indians who accompanied de Vaca, when he finally met with Spaniards in Texas, were astonished to learn—could not believe—that he was of the same people as the slave raiders. For Cabeza de Vaca's journey had transformed him—he developed sympathy, if not affection, for those among whom he wandered for many years, distinguishing between those who abased and those who helped him—realizing the complex humanity and diversity among the many peoples he encountered.

In de Vaca's book—a sober retelling of much misery and hardship—there is an absence of the fantasies and exaggerations of great cities of gold and other treasures typically recounted by adventurers to America and Asia. This led some contemporaries to believe that Cabeza de Vaca *must* have witnessed these wonders: Why else would he keep silent? De Vaca's story had the unintended consequence of inspiring the first wide-scale European exploration of the future United States.

From Mexico, Cortés sent an exploratory party north along the California coast, while others were sent into New Mexico. These probings led to the Coronado expedition, the first intensive European exploration of the American West. While Coronado headed northeast from Texas, another large Spanish force, led by Hernando de Soto, moved north from Florida. Together these two expeditions crossed much of the breadth of the future United States.

## De Soto's Entrada

Hernando de Soto was an experienced conquistador, having earned for himself a fortune in Peru. In 1537, the king authorized him to settle Florida. De Soto was unsuccessful in convincing Cabeza de Vaca to join him—the latter instead became governor of Paraguay. De Soto was so sure of Florida's riches that he invested his Peruvian fortune and borrowed great amounts to subsidize his over 600 man (and a few women) expedition.

Following in the footsteps of the earlier Narváez expedition, de Soto's landed at Tampa Bay in May 1539. The Spanish soon located Juan Ortiz, a survivor of the Narváez expedition who served him as translator. Any advantage de Soto might have reaped from Ortiz's linguistic and cultural expertise was negated by de Soto's brutality towards the numerous peoples he encountered. Wherever they went, the Spanish abused the natives. Women were taken as concubines, natives were forced to become *tamemes* (carriers of the Spaniards' goods), and many were sadistically murdered and mutilated by the conquistadors and their dogs. The enslavement of Indians was a planned affair: de Soto brought the iron implements necessary to secure coffles of slaves.

De Soto led his unwieldy army on a great trek through the Southeast. From Florida they headed north, along the way encountering militarily organized native peoples who fought them successfully, pushing the Spanish from their lands as much as the Spanish wished to move on in search of precious metals. As the Spanish proceeded, word of their impending arrival preceded them, thus Indians often abandoned their towns and waited for the Spanish in ambush. The Spanish did, however, receive a warm welcome from the great Queen Cofitachequi, who was carried in a litter by her people and graciously showered the Spanish with food and gifts. Among her people the Spanish found no gold, but the queen possessed many pearls. The Spanish stole from her temples 200 pounds of pearls. For 15 days the Spanish stayed with these Indians, ancestors to some of the modern-day Creek people. They got along well until de Soto demanded women. As they continued on their journey, the process was repeated—friendly relations turned sour when de Soto placed unreasonable demands on his hosts.

After scouring the Carolinas, de Soto headed west through the Tennessee River Valley and into modern-day Alabama. The powerful Coosa chiefdom, also ancestors of the Creek, inflicted a great defeat on the Spanish, who lost most of their supplies and horses. Many Spanish wanted to quit these lands and head to the Gulf of Mexico, where Spanish ships waited, but de Soto pushed on. They marched into the rolling hills of northern Mississippi, where the powerful Chickasaw almost destroyed the Spanish expedition. The survivors built barges and crossed the Mississippi River into Arkansas—de Soto considering whether to continue on to the Pacific Ocean—he was unaware not only of the huge breadth of the continent, but that Coronado's expedition was only 300 miles to the west. De Soto decided to turn back. Upon reaching the Arkansas Plains, he beat a retreat to the Mississippi and the Spanish encountered the great Moundbuilder cultures along that river, particularly the Natchez, who offered the Spanish no succor.

When de Soto fell ill and died in the spring of 1542, the remnants of his entrada marched towards Mexico across Louisiana and Texas. Running out of food, they returned to the Mississippi, which they descended to the Gulf of Mexico, and eventually 300 survivors reached Mexico. All told, the expedition had lasted 3.5 years from the time it entered Florida to its exit from the Mississippi.

The Spanish reaped no benefit from this costly enterprise. The information attained about the South and its peoples was of little practical value, for the Spanish would not send more expeditions—the region did not appear promising in terms of providing a financial windfall. Moreover, the Spanish alienated every Indian group they met; it is doubtful they would receive a warm welcome anywhere.

Many Indians of the region were left in disarray by the Spanish. The Europeans introduced pathogens that had deadly impact on native peoples, as new diseases and illnesses spread from one group to the next. Hitherto unexposed to these pathogens, the natives had no protection from them. Fortunately for many, since the Spanish and other Europeans did not return to most of the American Southeast outside of Florida and coastal Georgia and Carolina for a half-century to a century and more, many groups recovered their numbers and developed resistance to the illnesses, so that they did not suffer as much as those subject to sustained contact, as in Florida, where upwards of 90% of the native population lost their lives from Spanish-borne diseases.

The de Soto entrada was a scandal in Spain, and led many to question the purpose and conduct of Spanish overseas settlement. De Soto's contemporaries almost universally condemned him. His abuse of Indians particularly stood out, and many from within the Church called for better treatment of native peoples and their conversion to Christianity. The avaricious goals of men like de Soto were transparent, and it was indicative of his entrada, and a special point of criticism, that it wandered from place to place; by the 1540s, Spain wanted colonies, not roving bands of treasure hunters. The age of the conquistador was coming to an end, and the crown refused to license such men. Instead, the age of the *adelantado* was born, who was more of an administrator over a given territory of which he held many rights and privileges. The adelantado was to subdue native people in a single place, employ priests to bring them to Christianity, and import Spanish to settle the land and strengthen it defensively.

## Coronado and the Search for Cibola

As de Soto explored and ravaged the Southeast, Francisco Vázquez de Coronado, with similar goals, explored the Southwest. A friar, Marcos de Niza, earlier had reported finding the great city of Cibola in the Sonora Valley, Arizona. Cibola was reputed in medieval legends to be one of the seven great cities of the world, and Fray Marcos declared it more magnificent than Mexico City.

The viceroy of New Spain authorized Coronado to seize Cibola. Coronado invested money from his wife's great fortune to outfit over 300 Spaniards, 1,000 Indians, and 1,500 horses and pack animals. They departed northwest Mexico in February 1540 and invaded Cibola in July. Cibola was nothing like what Fray Marcos had described. Instead of a great city, they found a Zuni town of a few hundred inhabitants. The friar was sent home in disgrace, but Coronado persevered. He sent small exploring parties to the west, which reached the Colorado River, and to the east to the Rio Grande River. Hearing good things about the Rio Grande Valley, he took his expedition east to winter. Most everywhere they went, the natives were friendly and helpful.

But in Texas, the Spaniards overtaxed the Indians' resources and a dozen pueblos took up arms against the invaders. A Plains Indian, possibly a Pawnee, who had befriended the Spanish, promised to guide them to Quivera, which he claimed contained much gold. Coronado headed northeast in the Spring of 1541, encountering great herds of buffalo and Indians who might have been Apache. They also met with the Teyas, from which Texas received its name. Sending most of the men to camp at the Pecos River, Coronado crossed the high plains of western Texas, northeast to Oklahoma. They followed the Arkansas River east to the land of the Wichita, then headed northeast again. Having reached Kansas, Coronado claimed the land for Spain by erecting a wooden cross. But having found no cities of gold, he and his forces retreated to Mexico.

Despite discovering friendly Indians who inhabited rich lands, and who graciously shared their food and provided guides and other assistance, the expedition was considered a failure because no gold was found. Coronado was tried but declared innocent of mismanagement. Although the Spanish would soon expand their domain into New Mexico, it would be well over a century before they returned in numbers to Texas.

## THE IMPORTANCE OF FLORIDA

After de Soto, it was difficult to convince anyone in Spain of La Florida's value. In March 1562, King Philip made a formal declaration that he would not support any expedition to La Florida. But if La Florida had no intrinsic value as a source of precious metals or other valuable commodities, the Florida peninsula had great geopolitical significance. Florida's location was key to guarding the sea route that connected Spain to its New World Empire.

## Protecting the Sea Lanes

Jealous of Spain's Atlantic empire and Portugal's Asia empire, English, French, and Dutch all sought a share of the riches through privateering. Privateers were licensed pirates, usually called corsairs in the 16th century—government authorized (and sometimes funded) to assault the ships and possessions of other nations. They did considerable damage against Spanish and Portuguese shipping and coastal communities in the Atlantic, Pacific, and Indian Oceans. Privateering led to great profits for governments and private investors, while employing huge numbers of men. The Spanish and Portuguese responded by strengthening their shipping lanes, but they never were able to completely end assaults upon their far-flung empires.

The attacks of corsairs upon Spanish shipping forced the crown to organize the shipment of goods within the empire. As early as 1526, merchant vessels were required to sail in convoys. By the early 1540s, the crown had organized a system that would remain in effect, with various adaptations, for the next two and a half centuries. The Spanish Navy would guard merchant convoys to and from the Americas. Initially, one fleet sailed each year to the West Indies, and upon reaching the Caribbean, it divided into two: one went to Mexico and the other to South America and then to Panama. This was succeeded by two heavily armed convoys annually. For the return each spring, ships from Panama, Columbia, and elsewhere in the Americas sailed for Cuba, and from there, they received an armed escort to Spain. (The Potosí silver ships received their escort the moment they left port.) The safest and quickest sailing route from Cuba to Spain was north along the Florida coast before heading east. Thus, if the Florida coast was in the hands of Spain's enemies, it would provide a convenient locale from which to attack Spanish treasure ships. Moreover, Florida could provide a base for direct attacks upon Spanish colonial settlements, in Cuba and other islands in the West Indies, as well as Mexico and Central America. Englishman Sir Francis Drake, for instance, led assaults upon Spanish towns in the Caribbean, and on mainland American Atlantic and Pacific coasts. He forced inhabitants to pay ransoms to stop him from destroying all of a town's buildings and to return captives.

## French and Spanish in Florida: The Violent Competition of Empires

Believing the Spanish had given up on settling Florida, the French determined to seek treasure there, landing a large force in 1562. King Philip II of Spain quickly determined to destroy the French colony. The king selected for the task one of his most competent naval captains, Pedro Menéndez de Avilés. Menéndez had proven his skills by commanding the squadron that guarded the treasure ships that yearly sailed from the Americas to Spain through the straits of Florida. Philip ordered Menéndez to remove the French and build a permanent Spanish colony. The episode that unfolded had great repercussions for the future of Spanish, French, and English settlement in North America.

The French constructed Fort Caroline to the north of modern-day St. Augustine. Jean Ribault, the French commander, after establishing the colony returned to France to gain more supplies and support. Captured and temporarily imprisoned in England, Ribault piqued English interest in the region to copy the French and also establish a permanent base along the Atlantic Coast, ultimately leading to the settlement of Roanoke.

Ribault returned to Florida just before Spanish arrival in 1565. The French took to their ships believing they would have greater firepower against the Spanish at sea. For five days they unsuccessfully sought the enemy, then a storm dispersed the French ships against the Florida coast. Menéndez came up behind them and easily captured Fort Caroline. He hung its men. The Spanish learned from local Indians, whom the French initially had befriended but then betrayed, that hundreds of French had shipwrecked in various areas along the coast. Although outnumbered, the Spanish had the upper hand—for their forces were all together. The groups of dispersed French sailors, who numbered between 300 and 500, all made the same decision: without their ships they had no choice but to surrender. Menéndez offered no terms—the French would have to accept whatever fate he determined for them.

Ordered to submit in parties of ten, the French were each questioned as to their religion and skills aboard ship. Then, with their hands tied behind their back, they were stabbed to death. The process was repeated for the next ten—their comrades unaware of the previous ten men's fate. This continued until almost all were killed. Only 16 were spared. Menéndez justified the cold-blooded murders to his king, claiming the French had been spreading "the odious Lutheran [Protestant] doctrine in these Provinces, and that I had [to make] war [with] fire and blood against all those who came to sow this hateful doctrine." In spite of his professed religious motives, the 16 whom he spared were of the heretical faith, but Menéndez required their special skills.

The first meeting of two European groups intending to colonize the same locale in the future United States had ended in a bloodbath. The competition for European settlement of the New World would hereafter be defined largely by warfare. Legal claims to territory had little meaning—brute force was the deciding factor. Whatever civility men may have displayed at home, they would show even less in the New World, where distance from traditional societal institutions seemed to give license for all sorts of acts of inhumanity.

Menéndez's colony survived as the oldest permanent European settlement in what is now St. Augustine, Florida. Though Spanish Florida was important for protecting the sea lane, the colony never came close to fulfilling the economic goals of the Spanish crown, and in fact, long drained the Spanish treasury. From 1564 to 1577, Florida consumed a quarter of the empire's entire outlay for defense. And although that percentage declined, the colony remained enormously expensive—forts had to be built and constantly maintained in the inhospitable environment; soldiers, settlers, and supplies had to be sent; and priests and presents had to be provided for the Indians, who hopefully would be lured into missions to be converted to Christianity and then would provide labor and defense for the colony. The crown intended the colony to be self-supporting through agriculture and livestock, which could be sent to the West Indies.

## SPANISH AND INDIANS

By the second quarter, and even the third quarter of the 16th century, most American Indians had yet to develop views of the Spanish and other Europeans—they had yet to meet them, and knew little, if anything about them. The Spanish had formed a much more distinct picture of Native American societies. They knew these varied greatly one from the next, but were similar in their heathenism and perceived savagery. Even more important to the Spanish: the Indians could be a source of great wealth. Some possessed massive quantities of precious metals and gems; that many Indian civilizations had marvelous craftsmen who turned gold and silver into valuable objects was unimportant—the Spanish melted these items down. If the Indians did not have precious metals, then they could be put to work to wrest wealth from the land. But many Spanish also feared that if they did not convert the heathen to Christianity, then God would not bless their enterprise. God, they believed, had hidden knowledge of the Americas from Europeans for centuries and then revealed the New World for a purpose—he expected his people to enlarge the Church of Christ. Spain above all other nations of Europe had been blessed with a great empire in America, and must fulfill its duty to serve God and his Church.

## Spanish Conversion of American Indians

Conversion of the natives would not be easy. Spanish and Indians viewed one another across a vast cultural divide. Differences in ways of life—customs, work, play, and religion made distinctions that often created suspicion and hostility rather than curiosity. Some native practices, like frequent bathing, though inscrutable to Europeans, probably were not a focal point for hostility; indigenous peoples were probably more offended by the lack of frequency with which Europeans bathed. The Iberians took greatest offense at cannibalism, which they encountered in the Caribbean, Central America, Mexico, and Brazil. This practice alone earned American Indians a badge of inferiority in European eyes, compounded by negative perceptions of Indian nudity or near nudity as indicative of a wanton nature. The thoughtful among the Spanish pondered the sources of native "savagery": Were Indians naturally inclined to their alleged debaseness, or was it a product of their heathenism and ignorance? Whatever the answer, churchmen agreed, conversion would rectify a host of faults.

By the time Florida was colonized, Philip II insisted that the cross accompany the sword. Menéndez brought six Jesuits to Florida—the first Jesuits to work in Spanish America—to preach the gospel. As often was the case in colonies, religious and military interests clashed, retarding conversions. Nevertheless, Spain built an extensive mission system designed to Christianize Indians and "civilize" them to Spanish ways. Beginning in the province of Guale, the coastal region of modern-day Georgia, sweeping south to Mocama in northeast Florida, and then west across northern Florida, the Spanish created over 30 missionary communities by 1675.

Missionaries often took it upon themselves to defend the interests of their Indians against civil and military authorities. Missionized Indians were expected to provide labor and military service, and demands upon them could be oppressive. Priests—and Indians themselves—wrote letters to the king and his ministers to redress grievances, and they often received a sympathetic reply. Many Spanish sought to rectify the worst abuses of conquest and colonialism, and it was not unusual for priests and their allies to consider converted American Indians as better Christians than their own colonists and colonial officials, especially in places like northern Florida where the priests had great success.

## Indians and Missions in La Florida

Those natives who accepted mission life often did so because their own societies were crumbling amidst the onslaught of disease, and the political and social changes brought about by the Spanish. Indeed, to many Indians, they were the last hope for survival. Missions ordinarily included not just the converted, but "heathen" of different ethnicities seeking refuge from their enemies. The transformation of life could be slow. Missionaries rarely tried to radically alter native culture. The natives would not tolerate radical change. Instead, the missionaries focused upon baptism, teaching catechisms, regular attendance at religious ceremonies, and eliminating native cultural practices they found reprehensible, such as polygamy, idol worship, and immodest dress. In Florida, the missionaries undertook a sustained program to end the playing of pelota, a violent ballgame that pit Indian communities against one another. To the Spanish, the game signified Indian savagery, but perhaps, too, they perceived the game as reinforcing Indian ties to their communities, rather than to the Spanish and Christianity. Certainly they opposed the injuries from playing that prevented the men from working.

Mission Indians were expected to labor. Abuse of Indian labor had come under attack from within the Church as early as 1511, and Spain enacted laws to protect laborers in the following years. The "New Laws" officially ended the enslavement of Indians—but not Africans—in 1549, but Spanish officials kept Indians in various forms of forced labor through the centuries.

*Repartimiento* was one loosely defined form of labor practiced by the Spanish in Florida and elsewhere in the empire. Generally, Indian adult males were required to work for the king two weeks per year in the fields, though they often worked for months at a time unloading ships, building forts, procuring lumber, and so on. The priests also assigned Indians to work in fields—mostly women—to maintain the Church, while tithing a portion of each family's farm products. Indians were forced to sell their crops to the government, a system fraught with abuse. Most arrangements were negotiated with caciques (chiefs), a practice common within the Spanish colonies.

The benefits of the Florida missions to Spain were immense, for mission Indians provided much of the colony's defense, labor, and foodstuffs. And the Spanish had much success converting Florida natives, especially in comparison with later efforts by the English and French to the north. But ultimately, the Florida missions were a failure, as most were destroyed from 1660 to 1710 by Indians, English, and pirates intent on enslaving mission Indians.

## Conclusion

Spain was the most important nation creating an Atlantic World empire in the 16th century. The conquests of Mexico and Peru, in particular, fueled Spain's continued expansion into the Americas. American gold, and more importantly, silver, made colonialism a paying proposition. A large portion of the income obtained from precious metals was funneled to Spain's military needs in Europe, where Spain was the most significant power. But much American silver also made its way to the Spanish Philippines, and from there to China, the Spice Islands, and elsewhere in Asia, prompting globalization of trade. Asia, Europe, and Africa had already been connected by trade, but now the Americas became an important component of commercial networks that circled the globe. The subsequent creation of plantation agriculture in the Americas, producing crops such as sugar and tobacco, would further integrate the Americas into world markets, and increasingly tie Africa into both globalization and European empire-building, as millions of Africans were transported to the Americas to work as slave laborers.

Spain would not be at the forefront of this agricultural expansion, though they would participate in it. The Portuguese in Brazil, and the French and English in the West Indies, eventually played pre-eminent roles in establishing the plantation complex of sugar and slaves that became the cornerstone of the Atlantic economy. Nonetheless, in terms of Atlantic empires, Spain's became the largest and most geographically far-reaching, extending south from Mexico through Central America and much of South America, and north into New Mexico, California, and Florida, as well as into the West Indies, where it included Cuba, Puerto Rico, Hispaniola, and other islands. Although a centralized empire receiving much direction from Spain, Spanish success owed to its adaptability. The ending of the age of the conquistador inaugurated more rationale approaches to colonization. Spanish political officials and priests employed a variety of methods to integrate new territories and peoples into the empire. Conversion of American Indians was key and a cornerstone of Spanish success. Abuse of native peoples did not end, as Indian labor was exploited in a variety of ways. But in many places, accommodation between the colonized and the colonizer was reached, giving the empire stability and permanence: the Spanish empire largely outlasted the empires of other Europeans in the Americas.

Spanish success north of Mexico was more limited than to the south, though there too the presence was lengthy and widespread. With the de Soto and Coronado expeditions, the Spanish explored the inland continent from California to Florida. Not until the Lewis and Clark expedition over two and a half centuries later did Europeans or their descendants again undertake cross-continental exploration. The expeditions of Coronado and de Soto had but fleeting impact on Spanish expansion, but they introduced many Europeans to American Indians, as well as deadly pathogens that spread disease. Nonetheless, by not sustaining contact in the aftermath, this could have helped many inland Indians develop resistance for when Europeans ultimately returned.

Spain did not completely give up settling North America above Mexico after the failures of de Soto and Coronado. Most notable was the settlement of Florida, largely to defend the sea lanes, and to prevent other Europeans from using Florida as a base to threaten Mexico, Cuba, and other Spanish colonies. In the 17th century, Spain also established a more permanent presence in New Mexico, and in the 18th century, it returned to Texas. For the most part, however, Spain had little reason to expand north of Mexico. Strategic imperatives aside, these lands held little economic promise. The opportunity to mine precious metals or cultivate tropical crops was the major lure to colonize new areas. The Spanish would have liked to expand into California, for there were many Indians there and the cultivation of crops would support other regions, but the Spanish feared that settling the California coast would attract English, Dutch, and French interlopers who could then interfere with the profitable trade between Mexico and Asia.

By the end of the 16th century, competitor European powers cast their eyes on colonizing in the north Atlantic at places where Spain had shown little interest. Spain was alarmed by the entry of France into Florida, but not overly concerned when French, English, and Dutch attempted to colonize further north. The Spanish expected these endeavors to fail—they did not believe that colonies in places like the future Virginia, New York, New England, or Canada would be financially viable. The ecology of these places would not permit the production of tropical crops, and there likely was no gold or silver since the Indians of these regions possessed little or no precious metals.

# DOCUMENTS

## 2.1. An Eyewitness Account of the de Soto Expedition

*Hernando de Soto arrived at Tampa Bay in 1539 with approximately 600 men. His shortsightedness and brutality towards American Indians played a significant role in the failure of his expedition. For three years, de Soto led his men through the Southeast in search of El Dorado. They traveled as far north as Tennessee and as far west as Texas. Soto died along the way. The failure of his expedition and a later one by Tristan de Luna y Arrellano led Philip II to announce that no more Spanish attempts would be made to settle Florida. The following account was written by Rodrigo Ranjel, who accompanied de Soto as his private secretary. How did the Indians respond to the Spanish when first encountering them? How did their behavior change when the Spanish became abusive?*

On Sunday, May 8, the Governor Hernando de Soto departed from the City of Havana with a noble fleet of nine vessels, five ships, two caravels and two brigantines; and on May 25, which was Whitsuntide, land was seen on the northern coast of Florida; and the fleet came to anchor two leagues from shore in four fathoms of water or less. . . .

On Trinity Sunday, June 1, 1539, this army marched by land toward the village, taking as guides four Indians that Johan de Anasco had captured when in search of the harbour; and they lost their bearings some what, either because the Christians failed to understand the Indians or because the latter did not tell the truth. . . .

Some paths were found, but no one knew or was able to guess which to take to find the natives of the country. The four Indians understood very little, and then only by signs, and it was not easy to guard them as they had no fetters. Tuesday, June 3, the Governor took possession of the country in the name of their Majesties, with all the formalities that are required, and dispatched one of the Indians to persuade and allure the neighbouring chiefs with peace. That same night two of the three Indians that remained ran away, and it was only by great good luck that all three did not get away, which gave the Christians much concern.

This Governor [Soto] was much given to the sport of slaying Indians, from the time he went on military expeditions with the Governor Pedrarias Davila in the provinces of Castilla del Oro and of Nicaragua. . . .

So then, continuing his conquest, he ordered General Vasco Porcallo de Figueroa to go to Ocita because it was reported that people had come together there; and this captain having gone

*(Continued)*

there, he found the people departed and he burned the village and threw an Indian, which he had for a guide, to the dogs....

The Governor decided to go further inland, because an Indian lad gave great reports of what there was in the interior....

[T]hey came to a village where some principal Indians appeared as messengers from Ichisi; and one of them addressed the Governor and said three words, one after the other, in this manner: "Who are you, what do you want, where are you going?" And they brought presents of skins, the blankets of the country, which were the first gifts as a sign of peace. All of this took place on Holy Thursday and on the Day of the Incarnation. To the questions of the Indian the governor replied that he was a captain of the great King of Spain; that in his name he had come to make known to them the holy faith of Christ that they should acknowledge him and be saved and yield obedience to the apostolic Church of Rome and to the supreme Pontiff and vicar of God, who lived there; and that in temporal affairs they should acknowledge for king and lord the Emperor, King of Castile, our Lord, as his vassals; and that they would treat them well in every thing and that he would maintain toward them peace and justice just the same as towards all his Christian vassals....

Friday the last day of April the Governor took some horse, those that were most refreshed, and the Indian woman that Baltasar de Gallegos brought for a guide, and went along the road to Cofitachequi, and spent the night near a large, deep river; and he sent on Johan de Anasco with some horsemen to secure some interpreters and canoes for crossing the river, and he got some. The next day the Governor came to the crossing opposite the village, and the chief Indians came with gifts and the woman chief, lady of that land whom Indians of rank bore on their shoulders with much respect, in a litter covered with delicate white linen. And she crossed in the canoes and spoke to the Governor quite gracefully and at her ease. She was a young girl of fine bearing; and she took off a string of pearls which she wore on her neck, and put it on the Governor as a necklace to show her favour and to gain his good will. And all the army crossed over in canoes and they received many presents of skins well tanned and blankets, all very good; and countless strips of venison and dry wafers, and an abundance of very good salt. All the Indians went clothed down to their feet with very fine skins well dressed, and blankets of the country, and blankets of sable fur and others of the skin of wild cats which gave out a strong smell. The people are very clean and polite and naturally well conditioned.

On Friday, May 7, Baltasar de Gallegos, with the most of the soldiers of the army, arrived at Ilapi to eat seven barbacoas of corn, that they said were there stored for the woman chief. That same day the Governor and Rodrigo Ranjel entered the mosque and oratory of this heathen people, and opening some burying places they found some bodies of men fastened on a barbacoa. The breasts, belly necks and arms and legs full of pearls.... They took away from there some two hundred pounds of pearls; and when the woman chief saw that the Christians set much store by them, she said: "Do you hold that of much account? Go to Talimeco, my village, and you will find so many that your horses cannot carry them." The Governor replied: "Let them stay there; to whom God gives a gift, may St. Peter bless it." And there the matter dropped. It was believed that he planned to take that place for himself. . . .

The Indians spent fifteen days with the Christians in peace, and they played with them, and likewise among themselves. They swam with the Christians and helped them very much in every way. They ran away afterwards on Saturday, the 19th of the month, for something that the Governor asked of them; and in short, it was because he asked for women. The next day in the morning the Governor sent to call the chief and he came immediately; and the next day the Governor took him off with him to make his people come back, and the result was they came back. In the land of this Chiaha was where the Spaniards first found fenced villages. Chiaha gave them five hundred carriers, and they consented to leave off collars and chains. . . .

Thursday they passed another small village, and then other villages, and Friday the Governor entered Coca.

This chief is a powerful one and a ruler of a wide territory, one of the best and most abundant that they found in Florida. And the chief came out to receive the Governor in a litter covered with the white mantles of the country, and the litter was borne on the shoulders of sixty or seventy of his principal subjects, with no plebian or common Indian among them; and those that bore him took turns by relays with great ceremonies after their manner.

There were in Coca many plumes like the early ones of Seville, very good; both they and the trees were like those of Spain. There were also some wild apples like those called canavales in Extremadura, small in size. They remained there in Coca some days, in which the Indians went off and left their chief in the power of the Christians with some principal men, and the Spaniards went out to round them up, and they took many, and they put them in iron collars and chains. And verily, according to the testimony of eye-witnesses, it was a grievous thing to see. But God failed not to remember every evil deed, nor were they left unpunished, as this history will tell.

The historian asked a very intelligent gentleman who was with this Governor, and who went with him through his whole expedition in this northern country, why, at every place they came to, this Governor and his army asked for those tamemes or Indian carriers, and why they took so many women and these not old nor the most ugly; and why, after having given them what they had, they held the chiefs and principal men; and why they never tarried nor settled in any region they came to, adding that such a course was not settlement or conquest, but rather disturbing and ravaging the land and depriving the natives of their liberty without converting or making a single Indian either a Christian or a friend. He replied and said: That they took these carriers or tamemes to keep them as slaves or servants to carry the loads of supplies which they secured by plunder or gift,

*(Continued)*

and that some died, and others ran away or were tired out, so that it was necessary to replenish their numbers and to take more; and the women they desired both as servants and for their foul uses and lewdness, and that they had them baptized more on account of carnal intercourse with them than to teach them the faith; and that if they held the chiefs and principal men captive, it was because it would keep their subjects quiet, so that they would not molest them when foraging or doing what they wished in their country; and that whither they were going neither the Governor nor others knew, but that his purpose was to find some land rich enough to satiate his greed and to get knowledge of the great secrets this Governor said he had heard in regard to those regions according to much information he had received; and as for stirring up the country and not settling it, nothing else could be done until they found a site that was satisfactory.

Source: Rodrigo Ranjel, Diary, in *Narratives of the Career of Hernando de Soto*. 4 vols. Translated and edited by Edward C. Bourne (1904), 2: 51–52, 55–56, 59–60, 69, 78–80, 86, 88, 91–92, 98–99, 112–113, 117–118.

## 2.2. Pedro Menéndez de Avilés Explains to King Philip II Why He Put the French in Florida to Death

*When in 1563 King Philip II of Spain chose to establish a permanent colony in Florida, he selected one of his most competent naval captains, Pedro Menéndez de Avilés. Menéndez had proven his skills by commanding the squadron that guarded the treasure ships that yearly sailed from America to Spain through the straits of Florida. When a French force landed in Florida in 1562 to establish a colony, the Spanish had to destroy it, otherwise the French could use Florida as a privateering base to assault the treasure fleet, and perhaps as a staging ground to take Cuba, the center of Spanish power in the Caribbean. Menéndez chose to put almost all the French he captured to death, which he justified in letter to the king. On what grounds did Menendez put almost all the French to death?*

### Pedro Menéndez de Avilés to King Philip II

On the 28th of September [1565] the Indians notified me that many Frenchman were about six leagues from here on the coast, that they had lost their vessels and escaped by swimming and in boats. Taking fifty soldiers I was with them next morning at daylight, and leaving my men in ambush, I took one with me to the banks of the river, because they were on one side and I on the other bank. I spoke to them, told them I was Spanish; they said they were French. They asked me to come over to them either alone or with my partner, the river being narrow. I replied that we did not know how to swim, but that they could safely come to us. They agreed to do so, and sent a man of some intellect, master of a boat, who carefully related to me how they had left their Fort with four galleons and eight small vessels, that each carried twenty-four oars with four hundred picked soldiers and two hundred marines and John Ribault as General and Monsieur Le Grange, who was General of the Infantry, and other good captains, soldiers, and gentlemen, with the intention of finding me on the sea, and if I attempted to land, to land their people on the small boats and capture me . . . that they were overtaken by a hurricane and tempest and were wrecked about twenty or twenty-five leagues from here. . . . He asked for himself and companions safe passage to their Fort, since they were not at war with the Spaniards. I then told him how we had taken their Fort and hanged all those we found in it, because they had built it without Your Majesty's permission and because they were scattering the odious Lutheran doctrine in these Provinces, and that I had [to make] war [with] fire and blood, as Governor and Captain-General of these Provinces, against all those who came to sow this hateful doctrine; representing to him that I came by order of Your Majesty to place the Gospel in these parts and to enlighten the natives in all that the Holy Church of Rome says and does so as to save their souls. That I would not give them passage; rather would I follow them by sea and land until I had taken their lives. He begged to be allowed to go with this embassy and that he would return at night swimming, if I would grant him his life. I did to show him that I was in earnest and because he would enlighten me on many subjects. Immediately after his return to his companions there came a gentleman, a Monsieur Laudonnier, a man well versed and cunning to tempt me. After much talk he offered to give up their arms if I would grant their lives. I told him he could surrender the arms and give themselves up to my mercy, that I might do with them that which our Lord ordered. More than this he could not get from me. And that God did not expect more of me. Thus he returned and they came to deliver up their arms. I had their hands tied behind them and had them stabbed to death, leaving only sixteen, twelve being great big men, mariners whom they had stolen, the other four master carpenters and caulkers — people for whom we have much need, and it seemed to me to punish them in this manner would be serving God, our Lord, and Your Majesty. Hereafter they will leave us free to plant the Gospel, enlighten the natives, and bring them to obedience and submission to Your Majesty. The lands being extensive, it will be well to make them work fifty years — besides, a good beginning makes a good end, so I have hopes in our Lord that in all He will grant me prosperity and success, so that I and my descendants may give to Your Majesty those Kingdoms full and return the people Christians. My particular interest as I have written Your Majesty is this: We are gaining great favor with the Indians and will be feared by them, although we make them many gifts.

Source: A. M. Brooks, The Unwritten History of St. Augustine (1909), 133–134.

## Bibliography

Burkholder, Mark A., and Lyman L. Johnson. *Colonial Latin America* (2004).

Bushnell, Amy. *The King's Coffers: Proprietors of the Spanish Florida Treasury, 1565–1702* (1981).

Cabeza de Vaca, Alvar Núñez. *Castaways: The Narrative of Alvar Núñez Cabeza de Vaca*, ed., Enrique Pupo-Walker, trans., Frances M. López-Morillas (1993).

Clayton, Lawrence A., Vernon James Knight, Jr., and Edward C. Moore. *The De Soto Chronicles: The Expedition of Hernando De Soto to North America in 1539–1543* (1993).

Diffie, Bailey W., and George D. Winius. *Foundations of the Portuguese Empire, 1415–1580* (1977).

Flint, Richard. *No Settlement, No Conquest: A History of the Coronado Entrada* (2008).

Flint, Richard, and Shirley Cushing Flint, eds. *The Coronado Expedition to Tierra Nueva: The 1540–1542 Route Across the Southwest* (1997).

Floyd, Troy S. *The Columbus Dynasty in the Caribbean, 1492–1526* (1973).

Gallay, Alan, ed. *The Colonial Wars of North America, 1512–1763: An Encyclopedia* (1996).

Hoffman, Paul E. *A New Andalucia and a Way to the Orient: The American Southeast During the Sixteenth Century* (1990).

Hoffman, Paul E. *The Spanish Crown and the Defense of the Caribbean, 1535–1585: Precedent, Patrimonialism, and Royal Parsimony* (1980).

Hudson, Charles. *Knights of Spain, Warriors of the Sun: Hernando De Soto and the South's Ancient Chiefdoms* (1997).

Lyon, Eugene. *Enterprise of Florida: Pedro Menendez Aviles and the Spanish Conquest of 1565–1568* (1983).

Parry, J. H. *The Age of Reconnaissance* (1963).

Parry, J. H. *The Spanish Seaborne Empire* (1966).

Phillips, William D., and Carla Rahn Phillips. *The Worlds of Christopher Columbus* (1991).

Reséndez, Andrés. *A Land So Strange: The Epic Journey of Cabeza de Vaca* (2007).

Russell, Peter. *Prince Henry the Navigator* (2000).

Sauer, Carl Ortwin. *Sixteenth-Century North America: The Land and People as Seen by the Europeans* (1971).

Weber, David J. *The Spanish Frontier in North America* (1992).

# 3

# Early Stages of English Overseas Expansion, 1508–1622

## INTRODUCTION

No European nation had as great an impact on the future United States as England. English political and legal institutions indelibly shaped American civil society; English language, history, and culture provided the window through which many colonists viewed and understood the New World. Although two of the most notable characteristics of the United States have been the diversity of its people and environment, Anglo culture is stamped upon American society in just so many ways. English colonists viewed the land and its peoples through English eyes, and most hoped to re-create England in the New World.

But America could not become England. An abundance of land that could produce plantation crops, plenty of food, and contained great forests, the long distance from Europe, and entirely new circumstances precluded an exact mirroring of English society. Some of the changes owed to demography. A plethora of native peoples and the arrival of immigrants from other lands—especially from Africa and Europe—all interacted to create new cultural forms. English colonists would not even form a majority in many English colonies, as Scots, Scots-Irish, Dutch, Angolans, Irish, Bantus, French, Germans, Ibos, Swiss, Senegambians, and dozens of other peoples arrived on American shores—free or in bondage—bringing with them their own culture. But the political sinew was English in English colonies—in the formation of local, colonial, and imperial governments. English political culture also prevailed in terms of free peoples' understanding of rights and privileges, liberty and justice, political participation, and dissent. English political forms provided the philosophic underpinnings for much of civil life, even as they were contested, enlarged upon, and altered.

There was, of course, no one English way of doing things. The English varied by class, gender, religion, and geography. And English colonies varied immensely due to environmental, institutional, and demographic factors. Virginia, Barbados, and Massachusetts were all English colonies, yet differed tremendously in terms of local government, economy, settlement patterns, religion, and class relations. A European visiting them would note their English character, yet—and travelers often would—stand amazed at their disparity.

Diversity was inevitable, and within England itself people were both aware and proud of regional diversification, but the thrust of history was towards unity. England, France, and Spain all were in the process of centralizing through administrative and legal measures, reducing the nobility's regional power, and increasing central government authority. These nations developed national armies and national economic policies, while cultural uniformity began to prevail over regional distinctiveness. Monarchy was getting stronger not weaker.

## ENGLISH POLITICAL CULTURE

When Columbus sailed for America, England was a mid-level nation in western Europe, where Spain and France were the two most powerful nations. The Spanish monarch held large territorial claims in Italy and the Low Countries (Netherlands and Belgium) and possessed close kin ties with the Holy Roman Emperor in Central Europe. France, too, held lands in Italy and other parts of Europe. England possessed portions of western France, but was far more involved in the affairs of the British Isles than the European mainland. England's main extra-territorial concern usually lay in reducing French influence in Scotland, England's neighbor to the north, and to that end, in the first half of the 16th century England maintained close ties with Spain.

During the course of the 16th century, however, the ties between Spain and England came undone—first by Henry VIII's divorce of his Spanish wife, Catherine of Aragon, daughter of the Spanish monarchs, Ferdinand and Isabella, and second by England's break with the Catholic Church and the creation of its own national Protestant Church, the Church of England. England's subsequent support for

Protestants in the Germanies and the Low Countries against the Spanish would lead England to challenge Spanish supremacy in the New World any way they could, ultimately prompting English expansion in Ireland and the Americas.

Foreign affairs often preoccupied the English government in the 16th century, but turbulent domestic matters provided an equal threat; sometimes the two merged. The suppression of English Catholics led to widespread discontent and sometimes rebellion. The specter of Catholic Spain allying with English Catholics haunted English Protestants. Discontent over high taxes and impoverishment caused by the Enclosure Movement forced many peasants to leave the countryside looking for work. Fear of the dispossessed played a role in the English government pursuing overseas activities, such as colonization of Ireland and the Americas, and expansion of mercantile and privateering enterprise: these would usefully employ young men who might otherwise engage in crime and undermining the social order. England sought a variety of solutions to its religious and economic problems, but what made England unusual in Europe was the politicization of the nation: over the course of the 16th and 17th centuries, people of all classes engaged in debates not only over public policies, but the proper form of government—a tradition carried by English colonists to the New World.

## The Monarch and Parliament

At the end of the 15th century, no one could foresee the revolutionary political changes in store for the nation: the rising political and economic importance of the middle class followed by increasing demands from the lower classes for even more radical changes in the English polity. The period began with a thrust toward centralization and the increased power of the monarch that followed Henry Tudor's victory at the Battle of Bosworth in 1485, which led to the end of the Wars of the Roses, civil wars that had begun 30 years before. Henry VII (1457–1509) and his son, Henry VIII (1491–1547), were not "absolute" monarchs in the style of later 17th-century kings, but they ruled their domains effectively, perhaps even more absolutely. Tudor kings did not need to define their "divine right to rule" as later Stuart kings did: they assumed that right. Henry VIII's daughter Elizabeth I (1533–1603) was forced to contend with Parliament—the legislative body that represented the nobility and commoners—in ways that her father and grandfather never did, and sometimes to remind Parliament of God's appointment of her to rule, but she proved even more effective in manipulating the reins of government than they. Future monarchs were not so skillful, and powerful forces in society pressured for change, seeing Parliament as the engine for whatever social, religious, economic, or political alteration they desired.

The Tudor dynasty gave way to the Stuart in 1603 when James I (James VI of Scotland, 1566–1625) assumed the throne. James articulated the reasons and extents for a monarch's great power in tracts such as *Basilicon Dorn*. Kings possessed "Divine Rights": they were selected by God to rule lesser people. A king's power was to be neither questioned nor limited; he had only to answer to God. The king's will was law. But Parliament possessed the power of the purse: they controlled taxation. The king possessed many sources of income, but governing the state became increasingly expensive, especially to purchase the weaponry and men to conduct war, and the costs of maintaining the court in a regal fashion so that it could rival the courts of richer Spain and France. Stuart monarchs often tried to rule without calling Parliament, but faced with the need for money, they found that they could not rule alone. Parliament thus increased its influence in government against monarchs' pretensions to absolute rule.

Defining political power in the realm was no easy task. In Elizabeth's reign, both monarch and Parliament looked to the past for guidance. English law was codified at the end of the 16th century by the great jurist Francis Bacon, who collected and organized laws and legal cases going back hundreds of years; laws had an ancient lineage like kings, and their age legitimated their authority. Many began to see "the law" as the cornerstone and guarantee of all rights and privileges, while ensuring the proper ordering of society. The law received a special sanctity in English society, a sanctity that kings could not disregard. In this scenario, the monarch was just a part, albeit a very important part, of the governing process and subject to the same laws as other men.

## The Spread of Ideas Through Publication of the Printed Word

If the 16th century marked the unification of England, the codification of law, the growth of English nationalism, and the centralization of political power, the 17th century saw the splintering of the nation into just so many factions and interest groups, the rise of Parliamentary power, and one of the most fruitful public discussions of power and the state to take place in human history. The overthrow and beheading of King Charles I in the English Civil War (1642–1651) opened the possibility to completely remake government and society. Social and economic radicals called for wholesale changes such as the elimination of private property and the elimination of monarchy. Political conservatives called for a re-ordering of the state to restore the "proper" order of things. From Thomas Hobbes's *The Leviathan* (1651) to John Locke's *The Second Treatise on Government* (1690), people from all walks of life contributed to the debates that took place in pamphlets and books, taverns and churches. The English considered the nature of man in society, the proper forms of government, and the relationship that should exist between the ruler and the ruled. Law and justice, liberty and virtue, and rights and responsibilities all were debated and defined at great length. The English carried these ideas and the tradition of public discourse overseas. Their own colonists, particularly in mainland North America, would excel at the practical and theoretical aspects of politics and argue for the supremacy of the "rule of law."

The spread of political ideas and discourse was facilitated by the printing press. The printing press provided the public with greater access to law codes, to news of other parts of the realm and the world, to the debates that divided men in government, and to the ideas of great thinkers. Printing provided a medium for wide distribution of a diversity of opinions, including a venue for the expression of common peoples' ideas, as broadsheets (large public notices attached to walls) and pamphlets were relatively inexpensive to publish. Printers could be punished for libel and for printing items that criticized the government, but print they did, and no other medium played such an important role in politicization—that is, the education of, and promotion of interest in, politics by common people.

Printing was one of the many factors that helped foster nationalism among the English. Published poetry, lyrics, books, plays, and political pamphlets all contributed to the idea of an English "specialness"—that the British Isles were not a part of Europe, that England possessed superior political and legal institutions, that England had a destiny to lead resistance to the "tyranny" of Spain and the Catholic Church, including the liberation of people overseas, whether Irish or American Indian. In actuality, the English did little liberation and were inclined to repress native peoples who stood in their way. The search for profits usually, but not always, trumped all other factors. A favorite method of procurement from the mid-16th-century through the mid-18th-century involved pirating the riches of the Spanish or Portuguese empires. The English, Dutch, and French captured Iberian ships returning from the Americas and Asia loaded with valuable cargoes. But they also established their own colonies. In the 17th century, England evolved from an economic backwater into an economic power-house. It largely accomplished this through the subjection of non-English peoples and their lands. The accumulation of inexpensive raw materials and the appropriation of cheap labor fed a manufacturing revolution. Whereas the Spanish relied on American treasure to fund their empire, allowing a steep decline in their own manufacturing, the English developed an economic infrastructure that became the envy of Europe. To make that transformation, England first had to become a trading nation.

## ENGLAND ON THE SEAS

English overseas expansion moved in fits and starts under the Tudor dynasty (1485–1603). As early as the 1480s, Bristol fishermen likely plied their trade in American waters off Newfoundland, but fishing there apparently ended in the 1490s. English voyages of exploration were undertaken by John Cabot in 1497, and by 1502 English ships were returning from Newfoundland with Eskimos. Only a few years later, the English began considering opening a Northeast Passage over Europe to trade with Asia.

### The Search for New Markets in the East

In the early 16th century, England's exports mostly were carried to continental Europe by Hanseatic (German) traders. England's great export was unfinished wool shipped to western and northern Europe. In the first half of the 16th century, the key destination was Antwerp (in modern-day Belgium), the most important entrepôt in western Europe. Henry VII promoted the growth of the English merchant class early in the century, but not until the collapse of the Antwerp market mid-century did English merchants begin seeking new markets, which planted the seeds for England building an overseas empire.

The crown charted private joint-stock companies, whereby merchants and other investors pooled their resources so that losses would not bankrupt individuals. In exchange for a share of the profits, the companies received from the government monopolistic rights to trade routes in particular geographic areas. Many investors hailed from London, the city that increasingly dominated English overseas trade. Since the Italians, Spaniards, and Portuguese would not let traders of other nations use their routes to Asia, in 1553 the explorer Sebastian Cabot and the city of London joined forces to open a Northeast Passage to Asia. This led to the creation of the Muscovy Company, which established an important trade with Russia through the North Sea. The Muscovy Company sponsored the collection of geographic knowledge and the development of geographical science, of which England lagged far behind Portugal and Spain. Although Russia did not become a major market for English goods, the English were able to obtain much needed naval stores, especially rope and cable, which facilitated the growth of the navy. The Russian trade also prompted English merchants to travel overland through Russia to open a trade with Persia for valuable gems.

The overland route to Persia was too expensive due to carriage costs, but it spurred the creation of the Levant Company to trade for Asian goods with the Ottoman Empire. The Levant Company's success allowed the English to bypass the Venetian merchants who previously controlled this trade. The Levant Company became an important link in the eventual establishment of the East India Company, the most important organization that England formed for extending its presence into Asia, and ultimately to the extension of the English Empire into India. But the merchants and the government still sought an easier and quicker way to reach the Far East.

## The Search for a Northwest Passage

The search for a Northeast Passage to Asia was ultimately a failure. Ice prevented ships sailing north of Russia from reaching China and Japan. By the late 16th century, and continuing for over 100 years, English efforts to reach Asia turned to searching for a Northwest Passage over or through North America. Given this task, Martin Frobisher explored Labrador for England in 1576 and 1577. He became a cause célèbre at Queen Elizabeth's Court, when he claimed to have found one of the world's greatest deposits of gold. He returned to Labrador with shiploads of men to mine what turned out to be worthless dirt in this barren, inhospitable land, and never went beyond Labrador to search for the passage for which he had been charged. It would have been fruitless—ice prevents ships' passage above North America, though future English (and French) explorers would locate Hudson Bay in Canada and initiate a very profitable trade in furs and other items.

Michael Lok, the London merchant who organized Frobisher's expedition, published a popular map of North America prototypical of most maps of the continent in the 16th century. Ignorant of American topography, these maps display the wishful thinking of the era. They depict water passages to Asia, not only above North America, but through it. The continent is depicted as a narrow land mass, often with Japan just off the west coast. Lok's map, and those of his lesser-known contemporaries, led subsequent generations of explorers and early colonists to mistakenly believe they would find Asia at the end of the St. Lawrence Seaway in Canada, or the Hudson River in New York, or the James River in Virginia.

An important by-product of the search for a Northwest Passage was the first encounters of the English with America's native peoples. In Labrador, the natives harassed and restricted the movement of Frobisher's men. Frobisher did succeed in kidnapping several, whom he brought to England as curiosities. All died shortly after arrival. Nevertheless, Frobisher began a pattern that continued for hundreds of years: English bringing American Indians and their artifacts to England as symbols of the exotic New World to which the nation had access, and portions of which they intended to control.

## RALEGH AND ROANOKE

The actual settlement of English colonies overseas began not with America, but with Ireland. Ireland was a threat to England as a launching ground for invasion by Spain. English–Spanish relations had deteriorated in the mid-16th-century under Elizabeth, in large part due to English privateering, but also because of her support for Dutch and German Protestants against Catholic Spain. Elizabeth's solution was not merely conquest of Ireland—but colonization. Irish were removed from the land and forced southward, while the English established "plantations" with English settlers. The Irish were considered a "savage race . . . beyond the pale of civilization"—incapable, perhaps, of assimilation into Anglo society.

Colonization of Ireland by English (and later Scots) would continue for centuries. But it also became the English model for future settler societies: colonizers move to a new land, remove the "savages" from their homes, and establish plantations with their own colonists. It is no coincidence that many of the first English involved in colonizing America previously had colonized or served in the army in Ireland.

One young man, who made a reputation for himself as a dashing captain possessed of much acumen about Irish affairs, was Sir Walter Ralegh (sometimes spelled in the United States as Raleigh, but generally considered by scholars as an improper spelling), who became a favorite of Queen Elizabeth. Ralegh hailed from a sea-faring family. He and his half-brothers, John and Humphrey Gilbert, as well as other relations and neighbors from Devonshire, actively engaged in privateering, naval service, overseas trade, and Atlantic exploration. John Gilbert received a patent to plant a colony in North America but died before seeing it to fruition. Ralegh then received from the queen a patent to establish his own colony, thus beginning the process by which England became an imperial power in the Americas.

## England's Rationale for Colonies

Ralegh turned to noted exploration expert and propagandist, Richard Hakluyt, to compose a paper to convince Queen Elizabeth, her ministers, and private men to invest in his enterprise. This document, labeled "Discourse on Western Planting," provided what amounted to a blueprint for English overseas expansion for the next several centuries. Hakluyt argued that colonies would provide England with many distinct advantages. They offered places from which to establish bases to attack the Spanish in the New World. American colonies would also "yelde unto us all the commodities of Europe, Affrica, and Asia, as far as wee were wonte to travell, and supply the wantes of all our decayed trades." These included trees, valuable not only for their lumber but as a resource for producing naval stores; sassafras, which was believed to cure venereal disease; and sub-tropical items such as silk, dyes, and fruits. Hakluyt also foresaw that colonies would provide England a place to ship its excess population. Many in England believed the nation was overcrowded with unemployed and underemployed people who could be useful in building colonies. Colonies could become a dumping ground for other people unwanted at home—political and religious dissenters, prisoners, and orphans. All these people would be shipped to colonies in the coming centuries.

Colonies had another advantage: they would provide a marketplace for English goods, which would increase employment at home. England's North American colonies and native purchasers indeed would become England's best customers. But Hakluyt's purpose was not entirely materialistic. This minister of the Church of England believed that England should convert the natives to Christianity. He included not only "heathen," in this projection, but those natives already converted to "false" Christianity, by which he meant those whom the Spanish had brought to the Catholic

Church. Although the English record in converting natives was ultimately abysmal, especially in comparison with the Spanish and French, every English colony included in its charter that conversion of the natives was a central goal.

## England's First Colony in America

To fulfill the terms of his patent, Ralegh wasted little time in establishing men at Roanoke, which he named Virginia in honor of his Virgin Queen. He sent a preliminary expedition to choose a place to settle, survey the economic possibilities, and establish friendly relations with the local natives. The expedition returned with a report to attract investors: colonization was an expensive endeavor and Ralegh needed capital. In England, Ralegh made careful preparations to insure the building of a successful colony—no mean task given the distance from England and English unfamiliarity with the land. Ralegh gathered together many of the nation's foremost experts in navigation, ship building, fort construction, and mining. His key advisor was Thomas Hariot, England's foremost physicist and mathematician. Hariot trained Ralegh's men in the art of ocean-going navigation, prepared charts for them, and taught them how to use navigation instruments of his own devising. He also worked with master shipbuilders to construct new ships, one of which, the *Bark Ralegh*, eventually became the most advanced ship in the English Navy.

The initial reconnaissance expedition was followed by a more substantial one to pave the way for ultimate colonization. Ralegh sent Hariot to Roanoke: his skills of observation of the natural world were indispensable. Hariot was accompanied by the painter John White, who was charged with making visual representations of the natural world and the native peoples. Joachim Ganz, a Jew from Prague, was also sent to assay the mineral potential of the land. Ralph Lane, an experienced soldier from Ireland, was put in charge of the colony on land and instructed to build defensive works. Ralegh's cousin, the experienced seaman, Sir Richard Grenville, was in charge of the entire expedition, and he commanded it at sea.

This second expedition of 107 men stayed at Roanoke for almost a year and collected much valuable data. White's surviving paintings of local Indians form the most important visual representation of American Indians above Mexico until the age of photography. Theodore de Bry, a German publisher and engraver, transformed White's representations to the printed page: the numerous editions published in English, Latin, French, and German found a wide audience in Europe and publicized English colonialism. Hariot provided text to accompany the engravings, as well as a descriptive pamphlet—these provided important ethnographic accounts of North Carolina's coastal Indian population. Hariot was also a master linguist and studied the local native language; he was much assisted by two Indians, Manteo and Wanchese, who had been brought to England on the return of the first expedition. After their visit to England, they returned to Roanoke with the second expedition: Wanchese became an inveterate enemy of the English, while Manteo became a great friend and provided much help to the English in negotiating their way culturally and diplomatically with the coastal Indians.

Although the expedition was a great success in terms of gaining information, it was also a great failure. Lane was unable to adjust culturally to the local Indians, alienated local leaders, and initiated a war with a former native ally, Pemisapan. The war had disastrous consequences for the English: it showed the Roanoke-area Indians that the English were untrustworthy and brutal. The second expedition abandoned Roanoke, and Ralegh determined that the next expedition would settle in a different place and also create a permanent colony. He recruited farmers, craftsmen, and few soldiers. Instead of putting a military man in charge, White was appointed governor. And this time, the colony was supposed to be planted along Chesapeake Bay in modern-day Virginia, rather than on the sea islands of present-day North Carolina. The second expedition had (correctly) recommended this area as being much better suited to agriculture and the English had not alienated the Indians there.

## The Failure of Roanoke

Ralegh succeeded in attracting investors for the colony, but the way the first two expeditions made money was not through the products of the land but by privateering. English ships going to or returning from Roanoke captured Spanish "prize" ships and returned to England where the booty was sold at great profit. This provided the quick return desired by investors and sailors, but it deterred the English from developing permanent settlements that required long-term investment. The desire for prizes doomed Ralegh's third expedition to settle a permanent colony in Virginia. In 1587, Simon Ferdinando, the Portuguese captain charged with delivering White's colony to Chesapeake Bay, stopped at Roanoke to pick up 18 Englishmen who had been left there by Grenville to secure the place after Lane had removed the second expedition. The English upon arrival learned that all had been killed by local Indians or drowned attempting to escape. Instead of moving on to Chesapeake Bay, Ferdinando decided to instead go privateering and left the colonists in this hostile and unproductive environment. White departed with Fernandez to return to England to obtain more support for the colonists. He left behind his daughter and grand-daughter, Virginia Dare, the first English child born in America. Ralegh made preparation to relieve the colonists and probably to remove the colony to Chesapeake Bay, but the expedition was cancelled by the impending arrival of the Spanish Armada in 1588—a massive array of ships and soldiers intent on conquering England and restoring it to the Catholic Church. No ships could leave England without special permission. England defeated the Armada, but by the time White returned in 1590, an expedition further delayed by privateering, the colony had disappeared and became known in history as the famous "Lost Colony" of Roanoke. Although we may never know what happened to the colonists, the evidence points to them having joined local Indian groups and later being killed on the eve of England's next attempt to settle Virginia almost 20 years later.

As for Ralegh, he turned his attention to building plantations in Ireland and then to a fruitless search for El Dorado, the "Lost City of Gold," in Guiana (modern-day Venezuela). Unlike most of his peers, Ralegh was sympathetic to, and curious about, American Indians, as he believed in the universalism of man, and that Europeans could learn much from native peoples. He published a book, *The Discoverie of the Large, Rich and Bewtiful Empyre of Guiana*, which earned him infamy from a public unwilling to examine Indians on their own terms—he reprinted *their* stories as being of interest and value, but most Europeans could not see the point.

Ralegh also made it a practice to bring Indians to England, or to have his ship captains do the same, with the Indians' permission, where they could teach him and his associates about their culture and language, and in return learn about English culture and language. Some of these Indians became lifelong friends of Ralegh; all were permitted to return to America. Ralegh's long-term imprisonment under King James I prevented him from becoming involved in England's next attempt to settle Virginia, though he invested money in the enterprise. A group of merchants formed the London Company (later renamed the Virginia Company) in 1606 and convinced James I to allow them to once again attempt a settlement, named Jamestown for their monarch.

## VIRGINIA: THE FIRST PERMANENT ENGLISH COLONY IN THE AMERICAS

Three ships brought 104 colonists in 1607 to Chesapeake Bay, a much better place to settle than Roanoke due to the quality of the land and suitability for defense and expansion. Nevertheless, the colony barely survived its early years. The first settlers were mostly soldiers, "adventurers," and their servants. The adventurers were largely "Second Sons." In England, the laws of primogeniture and entail provided that first-born males inherited their father's land, so estates would not be divided. The second sons of elites ordinarily became military officers, lawyers, merchants, or clergymen. In Virginia, they hoped to gather an estate and return to England. Few intended to stay—what would be the purpose of being rich in Virginia. The settlers spent much of their time looking for precious metals and a passage to Asia, and little time securing their survival.

### The Starving Times

Survival was difficult and the men ill-suited to the task. The colony faced starvation. John Smith, the colony's leader, cajoled, intimidated, and forced the men to work, while seeking a variety of ways to obtain food from the Indians. But when Smith hurt his arm and returned to England for medical treatment, the colony floundered.

Relations with the neighboring Powhatan were never good. These Indians comprised a chiefdom of many peoples led by Powhatan, whose daughter Pocahontas, according to Smith, had saved him from death at the hands of her father, and who later married John Rolfe and went with him to England where she died of illness. Relations deteriorated when the English arrogantly demanded corn and other assistance from the Powhatan, who moved inland, leaving the English to their own devices.

The settlers were frustrated. They had learned from Cortés's experience that if one encountered "bad" Indians, then seek an alliance with their enemies, but Powhatan's enemies were distant from Jamestown and could not be located. The settlers again starved—one man even cut up his wife, salted the pieces, and ate her. Some English abandoned the colony and joined the Indians. This was intolerable to the English. They demanded that the Powhatan turn over their settlers, and when the Indians refused, they cold-bloodedly murdered Queen Pamunkey and her children. The English could not accept that their own people would prefer Indian society to their own: throughout early American history, colonial governments employed force to make their people who lived with Indians return. The English believed that those who chose Indian society over their own must have lost their minds. For the English to accept that their people might prefer Indian life to their own, they would have had to question their own superiority and right to take possession of "inferior" Indians' land. But they could not question their basic views of themselves and their world.

Nor would they work to survive. The settlers became listless and spent their time idly, bowling in the streets and playing cards. Even when they received supplies from England, they refused to prepare a harvest for the next year and potential future shortages. Though they knew how to grow corn, they did not—that was an Indian crop. Soldiers, by their profession, refused to labor on the land. The Second Sons also refused. These gentlemen had not come to America to be farmers and perform manual labor. To them, survival was a matter of diplomacy—finding a way to convince Indians to take care of their needs. Unable to do so, the colony squandered.

The English found neither gold nor silver in Virginia. Nor did they locate a passage to the Orient. But they did find tobacco. Rolfe introduced some seeds from the West Indies and the planters produced a crop. Earlier Ralegh popularized what James I called the "Stynking Weed," and tobacco became fabulously popular at court, and then among the masses in England and elsewhere in Europe. Virginians grew tobacco as planters, not farmers, employing poor workers who the Virginia Company sent to labor in the fields. The colony had found its gold: the colony became obsessed with tobacco.

## Populating a Colony

Jamestown became the future United States' first boom town—fortunes were made and quickly lost as the men gambled their earnings or spent their gains on Dutch ships that pulled into port and were no less than floating saloons and brothels. The Virginia Company was pleased with having a way to earn profits, but saw little due to the corruption of their officials in the colony. In 1619, Sir Edwyn Sandys took control of the company in England, hoping to give Virginia direction and stability. Many of his efforts set precedents for future English colonies.

To build population, Sandys introduced the headright system, whereby every settler received 50 acres of land upon arrival in the colony. This led to the institution of indentured servitude, as planters obtained 50 acres for every servant they imported from England. The servants ordinarily worked four to seven years and then received their own 50 acres. Over the next century and a half, about half of all Europeans who immigrated to the English colonies came as indentured servants or in other forms of servitude. Many impoverished Europeans agreed to become indentures because they could eventually own land—an opportunity largely unattainable in Europe.

Virginia became a cause célèbre in England, as ministers promoted sending the poor, particularly orphans, to the colony, where employment and thus a promising future awaited. They believed that the colony could save these youths from a life of crime, as the Protestant Work Ethic held that steady hard work was good for the soul, and make them good Christians. Sandys rounded up hundreds of orphans from London alone, and 3,500 persons in total were sent within three years.

Sandys also recruited many impoverished women, who were auctioned off by the company to become wives for the men. Sandys believed that if the men began families, they were less likely to return to England, and that marriage would settle down the unruly bachelors to become responsible citizens. The women took advantage of the situation as best they could. Many began bidding wars to obtain their betrothal, and laws were passed to prevent them from making agreements with more than one man.

The central fact of life in Virginia was that it was a "dying place," as the average length of life in the colony was about 3.4 years and would remain so until mid-century.

The most dangerous period was the first year, called the "seasoning period," as colonists adjusted to the new environment. It is unclear why the newcomers died in such large numbers, but it might have been due to the water, as well as the unhealthy conditions under which laborers worked. When the settlers turned to cider in mid-century, health improved. Women survived in Virginia better than men, and some became rich widows who married two, three, four, or more times. Another common way to wealth was to become the trustee for a wealthy orphan and then ravage the estate.

## Developing the Virginia Economy

Sandys tried to diversify the economy by sending specialists to develop wine and silk cultures and an iron foundry. A glass works was established as well as an incipient naval stores industry. The company tried to restrict tobacco cultivation, to create a more balanced economy, but to no effect as tobacco remained the best way to make money.

In 1619, the first recorded Africans arrived in Virginia, brought by a Dutch ship. Almost nothing is known of these "20 and odd Negroes," though it is presumed that they were either slaves or treated akin to indentured servants. In the coming years, some of the Africans gained freedom, and some would be treated as slaves, as there were no clear lines drawn between people according to skin color—status as free or servant was the most important demarcation between people—Africans, Europeans, and natives worked side-by-side in the fields, socialized together, and were treated brutally by their masters, whose main concern was wringing as much labor as possible from them before they died or attained freedom.

The Virginia Company established an assembly, but it had virtually no power until the last quarter of the century. More important was the Company's ending of martial law and guaranteeing colonists that they would enjoy all the rights of Englishmen—that is to say, whatever rights settlers had in England, they would possess in Virginia. This established a precedent followed by future colonies, though some-times the king had to step in to protect colonists in places like New England, where colonists were denied religious rights they enjoyed in the mother country.

Money was raised in England for a school to educate and convert American Indians in Virginia. It was expected that such a school would ease relations between the native peoples and the English, but no Indians attended. Colonists believed that rela-tions had improved with the Powhatan, and as in future colonial settlements, Indians came and went among the settlers on a daily basis. Jamestown was thus ill-prepared for a coordinated Indian attack that took the lives of 347 settlers in 1622. This put an end to any thought of assimilating local Indians into colonial society. Within three years, Virginia took its vengeance many times over against the Powhatan, with whom they warred periodically in the coming decades.

The Indian assault on Jamestown brought the colony to the attention of the English crown. It was noted that there were 4,270 colonists in Virginia from 1619 to 1622, and with 347 killed by the Indians, there should have been 3,923 English left. But there were only 1,240. Thus, not including the 347 killed by Indians, over 68% of the population had died in three years. Citing gross negligence on the part of the Virginia Company, the crown took away its charter and made Virginia the first royal colony.

With the demise of the Virginia Company, the attempt to diversify the economy also ended. Virginia, indeed, became a tobacco colony with most producers devoting their efforts to the cultivation of this valuable cash crop. The King of England earned 10% of his personal income from a tax on tobacco, and thus had no reason to steer colonists to other enterprises. Virginia became a model for future English colonies in the West Indies and the American South, which hoped to repeat Virginia's economic success by finding their own crop that they could profitably produce for world markets.

## Conclusion

English overseas expansion moved in fits and starts through the 16th century. Mercantile enterprise became more significant in the second half of the century, as England carried a greater share of its own products to European markets and extended its reach to Russia and the eastern Mediterranean. Privateering of mostly Spanish and Portuguese ships, but also the ships of other nations, expanded English wealth and provided a training ground for captains and sailors. Colonization in Ireland and at Roanoke were building blocks for future colonization efforts, but in the early 17th century England still lagged far behind Spain and Portugal in establishing colonies and creating networks for world trade.

As England more actively engaged in overseas enterprise, so, too, did the Dutch and French. The 17th century witnessed the rise of the Dutch as one of the world's great trading powers, particularly in Asia where they effectively competed against the Portuguese. France, preoccupied with affairs at home and in Europe, tentatively colonized in Canada (and the Dutch moved into New York) as the English settled at Jamestown. Both France and England soon turned their attention to other locales in North America, but also to the islands of the West Indies, where they could establish plantations to produce the most important New World crop of the 17th and 18th centuries: sugar. If the story of European overseas expansion in the 16th century was largely a story of Spain and Portugal, the 17th century saw the rise of the Dutch and English. The Protestant powers would not occupy the large expanses of territory that the Spanish did in the Americas (and Spain continued to extend its dominion in the 17th century), but the Dutch and English greatly expanded their commercial and manufacturing capabilities to make profits not only from their own colonies but also from the colonies of other European powers. Of course, none of this could be foreseen in 1622 when Jamestown seemed to be falling apart at the seams. English colonization in the Americas was inconsiderable compared to Spain and Portugal. Yet the Jamestown colony was very important. The success of tobacco meant that the English could build profitable colonies without the land possessing precious metals. The prospect of free land proved incredibly attractive to English of all classes—the dispossessed and landless poor, the middle-class families, and the well-born hoping to increase their wealth and prospects. The English promotion of colonization as a way to rid the mother country of undesirables—political and religious dissidents, orphans, and criminals became a boon to the nation. In conjunction with relatively open emigration policies that permitted and promoted migration of non-English Europeans, the English colonies in North America rapidly increased their population, which provided them strength against hostile forces and a strong foundation for future development.

# DOCUMENTS

## 3.1. Richard Hakluyt on the Usefulness of Colonies to Solve Employment Problems in England

*Richard Hakluyt's "Discourse of Western Planting" was designed to rally support, political and financial, for Walter Ralegh's Roanoke colony. The following short excerpt discusses one of the key aspects for English colonization—to provide employment for poor Englishmen who otherwise would become a social problem in the mother country. The use of colonies as a solution to England's social and economic problems remained a driving force through the centuries. Compare this document with the Parliamentary law of 1718 reproduced in chapter six, which not only forced the migration of criminals to the colonies, but provided rules for shipping young people who otherwise might undertake criminal activities in England. How will colonization solve England's unemployment problem? Why did Hakluyt consider unemployment such a great threat to the realm?*

Cap. IV. That this enterprise will be for the manifolde ymployment of numbers of idle men, and for bredinge of many sufficient, and for utteraunce of the greate quantitie of the commodities of our realme.

It is well worthe the observation to see and consider what the like voyadges of discoverye and plauntinge in the Easte and Weste Indies hath wroughte in the kingdoms of Portingale and Spayne; bothe which realms, beinge of themselves poore and barren and hardly able to susteine their inhabitaunts, by their discoveries have found suche occasion of employmente, that these many yeres we have not herde scarcely of any pirate of those twoo nations; whereas wee and the Frenche are moste infamous for our outeragious, common, and daily piracies. Againe, when hearde wee almoste of one theefe amongst them? The reason is, that by these, their newe discoveries, they have so many honest wayes to set them to worke, as they rather wante men then meanes to ymploye them. But wee, for all the statutes that hitherto can be devised, and the sharpe execution of the same in poonishinge idle and lazye persons, for wante of sufficient occasion of honest employmente, cannot deliver our commonwealthe from multitudes of loyterers and idle vagabondes. Truthe it is, that throughe our longe peace and seldome sicknes (twoo singular blessings of Almightie God) wee are growne more populous than ever heretofore; so that nowe there are pf every arte and science so many, that they can hardly lyve one by another, nay rather they are readie to eate upp one another; yea many thousandes of idle persons are within this realme, which, having no way to be sett on worke, be either mutinous and seeke alteration in the state, or at leaste the very burdensome to the commonwealthe, and often fall to pilferinge and thevinge and other lewdnes, whereby all the prisons of the lande are daily pestred and stuffed full of them, where either they pitifully pyne awaye, or els at lengthe are miserably hanged, even XX. at a clappe oute of some one jayle. Whereas yf this voyadge were put in execution, these pety theves mighte by condempned for certen yeres in the westerne partes, especially in New-efounde lande, in sawinge and fellinge of tymber for mastes of shippes, and deale boordes; in burninge of the firres and pine trees to make pitche, tarr, rosen, and sope ashes; in beatinge and workinge of hempe for cordage; and, in the more southerne partes, in settinge them to worke in mynes of golde, silver, copper, leade, and yron; in dragginge for perles and currall; in plantinge of suger canes, as the Portingales have done in Madera; in mayneteynaunce and increasinge of silke wormes for silke, and in dressinge the same; in gatheringe of cotton whereof there is plenty; in tillinge of the soile there for graine; in dressinge of vines whereof there is greate adoundaunce of wyne; olyves, whereof the soile ys capable, for oyle; trees for oranges, lymons, almon-des, figges, and other frutes, all which are founde to growe there already; in sowinge of woade and madder for diers, as the Portingales have don in the Azores; in dressinge of raw hides of divers kindes of beastes; in makinge and gatheringe of salte, as in Rochel and Bayon, which may serve for the newe lande fisshinge; in killinge of the whale, seale, porpose, and whirlepoole for trayne oile; in fisshinge, saltinge, and dryenge of linge, codde, salmon, herringe; in makinge and gatheringe of hony, waxe, turpentine; in hewinge and shapinge of stone, as marble, jeate, christall, freestone, which will be goodd balaste for our shippes homewards, and after serve for noble buildinges; in makinge of caske, oares, and all other manner of staves; in buildinge of fortes, townes, churches; in powdringe and barrellinge of fishe, fowles, and fleshe, which will be notable provision for sea and lange; in dryenge, sortinge, and packinge of fethers, whereof may be had there marvelous greate quantitie.

Besides this, such as by any kinde of infirmitie cannot passe the seas thither, and are now chardgeable to the realme at home, by this voyadge shal be made profitable members, by employ-inge them in England in makinge of a thousande triflinge thinges, which will be very goodd marchandize for those contries where wee shall have moste ample vente thereof.

And seinge the savages of the Graunde Baye, and all alonge the mightie ryver that ronneth upp to Canada and Hochelaga, are greately delighted with any cappe or garment made of course wollen clothe, their contrie beinge colde and sharpe in the winter, yt is manifeste wee shall finde in greate utteraunce of our clothes, especially of our coursest and basest northerne doosens, and our Irishe and Welshe frizes and rugges; whereby all occupations belonginge to clothinge and knittinge shalbe freshly sett on worke, as cappers, knitters, clothiers, wollmen, carders, spynners, weavers, fullers, sheremen, dyers, drapers, hatters, and such like, whereby many decayed townes may be repaired. . . .

Nowe if her Majestie take these westerne discoveries in hande, and plante there, yt is like that in shorte time wee shall vente as greate a masse of clothe yn those partes as ever wee did in the Netherlandes, and in tyme moche more.

Source: Richard Hakluyt, A Discourse Concerning Western Planting, in Collections of the Maine Historical Society, Second Series (1877), 36–39, 42.

*(Continued)*

## 3.2. Lady Mary Wyatt Writes to her Sister from Jamestown, Virginia

*The wife of Sir Francis Wyatt, Mary Wyatt settled in Virginia in 1623. The following letter describes her journey to Virginia and the need for supplies in the colony. What kind of help could people in England provide for their relations in the New World?*

**Lady Mary Wyatt to her Sister Sandys 4 Apr. 1623.**

Dear Sister,

You would have heard from me earlier if not for the extremity of sickness that has hindered me till now. For our ship was so pestered with people and goods that we were full of infection, and that after a while we saw little but throwing folks overboard; it pleased God to send me my health till I came to shore and 3 days after I fell sick but I thank God I am well recovered. Few else are left alive that came in our ship: for her have died husbands, wives, children and servants. They told me they sent a Ship less pestered for me, but there never came a Ship so full to Virginia as ours. I had not so much as my cabin free to myself. Our captain seemed to be troubled by it. . . . Our beer stunk so I could not endure. . . . This was our fortune at sea, and on land we did little better, for our people as well as our cattle have died, so that we are all undone, especially we that are newcomers. If our friends do not help it will go hard with us next winter. I know not who to send to for help but you, for my mother is so far that she could help me none when I left. You and my sister helped much: if she desires to send me butter and bacon, tell her I prefer butter and cheese. Since the Indians and we fell out we dare not send a hunting party except with so many men that it is not worth the labor. Whatever you send, include a bill of lading. If my mother talks of sending me anything let it be malt put in very good casks. It must not be ground. If I should take upon me to thank you for your love to me when I was in England, I have not left room, or had I, I could not express my love but in being.

Your sister and servant
Mary Wyatt

Source: *Records of the Virginia Company.* 4 vols. Edited by Susan Kingsbury (1935), 4: 232–233.

# Bibliography

Andrews, Kenneth R. *Trade, Plunder and Settlement: Maritime Enterprise and the Genesis of the British Empire, 1480–1630 (1984).*

Chaplin, Joyce. *Subject Matter: Technology, the Body, and Science on the Anglo-American Frontier, 1500–1676* (2001).

Horn, James. *Adapting to a New World: English Society in the Seventeenth-Century Chesapeake* (1994).

Hume, Ivor Noël. *The Virginia Adventure* (1994).

Kupperman, Karen Ordahl. *The Jamestown Project* (2007).

Kupperman, Karen Ordahl. *Roanoke: The Abandoned Colony* (1984).

Kupperman, Karen Ordahl. *Settling with the Indians: The Meeting of English and Indian Cultures in America, 1580–1640* (1980).

McDermott, Martin. *Martin Frobisher: Elizabethan Privateer* (2001).

Mancall, Peter C. *Hakluyt's Promise: An Elizabethan's Obsession for an English America* (2007).

Moran, Michael G. *Inventing Virginia: Sir Walter Raleigh and the Rhetoric of Colonization, 1584–1590* (2007).

Morgan, Edmund S. *American Slavery, American Freedom: The Ordeal of Colonial Virginia* (1974).

Oberg, Michael Leroy. *The Head in Edward Nugent's Hand: Roanoke's Forgotten Indians* (2008)

Parks, George. *Richard Hakluyt and the English Voyages* (1961).

Quinn, David Beers. *England and the Discovery of America, 1481–1629* (1973).

Quinn, David Beers. *Raleigh and the British Empire* (1947).

Quinn, David Beers. *Set Fair for Roanoke: Voyages and Colonies, 1584–1606* (1985).

Rountree, Helen C. *The Powhatan Indians of Virginia: Their Traditional Culture* (1989).

Vaughan, Alden T. *American Genesis: Captain John Smith and the Founding of Virginia* (1975).

Vaughan, Alden T. *Transatlantic Encounters: American Indians in Britain, 1500–1776* (2006).

# 4

# Europeans and Indians in the Northeast, 1620–1670

## INTRODUCTION

Although the Spanish opposed English colonization of Virginia, claiming the exclusive right to colonize North America, the colony did not seem a grave threat to Spanish interests, and they made little attempt to remove it, as they had done with the French settlement in Florida. Likewise, the Spanish did not prevent other European powers from colonizing to the north of Virginia. The Spanish did not consider these lands strategically or economically valuable, as they lay distant from Spanish colonies in the Caribbean, South America, and Mexico and were believed to possess no precious metals. The English, French, and Dutch, however, set their sights on the lands to the north. For even if these lands did not have gold and silver, they might bear other valuable commodities. The economic gains Spain made from its American colonies were too hard to ignore; other European powers hoped to reap similar benefits. Precious metals and finding a new route to Asia remained as goals. But the chances of finding either were remote. Nevertheless, valuable commodities might be available given the presumed riches of the land and the abundance of animals.

Each colony's success would depend on a variety of factors, most notably the natural resources, and the demography, desires, and cultures of both the indigenous peoples and the colonizers. The Dutch, for instance, drawing on their experience in Asia, and funded by private companies, looked to establish trade with the indigenous peoples, while the French engaged in a much more imperial adventure, seeking to expand their monarch's domain. The English in the north comprised the most unusual settlements of all. Unlike the English in Virginia, and also differing from the European colonists in other American settlements, the emigrants to New England largely arrived in family units, mostly engaged in family farming, and intended to replicate the material life of the Old World in the New World. Driven by religious and political persecution, as well as by declining economic opportunities, they held dreams of transforming the American landscape into their ideal of utopia.

## PURITANS AND PILGRIMS

One of the great forces for social and political change in 16th- and 17th-century England was a Protestant religious movement known as Puritanism. The Puritans were Calvinists who believed the Church of England had not gone far enough in ridding itself of all remnants of the Catholic Church, hence they wished to "purify" the Church of its Catholic, non-biblical elements, to return to a "primitive" Christianity as they believed existed in biblical times. This meant a reduction in the number of sacraments, elimination of religious iconography, particularly representations of Christ and the Saints, and emphasis upon the necessity of each Christian reading the Bible themselves—not having a priest mediate the relationship between man and God.

### Religious Persecution in England

Queen Elizabeth and other conservative Anglicans opposed and then persecuted the Puritans for a variety of reasons, not least of which was that they were viewed as troublemakers. As head of the Church of England, the Queen wished her Church to include *all* English within the fold, and in fact, all were required to attend worship once in four weeks, a law designed to force Catholics into the Protestant Church. The Puritans were ideologically driven to brook no compromise and demanded all sorts of changes to the Book of Common Prayer, in church governance, and in calling for England to lead international Protestantism against the Catholic Church. Not all Puritans were alike. There were various sectarian and theological strains, so that nonconformity, that is to say, Protestant dissent from the Church of England, proliferated in England and threatened the very fabric of society, for Dissenters not only challenged the form of religion at a time when most people believed that everyone in a nation must be of the same religion, but also posed social and political challenges, challenges that would brew for decades and ultimately lead England into Civil War (1642–1651).

Although mostly any Protestant dissenter from the Church under Elizabeth was called a Puritan, by the early 17th century the movement gained more coherence through two generations of publishing and discussing what they stood for: worship of a God who accepted neither faith nor good works as able to open the gates of heaven. An all-powerful, all-knowing God decided from time immemorial who would receive salvation; people must live according to Christian precepts, accept their fate, and not alienate their God, the author of all things.

Puritanism's strict discipline, which emphasized self-control and individual responsibility, had great appeal among the educated middle class, upwardly mobile families demanding a greater voice in Parliament and county governments. Many were millennial—believing the end of the world imminent—and hoped to do all they could to prepare the way. Self-discipline and millennialism convinced Puritans that they must actively engage themselves into transforming this world: to know God's truth and not act upon it was to live in sin and give the lie to them being a God-fearing people.

Facing persecution for establishing churches separate from the Church of England, some Puritans migrated to Holland, which offered religious tolerance. These included poor farmers who moved to Leyden from northern England beginning in 1607. They found Leyden's urban environment not to their liking and missed being among English people. They decided to migrate to Virginia but were too poor. Eventually they received help from an English merchant, Thomas Weston, who received a patent for them for land in the colony and promised to defray a large portion of their expenses. In return, the migrants agreed to turn over to him their agricultural profits for seven years.

## Plymouth

Famed in history as the "Pilgrims," 102 left on the *Mayflower* in 1620. Only a third were actually Pilgrims from Leyden, as they invited others to join them. The ship was apparently blown off course and landed in Massachusetts Bay. Disease had so plagued them that the Pilgrims decided to not remove to Virginia, though some historians speculate that all along they intended to settle distant from Virginia to retain control over their lives and practice their religion as they saw fit. The Plymouth colony, as their settlement was called, marked the first of many emigrations from England for religious purposes.

A local Indian, Squanto, helped the Pilgrims establish an alliance between them and the Wampanoag, so that Plymouth did not experience the "troubles" with local Indians that beset the early years of the Virginia colony. The Pilgrims' alliance with the Wampanoag saved the colony, and the Indians helped the starving newcomers with food; each pledged to support the other militarily. This alliance led to the first "Thanksgiving."

The Pilgrims bound themselves to each other in the "Mayflower Compact," intending to prevent dissent among themselves, but they never succeeded at creating a community shorn of discontent religiously, civilly, or socially, particularly as all the settlers did not share the same values. The arrival of more settlers led to crowding and to the eventual establishment of 11 towns. This expansion prompted friction with local Indians, though major conflicts did not arise until several decades later when massive English migration to neighboring Massachusetts created a host of problems.

Plymouth was an insignificant colony. It never received from England the political right to be a separate colony, though individual titles to land were granted by the

English government. The Pilgrims themselves recognized their failures, particularly their religious ones, in creating an idealized Christian community—William Bradford's *Of Plimouth Plantation* documented the failure of their dreams, and the second and third generation looked elsewhere for inspiration than to the colony's founders. They looked to their powerful neighbors, the Puritans, who established Massachusetts Bay.

## MASSACHUSETTS BAY: CREATING A CHRISTIAN COMMONWEALTH

Unlike the Pilgrims, who believed the Church of England too corrupt to be purified, and therefore separated from it, most Puritans were non-separatists intending to purify the Church of England from within. If they fled persecution by removing to the New World, then they would have abandoned their charge. After wrestling with this problem for many months, the Puritan community decided that migration would be justified if they created a "New Jerusalem," a model for the rest of the world, especially England, on how to build a truly Christian society.

The Puritans received a charter from the English government to settle Massachusetts, the government only too happy to have these troublemakers leave England but remain useful to the nation by expanding its domain abroad. The mostly middle- and upper-middle-class settlers were highly organized and focused on the task before them. Thus they prepared well for the migration and did not experience the starving times faced by the Virginians and the Pilgrims.

### The Great Migration

One thousand Puritans, led by John Winthrop, a pious and talented lawyer, embarked for the New World in 1630. Even before they arrived, Winthrop worried about the Puritans keeping to their purpose. He feared the people's seduction by the New World's bounty and the lack of traditional social structures. In a long sermon preached aboard the flagship *Arabella*, Winthrop reminded the Puritans that they were not emigrating to escape the social classes they were born into, that the poor should not expect to rise above the rich. He said that God had ordained the social order, "in all times some must be rich, some poor, some highe and eminent in power and dignite; others mean and in subjeccion." The people were to possess the land, but not be possessed by it. To fulfill their mission, they had to forge a unity of purpose: "we must be knit together in this worke as one man." For if we "fall to embrace this present world and prosecute our carnall intencions seeking great things for our selves and our posterity, the Lord will surely break out in wrathe against us and be revenged."

To achieve their ends, the Puritans established a government based upon biblical precepts. Government would take an active hand in directing the commonwealth and enforcing proper Christian behavior. One of its foremost tasks would be suppressing heresy.

Intolerance became a cornerstone of Massachusetts. The Puritans fled England because of religious persecution but they had no intention of tolerating religious dissent. Nathanial Ward, in 1647, published the classic defense of intolerance, *The Simple Cobbler of Aggwam*. "He that is willing to tolerate any Religion, or discrepant way of Religion, beside his own . . . either doubts his own or is not sincere in it." If a society believed it possessed the truth, as the Puritans did, and tolerated other beliefs, then it consciously avowed falsehoods and sinned against God.

With 20,000 migrating to Massachusetts within the first 13 years, the Puritans quickly spread out from their main settlement at Boston and formed numerous towns. The town became the center of life—it acted as a corporation distributing land to families, which received portions according to their social status. Each town created a covenant by which the signers bound themselves to serve God and live in Christian brotherhood. No one could reside outside of a township's authority to escape the stringent rules all must live under.

The utopian idealism of the Puritans to create a Christian commonwealth can be seen in the towns' highest social value: consensus. At town meetings, everyone had the opportunity to speak, but once a decision was made all were expected to accept it. Townspeople were strongly encouraged to settle all personal differences amiably within the town, with the help of elected selectmen, if necessary.

All were required to attend church weekly, but relatively few became members. To become a church member, a Puritan had to experience grace, the mystical transformation of the individual by God that gave him or her eternal life. If a Puritan believed his or her spirit "regenerate," then he or she testified before other "visible saints," who voted whether they believed the experience true or delusional. If true, the visible saint became a member of the church. The Puritans expected that very few souls would be regenerated and that the mass of humanity was destined for Hell. Moreover, individuals had no role in bringing on grace. As with most 17th-century Protestants, Puritans believed that an omnipotent God knew everything and, since God's power could not be limited, every moment and every action had been premeditated by God in time immemorial. Nothing could alter God's mind: not prayer, not faith, not good works.

Puritans were filled with anxiety over whether they would receive grace, and if they had, whether it was real or the work of the Antichrist. They worried over family members and friends, particularly children who might die before becoming regenerate. This anxiety fueled a remarkable number of diarists—the Puritans left a rich accounting of their spiritual life—and have fascinated historians ever since for their deep reasoning and speculation on the nature of life and society.

Puritan theology created political and social problems. If the human was helpless to change his or her fortune to achieve salvation, then why behave or pray to God? Ministers and elders told their people that proper behavior *might* indicate grace approaching, and certainly improper behavior indicated that a claimed regenerate had had a false experience of grace. But the ministry had to admit that humans could not presume on God in any way, and that God chose whomever he wished to save, regardless of any outward appearances of a person's holiness. Thus, the government had to be forceful to insure good behavior, since an ethical life did not lead to grace. As in other Protestant communities, conformity and proper behavior was partly maintained by neighbors reporting on one another at Sunday meetings.

## Roger Williams and the Founding of Rhode Island

The greatest challenge to the Puritans in the first decade came not from dissenters from Puritanism, nor from reprobates, nor from those who succumbed to hopeless despair that nothing they could do could save their soul. The challenge came from orthodox Puritans.

Roger Williams arrived in Massachusetts in 1631. A rising star in the English Puritan community, his reputation for piety and learning preceded him to America. Williams attracted admirers wherever he went—Puritans found his holiness charismatic. Theologically brilliant, all expected Williams to become one of the leading ministers in Massachusetts.

But Williams was a dangerous man. For his piety and his conscience would not permit him to compromise, and the Puritans could not tolerate the independent spirit that publicly criticized common practices and beliefs. The root of the problem was Williams's extreme separatism.

Separatists believed the Church of England too corrupt to be purified and that the Puritans must publicly avow their separation. In actuality, separation had little practical meaning, for Massachusetts already operated its churches on a Puritan model. But it would be highly impolitic for the Puritans to officially separate from the Church of England, which would also alter the Puritan goal of purifying the Church from within. The Puritans wished to be free to create their New Jerusalem and separatism was likely to bring down the wrath of England on the colony: they feared revocation of their charter and English interference with their semi-independence. Williams publicly railed against association with the Church of England, by which the colony lived in sin. Massachusetts leaders tried to convince Williams of the error of his ways, and several churches barred him from preaching.

Williams's probing mind also led him to question the validity of the colony's charter. What right did the King of England have to grant Massachusetts land to the Puritans. Did not the land belong to its Indian inhabitants. No one had extinguished their prior claims. This challenge undermined every landholders' title in the colony. Massachusetts' leading men begged Williams to desist but he refused.

Williams tirelessly developed his separatist concepts in his search for purity. He arrived at the conclusion that church and state must be completely separated. This went against the age-old view that state and church must mutually support each other to the benefit of both. Williams's concern was the sanctity of the church. Why should civil authorities, people who might be corrupt and unregenerate, have any power over religion. The connection of civil authority to religion necessarily perverted the church. But the Puritan commonwealth of Massachusetts was built on the intertwining of church and state. The state must enforce conformity in religious life. Williams's cry of corruption called into question the nature of the entire Puritan mission. The colony's leaders, though they admired Williams, banished him from Massachusetts.

Williams moved south to Narragansett Bay, where he continued the search for purity: to separate the holy from the impure forces of the world. He considered that *all* institutions are by nature corrupt, as they are a gathering of people, some of whom must be impure. Thus, even the church could not escape corruption—as false Christians would be members. The only purity, he concluded, existed in the individual. Williams asserted complete freedom of conscience, that government should not interfere with the practice of any individual's religion—a radical concept.

Williams was not the only dissenter—or free thinker—at Narragansett Bay. Over the coming decades, other exiles from Massachusetts, many self-imposed, joined him. Williams returned to England and secured a patent for this new colony, Providence Plantation, which later changed its name to Rhode Island. Receiving the patent was a practical political move on Williams's part—but he insisted on the purchase of land from

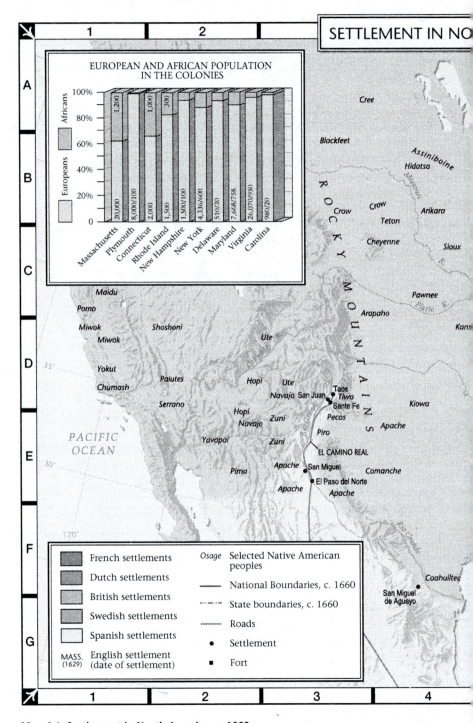

**Map 4.1  Settlement in North America, c. 1669**

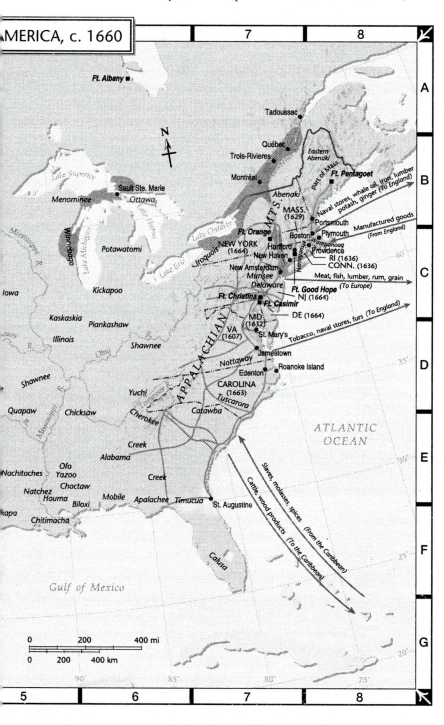

MERICA, c. 1660

Ft. Albany

Tadoussac

Québec

Trois-Rivieres

Montréal

Eastern
Abenaki

part of Mass.

Ft. Pentagoet

Sault Ste. Marie

Menominee

Ottawa

Abenaki

Naval stores, whale oil, iron, lumber
potash, ginger (To England)

MASS.
(1629)

Portsmouth    Manufactured goods
(From England)

Potawatomi

Ft. Orange

Boston

Plymouth

Winnebago

NEW YORK
(1664)

Hartford

Wampanoag

Providence

Kickapoo

New Haven

RI (1636)

Iowa

New Amsterdam

CONN. (1636)

Munsee

Meat, fish, lumber, rum, grain

Delaware

Ft. Good Hope (To Europe)

Kaskaskia

Ft. Christina

NJ (1664)

Piankashaw

Ft. Casimir

Illinois

MD
(1632)

DE (1664)

Shawnee

VA
(1607)

St. Mary's

Tobacco, naval stores, furs (To England)

Jamestown

Shawnee

Nottaway

Roanoke Island

Edenton

Quapaw

Yuchi

CAROLINA
(1663)

Chicksaw

Tuscarora

Cherokee

Catawba

Creek

ATLANTIC
OCEAN

Alabama

Ofo

Nachitoches

Yazoo

Creek

Natchez

Choctaw

Houma

Mobile

Apalachee

Timucua

St. Augustine

Biloxi

kapa

Chitimacha

Slaves, molasses, spices (From the Caribbean)

Cattle, wood products (To the Caribbean)

Calusa

Gulf of Mexico

0    200    400 mi

0    200    400 km

local native peoples. Rhode Island developed excellent relations with Native Americans, a far different situation than most other colonies, with the notable exception of the early years of the Pennsylvania colony. It is clear from Rhode Island's and Pennsylvania's history that conflict between the English and native peoples was not inevitable, but depended on local circumstances, and particularly colonial governments' willingness to restrain their colonists from taking Indian land and initiating and provoking wars.

In the coming decades, Rhode Island continued to attract religious dissenters of many traditions and the politically disaffected. The colony maintained a weak government so as not to interfere with individuals and towns, and they formed a more democratic style of government than elsewhere in English America. Rhode Islanders even had the right to choose their own governor—only Connecticut shared that distinction—and maintained that right through the colonial period.

## Anne Hutchinson and the Challenge of Antinomianism

Another threat from the orthodox arose in Massachusetts soon after Williams's banishment. Some Puritans heckled clergymen whom they believed preached a false doctrine of salvation through works, rather than by grace. The controversy so divided the community, John Winthrop wrote, it was "as common here to distinguish between men as being under a covenant of grace or a covenant of works, as in other countries between Protestants and papists."

Many believed Anne Hutchinson was the root of the problem. Born in 1591, Hutchinson was highly educated by her theologian father—who frequently was arrested for his non-conformity in England. Extremely pious, she immigrated to Boston in 1634 from Lincolnshire, England, to be near the zealous and pious minister John Cotton, whom she greatly respected and with whom she allied in Boston. Hutchinson's midwifery practice permitted her much intimacy with Boston women, and weekly prayer meetings at her home attracted increasing numbers of women; her meetings for men were equally successful. Charismatic, zealous, and theologically brilliant, Hutchinson earned respect throughout Boston, her husband's election to the colonial assembly probably reflecting her status in the community rather than his.

Worse than the charge of heckling ministers was the accusation against Hutchinson and her followers of antinomianism. Antinomianism encompassed the belief that when an individual achieved salvation, they were no longer human: they had become a visible saint—one of the chosen few. Some argued that having discovered God's will through grace that they no longer needed to obey laws—for they knew what was right; nor should they listen to unregenerate ministers, for grace allowed them to know the true meaning of the gospel. In the Netherlands, antinomians were reputed to have become hedonists: secure in the knowledge that God never changed His mind—they had no worry of losing God's gift of grace, and thus they entered a life of pleasure-seeking, which included abandonment of spouses.

The true threat of antinomianism in Massachusetts was that it could sever the community between those who experienced grace and those who did not. How could the unregenerate be expected to heed their leaders and obey the laws, when the antinomians flaunted their privileged status and disrespected civil and religious institutions. The antinomians' separation of themselves as the chosen few threatened the consensus that was the community's highest social value.

The young governor, Sir Henry Vane, a supporter of Hutchinson, was intimidated by critics into resigning his position. John Cotton also moved away from the antinomians, though he did not completely abandon Hutchinson. As the Puritans were wont to do when facing grave religious problems, they called a synod, a meeting of ministers to discuss the dreaded doctrines allegedly being espoused in Boston. Over 100 heresies were detailed and condemned over several weeks—but no individual associated with any of them. The synod denounced the holding of private religious meetings and the heckling of ministers.

In November 1637, the General-Court, the colony's legislative body, met to discuss the synod's findings. Many of Hutchinson's followers were brought before them and found guilty of sedition and contempt. Some were heavily fined, others disqualified from voting and holding public offices; 58 men were disarmed until they acknowledged their seditions. Many others were banished from the colony: the cancer was being cut from the community.

Hutchinson herself was then brought before the court. For two days she was questioned and berated. Offended that a woman should have so much influence, one elder stated, "yow have slept owt of yor place, yow have rather bine a Husband than a Wife, & a preacher than a Hearer; & a Magistrate than a Subject." But none could trap her into admitting any heresy, and many exploded in anger at her clever responses to their questions. Hutchinson's triumph was virtually complete, the case against her almost closed, when she lost her composure and unleashed a tirade against her persecutors. She told her shocked audience that she knew what she knew through divine revelation; that God had thrust into her mind knowledge of the Bible and his will: that God had told her to go to Massachusetts, where she would be persecuted, but he would punish the colony.

The magistrates had to meet Hutchinson's challenge. Either she or they were deluded that they did God's will. Her admittance that God spoke to her was heresy—most Christians believed that God does not literally speak to humans since the close of the Bible. But in fact, Hutchinson only said that God's voice had spoke to her soul—not that she actually had heard his words—but the magistrates used this, and her numerous alleged seditions to declare her "unfit for our society." The Reverend John Wilson raged at her, "in the name of our Lord Jes[sus] Ch[rist] and in the name of the Church . . . I doe cast you out . . . I doe deliver you up to Satan . . . I command you . . . as a Leper to withdraw your selfe."

Hutchinson's banishment came under temporary reprieve, as she was pregnant, during which time the elders tried to get her to repent—which might bring her followers back into the fold. She would not. She and others headed south to Narragansett Bay where they formed their own quarrelling community. Hutchinson eventually moved to Long Island, and then to New Netherland, where she died in an Indian attack in 1643.

## INDIANS AND ENGLISH IN NEW ENGLAND

When the Pilgrims arrived at Plymouth, the native people of the region had long had contact with European fishermen, many who dried their catch on shore. Fortunately for the Pilgrims, they met Squanto, a local Indian who is believed to have spent 10 years in England, having been captured, and then returned home in 1615. Squanto was then sold into slavery in Spain by an English sailor; he eventually escaped to England, and again reached home in 1618, only to find his people destroyed by small pox. He found refuge with the Wampanoag, and worked for them as a translator with the Pilgrims, playing a critical role bringing the two peoples into alliance.

The character and experience of individuals like Squanto went a long way to smoothing relations between the culturally diverse indigenous peoples and the Europeans, especially when they possessed language skills and could explain the needs and desires of each to the other. But skillful mediators like Squanto were few in the early stages of colonization. Bridging the cultural divide was difficult, though mediated by ceremonies, the exchange of goods, and a show of mutual goodwill. Prejudice was difficult to overcome, particularly for Europeans situated in an unfamiliar environment, and in need of food and military aid. The Europeans were also hampered by notions of their superiority, which made it difficult for them to work with people who could and did help them in so many ways. In New England, as in other colonial areas, Indians and Europeans had to interact with one another; those interactions not only had physical and social consequences for all, but posed an array of cultural challenges as each had to incorporate the other into their world view.

## Cultural Challenges

Many Europeans were offended by native dress, or lack thereof, and interpreted native appearance and manners, and the natives themselves, as "savage." The word *savage* means "wild man," and Europeans attributed native savagery to the Indians' lifestyle, to their civil society, and to their lack of Christianity. The common native practice of scalping enemies offended European sensibilities and further indicated savagery; Europeans preferred to take the entire head of their enemies. Savagery was often interpreted as diabolical: Puritans perceived Indian medicine men as agents of the Devil, who tricked gullible Indians into performing religious ceremonies in his service.

The Puritans (and other Europeans) were further confounded by native gender roles, whereby women tended the fields and men hunted. In Europe, hunting was the sport of kings, and common people were restricted from hunting. Native men were thus seen as lazy and presumptuous for spending so much time in a leisure activity that should be reserved for nobility. The natives, too, were surprised and disturbed by gender role differences. Englishmen performed women's work by planting the fields, and Englishwomen, they believed, did little or no work and must rule their husbands.

The desire to trade and the need for alliances encouraged, if not pushed, natives and English to overcome cultural differences and hostilities. As long as no one wielded a preponderance of power, or competed too strenuously for valuable resources, then a level of tolerance and positive interactions could occur. In the first decades of settlement, Puritans were aided by circumstances that defused potential conflict and permitted relatively unimpeded development and expansion. Normally, heavy migration would lead to conflict with indigenous peoples over land, but natives of the New England coast had been decimated by diseases. As historian Francis Jennings noted, the Puritans did not enter a "wilderness," as they described it, but a "widowed land" whose occupants had died.

The Puritans interpreted Indian deaths from disease in providential terms, that God was clearing the land of heathens for Christian occupation. Some Puritans contemplated converting the Indians to Christianity, but these attempts were quite limited, especially in comparison with the Spanish and French, in large part owing to differences between Catholicism and Protestantism. The Catholic Church hoped to be a universal church that would someday include all humans. Protestants were much more exclusive. Only the chosen few were going to heaven, and they found it difficult to imagine savage Indians among the elect.

Yet the Puritans made some effort, establishing "Praying Towns," mostly inhabited by Indians from groups that had been ravaged by disease and warfare. Praying Towns, in effect, were reservations. Although "Praying Indians" were expected to convert to Christianity, the town's purpose was less religious than political, social, economic, and military. Praying Indians had to give up their hunting way of life, thus leaving more land for the English. They also had to accept English gender roles—the men became farmers instead of hunters. The English demanded that Praying Indians cut their hair and wear English clothes—they had to look English. By transforming Indians into English (at least by appearance), and limiting Indian mobility by confining them to the towns, the English intended to diminish the native threat militarily and culturally. As the Puritans feared the bounty of the land diverting them from their holy experiment, they also feared the example of the Indian diverting them from Christian ways: they could not afford having their own people display the same independent spirit as the natives, and thus wanted to crush that spirit when they could.

English religion had little impact on native peoples, and in the first few decades of colonization, trade goods had yet to transform native life. Yet the English arrival was disastrous, notably because of the unintentional spread of disease. By the end of the 17th century, the European-borne pathogens had reduced the native population of New England to 10% of what it had been 100 years before. Much of this devastation occurred along the coast, the area with the longest and most sustained contact with Europeans, while inland, powerful native peoples remained. These included various Abenaki groups in northern New England and southern Canada, the Pequot in modern-day Connecticut and Long Island, New York, and the Narragansett and Wampanoag in southern New England. The Puritans engaged in military conflict with all these peoples.

## The Pequot War (1636–1637)

The Pequot were the first to war with the English, only six years after Massachusetts' founding. The origins of the so-called Pequot War are obscure. The Pequot were the most powerful native group in central and southern New England, collecting tribute from other natives in the area. When Dutch traders established a post on the Connecticut River, they undermined the Pequots by trading freely with neighboring peoples over whom the Pequots claimed authority. English traders from Plymouth moved into the area and soon did the same.

Hostilities escalated when the Dutch kidnapped and killed a Pequot sachem (a paramount chief) and the Pequot killed a Virginia trader who had just arrived in the area. Before events could spin out of control, the Pequots and Massachusetts tried to patch things up—both were concerned about growing Dutch power to the west and the possibility of a Dutch alliance with the Narragansett of Rhode Island. The Narragansett worked diligently to keep the Pequot and English apart and established an alliance with Williams's Rhode Island colony. The Pequot, feeling betrayed and surrounded, attacked English settlements in the new Puritan colony of Connecticut, and by 1637, full-scale warfare had begun.

As with most wars between the Europeans and Indians, Indians ordinarily comprised a majority of those who fought on the European side. Sometimes these Indians fought as auxiliaries for pay, but usually they participated in these conflicts because of their own political, diplomatic, and economic goals. Mohegans and Narragansetts joined the English against the Pequots, not because they were subordinates to the English, but because of their own enmities with the Pequot. The Mohegans had been subjects of the Pequot, their leader Uncas was son-in-law to the great sachem of the Pequot, and apparently Uncas wanted to turn the tide and make the Pequot subordinate to him. In the war, the Mohegans and the Narragansetts provided reconnaissance and most of the soldiers. But it was English brutality that was most startling.

At one Pequot village, Captain John Mason decided not to risk untested troops in battle, but still wished to find a way to massacre the enemy and crush their will to fight. With Narragansetts and Mohegans looking on, the English set fire to the village and then killed almost all those who tried to escape. Somewhere between 300 and 700 were killed, the vast majority women and children. Captain John Underhill, Mason's second-in-command, recorded Narragansett dismay with the English form of warfare. He said, although the Narragansett "much rejoiced at our victories . . . [they] cried Mach it, mach it; that is, It is naught, it is naught, because it is too furious, and slays too many men."

The Pequots began disintegrating, some migrating southward, others hiding in swamps. In 1638, the survivors surrendered. The Mohegans and the Narragansetts each received 80 Pequots, the Niantics 20, and others were sold by the English into slavery in the West Indies. The Pequots lost most of their land, though small groups survived, and in the 20th century, they received official recognition as a native people from the United States government.

In the aftermath of the war, the Mohegans emerged as the major power in Connecticut, asserting their dominance over the smaller tribes, much as the Pequot had done, with the important difference that the Mohegan maintained excellent relations with the English. Relations between the Mohegans and the Narragansetts, however, were unstable. They had been enemies before the English arrived, allies in the Pequot War, but afterwards relations again deteriorated so that the two frequently fought, with the English usually tacitly supporting the Mohegans. A delicate balance was maintained between the major powers until the last quarter of the 17th century.

There was no such thing as English military dominance or superiority in the early stages of colonization. Success in warfare depended upon alliances with Native Americans, who provided manpower, military skills, and knowledge of the land. Native allies of the English possessed their own motives and goals and manipulated the English as much as the English manipulated them. Nevertheless, the terms of warfare were changing, as the Puritans introduced a strategy of massacring the belligerents and enslaving some, whereas the natives tended to kill relatively few and enslave or incorporate the captives.

## NON-ENGLISH EUROPEAN SETTLEMENTS IN THE NORTHEAST

The English were not the only power to significantly expand in the North. Other Europeans, particularly the French and Dutch, hemmed in the English from the north and west, while the Five Nations of Iroquois, in response to the European presence and the introduction of a new international market economy, militarized and extended their influence in modern-day New York and over native peoples to the west. Given the competitive nature of colonization, it was inevitable that the Europeans would come into conflict with one another in the Northeast, but in the early stages of colonization they did not necessarily seek out armed conflict. The Europeans' main concerns lay in securing their settlements, maintaining subsistence, and turning a profit, if possible. None were shy, however, at using force to achieve their ends.

## Origins of New France

French interest in North America emerged within a decade of Columbus reaching the West Indies. French fishermen exploited the Newfoundland fisheries in the North Atlantic—the world's greatest fisheries—for cod, and Giovanni da Verrazano sailed the Atlantic Coast for France in 1524 as far south as Florida. In 1534, Jacques Cartier provided a more systematic exploration of the North Atlantic Coast in search of a Northwest Passage to Asia. When Cartier encountered the Micmacs at the Gulf of St. Lawrence, he found people not only eager to trade, but experienced at trading with Europeans, indicative that contact with Europeans preceded the "official" expeditions sent by governments.

On Cartier's second voyage in the summer of 1535, he sailed up the St. Lawrence Seaway to modern-day Quebec and gave the region its name, Canada. But French interests were not confined to the far north, as they made inroads into Brazil and Florida, though their major overseas activity, as with the English and Dutch, was attacking Spanish shipping and colonies. French colonization attempts in Brazil and Florida were destroyed by the Portuguese and Spanish, respectively, and the Wars of Religion in France effectively forestalled subsequent efforts in the 16th century.

In 1608, the French established a permanent colony at Quebec under Samuel de Champlain. Champlain commanded the colony for most of the next 25 years, and he ably extended French knowledge of the region. Despite the arrival of few colonists, the colony's economy became important to France through the profitable fur trade.

To facilitate trade, Champlain sent young men to live with Indians and learn their languages and customs. These men became the coureurs de bois, who eventually spread throughout the Great Lakes region, even as far west as Montana and South Dakota, though most distant trade was conducted with Indian middlemen, such as the Odawas. Native peoples generally welcomed the traders, so that they did not have to travel long distances to obtain trade goods. European traders generally married native women to secure kinship ties to the Indian community, which also strengthened French–native relations.

Missionary societies followed trade routes to native peoples. The early efforts by Ursiline nuns and Jesuit priests were mostly failures. The French then created the reserve, a reservation to confine Indians to a single place, much like the English Praying Towns. Whereas the English pressured Indians to move to Praying Towns to take their land, the French relied on voluntary removal to generally productive lands closer to their own settlements, in part, to provide a mutually protective ring against enemies. Because the missionaries feared French colonials corrupting Indians with their morality, many of the missions were later moved away from

European settlements. Although French success was limited in converting natives to Christianity, and in transforming natives culturally into French, they did succeed in creating staunch allies out of many.

In 1628, the Kirke brothers of England determined to conquer French Canada. They captured 18 French ships in the St. Lawrence River, many of which carried supplies for the colony. The loss of the supply ships led to near starvation, and in 1629, the brothers forced the French to surrender. Three years later, however, the English government made the Kirkes relinquish the colony as part of a new peace treaty between England and France, and Champlain returned once again to govern Canada.

Not until the end of the 17th century would the French–English conflict again reach a heated stage, and then warfare between the northern English colonies and French Canada would be near constant for six decades. But through most of the 17th century, the competition between the French, English, and Dutch for control of the fur trade ensnared native peoples from the Atlantic to the Great Lakes into various forms of military engagement, from raids and skirmishes to all-out war, conquest, and removal. The French allies, the Huron, were the first major victims. They were forced by the Iroquois, trading partners of the Dutch, to abandon their lands near Lake Ontario, for lands further west in Wisconsin, and east in Quebec, some even moving to Iroquoia as allies of their old enemies. The removal of the Huron allowed the Iroquois to subject numerous smaller native groups in modern-day New York and Pennsylvania, forcing many to flee to the Ohio Valley, and further west and north into the Great Lakes region. Most of these refugees allied with the French, formed new villages, and sought ways to resist growing Iroquois power. Thus the impact of European settlements, though distant from many native peoples, still had tremendous impact on their lives through the economic power of trade.

## Dutch, Iroquois, and Swedes

Dutch and Swedes also undertook empire-building in the vast lands of the north. While the English were settling Virginia, in 1609 Henry Hudson, employed by the Dutch, explored the river named for him in the modern-day state of New York. A little over ten years later, the Dutch West India Company received monopoly rights from their government to the area, to which they sent settlers in 1624.

The Dutch empire was expanding by leaps and bounds. They kicked the Portuguese out of many of their Asian possessions to become the world's greatest trading power. The Portuguese–Dutch Asian model of overseas expansion differed greatly from that practiced by Spain, England, and France and even by Portugal in the West. In Asia, the Portuguese and Dutch relied on trading factories—coastal forts—built in advantageous locations for conducting trade on sea and with inland peoples. Unlike in the West, there was little emphasis placed on settlement of colonists, exploitation of mines, or conversion of indigenous peoples to Christianity. Trade—and control of trade routes—was the focus of expansion.

The Dutch East India Company directed Dutch expansion in Asia, and the Dutch West India Company followed a similar path in the Atlantic. The latter developed trading forts in Brazil, in West Africa, on the Amazon River, and elsewhere. At the mouth of the Hudson River, the Dutch purchased Manhattan Island from the Manhate Indians.

A village was erected at the south end of the island and enclosed by a wall, which gave birth much later to the famed Wall Street. The small community quickly became one of the most diverse on the North American continent, as Dutch, French, English, Swedes, Portuguese, Afro-Brazilians, and Jews all found their way to the trading center. At least 18 languages were spoken on Manhattan Island by 1650.

Although New Netherland, as the colony was called, was not nearly as profitable as other parts of the Dutch West Indies Empire, money was to be made there. Manhattan possesses one of the world's great harbors, and from there ocean-going vessels could sail up the Hudson River for 100 miles, to a point where Dutch traders established Beverwyck, later renamed Albany by the English. Native Americans brought valuable furs there, which then easily entered the Atlantic economy.

The Iroquois used their access to Beverwyck to improve their own position in the region. They became middlemen between the Dutch and native peoples to the west, as furs were transported over 1,000 miles to Beverwyck. To secure their advantageous economic position, the easternmost Iroquois, the Mohawk, went to war with the Mahican, with whom the Dutch earlier had established a trade. Enmity between the Mohawk and Mahican preceded the Dutch arrival in New Netherland, but the Mohawk could not abide the strengthening of the Mahican and their allies. Despite Mahican superior numbers, after four years of fighting the Mohawk prevailed, and the Dutch were forced to accept the outcome. Although the Iroquois then monopolized access to Dutch trade at Beverwyck, their success enmeshed them in over 70 years of warfare with Algonquins and French, to control the fur trade and lands all the way to the Mississippi River and beyond.

Closer to Manhattan Island, the Dutch initiated war with the Indians of Long Island, as well as those west of the Hudson River and to the north. A new company administrator, William Kieft attempted to exterminate these Indians out of simple hatred and a desire for their land. Kieft's War (1639–1645) saw the Dutch indiscriminately massacre Indians, ultimately leading to Kieft's recall by the company, but not before the damage had been done and the war ended. Over 1,000 Delawares lost their lives, as well as members of about a dozen other groups. The colonial population of New Netherland also declined as many Dutch left the colony to escape the violence. Moreover, the war severely overtaxed the Dutch West India Company's finances, and the company lost interest in the colony, though its appointment of the devoted Peter Stuyvesant helped hold the colony together until English conquest.

The Dutch were also heavily involved in Sweden's establishment of a colony in North America. With the Dutch West India Company as its model, and half of its funding coming from Dutch merchants, the New Sweden Company settled on Delaware Bay on December 31, 1637. The company employed Peter Minuit, a former governor of New Netherland, as its governor. The colony occupied southern New Jersey and parts of eastern Pennsylvania and built several primitive forts from which to conduct trade. Early colonists unsuccessfully cultivated tobacco and had great difficulty producing enough food to support themselves. Relations with local natives were generally amiable, as the colony remained small and was unable to become militarily aggressive. In 1644, the colony had fewer than 100 colonists, though the number nearly doubled in the next three years. Jealous at Swedish trading success, the Dutch in New Netherland, led by Peter Stuyvesant, conquered the colony in 1655.

## Conclusion

The first century and a half of empire-building led to incredible acts of inhumanity by Europeans against native peoples. America was viewed as a place from which to wrest riches, and the indigenous inhabitants usually considered inferior people who should be killed, removed, or forced to labor. The desire to convert Indians to Christianity sometimes elevated views of natives as possessing the same basic character of all humanity and capable of improvement that might warrant more humane treatment. The need for native assistance, particularly military alliance, also mitigated the worst aspects of exploitation, and positive relations developed where mutually beneficial trade was welcomed by all parties. Although disease, warfare, and enslavement greatly reduced native numbers, and entire areas became depopulated, many native peoples retained their independence and power and would continue to do so for centuries.

Despite intense cultural prejudice towards native peoples, and towards the New World itself, colonists adapted to both. Most Spanish, French, and English would have preferred to re-create Europe in America, when they founded New Spain, New France, and New England, but this was impractical. They erected towns, churches, and houses to make the New World familiar, but available food and building materials and a vastly different landscape induced them to learn from the Indians how best to live in their new homes. The desire for profits led them to erect new economies and create new labor systems. The way to wealth in the New World usually involved harnessing large numbers of laborers for employment in extractive industries like mining and fishing, or in agricultural production of food and

cash crops for sale in distant markets. Slavery and other forms of forced labor, though known and practiced in Europe, became central to most colonial societies. But trade with native peoples was also important in many regions, particularly in large areas of the future United States. Europeans learned to adapt to natives to trade and earn alliance. They had no other choice, especially in places where natives could trade and ally with European competitors.

Native peoples were transformed by the arrival of Europeans. Disease decimated many and forced the survivors to adapt to a rapidly changing landscape. Some entered missions and became Christians, many joined with other refugees to create new towns and ethnicities. Almost all were affected by the influx of European immigrants, goods, and ideas. Still, just as Europeans remained rooted in European culture, even as they became Americans, so too did the indigenous peoples retain many of their ancient ways even as they adapted to and from the newcomers.

The process of colonization in the North differed from the areas to the south in significant ways. Except in southern New England, Indians held a preponderance of military power that lasted well into the 18th century. Relatively few Indians were directly exploited by the Europeans for their labor as slaves, servants, or mission Indians. Instead, Indians entered the European economy through trade of animal pelts that they hunted and processed. Although the Europeans of the north could not establish either a plantation or a mining economy, as characterized so many other areas of European colonization in the New World, there were advantages to settlement in the North. The environment was relatively healthy, there were huge swaths of productive land, and tremendous forests yielded quality wood for construction and plenty for heating. The river system facilitated travel and movement of goods to ports that could trade with other ports in the Atlantic economy. And the environment included great numbers of animals that could be harvested for food and their valuable pelts. If few Europeans in the north could obtain the great riches available in tropical and sub-tropical America, many could carve out a comfortable living: many areas of the North would attract large numbers of European immigrants hoping to own land.

# DOCUMENTS

## 4.1. John Winthrop's Concern for Puritan Settlement of New England

*John Winthrop's lay sermon, "Christian Charity. A Modell hereof," was delivered aboard the flagship* Arbella *on the passage to Massachusetts from England. Much of the sermon reflects Winthrop's fear that in America the Puritans would pursue individual interests rather than their "errand into the wilderness" to create a New Jerusalem that would be a light unto the nations. He implores the migrants to live a life of charity to one another, which can only be accomplished by living "knit" together as one community. What must the colonists do to remain a community?*

ANNO 1630
CHRISTIAN CHARITIE
A Modell hereof

GOD ALMIGHTY in his most holy and wise providence, hath soe disposed of the condition of' mankind, as in all times some must be rich, some poore, some high and eminent in power and dignitie; others mean and in submission.

*The Reason hereof*

**1.** *Reas.* First to hold conformity with the rest of his world, being delighted to show forth the glory of his wisdom in the variety and difference of the creatures, and the glory of his power in ordering all these differences for the preservation and good of the whole; and the glory of his greatness, that as it is the glory of princes to have many officers, soe this great king will haue many stewards, Counting himself more honoured in dispensing his gifts to man by man, than if he did it by his owne immediate hands.

**2.** *Reas.* Secondly that he might haue the more occasion to manifest the work of his Spirit: first upon the wicked in moderating and restraining them: soe that the riche and mighty should not eate upp the poore nor the poore and dispised rise upp against and shake off theire yoake. 2ly In the regenerate, in exerciseing his graces in them, as in the grate ones, theire love, mercy, gentleness, temperance &c., in the poore and inferior sorte, theire faithe, patience, obedience &c.

**3.** *Reas.* Thirdly, that every man might have need of others, and from hence they might be all knitt more nearly together in the Bonds of brotherly affection. . . .

*(Continued)*

It rests now to make some application of this discourse, by the present designe, which gaue the occasion of writing of it. Herein are 4 things to he propounded; *first* the persons, 2ly the worke, 3ly the end, 4thly the meanes. 1. For *the persons*. Wee are a company professing ourselves fellow members of Christ, in which respect onely though wee were absent from each other many miles, and had our imployments as farre distant, yet wee ought to account ourselves knitt together by this bond of loue, and, live in the exercise of it, if wee would have comforte of our being in Christ. . . . 2nly for the *worke* wee have in hand. It is by a mutuall consent, through a speciall overvaluing providence and a more than an ordinary approbation of the Churches of Christ, to seeke out a place of cohabitation and Consorteshipp under a due forme of Government both ciuill and ecclesiasticall. In such cases as this, the care of the publique must oversway all private respects, by which, not only conscience, but meare civill pollicy, dothe binde us. For it is a true rule that particular Estates cannot subsist in the ruin of the publique. 3ly The *end* is to improve our lives to doe more service to the Lord; the comforte and encrease of the body of Christe, whereof we are members; that ourselves and posterity may be the better preserved from the common corruptions of this evill world, to serve the Lord and worke out our Salvation under the power and purity of his holy ordinances. 4thly for the *meanes* whereby this must be effected. They are twofold, a conformity with the worke and end wee aime at. These wee see are extraordinary, therefore wee must not content ourselves with usuall ordinary meanes. Whatsoever wee did, or ought to have,

done, when wee liued in England, the same must wee doe, and more allsoe, where wee goe. That which the most in theire churches mainetaine as truthe in profession onely, wee must bring into familiar and constant practise; as in this duty of loue, wee must loue brotherly without dissimulation, wee must loue one another with a pure hearte fervently. Wee must beare one anothers burthens. We must not looke onely on our owne things, but allsoe on the things of our brethren. Neither must wee thinke that the Lord will beare with such faileings at our hands as he dothe from those among whome wee have lived. . . .

Now the onely way to avoyde this shipwracke, and to provide for our posterity, is to followe the counsell of Micah, *to doe justly, to love mercy, to walk humbly with our God.* For this end, wee must be knitt together, in this worke, as one man. Wee must entertaine each other in brotherly affection. Wee must be willing to abridge ourselves of our superfluities, for the supply of other's necessities. Wee must uphold a familiar commerce together in all meekeness, gentlenes, patience and liberality. Wee must delight in eache other; make other's conditions our oune; rejoice together, mourne together, labour and suffer together, allways haueving before our eyes our commission and community in the worke, as members of the same body. Soe shall wee *keepe the unitie of the spirit in the bond of peace.* The Lord will be our God, and delight to dwell among us, as his oune people, and will command a blessing upon us in all our wayes. Soe that wee shall see much more of his wisdome, power, goodness and truthe, than formerly wee haue been acquainted with. Wee shall finde that the God of Israell is among us, when ten of us shall be able to resist a thousand of our enemies; when hee shall make us a prayse and glory that men shall say of succeeding plantations, "the Lord make it likely that of *New England.*" For wee must consider that wee shall be as a citty upon a hill. The eies of all people are uppon us. Soe that if wee shall deale falsely with our God in this worke wee haue undertaken, and soe cause him to withdrawe his present help from us, wee shall be made a story and a by-word through the world. Wee shall open the mouthes of enemies to speake evill of the wayes of God, and all professors for God's sake. Wee shall shame the faces of many of God's worthy servants, and cause theire prayers to be turned into curses upon us till wee be consumed out of the good land whither wee are a goeing.

I shall shutt upp this discourse with that exhortation of Moses, that faithfull servant of the Lord, in his last farewell to Israell, Deut. 30.

*Beloued there is now sett before us life and good, Death and evill, in that wee are commanded this day to loue the Lord our God, and to loue one another, to walke in his wayes and to keepe his Commandements and his Ordinance and his lawes,* and the articles of our Covenant with him, that *wee may liue and be multiplied, and that the Lord our God may blesse us in the land whither wee goe to possesse it. But if our heartes shall turne away, soe that we will not obey, but shall be seduced, and worshipp and serue other Gods,* our pleasure and proffitts, *and serue them*; it is propounded unto us this day, *wee shall surely perishe out of the good land whither wee passe over this vast sea to possesse it.*

Therefore lett us choose life that wee, and our seede may liue, by obeyeing His voyce and leaveing to Him, for Hee is our life and our prosperity.

---

Source: John Winthrop, Christian Charity. A Modell hereof (1631).

## 4.2. Anne Hutchinson's Trial for Heresy

*Anne Hutchinson's ability to answer critics at her trial for heresy in Boston irritated both civil and religious authorities to no end. In the following short excerpt, we find that her exciting her opponents' anger was due in no small part to her gender—men had difficulty accepting that a woman could intellectually challenge them so effectively, hence the vehemence with which they denounced her. Why was Hutchinson's pride, her seeming lack of "humiliation," (by which the Puritans meant humility) such a threat to her accusers?*

Mr. Simes: I should be glad to see any Humiliation in Mrs. Hutchinson . . . for I fear thease are no new Thinges, but she hath ayntientlye held them, and had need to be humbled for her former Doctrines. . . .

Mr. Peters: We did not thinke she would have humbled herselfe for denyinge Graces this day, for her

opinions are dayngerous & fundamentall & such as takes downe the Articles of Religion, as denying the Ressurection, & fayth, & all Sanctification. . . .

Governor: I must put Mrs. Hutchinson in minde of a paper that she sent me, wherein she did very much slight fayth. . . .

*(Continued)*

Mrs. Hutchinson. Those papers were not myne. . . .

Brother Willson. I must needs say this & if I did not say soe much I could not satisfie my owne contience herin, for wheras yow say that the Cawse or Root of thease yor Errors, was yor slightinge & Disrespect of the Magistrates & yor unreverent Carriage to them,/ wch though I thinke that was a greate Sine, & it may be one Cawse why God should thus leave you, but that is not all, for I fear & beleve ther was another, & a greater Cawse, & that is the slightinge of Gods faythfull Ministers & contemninge & cryinge downe them as Nobodies. . . . I doe not deny but it may be yow might have an honorable Esteme of some one or 2. Men, as owr Teacher & the like, yet I thinke it was, to set up yor selfe in the Roome of God: above others, that yow might be extolled & admired & followed after, that yow might be a greate Prophites . . . it grives me, that yow should soe mince yor dayngerous, fowle & damnable Herisies, wherby yow have soe wickedly departed from God & done soe much hurt.

Mr. Shephard. I think it is needles forany other now to speake & useless, for the Case is playne, & hear is Witnesses enough. . . .

Mr. Peters. I would desire Mrs. Hutchinson in the name of the Lord that she would serch into her hart farther to helpe on her Repentance/, for though she hath confessed some Things yet it is far short of what it should be, & therefor

1. I fear yow are not well principled & grownded in yor Catechisme.
2. I would commend this to yor Consideration that yow have

slept owt of yor place, yow have rather bine a Husband than a Wife, & a preacher than a Hearer; & a Magistrate than a Subject, & soe yow have thought to carry all Thinges in Church & Commonwealth as yow would, & have not bine humbled for this.

Brother Willson. The Church consentinge to it we will proceed to Excommunication.

Forasmuch as yow, Mrs. Hutchinson, have highly transgressed & offended, & forasmuch as yow have soe many ways troubled the Church wth yor Erors & have drawen away many a poor soule, & have upheld yor Revelations: & forasmuch as yow have made a Lye, &c. Therfor in the name of our Lord Je: Ch: & in the name of the Church I doe not only pronownce yow worthy to be cast owt, but I doe cast yow owt & in the name of Ch. I doe deliver you up to Sathan, that yow may learne no more to blaspheme, to seduce & to lye, & I doe account yow from this time forth to be a Hethen & a Publican & soe to be held of all the Brethren & Sisters, of this Congregation, & of others: therfor I command yow in the name of Ch: Je: & of this Church as a Leper to wthdraw yor selfe out of the Congregation; that as formerly yow have dispised & contemned the Holy Ordinances of God, & turned yor Backe one them, soe yow may now have no part in them nor benefit by them.

Source: *Proceedings of the Massachusetts Historical Society*, Second Series, Vol. 4 [Vol. 24 of continuous numbering] (1887–1889), 184, 185, 186, 187, 190–191.

## 4.3. A Puritan view of the Pequot War

*Thomas Shepard was a leading minister in colonial New England, who in his writings documented much of the persecution Puritans faced before arriving in America. His "confessions," sermons, and autobiography were inspirational to subsequent genera-tions of Puritans. The following excerpt provides some of his observations on the Pequot War. Was Pequot "pride" an issue for the Puritans, as it was with Anne Hutchinson in the previous document? What kind of pride does Shepard display for Puritan military prowess against the Indians?*

At this time I cannot omit the good-ness of God, as to myself so to all the country, in delivering us from the Pequot furies. These Indians were the stoutest, proudest and most suc-cessful in their wars of all the Indians; their chief sachem was Sasakus, a proud, cruel, unhappy and headstrong prince, who, not willing to be guided by the persuasions of his fellow, an aged sachem Momanattuck, not fear-ing the revenge of the English, having first sucked the blood of Captain Stone and Mr. Oldam, found it so sweet, and his proceedings for one whole winter so successful, that having besieged and killed about four men that kept Seabrook fort, he adventured to fall upon the English up the river at Weathersfield, where he slew nine or ten men, women, and children, at una-wares, and took two maids prisoners, carrying them away captive to the Pequot country. Hereupon, those upon the river first gathered about seventy men and sent them into Pequot country, to make that the seat of war and to revenge the death of those innocent whom they barbarous-ly and most unnaturally slew. These men marched two days and nights from the way of the Narragansett unto Pequot, being guided by those Indians then the ancient enemies of the Pequots. They intended to assault Sasakus' fort; but falling short of it the second night, the providence of God guided them to another nearer, full of stout men and their best soldiers, being as it were cooped up there to the number of three or four hundred in all, for the divine slaughter by the hand of the English. These therefore, being all night making merry and singing the death of the English the next day, toward break of the day being very heavy with sleep, the English drew near within the sight of the fort, very weary with travail and want of sleep, at which time five hun-dred Narragansetts fled for fear and only two of the company stood to it to conduct them to the fort and the door and entrance thereof. The English being come to it, awakened the fort with a peal of muskets directed into the midst of their wigwams; after this, some undertaking to compass the fort without, some adventured into the fort upon the very faces of the enemy standing ready with their arrows ready bent to shoot whoever should adven-ture. But the English, casting by their pieces, took their swords in their hands (the Lord doubling their stren-gth and courage), and fell upon the Indians, where a hot fight continued about the space of an hour. At last, by the direction of one Captain Mason, their wigwams were set on fire, which, being dry and contiguous one to another, was most dreadful to the Indians: some burning, some bleeding to death by the sword, some resisting till they were cut off, some flying were beat down by the men without, until the Lord had utterly consumed the whole company, except four or five girls they took prisoners and dealt with them at Seabrook as they dealt with ours at Weathersfield. 'Tis verily thought, scarce one man escaped, unless one or two to carry forth tidings of the lamentable end of their fellows. Of the English, not one man was killed but one by the musket of an Englishman (as was conceived). Some were wounded much, but all recovered and restored again.

Source: Thomas Shepard, *Autobiography* (c. 1649).

## Bibliography

Axtell, James. *The European and the Indian: Essays in the Ethnohistory of Colonial North America (1982).*

Eccles, W. J. *France in America* (1990).

Gallay, Alan, ed. *The Colonial Wars of North America, 1512–1763: An Encyclopedia* (1996).

Hall, David, ed. *The Antinomianism Controversy, 1636–1638* (1968).

Jaenen, Cornelius J. *The French Relationship with the Native Peoples of New France* (1984).

Jennings, Francis. *The Invasion of America: Indians, Colonialism and the Cant of Conquest* (1975).

Kupperman, Karen Ordahl. *Settling with the Indians: The Meeting of English and Indian Cultures in America, 1580–1640* (1980).

Langdon, George D. *Pilgrim Colony: A History of New Plymouth, 1620–1691* (1966).

Laplante, Eve. *American Jezebel: The Uncommon Life of Anne Hutchinson, the Woman Who Defied the Puritans* (2004).

Merwick, Donna. *Possessing Albany, 1630–1710: The Dutch and English Experience* (1990).

Merwick, Donna. *The Shame and the Sorrow: Dutch-Amerindian Encounters in New Netherland* (2006).

Miller, Perry. *Errand into the Wilderness* (1975).

Morgan, Edmund S. *The Puritan Dilemma: The Story of John Winthrop* (1998).

Morgan, Edmund S. *Roger Williams: The Church and the State* (1967).

Oberg, Michael Leroy. *Uncas: First of the Mohegans* (2003).

Otto, Paul. *The Dutch-Munsee Encounter in America: the Struggle for Sovereignty in the Hudson Valley* (2006).

Rink, Oliver. *Holland on the Hudson: An Economic and Social History of Dutch New York* (1986).

Rutman, Darrett B. *Winthrop's Boston: A Portrait of a Puritan Town* (1965).

Salisbury, Neal. *Manitou and Providence: Indians, Europeans, and the Making of New England, 1500–1643* (1982).

Stoever, William K. B. *A Faire and Easie Way to Heaven: Covenant Theology and Antinomianism in Early Massachusetts* (1978).

Trudel, Marcel. *The Beginnings of New France, 1524–1663* (1973).

Vaughan, Alden T. *The New England Frontier, 1620–1675* (1995).

# 5

# Africans and the African Slave Trade

## INTRODUCTION

The international trade in African slaves was a momentous historic phenomena. It formed the linchpin around which the western European powers built empires in the New World. The slave trade provided mass amounts of labor to produce valuable agricultural products that Europeans sold throughout the world, further promoting the interconnectedness of the continents and globalization. The merchants who conducted the slave trade accumulated fantastic profits that, along with the earnings from New World crops produced by these slaves, heralded the rise of capitalism and stimulated the Industrial Revolution. The slave trade also "Africanized" the Americas—as Africans comprised the great bulk of emigrants to the New World in the 16th through 18th century.

Colonial New World societies can truly be said to be the product of African, American Indian, and European cultures. Enslaved Africans had profound impact upon the Americas not only through their labor, but culturally as well. Their influence ranged widely and deeply, from music to religion, and from agriculture to architecture. But as we measure the impact of African peoples on the Americas, we must not forget the impact of that forced migration and enslavement on the people themselves. For Africans, the transformation meant being wrested from their homes and transported through a deadly "Middle Passage," the survivors facing a life of hard labor.

This complex story has gained renewed scholarly attention. New studies of Africa and the slave trade have brought the colonial world and its peoples into sharper focus. We now have a much better picture of where slaves came from in Africa, in what numbers, and when. We also know where they went and who took them there. Scholars have documented how Africans were procured in Africa and sold to Europeans, the range of goods that facilitated transactions, and the role of Africans as both sellers and victims of enslavement. These areas of inquiry help clarify many issues surrounding African life in the New World: Who were these people? What did they bring with them to America? What impact did their lives in Africa have upon their subsequent lives in America?

## SLAVERY IN HISTORICAL PERSPECTIVE

Human enslavement was common in the early modern world. The concept that all humans should enjoy freedom, particularly the freedom to control their own labor, is a relatively modern construct of the late 17th and early 18th centuries, which did not gain wide currency until the 19th century. Slavery varied as an institution from one place to the next, but generally, in the early modern period, people kept as slaves those they considered as "others," people alien from their own society and culture. Some were enslaved for their labor, but people also were enslaved for use in religious ceremonies or human sacrifice. Sometimes people were captured and enslaved until they could be redeemed in exchange for captives taken from one's own group, or people were kidnapped for ransom, which if not paid resulted in enslavement. Captives taken in war could be enslaved or assimilated to replace lost members; in some societies, the presence of slaves as degraded humans reminded the free of the value of kinship and belonging. Slavery thus took many forms. All involved the denial of liberty, but treatment of slaves, slaves' rights, and the lives of slaves varied considerably from one society to the next, and even within societies.

### Slavery in Europe and North Africa

The European history of slavery is well documented. Greece and Rome both practiced slavery, and the institution, though it declined in the Middle Ages, survived into the early modern period through serfdom. Serfdom, which tied peasants to the land, had largely replaced slavery and was itself in great decline on the eve of New World colonization, though it remained a major form of labor in parts of Eastern Europe, particularly

Poland and Russia. Slavery had mostly disappeared from northern Europe, but the same was not true in the south. Spain, Portugal and Italy all kept Africans enslaved. For centuries, they had purchased slaves from Arab traders in northern Africa, who procured them from sub-Saharan Africa, from where they had been transported by horsemen and camel caravans. Not all, not even most, were shipped to Europe. Many remained in North Africa or were transported and sold to Southwest Asia.

Contemporary to the onset of the Atlantic slave trade was another slave trade that operated in the Mediterranean Sea that traveled north to south. Arabs from the Barbary Coast, particularly from Tunis, Algiers, and Tripoli, enslaved over 1 million Europeans from the 1530s to the 1780s. (Tens of thousands of additional Europeans, mostly from Eastern Europe, were enslaved in the Ottoman Empire in Europe and Asia.) The enslavement of Europeans in North Africa peaked in the 16th and 17th centuries, during which time it victimized more people than the African slave trade to the Americas. The majority of the victims came from southern Europe, but even English from northern Europe were captured, so that there were more English enslaved in Africa in 1650 than Africans enslaved in English colonies at that time.

The Europeans were captured on ships and through land raids. Over 90% of those taken were male. Owned by either rulers or private individuals, many spent their lives at hard labor on building projects or as rowers aboard galleys (until the use of galleys declined after 1700). A small number were permitted to operate businesses and turned over a share of the profits to their masters. Female slaves usually labored as domestics or became concubines.

One of the main differences between European enslavement in Africa and African enslavement in the Americas was that European slaves could be ransomed to obtain their freedom. Societies formed to redeem Christian slaves, and often governments became involved. Most, however, were not ransomed. Another difference: slaves enjoyed more rights under Islamic law than in Christian countries. They also worked a greater variety of jobs. Still, the differences may be less important than the similarities. Most slaves lived shortened lives laboring under dehumanizing conditions.

## The Desire for Slaves in New World Colonies

By no means was expansion of the African slave trade pre-ordained. In the 16th century, Spanish and Portuguese enslaved American Indians in large numbers, and in subsequent centuries they continued to rely heavily on Indians through a variety of labor arrangements. But the Iberians increasingly turned to African labor. The reasons were demographic, social, and economic. In the island of the West Indies, the native peoples had been utterly ravaged by myriad European-borne illnesses. But also, a reform movement inspired by Bartolomé des Las Casas led to the end of Spain's "official" enslavement of American Indians in 1549. Las Casas only opposed enslavement of American Indians, not Africans, an exclusion he regretted at the end of his life. Perhaps Spanish exclusion of Africans resulted from their centuries of keeping Africans enslaved in Spain, thus considering it natural for Africans to be slaves. The enslavement of Indians was relatively new for them. Many Spanish believed they had a special charge to convert America's heathen—a God-given opportunity to spread God's church—and by so doing Spain would receive God's blessing. Nevertheless, as discussed in the previous chapter, many Spanish colonials kept Indians as slaves in practice, if not in law. Still, there were not enough to satisfy planters' demands for slaves, particularly for the sugar plantations.

There was another source of labor available: European. Although the Spanish did not seriously consider the use of large numbers of European laborers in their American colonies, the English, French, Dutch, and Portuguese did (though the Portuguese shipped most of their Portuguese laborers to Asia). The Europeans employed huge numbers of indentured servants in their colonial economies, whereby people from their own countries or other European countries contracted to labor for a period of years, in exchange for passage to the New World. Prisoners, too, were shipped in large numbers from Europe, particularly by the English. But ultimately the preferred choice was African slaves.

The shift to African labor would not have occurred without the development of plantation agriculture. The Spanish and Portuguese, and later, when the Dutch, English, French, and Danes developed plantation colonies, all came to believe that Africans were better agriculture laborers than American Indians. This was the crux of the issue: in Brazil, Barbados, Jamaica, the Leeward Islands, and the other sugar-producing areas of the Americas, the demand for labor to cultivate and manufacture this most profitable of crops became insatiable. Just as the Canary Islands off the coast of Africa became the jumping-off point for Portuguese exploration and expansion in West Africa in the 15th century, it also provided the model for plantation agriculture in the Americas. Canary planters cultivated sugar with African slaves, setting the precedent for New World planters.

The simple fact was that Africans were available to enslave. Already familiar with the African slave trade through Arab middlemen, and then through Portuguese trade in Kongo and Angola, Europeans knew that the west coast of Africa could supply large numbers of slaves. But why there rather than elsewhere in the world? The West African coast was close to Europe and the New World, and many in West Africa were already kept as slaves and thus ready for purchase.

Additionally, the Portuguese, in particular, promoted wars and raids by Africans against Africans to obtain slaves, magnifying processes that already existed in West Africa, where slaves were kept as a major form of property. Africans accumulated wealth by raiding neighboring peoples and enslaving them. As in the Ottoman Empire, rulers owned slaves who served as soldiers, laborers, and administrators; some of these became powerful themselves in service to their ruler. But individual Africans also gained wealth through organizing raids on neighboring peoples. Land in Africa was owned by groups, not by individuals (except rulers). Slaves thus provided an alternate source of property and income for individuals. They worked producing goods or laboring on the land. The surplus slaves became the easily exchanged commodities of the African slave trade.

## WEST AFRICA AND THE SLAVE TRADE

Africans in the Atlantic slave trade almost entirely hailed from West Africa in three cultural zones, typically described as Upper Guinea, Lower Guinea, and Angola. Within these zones were numerous sub-cultures and over 50 different language groups. Despite language differences, cultural affinity arose from similarities in geography and ways of life. Diversity was more apparent in the Angola zone because of the political distinctions between kingdoms such as Kongo and Ndongo. Very little is known about how many people lived in West Africa before the onset of the Atlantic slave trade and during its formative centuries, but population was both rural and urban, with population densities low enough that there was little voluntary migration to seek new lands.

Kongo was almost the size of England, but most West African political units were small by comparison to those in Europe. A few of the larger political units were the size of Portugal and the German principalities, but many were no bigger than 500 to 1,500 square kilometers—or the size of a modern large American city. Disputes between states were rarely over land, as each owned enough to support their population. Instead, hostilities arose to obtain slaves and plunder. Rulers used slaving to increase their wealth, and sometimes to build power at home against local competitors.

## Slave Trading: A Local Affair

The vast majority of Africans victimized in the slave trade lived within 150 miles of the Atlantic coast along the middle two-thirds of West Africa—from Senegambia to Kongo. But the trade's dependence on local conditions led to even more concentration. For instance, despite Senegambia's proximity to Europe, which led to lower transportation costs, it was not a major supplier of slaves; that region's relative lack of interest in European goods retarded the trade in slaves. European preferences also directed trade from one area to the next. Planters in America preferred slaves from specific regions. Rice planters in South Carolina desired slaves from the rice-producing areas of Africa; many planters would not purchase Gambians because they believed that these heavily meat-eating peoples would cost more to maintain than slaves from other areas. Thus, even though slaves could be purchased along an extensive coast, four out of five slaves shipped to the Americas came from the west central part of Africa that extended from the "Slave Coast" to the Kongo.

Europeans did not prefer these areas because they enjoyed special influence. To the contrary, the Africans of the central coast prevented Europeans from controlling the trade there as elsewhere. Unlike in the Americas, Europeans, except in the Kongo, did not extend their military power into the continent. Thus, a small kingdom like Ouidah could play a pre-eminent role in the African slave trade. Ouidah had fewer than 200,000 people and a land area no more than 25 miles across. Ouidah offered low prices, slaves deemed acceptable to planters, and a large supply. Often French, Dutch, English, and Portuguese ships awaited in Ouidah's port for new supplies of slaves—and at times, Ouidah supplied 40% to 50% of those being sold along the entire West African coast. But at no time was Ouidah threatened with European conquest. Ouidah ably kept the Europeans at bay, making them compete with one another. When Ouidah eventually lost its independence in 1727, it was not to a European nation, but to Dahomey, an African country.

## African Strength in the Slave Trade

Modern confusion about Africans' active participation in the slave trade stems from the expectation that Africans should have felt kinship with one another based on racial identity and that they were intimidated and bamboozled into selling their own people. But Africans generally did not sell their own people—they sold "others"—aliens and enemies. A racial identity has to be constructed. In the 1500s, Europeans were just in the early stages of constructing a "white" identity. For Europeans, it was far more important whether they were French or Spanish; Protestant or Catholic; nobility or gentry; Christian or Muslim.

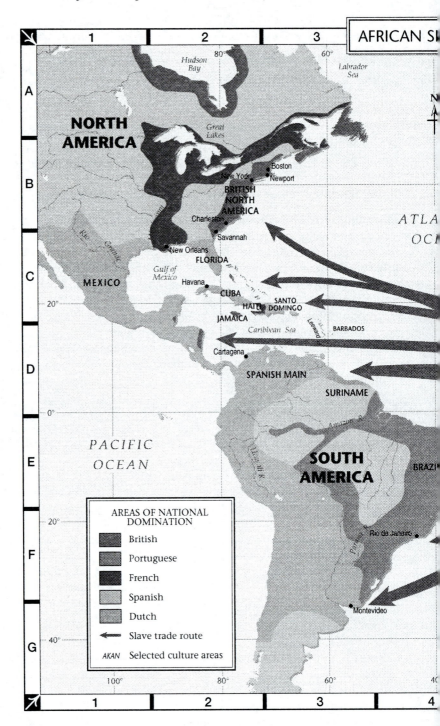

**Map 5.1 African Slave Trade, 1500–1870**

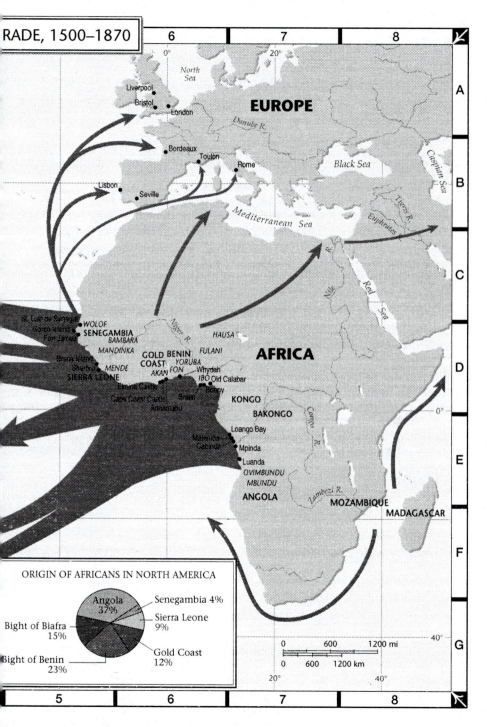

RADE, 1500–1870

EUROPE

Liverpool
Bristol
London
Bordeaux
Toulon
Rome
Lisbon
Seville

North Sea
Danube R.
Black Sea
Caspian Sea
Mediterranean Sea
Tigris R.
Euphrates

AFRICA

St. Luis de Sanaga
Goree Island
Fort James
SENEGAMBIA
WOLOF
BAMBARA
MANDINKA
Bunce Island
Sherbro
SIERRA LEONE
MENDE
GOLD
COAST
BENIN
AKAN
FON
Elmina Castle
Cape Coast Castle
Annamabu
Bance
HAUSA
FULANI
YORUBA
Whydah
IBO
Old Calabar
Bonny

Niger R.
Nile R.
Red Sea

KONGO
BAKONGO
Loango Bay
Malembo
Cabinda
Mpinda
Luanda
OVIMBUNDU
MBUNDU
ANGOLA

Congo R.
Zambezi R.

MOZAMBIQUE
MADAGASCAR

ORIGIN OF AFRICANS IN NORTH AMERICA

Angola 37%
Senegambia 4%
Sierra Leone 9%
Bight of Biafra 15%
Gold Coast 12%
Bight of Benin 23%

0    600    1200 mi
0    600    1200 km

American Indians and Africans likewise had numerous and overlapping identities—but being African or Indians was not one of them. These identities were constructed only when Africans and indigenous Americans faced vastly different outsiders who treated them not by their own identities, but by new ones they constructed and sought to impose. Africans had no concept they were African until Europeans ignored their identities and lumped them together by skin color. The same can be said of American Indians. Moreover, Europeans did not think of themselves as whites until they had categorized Africans, American Indians, and Asian peoples into non-white categories.

African participation in the slave trade as slavers arose from a position of strength. Europeans, except in a few instances, had little military or political power in West Africa and conducted trade only at the leisure of local African rulers who ensured competition between Europeans. Although Europeans participated in African wars as advisors and mercenaries, introducing new tactics and weaponry, their role was not decisive. Portuguese intervention in the wars of Angola provides the greatest example of Europeans engaging in African wars, and even there their presence was relatively unimportant. European artillery had little impact in Africa. The same was true of muskets, whose slow rate of fire offset the advantages of their range. Likewise, European forts on the Atlantic coast were of minimal value for offensive operations and, as Europeans themselves noted, not much use for anything other than storage of goods and slaves. Forts could only be maintained by the goodwill of local rulers. Until well into the 18th century, the European entry into the slave trade had limited impact on the course of African warfare.

African rulers set the terms of trade within their kingdoms. They established whether or not a group of Europeans could trade, the rate of customs taxes, and the conditions for trade. African leaders also determined which goods could or could not be exported—particularly slaves. Benin, for instance, prohibited the sale of male slaves, and ultimately of all slaves in the 16th century, preferring to keep their slaves working in their own domestic economy, and Europeans could do nothing about it. Kongo periodically barred all commerce with Europeans. Overall, the trade between Africans and Europeans was competitive, with no single group able to exercise dominance.

## West African Trade with Europe

Trade revolved around the exchange of goods. Earlier generations of historians assumed that Europeans *made* Africans dependent on their "superior" trade goods, inducing the sale of Africans from unwilling partners. Dependency was central to the African–European relationship in the 19th century, but did not occur through most of the earlier history of the Atlantic slave trade. The African economy was neither primitive nor unable to meet African needs as was previously assumed. Productive land, rulers' ability to effectively administer trade, and military power all contributed to economic independence, if not self-sufficiency in West Africa. Moreover, Europe shipped no essential commodities to Africa—nothing that Africans could become dependent on in the early modern period—which could give Europeans a leg up in the slave trade.

Africans produced their own iron and steel. In fact, African steel was likely the world's best before the 19th century. Yet Africans did import iron to supplement domestic demand for tools. This paralleled most African imports—supplements to items already produced: cloth, tools, jewelry, mostly luxury items. In other words, Africans imported cloth not because they were desperate to clothe themselves—contrasting the view of Africans as naked before Europeans arrived—but for reasons of fashion and prestige. Imported cloth accounted for only about 2% of the total cloth in West Africa. As in Europe, where foreign items, including African cloth, denoted status on its owner, the same was true of European cloth in Africa. Africans did not need European textiles. African textile workers were highly skilled and their work avidly sought throughout Europe. One 16th-century observer thought that cloth made in the Kongo was more beautiful and better worked than any in Italy, which produced much of the best textiles in Europe. African bedcovers were so prized that an Englishman tried to arrange for investors the purchase of over 1 million bed mats from Sierra Leone. With a flourishing textile and food economy, West Africans did not need to import European goods.

Textiles were the major item exported from Europe to Africa, though in some parts of West Africa they had little significance. Guns, gunpowder, and alcohol were hardly traded in the early centuries of the slave trade. Much more prevalent were metal goods—iron tools and cookery, mostly of brass and pewter, pots, pans, and basins. Also significant were cowries (shells used as money, mostly on the Slave Coast) and items for personal and household decoration. Africans exchanged for these the aforementioned textiles, as well as gold and ivory, and various worked metal pieces, such as spoons.

The trade between Europe and Africa exhibited neither dependency nor overwhelming power on either side. Europeans unable to procure desired commodities went elsewhere along the West African coast. African leaders traded with Europeans if they chose to, prevented monopolization by Europeans, and set the terms of trade. The scope of trade grew by leaps and bounds as Africans supplied a commodity, slaves, in great demand by Europeans. Africans parted with slaves to attain manufactured goods and prestige items. European threats to close-off either imports or exports, however, had little effect on African societies. Africans sold Africans not because they needed to, but because they had surplus that gained them exotic luxury items. Likewise, Europeans purchased Africans, not to produce necessities, but luxury goods, most notably sugar, which accounted for upwards of 90% of the slave trade. Never have so many suffered over so many centuries for such meager ends.

## CONTOURS OF THE AFRICAN SLAVE TRADE

The transportation of Africans to the New World was the largest forced trans-oceanic migration in human history. This mass diaspora had incredible human and historical consequences. For the Europeans, it meant a huge supply of labor that permitted them to build colonies and empires and to profitably exploit natural resources, particularly through agricultural production. It also led Europeans to dehumanize Africans as lesser humans, as peoples worthy of brutal treatment, initiating racist ideologies whose legacy continues to the present day.

For the victims of the slave trade, the horrors of the Middle Passage—the deadly transport to America—were followed by lives of hard labor, malnourishment, violent discipline, and high mortality rates. The survivors reconstituted their lives in the Americas under the most trying circumstances. They carried with them their identities and cultures, maintained their humanity, and adapted as best they could.

Each individual faced the slave trade in a personal manner, though all shared the experience of removal, transport, and enslavement in the Americas. The historian cannot re-create each person's experience—what they felt emotionally and physically, how they understood their lives and those who oppressed them, and certainly the hopes and fears they possessed. But we can address in general terms the contours of the slave trade from Africa to the Americas: how many were transported; where they were shipped and who carried them; what life was like on the slave ships.

## The Middle Passage: Resistance, Mortality, and Migration to America

Each slave resisted their enslavement and transportation to America as best they could but revolt was difficult. Slaves in Africa were shackled, imprisoned, and closely guarded as they awaited the ships' arrival, and then confined on board. Nevertheless, there were nearly 400 recorded cases of slaves revolting on ships during the course of the African slave trade from the 16th century to 1870. Most occurred at the port of debarkation in Africa or just after sailing. Regions that had the greatest likelihood of revolt also tended to be those avoided by the Europeans. Senegambia, Sierra Leone, and the Windward Coast accounted for less than 10% of the slave ships but more than 40% of the revolts.

Once on board the ships, Africans faced horrendous conditions. Overcrowding could devastate the people when diseases were present. Intestinal tract illnesses were the most common ailment and weakened Africans so that they more easily succumbed to epidemic diseases. The survivors then spread the diseases to New World ports. British and Dutch ships tended to be the most crowded, and of these, British ships operating out of the mainland colonies were often the most crowded of all, carrying two to three times as many slaves per tonnage than French ships. Slave mortality in the Middle Passage was roughly 20% before 1700, a number that declined to between 9% and 16% for the remainder of the history of the slave trade. Although the reasons for this decline are unclear, the most likely explanation is European cognizance of supplying enough food during the long Middle Passage, a concern expressed in many primary sources. The more slaves that could be delivered to markets, the greater the profits. The slave ships thus were overcrowded even as the traders tried to provide enough food, often failing, creating unhealthy conditions.

Contrary to popular belief, the ships did not carry a diversity of Africans. Slave ships usually made one stop in Africa, rarely two, to purchase human cargo. On board a ship, most or all of the slaves were of a single ethnic group, spoke the same language, and many personally knew others on board. Sales in America dispersed slaves to different estates, but it was likely that many found others speaking their languages in America, especially as most slaves lived on large estates. Moreover, different colonies tended to attract ships from particular areas of Africa. Thus, in the late 17th and early 18th centuries, almost four out of five slaves arriving in Virginia came from the Bight of Biafra or Senegambia, while over three out of four going to Antigua came from the Bight of Biafra or the Gold Coast.

## Females in the Slave Trade

Initially, slave owners preferred to purchase male slaves, but at the sources of supply many Africans preferred to sell females. European gender conventions placed men in agricultural labor and females in domestic labor. Nevertheless, some European female servants were put to work in the tobacco fields in Virginia and Maryland, where planters desperate for labor overlooked their gendered ideas of what was proper employment for females. Prejudice against employing African women in agriculture declined as they proved to be good workers. Moreover, as the status of Africans declined in the European colonies, and slaves became considered as property analogous to livestock, qualms against using African females in plantation production, in all but the heaviest labor, disappeared.

The status of African women should be contextualized alongside of the status and position of European women. Relatively few of the latter migrated to America, and those who did usually traveled connected to a family unit. With European women in short supply, most were heavily pursued for marriage and traditional household labor. But significant numbers of females emigrated from the northern European countries as servants. Despite their low social status, many may have been able to avoid field work because they remained in high demand as domestics and potential marriage partners. Nevertheless, European female servants also worked in the fields, and it was not uncommon for them to establish intimate relations with African males, including marriage. But when the status of European servants was elevated in the early 18th century (to be discussed in the next chapter), a trend developed to remove European females servants from the fields and place them in domestic labor.

Early buyers of imported African slaves were unconcerned with the reproductive capacity of their female slaves—masters were driven by short-term profits, not long-term gains to be made by ownership of slave progeny. In fact, most slaves in the New World were treated so brutally and the environmental conditions of hard labor so harsh, that the slave population would have declined without constant imports of more Africans. Despite planters' general preference for males, and Africans' general preference to sell females, compromises were made between buyers and sellers, so that many females entered the slave trade. Before 1800, females generally comprised from 37% to 41% of the imported slaves. This was a much higher ratio than European female migration to the Americas, which was closer to 10% in most areas. (New England and the Middle Colonies were an exception to this imbalance because many European families migrated there.) The imbalanced sex ratio, and the great power European masters held over their slaves, led to much inter-racial sexual activity with the result of many births: it was not unusual for masters to keep their own children as slaves. This trend persisted through the history of slavery in the Americas.

## The Slave Trade to the Americas

An estimated 9.3 million Africans were transported to the Americas before 1870. Almost 37% went to Brazil, 17% to Spanish America, 40% to the French, Dutch, British, and Danish Caribbean, 3.6% to British North America, and 2% to Europe. In the 16th century, Spanish America was the main destination, but was overtaken by Brazil in the 17th century. The British colonies took as many slaves as Brazil in the last quarter of the 17th century, receiving over one-third of the total, but Brazil again dominated imports until the end of the 18th century, when the British and French sugar islands sometimes passed Brazil in yearly imports. Only a relatively small number of Africans were exported to the English mainland colonies, with the peak period extending from the 1740s to the 1760s, when over 100,000 arrived, though this number was far surpassed during the first decade of the 19th century as a result of the cotton boom in the new United States.

Up until the mid-17th century, the Portuguese were the pre-eminent shippers of slaves to the Americas, largely supplying the colonies of other nations. Well over 1.5 million Africans were transported before 1700, with the English and Dutch steadily playing a more important role. The British became the premier traders in the 18th century, with the Portuguese, French, and Dutch right behind them. More than 75% of the slaves carried by the British went to British colonies, mostly to the West Indies. Before 1650, when the Portuguese dominated the slave trade, the majority of slaves went to Spanish colonies, though the single largest recipient was likely Portuguese Brazil. After 1650, the English sugar islands gained precedence, particularly Barbados and Jamaica, which together received over three-quarters of the total. One historian recently calculated that of the nearly 400,000 slaves transported to English colonies from Africa in the period 1662–1713, only 23,711 went to Virginia and Maryland. Even the tiny Leeward Islands more than doubled the imports of Virginia and Maryland in the early 18th century. This was owing to the high profitability of the sugar crop, beside which all other crops paled in importance. Without sugar plantations in the West Indies and Brazil, the magnitude of the slave trade would have been reduced by 75% or more, at least before 1800, and it might not have developed any significance at all. Without the sugar colonies fueled by African slave labor, other colonies' economy would not have developed so quickly. The economy of the New England colonies and South Carolina, for instance, depended on the sugar colonies, as to a lesser extent did the Middle Colonies of Pennsylvania and New York. The mainland English colonies provided the islands with foodstuffs and livestock, lumber, and other wood products such as shingles, barrels, firewood, and ships. The New England colonies received from the islands the necessary raw material for their very important rum industry. Their economy also benefited through development of a shipping industry that carried goods to and from the West Indies, including slaves from Africa. Even South Carolina, a colony whose economy revolved around slavery, was largely dependent on the sugar islands. A significant portion of Carolina's chief crop, rice, went to the West Indies to feed slaves.

Another way to consider the impact of the slave trade is in the total number of migrants arriving in the Americas: three out of four in the first half of the 18th century were Africans, including roughly 80% of the females. Africans comprised nine out of ten migrants to the sugar islands. By the first decade of the 18th century, one out of three arrivals in the English southern mainland colonies were Africans, a percentage that increased through the 18th century.

## The Slave Trade to the Mainland English Colonies

In the English mainland colonies, slavery had relatively little significance when compared to South America and the Caribbean in the 17th century. In the two Chesapeake colonies, Virginia and Maryland, where slavery had the greatest economic impact on the mainland before 1700, less than 10% of the population was African or of African descent. The slave trade became more important to the English mainland colonies in the 18th century. In the Chesapeake colonies, the slave population quickly rose to 25% by 1710 and close to 40% on the eve of the American Revolution. On the other hand, the percentage of slaves in New York remained nearly constant in the colonial period between 10% and 12%. Slaves could be employed in any number of jobs—not just on plantations—as craftsmen, domestics, and semi-skilled and unskilled labor. The key factor was availability and whether people had the money to purchase them.

One area of the colonial world where African slavery consistently had minimal impact was New England. That region's African slave population generally hovered between 2% and 3%. Most worked as domestics or laborers for prosperous farmers or merchants, often as a status symbol for their owners. The Puritans had few religious qualms about slavery, and actively engaged in the sale of American Indians, and as slave traders who carried Africans to other colonies. Puritans residing in other colonies were as happy to own slaves as their neighbors, but in New England the economy was much less supportive for owning slaves than elsewhere.

Despite the relatively small numbers of slaves imported by the English mainland colonies, the African population grew tremendously. These colonies had better living conditions for slaves and free people alike: fewer endemic diseases, better diet, and working conditions than in the West Indies and Brazil. Moreover, the greater profits of sugar led many callous planters to work their slaves to death and purchase new slaves, whereas Virginia and Maryland tobacco planters had a more difficult time affording and obtaining replacement laborers. The mainland colonies' African population grew by leaps and bounds in the 18th century from natural increase and new imports. The African slave population stood at about 30,000 in 1700, but by 1750 it had jumped to almost a quarter million, a number that nearly doubled 20 years later.

## WEST AFRICANS AND THEIR CULTURES IN DIASPORA

It used to be thought that because so many African Americans had lost their African languages and converted to Christianity, and had been subject to lives where they lived as little more than automatons, the cultural transmission from African to American was minimal. Yet the discarding of culture is not so easy, and studies have shown that the enslaved not only maintained many aspects of their cultures, but transmitted these to the Europeans and Indians in just so many ways. Slavery was dehumanizing, but the slaves carved out lives for themselves within the institution. They formed bonds of love, family, and community. They celebrated birth and death, sustained their spirituality, and maintained their material existence by adapting their own personal preferences to new circumstances.

### West Africans and Identity

Kinship relations were very important in African societies, providing the sinew that tied people together. Kinship provided a sense of belonging and often was connected to place. But kinship was also adaptable, and in the New World Africans and African Americans built new kinships, eventually overcoming the ethnic differences between them.

On the surface, ethnicity would seem an easy thing to identify, but in fact is quite difficult—ethnic identity is nothing more than what people construe to be a group identity. Language can tie people together, but not necessarily. Moreover, ethnic communities are rarely stable—as they are composed of various groups that come together, break apart, and so on. For instance, the English are not, as is commonly said, Anglo-Saxons, the product of two ethnicities forged into one. They are, however, a mix of Celtic, Roman, Danish, French, Norwegian, and Germanic peoples, among others, who themselves were mixes of various peoples. Ethnic identities form as people define themselves as to what they are not: an outsider group.

Despite being treated as "Africans"—an identity not their own, but simply a statement of which continent they came from—the peoples of Africa maintained and transformed their identities. Moreover, to say that people from Africa did not identify as Africans is not to say that people from regions within Africa did not share cultural traits: they did, as people living near one another in any geographical area tend to develop similarities of lifestyle, religion, social organization, and aesthetics. These shared beliefs and ways of life could allow cooperation to take place, if other sources of hostility could be overcome.

In the history of the slave trade, ethnic divisiveness among Africans was initially difficult to overcome. In potential and actual revolts aboard slave-trading ships and on New World plantations and in urban areas, ethnic division often, though not always, undermined the common status and interests Africans shared as slaves. Likewise, maroon communities—the enclaves of runaway slaves that existed in many New World areas—often were segregated by ethnic identity. These identities diminished over time as new identities were forged, much as the European immigrants to the United States in time replaced their Old World identities with new ones. These transformations depended on various factors and did not occur overnight. How strong was the ethnic enclave where one lived? What was the nature of exposure to new cultures? What advantages lay in retaining or discarding aspects of one's culture and adapting aspects of another?

## Cultural Transference to the New World

The process of cultural adaptation occurred for all the migrants to the New World, as it did for the native peoples. Cultures evolve, as they adapt from their neighbors. Cultural adaptation can be material, such as the use of new tools, the construction of new housing, and the wearing of different clothing, or they can involve the incorporation of new social practices, ideas, and languages.

Although languages ordinarily alter slowly over time, they changed rapidly for Africans who migrated to the New World where they were replaced either by creoles—mixtures of different languages—or by the adopted and adapted European language in the colony they resided. Creolization began in Africa where Africans of different languages living in close proximity to one another adopted lingua francas by which they could conduct basic communication. In the New World, creolization continued as Africans of different languages resided together on plantations. Creole languages, rather than European languages, flourished in the mainland colonies where the most heavy percentage of Africans resided, like South Carolina and Louisiana. Over time, these languages incorporated many elements of European languages so that communication between master and slave could take place.

African material culture survived in America in a variety of forms. Food items such as yams and rice crossed the Atlantic, European tools were converted by slaves into their African equivalents such as hoes and machetes, and instruments, particularly the banjo and drums, also made the crossing. European cloth was modified by Africans to suit their taste, and straw and grass baskets repeated workmanship and styles used in Africa.

Aesthetics easily transferred from Africa to the New World. Aesthetics involves a range of ideas and traditions denoting what a cultural group considers desirable, appropriate, and beautiful. These range broadly in styles and colors of decoration of material objects and are also expressed through music and dance, as well as the many ways people choose to fashion and represent the human body, through piercing and tattooing, and in hair styles and clothing. It is through aesthetic values in music, dance, and visual arts that Africans had some of their greatest influence on New World European cultures. It is only in recent years, however, that scholars have begun to document the materialistic influences, such as in agriculture, architecture, and food production. For example, scholars in recent years have disclosed the ways African planting and harvesting practices became common in many areas of the New World and that African housing styles and construction techniques became widely practiced in the American South while African cooking greatly influenced the creation of the region's distinctive cuisine.

## Africans and Religion

Africans also carried their religious beliefs to the New World, and though many eventually converted to Christianity, they maintained some of their African religious sensibilities, which ultimately influenced the Europeans' religious practices. As in Christianity, West African religions centered upon revelations. Unlike Christians, who believed that the age of revelation ended with the completion of the Bible, Africans perceived revelations as ongoing. The spirits of the dead, often associated with a particular place, were believed to have impact on the material world. These spirits could be appeased or offended, as well as directly communicated with and influenced by the living. Revelations came through dreams or divination, and spirits communicated through objects, people, and animals. Those with the gift of communicating with the spirit world could become priests. Three or four kinds of spirits have been identified: those tied to a particular place, lesser good and bad spirits, and a deified first human. In many areas of West Africa, secret societies were devoted to the worship of particular deities. Many Africans who converted to Christianity in Africa or the Americas did not give up their belief in present revelation and some of the secret societies transferred to the New World. Islam was also carried to America by Africans, but the number of followers is unknown. Nevertheless, there are numerous documentary references to slaves practicing Islam.

The process of African conversion to Christianity began in Africa, mostly in the Portuguese colonies. After arrival in America, the Catholic powers continued to devote much more effort to missionary activities than the Protestants. Two basic reasons exist for this discrepancy. The Catholics considered their church a universal church that should include all of humanity. Protestants, particularly the Dutch and English Calvinists, practiced a more exclusive religion. They believed God only chose a select few to enjoy salvation, and Africans and American Indians were not likely to be included. Moreover, the English and Dutch both thought that they might not legally be able to keep Christians as slaves, which led masters to block conversion of their bondpeople. Even when laws specified otherwise, masters continued to fear slaves suing for freedom on the basis of being Christians. In the Protestant countries, Africans had much less legal standing than they did in Catholic countries. For instance, Protestants (outside of a few places like Boston) refused to legally sanction slave marriages, slaves were denied all property rights, and under the law slaves were considered strictly as property. By contrast, in Catholic countries slaves' basic humanity was recognized and they enjoyed legal standing, though not on a par with Europeans. Not until the 1730s would Protestants avidly undertake conversion of their slaves, when new views of Africans formed. But conversion would face intense hostility from many masters until the end of the 18th century, when opposition began to decline, though it never was fully eradicated. Once Africans began to convert in large numbers to Christianity in the mainland British colonies (see chapter eleven), they greatly influenced Christian prayer styles, music, burial practices, and even concepts of the afterlife.

## Conclusion

Africans were not the only source of unfree labor in the Americas. American Indians continued to be exploited as slaves (see chapters eight and ten) and large numbers of Europeans labored as indentured servants and in other forms of bound labor (see chapter six). Africans provided the overwhelming bulk of labor in the West Indies and Brazil, while in the 17th-century English mainland colonies unfree Europeans comprised the major component of the labor force. Not until the second quarter of the 18th century did African slave labor form the economic foundation of the American South, where it remained so for over a century. African slavery was crucial to the English mainland's development in other ways as well—much of the export trade focused on meeting the needs of the West Indian plantations, and both New England and Middle Colonies merchants avidly engaged in the international slave trade (see chapter eleven).

Plantation agriculture along with mining was the engine that drove the economy of colonies and empires in the Atlantic world. At the heart of the plantation complex was the transport of millions of Africans to work on the plantations as slaves. Most came from West Africa, where slaves were the major form of property and surplus existed. Traded to the Europeans for textiles, metal goods, and other European manufactures,

as well as tropical products produced in the Americas, the victims were transported mostly to the sugar plantations of Brazil and the West Indies, though the desire for unfree labor drew them to all ports throughout the Atlantic world, to city and countryside in the Americas and Europe. Those who survived the brutal middle passage usually faced high mortality rates particularly in the West Indies and Brazil. In the mainland English colonies, the Africans fared much better partly owing to better environmental conditions and partly owing to mainland planters' comparative inability to replace laborers. Mainland colonists had less access to shipments of slaves from Africa and less capital to expend on purchases than sugar planters. Food quality and work conditions were generally healthier on the mainland than in the Indies, but in both, force and the threat of force were the main inducements to labor. Throughout the Atlantic world, few laws existed to protect slaves from brutality (see chapter six), but generally the legal systems of the catholic empires recognized more slave rights than did the Protestant empires, especially in terms of religion and family life.

Despite the inhumanity of their treatment and their debased status, the Africans maintained their humanity. The cultures they carried to the Americas were passed on to subsequent generations. Religious values and beliefs, aesthetics, craftsmanship, and numerous other aspects of culture not only were transferred across the Atlantic but shaped European and American Indian cultures. Cultural retention varied from place to the next. Its more obvious components, such as language, generally lasted longest in places that had overwhelming African populations (many of the islands of the West Indies), and where mostly African populations lived in relative isolation from Europeans and Indians (on the sea islands of South Carolina and Georgia and in some of the plantation areas of Louisiana). With language, many of the cultural influences of Africans on Europeans were subtle but pervasive. For instance, the distinctive southern drawl and the varieties of southern accents were recognized by contemporaries as distinctive from the northern English colonies by the end of the colonial period and owing to the large African population. In short, just as Africans were transformed into African Americans in America by their new lives and their exposure to other Africans and African Americans, and a variety of American Indian and European peoples, the Africans, in turn, influenced the cultures of those peoples and their lives. These influences can still be seen, heard, and experienced in the present day, in music and dance, in the cadences of language, in dress and hair styles, in an array of other visual arts, in celebrations of God, in the mourning of the dead, in storytelling, in cooking, in fishing, and in other forms of human activities: the cultural expressions and sensibilities of Africans remain a vital part of the fabric of American society.

# DOCUMENTS

## 5.1. Journal of the Slave Ship *St. Jan* Begun on March 4, 1659

(Spelling, punctuation, and grammar are modernized.) *This is an account of a Dutch slave ship that left Elmina, a Dutch trading post on the Gold Coast, to purchase slaves on the Slave Coast. It later was grounded at Curaçao off the coast of South America. Among the notable things recorded on its journey were the difficulty in obtaining food to feed the slaves, the over-50% mortality rate aboard ship before it was grounded, and the intervention of privateers who stole most of the surviving slaves. What issues on the voyage concerned the journal writer? Why might he have kept this journal?*

We weighed anchor by order of the Honorable Director, Johan Valkenborch, and the Honorable Director, Jasper van Heussen, to proceed on our voyage to Rio del Rey, to trade for slaves for the honorable company.

March 8. Saturday. Arrived with our ship before Ardra (a settlement on the Slave Coast), to take on board the surgeon's mate and a supply of tamarinds for refreshment for the slaves; sailed again next day on our voyage to Rio del Rey.

March 17. Arrived at Rio del Rey in front of a village called Bonny (near the mouth of the New Calabar River), where we found the company's yacht, named the *Vrede* (Peace), which was sent out to assist us to trade for slaves.

*(Continued)*

In April. Nothing was done except to trade for slaves.

May 6. One of our seamen died; his name was Claes van Diemen, of Durgerdam.

May 22. Again weighed anchor and ran out of Rio del Rey accompanied by the yacht *Vrede*; purchased there two hundred and nineteen head of slaves, men, women, boys, and girls, and set our course for the high land of Ambosius (north of the Kamerun River), for the purpose of procuring food there for the slaves, as nothing was to be had at Rio del Rey.

May 26. Monday. Arrived under the high land of Ambosius to look there for victuals for the slaves, and spent seven days there, but barely obtained enough for the daily consumption of the slaves, so that we resolved to run to Rio Kamerun to see if any food could be had there for the slaves.

June 5. Thursday. Arrived at the Rio Kamerun and the yacht *Vrede* went up to look for provisions for the slaves. This day died our cooper, named Pieter Claessen, of Amsterdam.

June 29. Sunday. Again resolved to proceed on our voyage, as there also but little food was to be had for the slaves in consequence of the great rains which fell every day, and because many of the slaves were suffering from the bloody flux (dysentery) in consequence of the bad provisions we were supplied at El Mina, amongst which were many barrels of groats (hulled or crushed grain), wholly unfit for use.

We then turned over to Adriaen Blaes, the skipper, one hundred and ninety five slaves, consisting of eighty one men, one hundred and five women, six boys, and three girls, for which bills of lading were signed and sent, one (copy) by the yacht *Vrede* to El Mina with an account of, and receipts for, remaining merchandise.

July 25. Arrived at Cape Lopez de Gonçalvez for water and wood.

July 27. Our surgeon, named Martyn de Lanoy, died of the bloody flux.

August 10. Arrived the company's ship, named *Swartem Arent* (Black Eagle), from Castle St. George d'el Mina, bound for Patria.

August 11. Again resolved to pursue our voyage towards the island of Annobon (in the Gulf of Guinea, off the central West African coast), in order to purchase there some refreshments for the slaves. We have lain sixteen days at Cape Lopez hauling water and wood. Among the water barrels, more than forty had fallen to pieces and were unfit to be used, as our cooper died at Rio Kamerun, and we had no other person capable of repairing them.

August 15. Arrived at the island Annobon, where we purchased for the slaves one hundred half tierces (casks) of beans, twelve hogs, five thousand cocoanuts, five thousand sweet oranges, besides some other stores.

August 17. Again hoisted sail to prosecute our voyage to the island of Curaçao.

September 21. The skipper called the ship's officers aft, and resolved to run for island of Tobago (off the Venezuelan coast) and to procure water there; otherwise we should have perished for want of water, as many of our water casks had leaked dry.

September 24. Friday. Arrived at the island of Tobago and hauled water there, also purchased some bread, as our hands had no ration for three weeks.

September 27. Again set sail on our voyage to the island of Curaçao, as before.

November 1. Lost our ship on the reef of Los Roques (off the north coast of Venezuela), and all hands immediately took to the boat, as there was no prospect of saving the slaves, for we must abandon the ship in consequence of the heavy surf.

November 4. Arrived with the boat at the island of Curaçao; the Honorable Governor Beck ordered two sloops to take the slaves off the wreck. One of the sloops, with eighty four slaves on board, was captured by a (an English) privateer.

Source: Elizabeth Donnan, ed., *Documents Illustrative of the History of the Slave Trade to America.* 4 vols. (1930–1935), 1: 141–144.

## 5.2. Customs at Whydah (1767)

(Spelling, grammar, and punctuation are modernized.) *These are instructions given to a captain on the payment of customs at Whydah. Note that the captain must buy the first group of slaves that he pays as customs, a slave's value noted as follows. He also receives a group of slaves to temporarily work as servants—they were paid for their work according to standards provided by the king. Why was so much detail provided to the captain? What do these instructions tell us about the operation of the slave trade?*

Eight slaves for permission of trade, gong gong beaters and brokers. These slaves paid to the Carborkees (village headmen). The slaves are each valued as 6 anchors (each worth 10 gallons) of brandy; or 20 cabesses of cowries (shell money, each cabess worth 4,000 shells); or 40 sililees (a unit of trade cloth); or 25 guns; or 10 long cloths; or 10 blue basts (coarse cotton from India); or 10 patten chintz (thick soled shoes made of painted or stained cloth from India); or 40 iron bars. Then the captain receives two small children of 7 or 8 years old, which the King sends as a return for the Customs.

The Carborkees then supply slaves to work in the fort. 1 for water and washer woman, 2 for the Factory house, and 7 for the canoe.

After the Customs are paid, which should be done as soon as possible, for the traders dare not trade till the King's Customs are paid, the Vice Roy gives you the following nine servants: one conductor to take care of the goods that comes and goes to and from the waterside . . . he's obliged to answer for things delivered to him. He's paid 2 gallinas (400) of cowries every time he conducts anything whether coming or going and one flask of brandy every Sunday.

Two brokers which are obliged to go to the traders' houses to look for slaves and stand Interpreter for the purchase. They are paid each two tokays (80) of cowries per day and one flask of brandy every Sunday and at the end of your trade you give to each of them one Anchor of brandy and one piece of cloth.

Two boys to serve in the house. They are each paid two tokays per day. At the end of your trade they receive one piece of cloth.

*(Continued)*

One boy to serve at the tent water side 2 tokays per day and one piece of cloth at the end of your trade.

One doorkeeper paid 2 tokays per day, and one piece of cloth at the end of your trade.

One waterman for the factory, 2 tokays per day. At the end of trade one piece of cloth.

One washerwoman, 2 tokays per day and six tokays every time you give her any linen to wash and one piece of cloth at the end of trade.

Note well: the last two servants are sometimes one, if so, you only pay one.

To the canoe men for bringing the captain on shore, one anchor of brandy, and to each man a hat and a fathom of cloth. To the boatswain, a hat, &frac12; piece of cloth, one cabess of cowries, a flask of brandy every Sunday, and a bottle every time they cross the bar with goods or slaves, and every time they carry a white man. At the end of trade one anchor of brandy and four cabesses of cowries for carrying the captain to his ship.

Note well. The above bottles, flasks, etc., was usually given to the canoe men, but now the captain gives them one anchor of brandy and one cabess of cowries every Sunday for the week's work. To the gong gong beater for announcing trade, 10 gallinas (2,000) of cowries and one flask of brandy.

To the King's messenger for carrying news of the ship's arrival and the captain's compliments to the King, 10 gallinas.

To the trunk keeper a bottle of brandy every Sunday and a piece of cloth when you go away if you are satisfied with his service.

To the Captain of the waterside on your arrival one anchor of brandy and at your departure one piece of cloth and one anchor of brandy.

To the six waterrowlers (men who hoist cargo on and off the ship), two tokays per day each and two bottles of brandy, besides which you pay them 2, 3, 4 tokays of cowries for each cask according to the size, and at the end of trade two pieces of cloth and one anchor of brandy.

To the Vice Roy who goes with his people to compliment the captain at his arrival and conduct him to the fort, one anchor of brandy and two flasks, but if Coke (?) be there, four flasks of brandy.

To the Vice Roy for his own Custom, one 15 yard piece of silk, 1 cask of flour, one cask of beef, but if you are short of these you may give him something else in lieu of them.

To making the Ten (?), one anchor of Brandy and 2 cabesses of cowries.

To the captain gong gong that looks after the house at night, one bottle per day and one piece of cloth, if you are content.

You pay 3 tokays of cowries for every load carried, such as one anchor of brandy, 20 sililees, 10 pieces of cloth, and so in proportion for small goods, but when loads are very heavy you pay more, such as 10 gallinas for a chest of pipes, etc.

Source: Elizabeth Donnan, ed., *Documents Illustrative of the History of the Slave Trade to America.* 4 vols. (1930–1935), 2: 531–532.

## 5.3. The Voyage of the *Little George*, 1730

*The following article appeared in the Boston* News-Letter *May 6, 1731. It recounts a successful revolt off the coast of Sierra Leone on a slave ship of Rhode Island. How did the slaves manage to escape?*

Since our last we have had a more particular Account of the Negroes rising and overcoming Capt. George Scott of Rhode Island, in his return from Guinea, which we have been desired to Insert: And it is as follows, *viz.*

I George Scott, (the Scriber) Master of the Sloop the *Little George*, belonging to Rhode Island; Sailed from the Bonnana Islands on the Coast of Guinea, the first of June 1730, having on Board Ninety six Slaves (thirty five of which were Men.) On the 6th of said Month at half an hour past four of the Clock in the Morning, being about 100 Leagues distant from the Land, the men Slaves got off their Irons, and making way thro' the bulkhead of the Deck, killed the Watch consisting of John Harris Doctor, Jonathan Ebens Cooper, and Thomas Ham Sailor; who were, thought, all asleep. I being then in my Cabin and hearing a Noise upon Deck (they throwing the Watch overboard) took my Pistol directly, and fired up the Scuttle which was abaft, which made all the Slaves that were loose run forwards except one or two Men (who seemed to laugh at the Cowardice of the rest, and defiance of us, being but 4 Men and a Boy) who laid the Scuttle, and kept us down confin'd in the Cabin, and passing by the Companion to view us, we shot two Men Slaves.

On so sudden a surprise, we were at a loss what to do, but consulting together, filled two round Bottles with Powder, putting fuses to them, in order to send them among the Slaves, with a Design at the same instant of Time, to issue out upon them, and either suppress them or lose our Lives; but just as we were putting our design in Execution, one of the Slaves let fall an Ax (either thro' accident or design) which broke the Bottle as Thomas Dickinson was setting fire to the Fuze, and taking fire with a Cagg of Powder, in the Cabin, rais'd up the Deck, blew open the Cabin Doors and Windows, discharged all our fire Arms but one, destroyed our Cloaths and burnt the Man that had the Bottle in his hand in a most miserable manner, and my self with the rest very much hurt thereby.

Upon this unhappy accident, we expected no less than immediate Death, which would have been unavoidable, had they at that Juncture of time, rushed in upon us. And being in this consternation and hopeless, sent up the Boy in order (if possible) to bring them to Terms, but they slighted our Message. And soon after (the Smoke clearing out of the Cabin) we found the other Bottle of Powder which by Providence had not taken fire, and which put new Life and vigour into us, that we were resolved to withstand them to the uttermost; and accordingly Loaded our Arms and Shot several of the Slaves, which occasioned all the Men Slaves to betake themselves to the Quarter Deck, over our Heads. The Slaves then got two Swivel Guns, and filled them almost full with Powder, which they found in the fore Hold, as

*(Continued)*

they were looking for Provisions, and designed to blow the Bulkhead in upon us, which they put fire to several times, but could not get off by reason of wet Weather. We had two Carriage Guns in the Boat, which we expected the Slaves would get out, and therefore watched them very narrowly; but in a dark Night they effected it, and brought them upon the Quarter Deck; they loaded one of the Guns, and pointed it directly down the Scuttle: we hearing them about the Scuttle and having prepar'd ourselves; so soon as they lifted it up, we Shot the Man dead that pointed the Gun, another of the Slaves standing by clapt a Match to it and fir'd it off, which blew the Scuttle all to pieces and some of the Deck, but did us no Damage. They then took pieces of Boards and laid them over the Scuttle and the Hole they had made in the Deck, and laid the Tarpawlin, with a great Weight upon them to prevent our coming up.

Then they made Sail (as they thought) towards Land and were continually heaving down Billets of Wood, and Water into the Cabin, with intention to Disable us and spoil our small Arms. And the Fourth Day after the Rising made the same Land we departed from, then stood off and on again for 4 or 5 Days more, in which time the Boy being forced by Hunger, run up among the Slaves, who immediately put him in Irons. They made several attempts to come down into the Cabin, but their Courage fail'd them. I then call'd to them to come down to decide the Matter, they answer'd by and by.

Finding our selves grow very weak, thro' these hardships, and for want of sustenance; we thought it proper before our Strength was quite spent to take some desperate Course. I proposed to cut away the Ceiling and bore some Holes thro' the Vessels Bottom, which being approved on, was directly done, and let in about three feet of Water, I then called to the Slaves, and told them, I would drown them all, which frightened them exceedingly: They then sent the Boy to the Cabin Door, to tell us, that they had but just made the Land, and that when they got a little nearer the Shore, they would take the Boat and leave them with the Young Slaves: I told them if they would do that I would not sink her. (My design in letting the Water in, was to force the Vessel on her side that we might get some advantage.) They stood in for the Land about 12 a Clock at Night, struck upon the Bar of Serrilone River, and were in great Danger of being lost. The Vessel being strong, beat over the Bar and they run Ashore about 3 Leagues up the River, on the North Side; being then High Water, and at Seven a Clock the next Morning there was not above a foot of Water along side.

The Natives waded from the Shore with fire Arms, wou'd have fain try'd to overcome us, but were persuaded from it by the Slaves on Board, who told them we should shoot them if they appeared in our Sight. They persuaded the grown Slaves to go Ashore, and drove the Young ones over board and then followed them, making the Vessel shake at their Departure. Our Boy assuring us the Slaves had all left the Vessel, we immediately went up with our Arms, and saw the Slaves just Ashore. We found our great Guns loaded quite full. And as we hoisted our Boat, the Natives mustered very thick on the Shore and fired at us divers time. We made what haste we could to the other side of the River, where we Rowed down about two Leagues, and found a Sloop riding in French-man's Bay belonging to Montserat, James Collingwood Commander, where we refreshed our selves, being all of us in a weak and miserable condition having, had nothing to subsist upon, during the Nine Days we were under this Affliction but Raw Rice.

Source: Elizabeth Donnan, ed., *Documents Illustrative of the History of the Slave Trade to America.* 4 vols. (1930–1935), 3: 118–120.

## Bibliography

Blackburn, Robin. *The Making of New World Slavery: From the Baroque to the Modern, 1492–1800* (1998).

Colley, Linda. *Captives: The Story of Britain's Pursuit of Empire and How Its Soldiers and Civilians Were Held Captive by the Dream of Global Supremacy, 1600–1850* (2002).

Curtin, Philip D. *The African Slave Trade: A Census* (1969).

Davies, K. G. *The Royal African Company* (1957).

Davis, Robert C. *Christian Slaves, Muslim Masters: White Slavery in the Mediterranean, the Barbary Coast, and Italy, 1500–1800* (2003).

Donnan, Elizabeth. *Documents Illustrative of the History of the Slave Trade to America.* 4 vols. (1930–1935).

Eltis, David. *The Rise of African Slavery in the Americas* (1999).

Klein, Herbert S. *The Atlantic Slave Trade* (1999).

Klein, Herbert S. *The Middle Passage: Comparative Studies in the Atlantic Slave Trade* (1978).

Law, Robin. *The Slave Coast of West Africa, 1550–1750: The Impact of the Atlantic Slave Trade on an African Society* (1991).

Lovejoy, Paul E. *Transformations in Slavery: A History of Slavery in Africa* (1983).

Manning, Patrick. *Slavery and African Life: Occidental, Oriental, and American Slave Trades* (1990).

Morgan, Jennifer L. *Laboring Women: Reproduction and Gender in New World Slavery* (2004).

Northrup, David. *Africa's Discovery of Europe, 1450–1850* (2002).

Rawley, James A. *The Transatlantic Slave Trade: A History.* Rev. ed. (2005).

Rediker, Marcus. *The Slave Ship: A Human History* (2007).

Smallwood, Stephanie E. *Saltwater Slavery: A Middle Passage from Africa to American Diaspora* (2007).

Thornton, John. *Africa and Africans in the Making of the Atlantic World, 1400–1800* (1998).

# 6

# Bound Labor in Early America

European Bound Labor
  Indentured Servitude
  Treatment of Indentured Servants
  Convicts and Redemptioners
Bound Labor in the Chesapeake Colonies
  Maryland
  The Development of Slavery in the Chesapeake
English and Africans
  English Views of Africans
  African Slaves and Indentured Servants
  Bacon's Rebellion
Slavery and the Law: Creating a Racialized Society
  Upholding the Color Line: Sex and Punishment
  Upholding the Color Line: The Slave Codes

## INTRODUCTION

The control and use of bound labor had a long history in Europe. Serfdom, the most prevalent form of labor control for hundreds of years during the Middle Ages, had bound people to work for a lord. Serfs possessed legal rights, and the lord had legal obligations to those bound to him. Serfdom had all but disappeared in western Europe by the 17th century, replaced in large part by tenant farming. Tenants possessed more mobility and independence than serfs, as they could contract to work for a different landowner after their tenancy agreement expired. With the disappearance of serfdom, forms of servitude did not end but were increasingly the fate of the young. Parents commonly bound their children, male and female, to work for others, whether on the land, in domestic service, or as apprentices. Though bound to labor, the servants possessed legal protections and the masters had legal obligations, such as to clothe and feed their charges and to educate them into the "arts and mysteries" of their master's profession. Both tenancy and servitude were carried to America and commonly practiced in all the colonies. Indentured servants often became farmers after their period of service expired. People became tenants in areas where there no longer was free land available, as in large portions of southern New England, or they did not possess the wherewithal to develop land, lacking capital to purchase tools, seed, and obtain subsistence until they could construct a self-supporting enterprise. Some colonials, particularly in New York, who possessed large tracts of land, paid individuals' passage to America if they would work for them as tenants. Both servants and tenants were not considered independent people, since they did not own their own land and were dependent on either a master or a landlord. Dependency precluded them from voting and proscribed to them a second-class status in society.

The largest pool of tenant and servant laborers could be found in the Chesapeake colonies. Most engaged in tobacco production or in producing food crops to support the tobacco plantations. Tobacco's success as a cash crop attracted the poor and ambitious from England in hopes of eventually becoming independent tobacco producers. Africans, too, arrived in the Chesapeake as servants to cultivate tobacco. Most, if not all, of the Africans arrived as slaves, though some achieved freedom in a fashion similar to indentured servants. Through most of the 17th century, European servants far outnumbered African servants in the mainland colonies, but a variety of forces were converging to effect a transformation by which few Africans became free, and more and more were imported, so that African slavery became the primary form of labor in the 18th century.

The transformation did not occur overnight. Racial views were not hard and fast in early Virginia and Maryland, and no ideology of racism designated enslavement of Africans to become the dominant form of unfree labor. In fact, there were numerous instances of free Africans receiving equal treatment in Virginia's courts, and much evidence exists of intimacy and cooperation among bound Africans and English that evince positive relations between these diverse peoples. To create a society based on the debasement and enslavement of Africans, laws and institutions had to be established to elevate poor English above Africans and to confine the latter to the lowest caste. The framework put in place not only persisted through the centuries of slavery but even after emancipation, as slavery was not the only way to bind labor. Eliminating the caste system was all the more difficult given the racist ideology that developed by the 18th century towards people of African descent.

## EUROPEAN BOUND LABOR

Despite the importance of slavery in European colonies, other sources of labor existed, and in some places predominated, particularly in England's North American colonies, most notably indentured servitude and convict labor. England was the main nation using indentured servants, though France and the Netherlands employed them in small numbers. Indentured servitude allowed free colonists to fill their labor needs, while presenting the mother country the opportunity to rid itself of unemployable young people. Those who chose to become servants hoped that when their indenture ended they would have opportunities to improve their lot in life. Some convicts were also given the choice of exchanging time in prison for servitude in America. They, too, received their freedom upon completion of their labor terms in America.

## Indentured Servitude

Indentured servants were recruited in Europe by entrepreneurs. In exchange for passage to America, maintenance, and "freedom dues," they worked for a specified term. Freedom dues were especially helpful for the released servants, as they provided a stake for them to get started as independent freemen. In some colonies, servants received headrights of 50 acres of land upon completion of their terms. But merchant shippers also claimed the headrights for shipping the servants. Servants did qualify for land under various laws in Maryland and Virginia in the 17th century, but this right steadily eroded and then disappeared before the onset of the 18th century. Afterwards servants received money and supplies when they became free, but no land. Headrights were meant for people who paid their own way to America, or brought people to America, not for the poor.

In the 17th century, the market for indentured servants was usually strongest in those English colonies where slavery predominated—in the West Indies and the Chesapeake. European indentured servants worked in the fields alongside slaves as laborers and in managerial positions directing labor. In the 18th century, more skilled artisans signed up as servants. Some emigrated to colonies with fewer slaves, such as Pennsylvania and New York, but many skilled workers chose the Caribbean islands—perhaps because they would receive higher wages after their servitude. (Skilled servants sometimes received wages during their period of indenture, but rarely did unskilled servants.) Length of service in the islands might also have played a role in choice of destination. Terms averaged nine months shorter in the Indies as an inducement for servants to go there.

The servant population was overwhelmingly youthful and male. Women comprised one in four indentured servants from 1650 to 1700, but that number declined to one in ten afterwards. Females were more likely to go to the Chesapeake colonies and Pennsylvania, and very few went to the West Indies. Two out of three indentured servants emigrated at the age of 15 to 25. It was very rare for servants to be younger than 10 or older than 40. Males age 25 to 40 tended to go to the islands—perhaps seeking different opportunities than the young heading to the mainland in hopes of eventually owning land. Those servants who arrived in the colonies without a contract, and many did, had their length of service regulated by law. In Maryland, for instance, those age 21 and over served five years, while those younger served longer.

Age thus played a critical factor in length of service. Those under 16 remained indentured until age 21, and thus tended to serve the longest terms. Those age 16 to 20 could also serve as many as six to eight years. Adult terms on the other hand usually lasted three to five years, with four the most common length, and with adjustments made for skill level and choice of destination. Carpenters and masons, in great demand, generally labored for masters nine months less than farmers, domestics, and workers in the textile trades, who in turn served fewer months than unskilled laborers.

## Treatment of Indentured Servants

One of the most notable aspects of the early system of indentured servitude was the extent of abuse heaped upon servants. The colonies lacked laws as existed in England to protect servants. In England, servitude was viewed as a form of apprenticeship. In exchange for learning the master's profession and receiving room, board, a small stipend, and moral instruction, a young person provided labor and obedience. In the colonies, however, rather than preparing servants for a life of economic independence and self-sufficiency, masters, particularly in the 17th century, often worked their servants brutally with little or no concern for their well-being. Many servants died before their terms expired.

The search for profits drove colonial masters. For many, their goal was to get rich and return to England, as is evident from the crude housing they continued to reside in even after they had accumulated great estates. Moreover, many thought that crossing the Atlantic gave them license for all sorts of behavior that would have been condemned and punished at home. Disregard of English and proprietary laws, rampant trade with pirates, brutal treatment of servants, trade with enemies during wartime, and attacks on allies in peace time were common components of colonial life. The New World lacked the institutions of civil society that regulated behavior—at least outside of New England—and the elite would create those institutions of church and state only when it was to their benefit to do so. Not until they became committed to their new homes and developed a sense of community did free colonists elect to support institutions that would stabilize society (and their place within it), while also providing protection for some of its least privileged members.

## Convicts and Redemptioners

Approximately 50,000 convicts were sent to the mainland colonies by the British government in the last 60 years of the colonial period. These comprised three out of four migrants from the British Isles in the 18th century. Less than a quarter were Irish and most of the rest were English. Scots had been sent in small numbers in the 17th century, but fewer than a thousand were sent in the 18th century. In the 17th century, convicts mostly migrated voluntarily as an alternative to prison, but in 1718 Parliament enacted a law forcing them to go. Both male and female convicts were transported, but as with indentured servants, most were men. Transported convicts who had committed capital offenses were pardoned from their death penalty and could return to Britain after 14 years. Felons who had not committed a capital crime could return after seven years. Many of the repeat felons sent to America may not have committed "serious" crimes in modern terms. These had participated in small-scale theft of food, household items, or small amounts of money. But certainly many were dangerous and some Americans resented their colonies being a dumping ground for criminals.

In many ways, the convict population was similar to the indentured servants: single men in their early twenties. As servants, they were governed by the same laws and regulations, served in the same occupations, and became free after their servitude. On the other hand, convicts had no choice in where they would serve and were chained and driven in lots like cattle to the marketplace. They were more likely to run away than indentured servants.

Another type of European servant in the English colonies comprised redemptioners. These were mostly Germans who traveled to America without paying their way, beginning in the 1720s. Upon arrival whoever paid for their passage controlled their labor for a period of years. Sometimes friends or families in the colonies paid, so they would not have to become servants. Many of the Germans went to Pennsylvania and later to Georgia, both of which developed sizable German populations.

## BOUND LABOR IN THE CHESAPEAKE COLONIES

Masters in the mainland plantation colonies initially preferred indentured servants over slaves. This began to change in the second half of the 17th century. A declining death rate in the Chesapeake colonies, the main importers of labor in the mainland English empire, meant that slaves became a better bargain because they could be worked harder and for a longer period of time. Some planters also considered the long-term profits from investing in slaves, who would increase their masters' wealth through reproduction. Availability also played a role in the transition from European to African labor. Towards the end of the 17th century, slave traders began bringing their human cargos to the mainland English colonies directly from Africa. Chesapeake planters no longer had to depend on an unreliable supply from the West Indies. Moreover, with the establishment of new colonies in the late 17th century, especially New York (conquered from the Dutch in 1664), South Carolina (1670), and Pennsylvania (1681), indentured servants had more colonies to choose as a destination. The influx of indentured servants remained high in the Chesapeake colonies, but the plantation system was expanding, so that in proportion to African imports, unfree European labor declined. Estimates of the total indentured servitude population in the 17th century range from 50% to 75% of all Europeans arriving in the English colonies after the 1630s, and in some places as high as 80%. Even in the mainland colonies where slavery was strongest, except for South Carolina, indentured servant migrants usually outnumbered African migrants before the mid-18th century, but because indentured servants ultimately attained freedom, slaves outnumbered European servants in the plantation colonies.

### Maryland

Maryland was founded across Chesapeake Bay from Virginia in 1637 as a refuge for English Catholics. The colony was owned by the Calvert family. They intended to establish large manors but could attract few tenants. Most early immigrants were either gentry or indentured servants, and the colony quickly followed Virginia's example and produced tobacco. Protestant settlers outnumbered Catholics, and to protect his co-religionists, Lord Baltimore enacted an Act of Toleration (1649) to prevent persecution of Catholics by Protestants.

Most labor in 17th-century Maryland was performed by indentured servants. Freemen who emigrated to the colony almost invariably became planters—leaving few free laborers available. If they did not have capital to begin a plantation, the freemen became tenant farmers producing tobacco. Land was fairly inexpensive to rent and the large landowners were happy to gain the rents or a share of their tenants' crops. Unlike sugar, tobacco can be worked by a single farmer and does not require a large labor force. As with Virginia, Maryland became a "tobacco colony."

Most slaves who arrived in Maryland, as in Virginia, came through the West Indies, and not Africa in the 17th century. Their purchase price was 2 to 2.5 times that of indentured servants. Slaves generally cost less coming from the West Indies than from Africa because planters rarely sold prime field hands and instead shipped older adult males with fewer years left to labor. Life years were relatively short for all in Maryland, though longer than in Virginia. Typhoid, dysentery, and an array of "agues" and fevers periodically struck Chesapeake colonies. An adult arriving in Maryland in his or her early twenties could expect to live about 20 more years.

The small planters rarely owned slaves. Over two-thirds of Maryland's slaves worked for only 6% of the planters from 1656 to 1720. Thus, slaves tended to live on very large estates, while indentured servants resided on smaller ones. Roughly 9% of Maryland's population was slave in 1680, a larger share than in Virginia, though Virginia had more total slaves. Virginia's slave population would increase at a faster rate as much more land was put into tobacco production. Its slave population reached 28% of the total in 1700, and 46% by 1750. Maryland's slave population also increased rapidly, but not as great in proportion to indentured servants and other Europeans. Nonetheless, slaves comprised 31% of the total in 1750.

## The Development of Slavery in the Chesapeake

The institution of slavery emerged in the Chesapeake colonies of Virginia and Maryland in a haphazard way. Planters concerned themselves with obtaining cheap labor—unfree labor—in any form. Unlike in Europe, where there was a surplus of labor and a limited amount of productive land, the reverse was true in the New World. Controlling scarce labor was the key to wealth. The main sources available were Indians, Europeans, and Africans.

Slavery was an option from first colonization. Englishmen were well aware of the institution through the enslavement of their own people in North Africa and their familiarity with Spanish enslavement of Indians in the Americas. Englishman Sir John Hawkins had famously supplied the Spanish with African slaves during Queen Elizabeth's reign. John Smith, the first leader of the Jamestown colonists, had been a slave in the Ottoman Empire. Once in Virginia, the English enslaved local Indians, many of whom they sold to the West Indies colonies. The Virginians only sporadically enslaved Indians from the 1620s to the 1670s, as the government mended relations with most of its native neighbors to entice them to defend the colony against hostile Indians. The colony remained reliant on European workers. With only a scattering of Indian and African slaves in Virginia in the first half of the 17th century, the institution had very loose roots. Steady supply of inexpensive indentured servants led this form of labor to predominate over slavery in the 17th century. Few ships arrived in the Chesapeake from Africa with slaves, as the tobacco planters could not pay as much for them as the West Indian sugar planters.

English Virginians understood slavery only in vague terms. They had neither laws nor customs to govern the institution. Slavery operated in an ad hoc way. Masters' power over their slaves was legally undefined—the first slaves were treated like indentured servants with little concern for their welfare. Some Africans remained slaves for life, and some did not. In the early years, no official determination was made regarding the status of slaves' children, perhaps because few slaves had children in Virginia's early years. The English simply purchased people who arrived in Virginia as slaves or captured native people and enslaved them—they did not consider what slavery meant beyond the immediacy of having slaves whose labor they could control.

## ENGLISH AND AFRICANS

Historians used to wonder: which came first for the English in Virginia, slavery or racism against Africans. In other words, did Englishmen enslave Africans because they were prejudiced against them, or did the enslavement of Africans lead to prejudice. We know that before colonization some Elizabethans held hostile feelings towards Africans, but were these attitudes strong enough to lead to the debasement of slavery. Queen Elizabeth issued three decrees to expel "Blackmores" from England, which obviously shows her hostility towards Africans. But when she issued a patent to Walter Ralegh to build a colony in the New World, there was no presumption that it should or would be built on African labor. Yet the example was there in the Atlantic World for the English to see. The English knew that the Portuguese and Spanish enslaved Africans and Indians—did this lead the English to consider slavery as a natural condition for both. Probably not. Ralegh was intent on establishing good relations with the Indians, and the labor for his colony would be provided by the colonists. With so many Europeans enslaved in Africa and the Ottoman Empire, it is unlikely that 17th-century Englishmen thought of slavery as a condition peculiar only to Africans and Indians. Yet, in the New World, the English only enslaved Africans and Indians, though they *considered* enslaving Europeans, and certainly many European indentured servants were treated as slaves.

Slavery was an ill-defined institution in the early decades of English colonization, and for over a half-century it was not apparent that African slavery would become the major source of labor. In early Virginia, a significant number of African slaves obtained freedom by making agreements with masters to produce a certain amount of tobacco over a period of time in exchange for freedom upon meeting these terms. Like the European indentured servants, they worked for a number of years and then became freemen. The early laws made no negative distinction against people of African descent, and free Africans were as likely to win civil cases against Europeans as to lose, illustrating a degree of color blindness in the Virginia courts. In the course of the 17th century, however, slavery did become associated with skin color. Enslavement of Africans and English racism towards Africans evolved as a result of both local and global circumstances. Global conditions created an extensive marketplace for Chesapeake tobacco in Europe, Africa, and Asia; global conditions moved tens of thousands of Africans to work on American plantations to produce crops mostly sold in other parts of the world. Yet we cannot attribute all to the large historical forces that led the European empires to employ African slavery on a massive scale in their colonies. Choices were made on a local level. In much of the Spanish empire, Indians rather than Africans were the major exploited labor groups. And in the Chesapeake, European indentured servitude long predominated over African slaves. So how did the transformation to African slavery take place?

## English Views of Africans

Just as slavery was not defined by law in Virginia's early years, there were no hard-and-fast views held by English towards Africans. Negative views of Africans undoubtedly existed throughout Europe, but these were not monolithic. One of the most popular works of literature in the Middle Ages, Wolfram von Eschenbach's *Parsifal*, included marriage between a European and African and did not hint at negative connotations. In 16th-century Central America, Englishman Sir Francis Drake forged an alliance with African slaves who had run away from the Spanish: mutual interests could trump any barriers that might otherwise have divided Europeans and Africans. Despite enslavement of Africans in the Middle Ages and Renaissance in southern

Europe, Spanish, Portuguese, and Italians all received delegations from African courts and made arrangements for educating African elites in Lisbon and Rome. In the 15th and 16th centuries, there even were marriages between African and European nobility. European concepts of race and prejudice towards Africans were amorphous.

European prejudice against Africans' skin color did exist. Although sub-Saharan Africans' skin color is an infinite array of brown hues, Europeans adopted variations of the Spanish word *negro*, signifying their color as black. Europeans associated black with the devil and impurity. (On the other hand, the English did not associate white with European skin color until close to the end of the 17th century.) Despite the lumping together of dark-skinned Africans by a color not their own, and the negative connotations associated with an identity thrust upon them, European development of an *ideology* of racism—an ideology of inferiority based upon skin color—occurred late in the colonial period. Seventeenth-century Europeans did not define "race" in modern terms. In early modern Europe, any group of people could be termed a race, such as the Irish, English, and Germans. Not until the 18th century did race become more generally associated with skin color, and even then the alleged characteristics of a race were limited and usually ill-defined. Today, racial categories have been dismissed by geneticists. Genetic differences among humans are so insignificant as to belie racialization. Yet humans continue to construct false categories and assumptions concerning races. The virulent persistence of racial prejudice in the modern world makes it all the more important to study its origins.

Prejudice can be overcome by intimacy and a forging of interests. The fact that some Africans received their freedom in Virginia (and other colonies) shows that racism towards Africans and the forms of slavery were not held hard and fast in early Virginia. Even though most Virginia Africans spent their lives as slaves, there existed all kinds of possibilities in the realm of English and African relations, especially given the intimacy that developed between them.

## African Slaves and Indentured Servants

Even more striking than the prosperity enjoyed by free Africans in Virginia, and near equal treatment by the early Virginia courts, was the extent of positive interaction between African and English laborers in the tobacco fields. Unfree English and African servants drew together from their brutal treatment by masters. They cooperated in ways that bespoke not only an overcoming of prejudice but the possibility for constructing a society where racism was not legitimized by law and custom.

One mode of cooperation between African and English servants was to commit crimes together. Together they stole from their masters, ran away, and eventually rebelled. Engaging in these illicit and dangerous activities makes evident a large degree of trust across the cultural borders that might otherwise have divided them. Almost as notable is that punishments for crimes were distributed fairly equally in early Virginia. English and Africans received similar or the same sentences when committing crimes together: in terms of numbers of lashes, periods of confinement, and remarkably, the extension of terms of servitude—further evidence that in the colony's early years, some Africans were treated as indentured servants.

Another form of intimacy among Africans and English occurred in sexual relations. Together they were found guilty of the crime of fornication (sexual relations between an unmarried man and woman) and marriage between the two was also common. Given the cooperation among African and English servants, and their mutual brutalization by the elite, the most significant dividing line between people in early Virginia was often class—not skin color. Whether one was free or bound to a master had the greater impact on one's life.

## Bacon's Rebellion

The familiarity and intimacy of European servants and Africans were deemed dangerous by the elite as the indentured servants and poor freemen increasingly undertook hostile action against the planters in the mid-17th century. With the improvement of health conditions in Virginia, more servants had gained freedom and expected to receive the fruits of their labor: to become planters. But the land they had contracted for when undertaking their indenture was either denied them or given them in areas too distant from market to be of use. Moreover, the freemen had neither money nor seed to develop their land. Many formed into groups of banditti and raided the plantations for supplies and livestock. Governor William Berkeley complained: "How miserable that man is that Governs a People where six parts in seaven at least are Poore Endebted Discontented and Armed."

The discontent exploded in 1676. Nathaniel Bacon, a recently arrived frontiersman, focused the discontent of the poor English on neighboring native peoples. Hostilities between Indians and English had been simmering for years, but Bacon and his allies had been unable to locate the enemy Indians—so they turned their guns on Indian allies of Virginia, whom they knew were innocent of hostile actions against the colonists. One reason for their military aggression: to capture Indians for enslavement. Bacon and his men then marched on the capitol at Jamestown and at gun point demanded a commission to fight Indians. After receiving the commission and departing, the governor declared them rebels and civil war broke out in Virginia.

The rebels burned Jamestown. Bacon soon died of dysentery. Although the rebels initially had expressed grievances against the government, with Bacon's death the rebellion lost its ideological focus and turned into raid and counter-raid for plunder. Some of the planters, who had long resented the governor's and his cronies' control over government and monopolization of the Indian trade, joined the rebels. By the time troops arrived from England to restore law and order, the rebellion had petered out. One of the last groups to be brought in comprised 80 men, 60 of whom were Africans or of African descent—again showing cooperation among the discontented regardless of skin color.

The King's Commission that investigated the rebellion reported unfavorably on the governor and his elite supporters for monopolizing the plums of office and trade and for maltreatment of the servants and freemen. They made many recommendations, some of which would be enacted, though slowly. They called for disbursement of political power into the House of Burgesses—the colonial assembly—so that more planters would have say in political and economic affairs. They also called for properly fulfilling the terms of indentures. Once servants became freemen, they should receive not only land, but seed, tools, food, and money: enough to cover their first year's expenses so they could establish their own plantations. But if the English government intended to stabilize society by preventing future rebellions of poor English, the Virginia government had very different ideas about the future of Africans.

# SLAVERY AND THE LAW: CREATING A RACIALIZED SOCIETY

Bacon's Rebellion provided a turning point in the treatment of Africans in Virginia. The possibilities for positive interactions between Africans and Europeans greatly diminished. The elite set about ensuring that the poor would not again unite against them, and began to create a society where skin color was the most important dividing line between people.

## Upholding the Color Line: Sex and Punishment

Laws governing people of color and slavery preceded Bacon's Rebellion. In 1643, African women were taxed, unlike European women. These taxes were placed on laborers, both free and servant, with the servants' tax paid by the master. European women probably were not taxed because most were presumed to be engaged in domestic labor, even if they were not, while African women mostly were slaves. In 1662, however, masters were taxed for their European women who worked in the fields, and another law was passed clarifying that all free African women would be taxed. Virginia in 1662 also enacted the single most important slave law ever passed in the colony. It provided perpetual bondage for the children of slave women. This broke with English tradition, where children held their father's status; indeed, they were their father's property. At the end of the decade, Virginia enacted the second most important piece of legislation the colony passed regarding slavery. Masters were protected by law in the event that they killed their slave. Africans were considered a "brutish sort of people," on whom it would be necessary to employ corporal punishment to make them work and behave. We can assume that most masters would not wish to destroy their slave property, but it was understood that brutal measures would be needed to keep bond-people in check and that deaths would occur. This permitted masters to kill recalcitrant slaves to provide an example to others. Later laws strengthened masters' control and provided that maiming was a suitable form of punishment as well.

In the 1660s, Virginia designed several laws to prevent sexual intimacy and other forms of interaction between Europeans and Africans. Europeans engaging in fornication with Africans were subject to double the ordinary fines for fornication. And English servants who ran away with African slaves suffered penalties of additional work time for themselves and for the time that the slaves missed from work. The legislature also made sure that Christian Africans could not claim freedom on the basis of religion.

Temporarily, the legislature in 1670 dealt differently with Native American slaves. It provided that enslavement would not be perpetual, but this was changed after Bacon's Rebellion so that Indians fared similarly to Africans and their descendants. One of the oddities of the biracial society that English Virginians wished to create was the position of Indians. Though the legislature occasionally referred to them as a distinct group, it was not unusual for Indians to be lumped together with Africans, and enslaved Indians were often described in legal documents as negroes in the coming centuries.

After Bacon's Rebellion, the Virginia legislature elevated the status of indentured servants vis-à-vis slaves. Any African who raised his or her hand to a European was subject to 30 lashes—thus giving indentured servants power over slaves, by whose side they still worked. Also, indentured servants could no longer be whipped naked, a demeaning punishment confined to slaves. The legislature took strides to prohibit inter-racial marriage—which occurred with some frequency in the colony. Early efforts to prevent these marriages failed, but punishment for the ministers who performed the marriage helped put them to an end. English women received severe sentences for bearing children out-of-wedlock by African men. Not only were these free and servant women punished, but their children were relegated to servitude until age 30. (Bastard children who were not the product of African–European unions served only until age 24.) This 1691 law was the first to use the term *white*, which now replaced *Christian* to refer to Europeans in the legislative record. It signified a growing racial consciousness in the colony—that skin color rather than religion divided Africans from Europeans.

Inter-racial bastardy cases remained fairly common in Virginia. In several counties for which records have survived, 17% of the cases in the 1690s and 30% in the 1700s involved unions between white women and black men. The few cases brought to magistrates' attention involving white men and black women went unprosecuted, and future laws would not interfere with the many children on plantations born of sexual relations between male masters and female slaves. The courts dealt only with African female sexual relations when the slave had sex with someone other than her master. This was considered a property crime and a master could sue for damages from the offending male. There was no such thing under law as the rape of a black woman.

## Upholding the Color Line: The Slave Codes

All together these laws, and others enacted in the West Indies, were adapted by other mainland English colonies and become known as "slave codes." The codes would grow more specific, defining slave behavior off the plantation. The plantation itself was considered the master's domain, which he could govern largely as he pleased. But some laws were passed restricting masters' power. For instance, masters could not teach their slaves to read. Some colonies (and later states) barred masters from emancipating slaves without removing them from the colony. Laws eventually were passed to protect slaves from murder by their masters, but since no black, slave or free, could testify against a white person, these laws were difficult to enforce.

The codes also proscribed whites' behavior to force their maintenance of the slave institution. Whites had to serve on slave patrols to regulate slave behavior—or pay a fine. The laws were also designed to prevent the growth of a free black population. Since a child inherited the mother's status, the children of white females and black slaves, termed mulattos, would be free. It was feared that mulattos would provide an example to slaves that some people with dark skins could be free. It was also feared that mulattos and free blacks would incite slave insurrections. Though the colonial legislatures were unwilling to enslave free blacks and mulattos, life was made difficult for them through heavy taxes, restrictions on employment, and a variety of legal penalties and disabilities. White society hoped to make free blacks' lives so miserable that they would leave.

The Virginia elite succeeded in creating a biracial society in which skin color became the most important dividing line between people. They enlisted poor whites by elevating their status and diminishing the status of African Americans. These laws led poor whites to believe that they did not share interests with blacks, even though they might live in similar depressed economic circumstances. Instead, they should take pride in their skin color, and know that however bad their lives became, they could not sink below the color line to the status of a slave or free black or mulatto.

## Conclusion

By the last quarter of the 17th century, most patterns of settlement in the English mainland colonies were in place. The vast majority of emigrants were servants, including Europeans, whether indentured, convict, or redemptioner. Slavery was emerging as the central form of labor, with a growing body of laws to regulate the behavior of all. A racial divide emerged that defined society for centuries to come—even after the emancipation of the slaves at the end of the American Civil War.

Bound labor was the most important form of labor in the European colonies throughout the Americas. Unfree Native Americans, Africans, and Europeans provided the bulk of the workforce in the most profitable sectors of the economy: mining and plantation agriculture. In many parts of the Spanish empire, Indians comprised the main source of labor. In the sugar islands of the West Indies and Brazil, Africans predominated. With less access to Africans, and the inability to produce the great profits of sugar production, the North American colonies above Mexico imported relatively few slaves in the 17th century. The Spanish in Florida and New Mexico depended on Indian labor. The English heavily relied on European bound labor, while the Dutch and French more actively engaged in trade with native peoples to produce profits.

All the European colonial societies welcomed African slave labor, but this was the most expensive form to purchase. Few Europeans had any qualms about working Africans hard, nor wrestled with the morality of possessing African slaves. Europeans also made excellent field and mining laborers, but their limited terms of service made them less valuable (though less expensive) than African slave laborers.

Indians were another potential labor source, and, as we will see in subsequent chapters, were heavily used in colonial America, especially as slaves, but there were other problems with supply. By the end of the 17th century, there was a notable shift in bound labor. Greater availability of African slaves contributed to the eventual predominance of slaves over indentured servants in Maryland and Virginia, a pattern to be followed in other plantation colonies, and which prevailed in the American South until the American Civil War. The transformation owed to economic forces: Africans proved to be a better investment than other forms of labor. The consequences, however, affected all aspects of society. With slavery as the foundation of wealth, the plantation-based societies had to transform their legal, social, and political systems to maintain slavery's predominance. The interests of slaveholders were secured by laws that circumscribed both slaves' and non-slaves' behavior, the legal construction of social relations that proscribed Africans and their descendants to the lowest caste, and by creation of polities designed to maintain this social and economic order. This process was not unusual and could be found wherever colonialism and slavery flourished in the Atlantic World.

In retrospect, one of the most remarkable aspects of the creation of new, highly proscribed slave societies that severely restricted human freedom was that it occurred in places where there was a remarkable degree of social mobility and great opportunity for Europeans to escape the rigid social systems of their mother countries. Although some colonists rued the inability of colonies to maintain Old World hierarchies, many welcomed the disorder. French coureur de bois left the

French colonies to pursue economic opportunities and adventures among Indian peoples. Landless English moved to Virginia to own their own land. Puritans sought not only land but to escape religious persecution. As we have seen, those seeking opportunities for themselves, and fewer restrictions on their chosen way of life, did not necessarily think that others should share in these benefits. Just as Puritans wished to practice their religion freely but no one else should, many who hoped for free land did not think that everyone should be granted the same entitlement. Not only did they want to prevent everyone from getting free land, but they wanted those denied the opportunity to work for them, whether as slaves, indentured servants, or tenants. And yet, seeds of long-term change had been planted. Simultaneous to the creation of repressive regimes that employed brute force to maintain security over bound labor in the planter colonies, or religious unity in New England, the legitimacy of hierarchy and limitations upon personal liberty, if not yet broadly questioned, were challenged, and examples bountiful, of other ways of doing things. Living in societies where many owned land meant that few would be poor. The liberties enjoyed by Indians, their mobile lifestyle, their social tolerance while maintaining strong societal bonds, these were condemned by colonists yet steadily assimilated into their cultures. An array of cultural constructs brought from Europe to America would be found wanting by colonists. But the most difficult hierarchical construct for Europeans to overcome was one they largely constructed themselves: a racialized system of slavery that debased Africans. No western European country had such a brutal system of labor control as the colonists created in the Americas. French and English would later affirm (incorrectly however) that slavery did not exist in their countries. In Spain and Portugal, slavery was more prevalent, but nowhere in Europe did it provide the bulk of labor as it did in many American colonies. Dependence on slavery was not the only significant difference between the Old and New World, but for Africans and African Americans the spread of New World slavery had disastrous consequences.

# DOCUMENTS

## 6.1. Virginia Laws of Servitude and Slavery (1643–1691)

*Virginia laws legislating servitude and slavery in the 17th century tended to focus on the interactions of European indentured servants with African slaves, providing punishment for sexual intimacy, such as fornication (sexual relations out of wedlock) and marriage, and the consequences of running away. For the most part, few laws in this period were passed regarding servant and slave behavior on the plantation, for masters were considered sovereign over their domain and could invoke whatever punishments they wished. What can we learn about the life of slaves from the laws enacted to regulate their behavior? What can we deduce from these laws about slaves relations with European servants?*

**March 1643**

Whereas many great abuses and much detriment have been found to arise both against the law of God and likewise to the service of manye masters of families in the collony occasioned through secret marriages of servants, their masters and mistresses being not any ways made privy thereto, as also by committing of fornication, for preventing the like abuses hereafter, Be it enacted and confirmed by this Grand Assembly that what man servant soever hath since January 1640 or hereafter shall secretly marry with any mayd or woman servant without the consent of her master or mistress if she be a widow, he or they so offending shall in the first place serve out his or their tyme or tymes with his or their masters or mistresses, and after shall serve his or their master or mistress one compleat year more for such offence committed, And the mayd or woman servant so marrying without consent as aforesaid shall for such her offence double the tyme of service with her master and mistress, And a ffreeman so offending shall give satisfaction to the master or mistress by doubling the value of the service and pay a ffine of five hundred pounds of tobacco to the parish where such offence shall be omitted. . . .

Whereas there are divers loytering runaways in the collony who very often absent themselves from their masters service, And sometimes in two or three monthes cannot be found, whereby their said masters are at great charge in finding them, And many times even to the loss of their year's labour before they be had, Be it therefore enacted and confirmed that all runaways that shall absent themselves from their said masters service shall be lyable to make satisfaction by service at the end of their tymes by indenture double the tyme of service soe neglected, And in some cases more if the comissioners for the place appointed shall find it requisite and convenient. And if such runaways shall be found to transgresse the second time or oftener (if it shall be duely proved against them) that then they shall be branded in the cheek with the letter R. and passe under the statute of incorrigible rogues.

**March 1658**

Whereas divers ill disposed persons do secretly and covertly trade and truck with other mens' servants and aprentices which tendeth to the great injurie of masters of ffamilies their servants being thereby induced and invited to purloine and imbezill the goods of their said masters, Bee it therefore enacted for redresse of the like disorders and abuses hereafter that what person or persons shall buy, sell, trade or truck with any servant, for any comoditie whatsoever without lycence or consent of the master of any such servant hee or they so offending against the premises shall suffer one monthes imprisonment without bail or mainprize and also shall forfeite and restore to the master of the said servant fower times the value of the things so bought, sold, trucked or traded for.

**March 1661**

Bee it enacted That in case any English servant shall run away in company with any negroes who are incapable of making satisfaction by addition of time, Bee it enacted that the English so

*(Continued)*

running away in company with them shall serve for the time of the said negroes absence as they are to do for their owne by a former act.

## June 1680

WHEREAS the frequent meeting of considerbale numbers of negroe slaves under pretence of feasts and burialls is judged of dangerous consequence; for prevention whereof for the future, Bee it enacted by the kings most excellent majestie by and with the consent of the generall assembly, and it is hereby enacted by the authority foresaid, that from and after the publication of this law, it shall not be lawfull for any negroe or other slave to carry or arme himselfe with any club, staffe, gunn, sword or any other weapon of defence or offence, nor to goe or depart from of his masters ground without a certificate from his master, mistris or overseer and such permission not to be granted but upon particuler and necessary occasions; and every negroe or slave soe offending not haveing a certificate as aforesaid shalbe sent to the next constable, who is hereby enjoyned and required to give the said negroe twenty lashes on his bare back well layd on, and soe sent home to his said master, mistris or overseer. And it is further enacted by the authority aforesaid that if any negroe or other slave shall presume to lift up his hand in opposition against any christian, shall for every such offence, upon due proofe made thereof by the oath of the party before a magistrate, have and receive thirty lashes on his bare back well laid on. And it is hereby further enacted by the authority aforesaid that if any negroe or other slave shall absent himself from his masters

service and lye hid and lurking in obscure places, comitting injuries to the inhabitants, and shall resist any person or persons that shalby any lawfull authority by imployed to apprehend and take the said negroe, that then in case of such resistance, it shalbe lawfull for such person or persons to kill the said negroe or slave soe lying out and resisting, and that this law be once every six months published at the respective county courts and parish churches within this colony.

## April 1691

And for prevention of that abominable mixture and spurious issue which hereafter may encrease in this dominion, as well by negroes, mulattoes, and Indians intermarrying with English, or other white women, as by their unlawfull accompanying with one another, Be it enacted by the authoritie aforesaid, and it is hereby enacted, that for the time to come, whatsoever English or other white man or woman being free shall intermarry with a negroe, mulatto, or Indian man or woman bond or free shall within three months after such marriage be banished and removed from this dominion forever, and that the justices of each respective countie within this dominion make it their perticular care that this act be put in effectuall execution. And be it further enacted by the authoritie aforesaid, and it is hereby enacted, That if any English woman being free shall have a bastard child by any negro or mulatto, she pay the sume of fifteen pounds sterling, within one moneth after such bastard child be born, to the Church wardens of the parish where she shall be delivered of such child, and in default of such payment she shall be taken into the possession of the said Church wardens and disposed of for five yeares, and the said fine of fifteen pounds, or whatever the woman shall be disposed of for, shall be paid, one third part to their majesties for and towards the support of the government and the contingent charges thereof, and one other third part to the use of the parish where the offence is committed, and the other third part to the informer, and that such bastard child be bound out as a servant by the said Church wardens untill he or she shall attaine the age of thirty yeares, and in case such English woman that shall have such bastard child be a servant, she shall be sold by the said church wardens, (after her time is expired that she ought by law to serve her master) for five yeares, and the money she shall be sold for divided as is before appointed, and the child to serve as aforesaid.

And forasmuch as great inconveniences may happen to this country by the setting of negroes and mulattoes free, by their either entertaining negro slaves from their masters service, or receiveing stolen goods, or being grown old bringing a charge upon the country; for prevention thereof, Be it enacted by the authority aforesaid, and it is hereby enacted, That no negro or mulatto be after the end of this present session of assembly set free by any person or persons whatsoever, unless such person or persons, their heires, executors or administrators pay for the transportation of such negro or negroes out of the countrey within six moneths after such setting them free, upon penalty of paying of tenn pounds sterling to the Church wardens of the parish where such person shall dwell with, which money, or so much thereof as shall be necessary, the said Church wardens are to cause the said negro or mulatto to be transported out of the countrey, and the remainder of the said money to imploy to the use of the poor of the parish.

Source: *The Statutes at Large, Being a Collection of All the Laws of Virginia, from the First Session of the Legislature in the Year 1619.* 13 vols. Edited by William Waller Hening (1810–1823), 1: 252–255, 445; 2: 26, 481–482; 3: 87–88.

## 6.2. A British Act of Parliament Forcing the Shipment of Criminals to the Colonies

*By act of Parliament, England promoted the forced migration of criminals to the colonies, where they would work as servants. It not only saved the expense of maintaining prisoners but provided a way for colonists to fill their need for labor. The act also included provision for the sending of children to labor as indentured servants and barred the transportation of pirates, who would be hung for their crimes. What kinds of crimes did Parliament find particularly heinous and hope to prevent through punishment by transport to the colonies?*

An Act for the further Preventing Robbery, Burglary and other Felons, and Unlawful Exporters of Wooll; and for Declaring the Law upon some Points relating to Pirates.

Whereas it is found by Experience, That the Punishments inflicted by the Laws now in Force against the Offences of Robbery, Larceny, and other Felonious Taking

*(Continued)*

and Stealing of Money and Goods, have not proved effectual to deter Wicked and Evil-disposed Persons from being Guilty of the said Crimes:And whereas many Offenders, to whom Royal Mercy hath been Extended upon Condition of Transporting themselves to the West-Indies, have often neglected to perform the said Condition, but returned to their former Wickedness, and been at last for New Crimes brought to a Shameful and Ignominious Death: And whereas in many of his Majesties Colonies and Plantations in America there is great Want of Servants, who by their Labour and Industry might be the Means of Improving and Making the said Colonies and Plantations more Useful to this Nation; Be it Enacted . . . That where any Person or Persons have been Convicted of any Offence within the Benefit of Clergy . . . and are liable to be Whipt, or Burnt in the hands, or have been Delivered to any Workhouse . . . as also where any Person or Persons shall be hereafter Convicted of Grand or Petit Larceny, Felonious Stealing or Taking of Money, or Goods and Chattels, either from the Person, or the house of any other, or in any other manner . . . It shall and may be Lawful for the Court before whom they were Convicted, or any Court held at the same place with the like Authority, if they think fit . . . shall be sent, as soon as conveniently may be, to some of hisMajesties Colonies and Plantations in America, for the space of Seven Years . . . as also of any Person or Persons Convicted of Receiving or Buying Stolen Goods, knowing them to be Stolen, for the term of Fourteen Years . . . [if they] shall Return into any Part of Great Britain or Ireland before the End of his or their said Term . . . [they] shall be liable to be Punished as any Person Attainted of Felony without the Benefit of Clergy; and Execution may and shall be Awarded against such Offender or Offenders accordingly. . . .

And whereas there are many sole Persons, who are under the Age of One and Twenty Years, lurking about in divers Parts of London, and elsewhere, who want Employment, and may be tempted to become Thieves, if not provided for: And whereas they may be inclined to be Transported, and to Enter into Services in some of his Majesties Colonies and Plantations in America: But as they have no power to Contract for themselves . . . [and are at least] of the Age of fifteen years . . . [and] are willing to be transported . . . It shall and may be Lawful for any Merchant or other, to Contract with any such Person for any such Service, not exceeding the Term of Eight Years. . . .

And be it hereby Declared, That all and every Person and Persons who have Committed or shall Commit any Offence or Offences, for which they ought to be Adjudged, Deemed, and Taken to be Pirates, Felons, or Robbers . . . [they] may be Tried and Judged for every Offence . . . and shall and ought to be utterly Debarred and Excluded from the Benefit of Clergy for the said Offenses; Any Law or Statute to the contrary thereof in any wise notwithstanding.

# Bibliography

Breen, T. H., and Stephen Innes. *"Myne Owne Ground:" Race and Freedom on Virginia's Eastern Shore, 1640–1676* (1980).

Brown, Kathleen. *Good Wives, Nasty Wenches, and Anxious Patriarchs: Gender, Race, and Power in Colonial Virginia (1996).*

Carr, Lois Green, Russell R. Menard, and Lorena S. Walsh. *Robert Cole's World: Agriculture and Society in Early Maryland* (1991).

Galenson, David. *White Servitude in Colonial America: An Economic Analysis* (1981).

Hatfield, April Lee. *Atlantic Virginia: Intercolonial Relations in the Seventeenth Century* (2004).

Heywood, Linda M., and John K. Thornton. *Central Africans, Atlantic Creoles, and the Formation of the Americas, 1585–1660* (2007).

Jordan, Winthop D. *White over Black: American Attitudes Toward the Negro, 1550–1812* (1968).

Main, Gloria. *Tobacco Colony: Life in Early Maryland, 1650–1720* (1982).

Morgan, Edmund S. *American Slavery, American Freedom: The Ordeal of Colonial Virginia* (1975).

Morgan, Kenneth. *Slavery and Servitude in Colonial North America: A Short History* (2000).

Morris, Thomas D. *Southern Slavery and the Law, 1619–1860* (1996).

Parent, Anthony. *Foul Means: The Formation of a Slave Society in Virginia, 1660–1740* (2003).

Smith, Abbot Emerson. *Colonists in Bondage: White Servitude and Convict Labor in America, 1607–1776* (1947).

Walsh, Lorena S. *From Calabar to Carter's Grove: The History of a Virginia Slave Community* (1997).

# PART 2

# Evolution and Adaptation of Early American Societies and Peoples, 1670–1730

# 7

# The Evolution of New England, 1670–1730

## INTRODUCTION

Within the Atlantic world each colony's development largely depended upon four basic factors: environment, labor, access to Atlantic world markets, and the cultures of all the inhabitants. The physical environment provided the realm of possibility—food for sustenance, resources for housing and clothing, and items that could be extracted, cultivated, or traded in the region or exported elsewhere. Labor—the skills and physical capacity to develop and process an environment's resources—could make the difference between colonists following a subsistence lifestyle or one where surpluses could be traded in the Atlantic economy. Labor could be accrued in several ways. In New England, for instance, large numbers of subsistence households relied on family labor, perhaps with an additional servant or two. In New England, most families produced modest surpluses, which they exchanged with their neighbors, or sold to merchants, who sent some of the commodities to other regions. Without substantial mineral resources that sold easily in world markets, such as silver or gold, and incapable of producing tropical crops, the New England economy could not afford to import large numbers of unfree laborers, nor participate in the Atlantic economy as a major exporter. Without creating the large surpluses that the plantation regions generated, there were relatively few extremely wealthy individuals. New England's economy was more middle class than the Chesapeake region, for instance, with fewer rich and poor. Another important factor that shaped New England lives and economy was the relatively healthy environment and plenty of food. This prompted dramatic population increase despite a great decline in migration to the region. The population explosion led to geographic expansion, as colonists moved north and west. This expansion and growth was not without its problems. It led to conflicts with Indians, vast ecological alterations with long-term consequences, and numerous challenges to Puritan values.

New England's economic development, as with other colonial regions, depended on its access by sea to other regions. New England was well-placed in this regard. Close to the rich fisheries of the North Atlantic, and in possession of excellent timber from its great forests for building ships, the fishing industry stimulated economic development in the region. Familiarity with the seas led New Englanders to engage in ocean-going commerce to the West Indies, Africa, and Europe, buttressed by avid participation in the carrying trade of goods to and from the mainland colonies. In other words, with limited natural resources compared to other colonial regions, the New Englanders found ways to actively engage in Atlantic world trade.

Much of this trade depended on New England's membership in the English empire. England provided protection for its colonies and for the trade routes through which goods were transported. England (and its colonies) also provided a marketplace for New England goods and offered their own in return. The English and Dutch empires effectively created commercial networks that promoted the flourishing of colonies and mother country. The French were somewhat less effective, and the Spanish much less so, particularly in supplying manufactured goods to suit colonial needs. By the late 17th century, the smaller Dutch, English, and French empires surpassed the Spanish in terms of economic development and naval power. The manufacturing center of Europe had shifted from south and central Europe to the northwest, and those three nations' commercial and military power increased as well. But colonists did not necessarily need access to markets within their own empire. Smuggling and piracy thrived in the Atlantic world, as colonists disregarded imperial law to trade with competitors. Piracy declined after the first quarter of the 18th century, as England, especially, sought to regulate New World commerce. But smuggling continued: market conditions prevailed over governmental restrictions. The mother countries were hampered in their efforts to stop smuggling because their empires were too large to firmly control. Colonial officials and colonists both disregarded imperial strictures with great regularity in pursuit of personal aims.

The economic aims of colonists were mostly formed by biological and cultural factors. Biology drives humans to eat, clothe, and shelter themselves, while culture influences what people choose to eat and wear, and the structures they live in. Culture also shapes the desire to accumulate secondary and non-essential things, such as items of personal adornment and for leisure. In short, it shapes patterns of consumption, though the ability to consume cannot be separated from the realm of the possible: what raw materials are available for processing, and what goods people can attain in the marketplace.

# TRANSFORMING NEW ENGLAND: ENVIRONMENT AND ECONOMY

When we speak of the "impersonal" forces of history, such as environment, empire, trade, and warfare, none of these have meaning disconnected to the humans who lived in, observed, shaped, and were shaped by the world they inhabited. It is necessary to consider the culture of humans—how people chose to live in an environment, and their responses to the physical and cultural challenges they faced. On a basic, but important level, cultural values impress upon people views of what food is acceptable to eat, gender roles in labor, patterns of land usage, and cues about which natural resources are worth cultivating or accessing. Many Native Americans, for instance, relied on deer for meat and clothing and developed an array of skills and strategies for procuring deer. Europeans residing in the same area generally preferred to import domesticated animals, such as cattle and sheep, and clothe themselves in wool, linen, and cotton. Cultural preferences led native peoples to adapt habitats to deer hunting, while English colonists built fences to hem in cattle. This difference takes on greater significance when we realize that thousands of colonists enclosing land reduced the habitat for deer, forcing Indians to either change their subsistence patterns or leave a region. Cultural values are not impermeable—many Europeans would don buckskin in the mid-18th century, while natives wore European-produced textiles; Indians undertook the plow, while many Europeans moved to open-field grazing of cattle.

## The Environment

The English of New England consciously transformed their homes, towns, and regions to suit themselves politically, culturally, and economically. Industriously, they used hard labor, often their own, while creatively adapting to the market conditions of the Atlantic world. They had relatively few rich and poor compared to other colonial regions and succeeded at creating a relatively stable society with a large middle class. And if their original dreams of building a New Jerusalem fell by the wayside, and the consensus and peace they yearned to maintain proved unrealistic and unattainable, they nonetheless took pride in becoming masters of their region and enjoying prosperity.

Generations of Europeans arriving in the Americas were struck, if not dazzled, by the agricultural potential of the land and its resources. In eastern America, along the Atlantic seaboard, the wealth of forests appeared as both opportunity and obstacle. Great forests of a diversity of trees were available for lumber and firewood. But for those intending to grow crops for consumption and export, trees were a nuisance. Early settlers preferred lands already cleared and abandoned by the native inhabitants, many of whom had succumbed to disease. Otherwise, much of the forest was fired— the quickest and easiest way to clear ground for planting.

New England Puritans viewed the "disappearance" of Indians as providential; that God had made room for his chosen people, who would make better use of the land than heathen. Religious values also deemed that the Christian's hard labor in transforming the land evinced proper piety and behavior. Reaping the fruits of hard labor was a sign of God's approval of both the enterprise of colonization and of individual lives. Christian views also shaped how the land should be cultivated: farmers practiced monoculture, the planting of but one crop in a field, because they believed it biblically ordained. But much of the cultural baggage Puritans carried to the New

World was "English" rather than Christian. Colonists hoped to re-create England in the New World, to make the countryside look like England's. They imported English animals, grasses, and other plants to feed their animals. They built English-style housing and surrounded their property with English-style fences. They purchased English goods: textiles, metal ware, and decorations, all in the latest fashion, if possible. The New Jerusalem and its inhabitants were not to appear new at all. Danger lay in the unfamiliar. The "savagery" of the Indians in their near nudity was all too remindful of Eden. Eden must be transformed, and the people should not fall prey to its charms. The serpent awaited to beguile with the apple; the Christian must counter with piety, hard work, and steadfast rejection of temptation—the temptation to live in Eden and not the New Jerusalem.

Native peoples, particularly those living near the Europeans, had to adjust to the rapidly altered environment. English farmers eliminated animal habitats by turning the forests into farmland, erecting mills on waterways, and introducing new crops and cultigens. They imported large numbers of domestic animals, particularly cows and pigs, which competed with the region's indigenous animals for food and living space. To obtain English goods, native peoples began over-hunting, further depleting the animal population, particularly beaver, which was highly valued by the Europeans for the furs used to make hats. Over-hunting led the fur trade to move west and north, leaving New England natives without ways to trade for the European goods upon which some had become dependent. More crucial was the decline of the deer population. Through selective burning of the forest, natives had created habitats to attract deer—these rapidly disappeared as English farmers deforested southern New England. Without deer, natives could no longer maintain their traditional way of life, because they needed the animals for food and clothing. Some Indians entered Praying Towns, where they took up the plow in hopes of maintaining themselves by adapting to European-style agriculture; others would be forced from the region by Puritans desiring their land. Throughout North America, native peoples proved adaptive to the market economy introduced by the Europeans, in terms of producing valuable items for exchange. But New England natives faced more difficult circumstances than natives in most other mainland colonial regions; the combination of swift European demographic growth, reduced animal populations and habitats, disease, and warfare, all led to declining numbers and power, particularly in the southern portion of the region.

## Economic Development

New England's economic development greatly differed from other colonial regions in the English colonial world—for that matter, it was unique in comparison with any colonial region in the Americas. Seventeenth-century colonies in the West Indies and North and South America were characterized by extraction of minerals or plantation agriculture, or as small outposts (such as French Montreal or Dutch Beverwijck) that subsisted on trade with indigenous peoples. Puritan New England differed by the diversity of its economy, its major form of labor, and its reliance on neither the Indian trade, extractive industries, nor plantation agriculture; its success lay in economic diversification and the ability to make profitable use of the seas' resources and to use the seas as highways linking diverse areas of the Atlantic world. But all these things were grounded on family agriculture: the ability of a rapidly growing populace to feed itself.

New Englanders actively participated in the fishing industry—an extractive economy—perhaps 10% of the economy revolved around this industry, and thus it became one cornerstone of the region. But in other colonial regions, the extractive economy could comprise 75% or more of income. When we add in forest products, the value of the extractive economy in New England increases, and certainly wood provided surplus that enabled New Englanders to purchase other regions' products. Nevertheless, the basis of the economy was agriculture, not plantation agriculture, but family farms and household production.

The chief form of labor in New England lay in the parents and children of each household. Farming families produced much of what the family needed, plus small surpluses for exchange in local and regional trade networks. Men labored in the fields to produce wheat and vegetables, kept livestock, and sold their surplus to merchants who traded with the West Indies. The inability of many New Englanders to produce enough surplus to earn credits to purchase imported goods led to establishment of local, small-scale operations to manufacture inexpensive lumber, shoes, iron, and a range of other products for regional consumption. Eventually, local manufacturers also produced surpluses that could be shipped to other regions.

New England women actively engaged in this economy through household manufacture of goods to exchange with neighbors and for export. They produced an array of textiles, spun and woven from wool, flax, linen, and cotton, which could be used for clothing, bedding, and curtains. Women also traded vegetables and herbs produced in their gardens, as well as soap, butter, cheese, candles, soup, meats, and baked goods. To earn credits from local storekeepers, they delivered their own and their daughters' labor—to wash, iron, and mend clothes, to tend young children, or to assist in a variety of household chores. In return, New England households received finished goods from England, such as ribbons, pins, scissors, shoes, stockings, and linen, as well as furniture, agricultural implements, and iron cookery. From the West Indies, they obtained sugar and molasses, and from more distant colonies, tea, coffee, and spices.

The Puritan emphasis on the virtue of labor led to many hardworking, industrious families who then desired to enjoy the fruits of their labor through purchase of imported luxury goods such as fine clothing and furniture, silver plate, and carriages. In the first generation, government attempted to restrict consumption. Sumptuary laws limited purchases of sugar and alcohol and legislated what garments people could wear, not only to prevent the wealthy from conspicuous displays of wealth, but also to keep common people in their place. These laws mostly failed from lack of enforcement; restrictions on clothing were periodically enacted and ignored. The government also set price controls to insure everyone a fair price for bread and wage controls and piecework rates to hamper how much people could earn. These too often were disregarded. The government then relied on ministers to exhort their flock against over-consumption and displays of status, and to warn laborers against charging high rates for their labor.

## Economic Position in the Empire

The Puritans recognized that they imported more than they exported and that measures must be taken to balance trade. The government promoted trade, manufacturing, and agriculture through a variety of means. They enhanced the economic infrastructure through road building, improved trade with the neighboring Dutch in

New Netherland, permitted higher limits on interest rates to prompt those with capital to lend their money to entrepreneurs, and offered bounties, subsidies, tax abatements, monopolies, and other special advantages to those who would initiate new industries and manufactories, particularly to produce flour, linen, finished clothing, shoes, iron and iron goods, salt, and lumber.

England viewed these developments as infringing on their own economy—that the mother country should provide finished goods in return for the colonies' raw materials. Otherwise New England would be competing directly with England in colonial markets. In the 1660s, England began legislating the imperial economy by enacting Navigation Acts. These laws initially were designed to eliminate foreign competition in the empire by controlling trade. All colonial goods had to be carried in English or colonial ships manned by crews of at least three-fifths English (including colonists). Many colonial goods had to be shipped to England before being re-exported elsewhere, thus ensuring that the mother country could tax the goods, and also creating employment for English workers in unloading and loading ships. The barring of foreign ships from colonial trade helped the New England economy. New Englanders could trade with English colonies without foreign competition, and shipbuilders, merchants, and sailors all benefited as they carried not only their own region's goods but those of other colonies in the burgeoning transatlantic commerce. Moreover, New England products were largely left off the list of enumerated goods that forced the plantation colonies to ship their products to England, so the New Englanders carried their goods to France, Spain, Portugal, and the colonies of those nations. Later Navigation Acts banned much of this trade, but enforcement was lax, so the New Englanders conducted illicit trade largely unimpeded.

By the early 18th century, renewed English fears of New England's success in manufacturing and trade led many to propose restrictions, though a few imperialists recognized that the region's prosperity benefited the empire. But not until the 1730s would England begin to limit New England production and trade through the Hat Act (1732), which placed high duties on some colonial manufactures, and the Molasses Act (1733), which was designed to force colonists to purchase English instead of foreign sugar and molasses. Thus, the New Englanders successfully built a prosperous economy without the benefit of plantation agriculture or by focusing as heavily as other colonial regions on intensive extraction of natural resources—though the value of wood to the economic health of the region remained enormous in terms of providing necessary firewood, building materials, and lumber for ship building. Instead of relying on a single item to trade—such as tobacco, rice, sugar, or wheat—or extraction of gold, silver, or iron—the New Englanders combined a variety of economic enterprises: fishing, lumber, household, small-scale manufacturing, family agriculture, and numerous enterprises related to shipping and international trade. New England's entry into the global economy was not spectacular—but creative and steady—its merchants developed knowledge of market conditions in numerous regions in the Atlantic world. Farmers and small craftsmen pursued their calling diligently to earn surpluses to gain items they could not produce themselves. Per capita income lagged way behind other English colonial regions, but unlike most regions, New England developed a large middle class, with a relatively small number of both the poor and the well-to-do.

## NEW ENGLAND SOCIETY

Economic prosperity challenged the harmony that New Englanders so highly valued. Many became more preoccupied with individual concerns than those of their community. Some resented their neighbors' success, or the pressures to conform religiously and socially. Yet cultural values tied the New Englanders together. An outsider viewing the hundreds of towns that comprised New England could not help but be impressed by how similar they appeared from one to the next physically, politically, culturally, and religiously. But by the last quarter of the 17th century, grave problems emerged undermining the ostensible unity. Wars with Indians were followed by conflicts with the French in Canada. Population growth led to the splintering of families and communities. And great anxiety filled many who wondered whether material success had led to a loss of purpose in America. To understand the development of these fissures, first we must examine the factors that held New England together.

### New England Towns

Most New England families lived in close proximity to other families. Unlike in Virginia and Maryland, where the English spread across the landscape on large tracts of land, the New Englanders settled in towns. In fact, the colonial governments ordinarily would not grant land to individuals, but only to towns. To become a town, a group of families bound themselves together with a signed document, a covenant. The "town" then petitioned the colonial government for a tract of land; families received portions within the tract according to their social status.

One historian has described these towns as "Christian, closed, corporate, utopian, communities." The towns were closed in that only members, those who signed the covenant and their children, received land. No one else could join the town—in effect, a corporation—without approval of its members. Outsiders were unlikely to gain entry (which would further divide the town's limited land base) unless they possessed needed skills, such as blacksmithing or carpentry. Through the covenant, the members promised to live with one another in Christian harmony and love, each town forming a microcosm of the colony as a whole—as Christian communities that would intentionally operate according to biblical precepts.

To fulfill its utopian ideals, towns had to provide and support a church and minister. They also yearly elected selectmen to whom townspeople could take their disputes. All were expected to accept and abide by the selectmen's decisions so that the community could remain in harmony. Ideally, the town should be self-contained, solving all its own problems, secure from the vagaries of the outside world. To forestall disputes, strict laws governed the fencing of land (which elected fence inspectors enforced) so that livestock trampling of crops, a major source of disturbance between neighbors in agricultural societies, would be minimized. Instead of living on their farms, everyone was required to occupy households around the town center to maintain the sense of community—and to keep a watchful eye on neighbors—daily the men traveled to their scattered portions of land, often miles away.

Political life revolved around the town meeting, where opinions could be expressed regarding issues before the town. Once a town reached a decision, everyone was expected to accept the outcome in a spirit of goodwill and consensus. Bickering, discontent with the proper order of things, and a contentious spirit were all held as unchristian and indicative of grave problems with individuals and the community. Achieving consensus, then, was a town's highest ideal.

## Women's Lives

Women formed the backbone of the New England towns. They cared for the children and instilled in them Puritan values. As a group, they sought to insure the moral values of the community. And they were producing much of the surplus New England traded in regional and Atlantic markets. Moreover, as producers of large numbers of healthy children, a rarity among Europeans, they ensured the region possessed future productive laborers.

Both custom and law proscribed females' place in society and restricted their ownership of property. Upon marriage, a woman's possessions became her husband's unless a pre-nuptial agreement specified continued ownership of particular property. Otherwise, husbands could legally dispose of all moveable property without their wives' consent. This would have placed women's property rights on a par with slaves, except that dower rights entitled women to one-third of their husband's estate upon his death, retaining ownership of the home and some land. This "right" rested upon the fact that a woman's family provided a dowry—property—for the marriage. Dower rights guaranteed that a wife had to legally approve her husband's sale of land and house.

Women occupied a dependent status, first upon their fathers, then upon their husbands, which barred them from political participation, as all dependents—women, children, servants, and non-property-holding adult males—could not vote. But even those women who achieved independent property-holding status were prohibited from voting. Custom, rather than law, delimited unmarried women into a social position as dependents. Never-married women were expected to live in another's household—if not their father's, then as a servant, or as a dependent in a sibling's household. Unmarried adult women received the moniker *spinster*, symbolizing that they spent their working hours spinning cloth in someone else's home. Only widows could enjoy an economic and social independent status, operating their deceased husband's business and living on their own. Thus, widowed women were found running taverns, dry-goods stores, and other enterprises. If their husbands were away, women could also fill male occupational roles.

Perhaps the greatest control a female possessed over the course of her life lay in the selection of a marriage partner. Parents arranged most marriages, as these were economic alliances between families that involved the exchange of property. But a woman could refuse a suitor. Parents might threaten to withhold a dowry to retain control over their daughter's choice of spouse—and many did—but daughters had the option of becoming pregnant and forcing their parents' acquiescence. Studies have shown that approximately half of New England women were pregnant at the time of a first marriage, displaying that many used this as a way to ensure their power over choice of a spouse, as parents wished to avoid the shame of a daughter becoming an unwed mother. Of course, the male's parents might oppose the match, but he still bore legal responsibility to support the child.

Before and after marriage, women's work revolved around the household. They bore responsibility for child care, food preparation, maintenance of the household, and gardens that produced herbs and vegetables. A strict division of labor marked New England households, as in other English households. Men worked the fields and provided firewood. Women tended the chickens, and if there were no women in the household, then there were no chickens. Women and men occupied separate spheres, in which much of their work and social lives were segregated. Women gathered with other women to perform a wide range of tasks, including textile production— clothing, bedding and table cloths, food preservation, midwifery, beer-making, and washing and mending clothes. They met with neighbor women for prayer meetings and in other social contexts, while men frequently worked and socialized with other men. Each knew little of the other's domain. Women often possessed limited knowledge of their family's scattered landholdings, while men were ignorant of household possessions, which their vague descriptions in legal documents bears out.

Although living in a patriarchal society that denied them political and legal rights of equality with men, and limited by custom to particular roles, society highly valued women's contributions to the family and society. As mothers and grandmothers, they were celebrated for the number of their progeny. In the community, they played the key role in socializing other females and males to societal expectations. The range of female labor spread more broadly than it would a century and a half later, when middle-class society hoped to shield women from blood and gore. In colonial America, women butchered animals, delivered babies, and provided a majority of the health care for women and children. Women received praise for their physical accomplishments and their contributions to home and hearth. Nevertheless, they occupied an inferior position to males that often worked to their disadvantage. An unhappy marriage was difficult to escape, though divorce was possible. A husband could hire a servant if his wife was a poor housekeeper or socialize away from the household if partnered in an unhappy marriage. Women's lives were much more physically confining than males—it was not unusual for women to have small children in the household well into their late forties and early fifties. Although women had recourse against a physically abusive husband, social custom and their work roles allowed them few or no alternatives to the domesticity expected of them. The household was their domain, but New England's strong communal bonds prevented isolation—whether a woman desired it or not—she must be neighborly, attend church, and was expected to engage in some chores with other women. The bulk of a woman's time was spent in household chores (including tending the family gardens) and in child care, but unless she lived on a frontier, she had much interaction with other women and their children.

## Demography

From the Puritan perspective, the development of towns and colonies provided evidence of great success in their godly settlement. With high migration during the first decades of settlement coupled with a low death rate, the Puritans filled up eastern Massachusetts and expanded west into the Connecticut Valley. Other Puritans moved south settling Rhode Island or into the New Haven and Connecticut colonies, which eventually combined. A significant migration also extended north into Maine and New Hampshire. The European population of New England increased 2.7% per year, so that the number of colonists doubled every 25 years, mostly through natural increase.

No healthier region for Europeans existed in the colonial world, and New Englanders enjoyed a longer life expectancy than people in England and France. A male child who reached 21 years of age could expect to live to 72 years. The healthy environment, and the fact that Puritans generally had emigrated to the region as families rather than individuals, led to near equal numbers of males and females, a rarity in colonial regions. Women generally bore children every two to three years, married relatively young, and thus produced more and healthier offspring. It was not unusual for women to bear 10 to 13 children.

Population growth placed great pressure on the land and communities. New Englanders, as with other colonists, believed the earth's bounty endless, and many took few measures to preserve and restore the land, as already was current in western Europe. Much of the rich forests were wasted—burned to clear land for agriculture and livestock. Flooding worsened as the land could no longer absorb as much water, and many native species disappeared as colonists imported preferred grasses for their livestock. The livestock themselves overpopulated southern New England, as these highly valued commodities not only provided for family needs, but could be a source of profit through sale to the West Indies. Ecological changes led to longer, colder winters and shorter, hotter summers.

Population growth of animals and humans, and declining agricultural fertility, forced out-migration from the older settled towns. By the third generation, at the end of the 17th century, the ideals of the Puritan communities were battered as towns could no longer provide for their own. Parents had neither enough land, dowries, nor cash bequests for all their children, many of whom had to migrate to distant places, often to never see their families again. Townsmen also moved away from town centers and consolidated their holdings for convenience, further splintering communities. In town after town, disputes arose, as those who lived distant from churches and schools wished to break away and form new towns. Usually those at the town center resisted, not wanting to reduce the town's tax base, forcing the outliers to seek relief by appealing to the General Court. Consensus broke down as bitter disputes arose from these threats to sunder the community. Usually, the General Court agreed to towns' breakups, but the contentiousness did not necessarily end, for the reduced towns often faced further divisions and breakups.

The ideals of the first and second generation could not survive unchanged into the third and fourth generation. The children and grandchildren of the founders had not experienced the persecution that their mothers and fathers had in England. The new generations had not made the great journey across the Atlantic to establish a New Jerusalem. Puritanism was losing its evangelical zeal to change the world. In England, the Puritans had won control of the government in the English Civil War (1649–1660). English Puritans then looked to New England for models to re-create English society, particularly the churches. But when the English discovered the great intolerance of their American Puritan cousins, they recoiled in horror at the New Jerusalem. With the Restoration of the Stuart Monarchy in 1660, all forms of religious zealotry came under attack in England, and the New England Puritans appeared to represent some of its worst excesses. As Puritanism lost power and public favor in England, New England became politically isolated and a source of disdain in the English-speaking world, the people referred to by the derogatory epithet, the Saints.

## The Salem Witchcraft Episode

The Salem witchcraft rage of 1692 confirmed New England's fanaticism to the region's outsiders. Accusations and trials for witchcraft were not unusual in New England. Excluding the Salem witchcraft rage, there were 93 trials in the 17th century. Rarely did trials occur elsewhere in the colonies. For instance, only a few cases have been found in Virginia. Compared to western Europe, witchcraft cases were more common by population in New England than in England, Spain, Italy, and the Low Countries, but occurred less frequently than in France, the Germanies, and the Swiss Confederation. What marked Salem as different was that it experienced virtually the last witchcraft rage in the western world: 141 alleged witches were brought to trial in a short period of time—the arrests began in March and the last hangings for witchcraft occurred in September.

Normally, individuals faced prosecution for witchcraft only after years of alleged practice. Plaintiffs accused defendants of afflicting them with pain, casting spells that prevented them from performing ordinary activities, and inflicting illness and death on their livestock. In New England, the accused witches tended to be childless women of middle age often in conflict with their neighbors. They were cantankerous individuals who refused to accept the ideal of the harmonious community. In Salem, however, the mania took on a life of its own. The accusers had not been subject to long-term afflictions—the first group of accusers were young girls—and the alleged witches were not believed to have been witches prior to the accusations.

Like in much of New England, Salem residents were torn between the old Puritan ideals of building a New Jerusalem and the materialistic aspirations to benefit from merchant capitalism. Salem also experienced the same divisiveness that existed throughout New England, whereby a section of the town petitioned the legislature to separate and form a new town. At the time of the Salem witchcraft rage, Massachusetts was in disarray—the charter had been taken away by the English government and the secessionists could receive no help for their petitions from the colonial government, which had no legal right to function. (England was in the midst of the Glorious Revolution, in which William and Mary replaced James II as monarchs.) The town had divided over support for a new minister, Samuel Parris. Families of those who began the witchcraft allegations supported the minister, whose own West Indian slave, Tituba, was one of the first accused. Parris played a major role in helping to spread the accusations to others. The accusers tended to be people experiencing economic decline. Their opponents represented the new economic success, opposition to the minister, and ostensibly expressed little interest in the old-style religion. Compounding anxieties were Indian threats in the region. Some historians have shown that fear of the devil and fear of Indians were intimately entwined in the minds of New England Puritans. The specter of capture by Indians haunted many: a reality confirmed by its real possibility and the popular published books by those who escaped or were freed from captivity. The devil, Puritans believed, was at work among the Indians, and extending his domain into Puritan communities by recruitment of witches. A perfect storm was brewing.

Once the initial accusations were made, they spread to surrounding towns as others joined in accusing both neighbors and strangers. The jails filled with accused witches. Many were convicted on spectral evidence—visions, rather than verifiable facts. Convicted witches could escape execution if they publicly confessed, but many refused to commit the sin of lying and instead asserted their innocence. Nineteen were executed before the mania ended. Colony leaders, many of whom supported the trials at first, altered their course and disallowed the use of spectral evidence, which led to the release from jail of the remaining accused and convicted witches. With the example of Salem, trials for witchcraft became rare in New England, as they had become in western Europe. Witchcraft became harder to prove in the courts of law. By 1735, England outlawed prosecution for witchcraft. By then, Salem had come to symbolize, as it does to this day, a gross example of fear, intolerance, and persecution.

## Conclusion

In terms of population growth and territorial expansion, Puritan New England was a great success in its second half-century. Hundreds of new towns were established, the land transformed to their needs, and people adapted themselves to the international market economy. The New England town structure proved resilient as the basic way to organize society on the local level, providing a sense of community as well as schools and churches. Secession of groups of people to form new towns was a painful process, repeated time and again throughout the region, but ultimately made life more convenient for the teeming population. The declining land base, however, forced out-migration of many to distant lands undermining family ties and striking townspeoples' confidence in their ability to take care of their own. Individuals' aspirations to improve their material circumstances, and the decline of the founders' fervor to create a New Jerusalem, also undermined Puritans' sense of purpose and their towns' ability to achieve consensus. Many individuals and families chafed under the communal ideal of living at the town center in close proximity to all other members of the community, and moved into the countryside to live on their own farmland.

The tension between individualism and community, and between materialistic aspirations and Christian piety, was experienced throughout Puritan New England. Though individualism often seemed to gain the upper hand, many of the Puritan ideals survived in New England. Town life remained more important in New England than in other regions, and the inhabitants retained a sense of themselves as possessing a moral purpose to shine a beacon of light for the world. It is no accident of history that a century later, in the 1820s and 1830s, the Puritans' descendants worried over the United States losing its moral direction and New Englanders avidly led or joined an array of movements to improve the nation's character, including abolition and temperance.

The Puritan sense of purpose, their cultural ideals, were in large part maintained by the homogeneity of the community. They were overwhelmingly English (unlike in most other English colonial regions), were middle class, and came from the same Protestant Dissenter tradition. But the Puritans, too, had to contend with people who were not like themselves, particularly Indians and Africans. The challenges and interactions of these diverse peoples in New England are the subject of the next chapter.

# DOCUMENTS

## 7.1. Cotton Mather on One of the Condemned Witches in Salem

*Cotton Mather was a leading Puritan minister in New England. During his long life, he published numerous sermons, pamphlets, and books on a range of religious matters, but also on science and a range of "worldly" affairs. His* The Wonders of the Invisible World *included much discussion on witchcraft, particularly the witchcraft panic that struck Salem in 1692. Mather believed that witchcraft existed, but held contradictory impulses regarding its presence at Salem. An initial supporter of the trials, he also played a leading role in ending them by urging the disregard of spectral evidence. In the following excerpt, he recounts the case of Bridget Bishop, the first person tried and executed for witchcraft in Salem. According to Mather, what kinds of evidence were acceptable and what were unacceptable for convicting a person of witchcraft?*

I. She was Indicted for Bewitching of several persons in the Neighbourhood, the Indictment being drawn up, according to the Form in such Cases usual. And pleading, Not Guilty, there were brought in several persons, who had long undergone many kinds of Miseries, which were preternaturally Inflicted, and generally ascribed unto an horrible Witchcraft. There was little Occasion to prove the Witchcraft, it being Evident and Notorious to all Beholders. Now to fix the Witchcraft on the Prisoner at the Bar, the first thing used, was the Testimony of the Bewitched; whereof several Testify'd, That the Shape of the Prisoner did oftentimes very grievously pinch them, choak them, Bite them, and Afflict them; urging them to write their Names in a Book, which the said Spectre called, Ours. One of them did further Testify, that it was the Shape of this Prisoner, with another, which one Day took her from her Wheel, and carrying her to the River side, threatened there to Drown her, if she did not Sign to the Book mentioned: which yet she refused. Others of them did also Testify, that the said Shape did in her Threats brag to them that she had been the Death of sundry persons, then by her Named; that she had Ridden a man then likewise Named. Another Testify'd the Apparition of Ghosts unto the Spectre of Bishop, crying out, You Murdered us! About the Truth whereof, there was in the matter of Fact but too much Suspicion....

V. To render it further Unquestionable, that the prisoner at the Bar was the Person truly charged in *this* Witchcraft, there were produced many Evidences of *other* Witchcrafts, by her perpetrated. For Instance, John Cook testify'd, that about five or six years ago, One morning, about Sun-Rise, he was in his Chamber assaulted by the Shape of this prisoner: which Look'd on him, grin'd at him, and very much hurt him with a Blow on the side of the Head: and that on the same day, about Noon, the same Shape walked in the Room where he was, and an Apple strangely flew out of his Hand, into the Lap of his Mother, six or eight foot from him.

VII. John Bly and his Wife testify'd, that he bought a sow of Edward Bishop, the Husband of the prisoner;

*(Continued)*

and was to pay the price agreed, unto another person. This Prisoner being Angry that she was thus hindred from fingering the money, Quarrell'd with Bly. Soon after which, the Sow was taken with strange Fits, Jumping, Leaping, and knocking her head against the Fence; she seem'd Blind and Deaf, and would neither eat nor be suck'd. Whereupon a neighbour said, she believed the Creature was Over-Looked; and sundry other circumstances concurred, which made the Deponents Believe that Bishop had Bewitched it. . . .

IX. Samuel Shattock testify'd, That in the Year 1680, this Bridget Bishop often came to his house upon such frivolous and foolish errands, that they suspected she came indeed with a purpose of mischief. Presently whereupon his eldest child, which was of as promising Health and Sense as any child of its Age, began to droop exceedingly; and the oftener that Bishop came to the House, the worse grew the Child. As the Child would be standing at the Door, he would be thrown and bruised against the Stones, by an Invisible Hand, and in like sort knock his Face against the sides of the House, and bruise it after a miserable manner. . . .

XII. To Crown all, John Bly and William Bly Testify'd, That being Employ'd by Bridget Bishop, to help take down the Cellar-wall of the old House, wherein she formerly Lived, they did in Holes of the said old Wall find several Poppets, made up of Rags and Hogs Brussels, with Headless Pins in them, the Points being outward. Whereof she could give no Account unto the Court, that was Reasonable or Tolerable.

XIII. One thing that made against the Prisoner was, her being evidently convicted of Gross Lying in the Court, several Times, while she was making her Plea. But besides this, a Jury of Women found a preternatural Teat upon her Body, but upon a second search, within Three or four hours, there was no such thing to be seen. There was also an account of other people whom this woman had afflicted. And there might have been many more, if they had been enquired for. But there was no need of them.

Source: Cotton Mather, *The Wonders of the Invisible World* (1693).

## 7.2. A New England Colonist's View of Indian Rights to the Land

(Spelling modernized. Italics removed.) *The New England author, "J.M.," published a pamphlet in 1722 to justify the right of those who "improve" the land to own it— an argument meant to rationalize both the taking of land from Indians and the injustice of allowing speculators to own large tracts. J.M. based his argument on his reading of the Bible and his understanding of God's intention that humans should cultivate the land and enjoy its fruits. As a European, J.M. could not understand or accept non-European ways of using the land—thus he never considers Indian hunting, for instance, as a legitimate use of the land. Despite his attempt to create a sober, and "reasonable," argument, he also lapsed into ridicule of American Indians and to sophistical assertions that Indians had accepted British sovereignty; that they had no understanding of owning land until the English arrived—and therefore really did not own it; and that their chiefs had sold tracts when they had no right to, but this illustrates the inability of Indians to be proper caretakers of their land. What is the role of God, according to the author, in determining who should own the land?*

1. That God hath given this American part of the Earth to the Indians, exclusive of all others; for if being born in the Country gives them the Property thereof, then they of English Extraction are possessed equally thereof with them, they being also born in the Country; and have equal reason to Exclude the Indians, as the Indians have to Exclude them.

2. As for their rightful Possession, it is granted, that where they have subdued, replenished, & are actually improving that is their Property; and to take that from them, is to Rob them; also to improve too near their Settlements, is annoyance that ought not to be tolerated. But

3. Is it not unaccountable, that the Natives or Indians should be invested with the Property of all this vast unsubdued, unreplenished, unimproved, unknown, and greatest part of this Creation, exclusive of all others; for they came here only Providentially as the English came....

If it cannot be proved, that god hath given the Property of all this vast un-subdued and unknown American part of the Creation to the Indians, exclusive of all others, nor that they have subdued or improved one hundred thousand part thereof; (they only were born and brought up in the Country, as also the wild savage Creatures were,

and preyed on every thing they could catch, a Rattle Snake could not escape their teeth) then the Natives have no more Property, save the Land they have subdued and improved; for no People have a right to Exclude the species Man from subduing, replenishing and improving the Earth.

If God in his Providence brought the English to this almost Vacant and Uninhabited part of the World, which was neither subdued, replenished nor improved; and the great Sachems submitted and surrendered to the Crown and Nation of England, and became our Kings Subjects; and all Opposing Powers and Rebels by the King of England's Subjects, both English and Indian extraction, were subdued and brought into subjection; and this part of the Earth subdued, improved and replenished by the Subjects of England, they bringing into this continent all sorts of Cattle, Grain, seed, Herbs, Roots, Fruits & Fowls, and all sorts of tools, Utensils, Arts and Sciences, with the true Knowledge and Worship of god, & also defended and protected the same; then it is manifest, that the Property is not invested in the Indian, but in the Crown and Nation of great Britain....

If we consider the Indians or Natives as communities, then this vast Continent either is their Property, exclusive of all others, or it is not; if it be the communities Property, what right have their Sachems to Sell it; for if Sachems, or any in Authority do

*(Continued)*

destroy, or alienate their innocent Subjects, their Liberties and Properties to Strangers (without their consent) by any device or colour whatsoever, Thereby they forfeit all right of Authority to govern, and are Manifested to be Tyrants; and then they ought to be deposed; for illegal Destruction and Alienation are contrary to, and inconsistent with both Moral virtue, Reason and government; and also destroys the end thereof, which is the Preservation of Life, Liberty and Property.

Before the English Arrived to this Continent, there was nothing in this Country, save Indian corn and Squashes, not one tame Creature, save cur dogs, nor any thing made of Metal, or the least step of Literature; nor did the Indians pretend to be invested with the property of the Soil, save where they had improved it . . . till the English possessed them therewith.

Source: J.M., *The Original Rights of Mankind Freely to Subdue and Improve the Earth* (1722).

## Bibliography

Axtell, James. *The European and the Indian: Essays in the Ethnohistory of Colonial North America* (1981).

Boyer, Paul, and Stephen Nissenbaum. *Salem Possessed: The Social Origins of Witchcraft* (1974).

Cronon, William. *Changes in the Land: Indians, Colonists, and the Ecology of New England* (1983).

Demos, John. *Entertaining Satan: Witchcraft and the Culture of New England* (1982).

Donahue, Brian. *The Great Meadow: Farmers and the Land in Colonial Concord* (2004).

Greven, Philip J. *Four Generations: Population, Land, and Family in Andover, Massachusetts* (1970).

Innes, Stephen. *Labor in a New Land: Economy and Society in Seventeenth-Century Springfield* (1983).

Johnson, Richard R. *Adjustment to Empire: The New England Colonies, 1675–1715* (1981).

Leach, Douglas E. *The Northern Colonial Frontier, 1607–1763* (1966).

Lockridge, Kenneth A. *A New England Town: The First Hundred Years, Dedham, Massachusetts, 1636–1736* (1970).

Martin, Calvin Luther. *Keepers of the Game: Indian-Animal Relationships and the Fur Trade* (1978).

Newell, Margaret Ellen. *From Dependency to Independence: Economic Revolution in Colonial New England* (1999).

Norton, Mary Beth. *In the Devil's Snare: The Salem Witchcraft Crisis of 1692* (2002).

Ulrich, Laurel Thatcher. *Good Wives: Image and Reality in the Lives of Women in Northern New England, 1650–1750* (1982).

# 8

# Indians, Africans, and English in New England, 1670–1730

**Cultural Transformation: Conversion and Adaptation**
Conversion of Indians to Christianity
Learning from and Converting to Native Ways of Life

**Debasing Others: Slavery and Warfare**
Enslavement of Indians: Victims of War
Enslavement of Indians: By Court and Decree
Enslavement of Africans

**Puritan–Indian Warfare**
King Philip's War (1675–1676)
Abenaki and Northern New England

## INTRODUCTION

Whether a new or established colony, the Europeans lived in a state of dependence on native peoples, who defended their colonies and conducted offensive operations against their enemies. Yet close alliance with the Europeans had great hazards. Europeans were not always the most steadfast of allies. The English, in particular, tended to treat non-Europeans as commodities—as people who could be bought and sold—even their "friends" became saleable. The English of New England and South Carolina had a propensity for turning on native allies: engaging a new group of Indians to assist them in enslaving old friends, waging war upon them, and dispossessing them of their lands. But the Europeans could not afford to alienate all native groups simultaneously. Native military power was often too strong, and with the Europeans frequently engaged in armed conflict with each other, the Europeans required Indian military assistance. Natives often bore the brunt of fighting in the imperial wars of France, Spain, and England, which began at the end of the 17th century and lasted over 100 years.

Although most Indians' lives and concerns had little to do with Europeans, the forces of the Atlantic world reached into native communities and had great impact. An Indian might never have met a European, but the influx of trade goods, and native wars to control trade or to procure Indian slaves, disrupted communities 1,000 miles distant from European settlements. The outside forces encroaching on native life are easy to identify: disease, European trade goods, dispossession of land, endemic warfare, slaving, and environmental transformation. Native peoples and experiences so varied from one place to the next that there were a multitude of responses to these external influences. But in general, we can say that Native Americans easily adapted new technologies and created new polities and successful diplomacies to treat with Europeans. Moreover, few Indians desired to "become" Europeans—as the latter hoped and expected—they maintained their traditional cultures. The European colonists did likewise, incorporating new technologies and trade goods, and adapting themselves to New World contingencies. They, too, maintained their basic cultural values though exposed to peoples far different from themselves.

Puritan New England's internal development was not unconnected to its relationship to both Indians within the region, and French and Indians to the north. Indian attacks near Salem, for instance, had heightened the anxieties that created the witchcraft episode. French assaults from Canada forced the Puritans to expend precious resources to secure frontier communities and to pay ransoms for captives. Within New England, native peoples also contested English expansion. Ideally, the English hoped to convert the Indians not only to Christianity, but to their way of life. Some were moved to Praying Towns, to transform them into English people. Despite the efforts at conversion, severe warfare broke out in New England as Indians were forced to protect themselves, their lands, and their ways of life.

## CULTURAL TRANSFORMATION: CONVERSION AND ADAPTATION

Conversion of Indians to Christianity was seen as solving a host of internal problems. Among other things, the Puritans perceived conversion as a way to make Indians less dangerous, while fulfilling their own mission as Christians. But conversion was a two-way street. Some English captives taken by Indians became "white Indians," choosing to remain with their new families even when given the chance to return. More common than conversion of Indians and English was cultural adaptation. Living in close proximity, Indians and English could not help but adapt from each other's cultures, even as they maintained most of their own cultural priorities.

### Conversion of Indians to Christianity

To most New England Puritans, the Indians were either devil-worshippers or people without religion. Intolerant to all forms of Christianity but their own, the Puritans were unlikely to tolerate Native American religion, when their practices and beliefs were so distant from Christianity. Many Puritans considered native religion dangerous, believing Indians did the devil's bidding, and thus must be removed from their presence so as not to pollute and corrupt their people. A few, however, thought the natives redeemable and called for their conversion to Christianity. Ironically, both natives and Europeans shared some religious concepts. Both believed in evil spirits that could be blamed for misfortune—a lost battle and the inability of a skilled individual to perform his skill; drought provided evidence of an improper fulfillment of ceremonies, indicating a people's shortcomings. Both sought other-worldly help to bring rain, cure the sick, and insure victory over enemies. But the Puritans would have seen no similarity. In their minds, Indians seeking help from their gods provided evidence of their superstitious nature. The key distinction for the Puritan was that they prayed to the true God and the Indians did not. If they needed further evidence for who was right and who was wrong, they looked at the large numbers of Indians succumbing to disease and concluded this an act of providence.

Some Indians felt the same way. Native communities wracked by sickness often turned to the Europeans and their God for help. The Puritans established Praying Towns for these refugees—an early form of the reservation. The Puritans used the Praying Towns not only to convert Indians to Christianity, but to instill into them English culture. They sought to alter Indian gender roles. Male Praying Indians were required to take up farming instead of hunting. If Indian men worked the plow, they would no longer require large hunting preserves, which could be turned over to the Europeans. Ending Indian mobility—confining them to one place—meant they could more easily be punished for misbehavior. The Puritans also induced male Praying Indians to cut their long hair. The cutting of hair, an Indian symbol of pride and individuality, presumably would reduce the Indians to humility, so that they could more easily accept Christ as their savior. Traditional Indian clothing was replaced with English clothing. If Indians looked and acted English, they ostensibly would be more familiar and less dangerous.

The Praying Towns were largely failures. The Puritans made little real effort to instill religious beliefs, and when they tried they expected the natives to make a complete religious and cultural transformation. Most natives interested in Christianity preferred to graft Christian beliefs onto their own. They also resented their tutors' racism and methods of discipline. No matter how much they accommodated to Puritan demands, they never would be treated as English. The Praying Indians saw little Christian spirit in the people who bore the message.

In comparison, the Catholic missionaries in neighboring New France had greater, though still limited success. When the reserve system failed in Canada, the priests went to live with the Indians, learn their languages, and attempted to alter only what they considered must be changed in Indian culture and religion: polygamy and certain burial practices, while trying to convince their charges to accept baptism and marriage as a sacrament. The priests' dress and manners set them apart as holy men who could appear interested in only the Indians' welfare and spirituality. Nevertheless, cultural arrogance and ignorance of Indian life marred their effectiveness. But as disease and warfare reduced native numbers, many did find comfort in the Church, and if nothing else, the Catholic missionaries succeeded in building strong political alliances between Indians and French.

### Learning from and Converting to Native Ways of Life

Despite New Englanders fear of Indians and their culture, they, like other Europeans, learned a great deal from native peoples. Europeans adopted native techniques of warfare—to move in single file, to hide behind brush, to travel on snowshoes, and to not meet the enemy in battle in open fields. They even adopted the native practice of scalping, as colonial governments offered bounties for the scalps of enemy Indians and French, including women and children, and then proudly displayed these scalps in their towns. Medicines were readily adapted so that almost 300 native remedies entered the European pharmacopeias. Indian behavior and lifestyle provided a model, often condemned, but nevertheless incorporated into Puritan life. Indian child-rearing practices were widely criticized for their leniency, but then adopted by Europeans. Native mobility was railed against as improper, but Puritans chafing under their own restrictions to reside in towns copied the Indians and moved to their farmland or to the frontier to escape established society. The Indians' "freedom" came under special castigation, as Puritans interpreted Indians as disregarding the social bonds so necessary to a proper ordering of society. This, too, would becamed a hallmark of "American" society and is represented even today in the way Indians have been appropriated as symbols of American freedom and courage, notably as mascots for sports teams.

Whereas Puritans never fully accepted Indians who wished to become English, the Indians assimilated as equals English who wished to be Indians. Hundreds of Puritans became white Indians. Though most began as captives, some joined voluntarily. Most captives who chose to stay with Indians were women or children, though adult males joined as well. To effect their conversion, captives ran through a gauntlet with Indians on either side of them, where they were struck by sticks, thorny brushes, and hands, to beat their culture out of them. Afterwards they were showered with gifts of food and clothing and given new names, receiving complete freedom in the community. Many were given new identities, replacing someone previously lost, and no position in Indian society lay unopened to them. Visitors often noted that they could not tell the white Indians from the others. White Indians stayed with the Indians for a variety of reasons—the kinships they established, the freedoms they enjoyed, and most notably, they welcomed the community bonds idealized in Puritan New England but rarely achieved.

It galled the English to have their people leave them. For instance, Connecticut provided a two-year imprisonment for anyone who lived with Indians. The English could not accept that their own people might find Indian society superior to their own—which would have forced them to question their lives, their societies, and their relations with Indians. Instead, they believed that white Indians had lost their minds: insanity must have led them to become Indians. At gunpoint and chained, when they could, the English forced the white Indians to return to English society—to save them from themselves. But the bonds remained and it was not unusual for their Indian families and friends to visit them.

## DEBASING OTHERS: SLAVERY AND WARFARE

The exclusiveness of their religion and culture made it difficult ideologically and culturally for Puritans to tolerate outsiders and alternative ways of life. Quakers, for instance, were barred entry into Massachusetts, their evangelical zeal seen as especially threatening to the religious life of the colony. As soon as they arrived, they were placed on ships and returned to England, but when they kept coming several were hung as examples to deter others. Indians posed greater problems, as they already lived in the region in great numbers, and possessed valuable land that the settlers desired. As in other colonial regions, the Puritans enslaved Indians, despite some possessing moral quandaries against slavery. Even after laws were passed barring Indian slavery, authorities skirted the legislation. African slavery, too, played a significant role in the region, as New England merchants avidly participated in the international slave trade by carrying slaves from one colonial region to another, and eventually opening a direct trade with Africa. Though only relatively small numbers of Africans were held as slaves in New England, their presence was visible enough that the Puritans wrestled with the meaning of having Africans in their communities and worried about them becoming rebels.

## Enslavement of Indians: Victims of War

In the 17th century, New England English outright enslaved over 1,200 natives of the region and subjected thousands more to limited periods of servitude that often extended into lifelong slavery. Until the end of the century, most Indian slaves comprised captives taken in war. Afterwards, colonial governments and courts condemned native "criminals" to slavery, and colonists purchased Indian slaves from other regions, most notably from South Carolina, where so many Indians were captured.

The Puritans rationalized enslavement of captives, as did other English, as the just deserts of prisoners taken in war. Yet European prisoners received only finite terms for their bondage, while natives were ordinarily committed to lifelong slavery, and, importantly, their children inherited their status. Moreover, European war prisoners serving periods of bondage were entirely male, while Indian prisoners included women and children. Roger Williams was one of the few to question enslavement of native women and children, since they were not combatants taken in war, but even he acquiesced to its necessity as a war measure and administered the public sale of captives.

Plymouth, in particular, engaged in enslaving native peoples. Children of "friendly" Indians were forcibly removed from their parents and "apprenticed" to English families, and hundreds were exported to Spain, Jamaica, and elsewhere. One ship alone, during King Philip's War (1675–1676), took 178 captives to Cadiz, Spain. Plymouth and other Puritan colonies did sometimes try to protect friendly Indians from enslavement by "manstealers"—but not always successfully.

Rationale for enslaving war captives was a slippery slope. In King Philip's War (discussed later), many Puritans declared that the Indians were not foreign, but rather subjects of the government. Therefore, governments and colonists declared them rebels committing treason—providing another rationale for punishment by enslavement. Governments then allotted slave captives to soldiers as a reward for service.

## Enslavement of Indians: By Court and Decree

With the end of King Philip's War, the Indians of southern New England could no longer be enslaved as prisoners of war, but this rationale continued in the northern reaches of the region. In Maine, Richard Waldron took over 200 Wampanoags and Penncacocks prisoner, though they arrived at his trading post under an offer of amnesty. The government in England complained to the New England governments about their laws and practices enslaving native peoples, particularly fearing renewal of warfare on the northern frontier. The King's Council occasionally ordered the release of Indian slaves taken in war. The French in Canada used the threat of English slaving as a way to gain the alliance of northern natives. Northern natives also responded to English slaving by taking English hostages, who were then either ransomed, or, if they chose to stay, incorporated into their groups.

As in other English areas, many New Englanders believed it reprehensible to deny freeborn people their freedom—they rationalized keeping Africans as slaves because they arrived in America as slaves or had been born into slavery. New England colonies thus banned the enslavement of Indians at various times, but the laws were constantly amended to allow its continuance. Rhode Island, for instance, banned Indian slavery in the colony in 1676 except for debt, for bringing up their children, and for export to other colonies. The legislature then allowed enslavement for up to 9 years, later amended to 30 years. In other words, the laws did almost nothing to bar enslavement of Indians, which was typical throughout the English colonies. In 18th-century New England, many Indians who became slaves did so through court action. Justices committed Indians to a life of servitude for crimes or failure to pay debts. For instance, in 1689–1690 one county court in Massachusetts condemned eight Indians for periods of servitude ranging from 6 months to 30 years—the length of the latter indeed a sentence of lifelong slavery. (The six-month sentence was punishment for theft of a handkerchief!) Although many court sentences were for limited periods of service, the Indians were often sold to other colonies and thus into perpetual slavery. The sale of Indian slaves became so common in New England that some colonists specialized in the business.

## Enslavement of Africans

Indian laborers, whether indentured servants or slaves, were classified as personal property, the same status as African slaves. Just as skin color became associated with slavery for Africans and their descendants, the same held true for Native Americans, many of whom became classified in legal records as black or mulatto. In 18th-century New England, Indian slaves could be found in both countryside and urban areas, as farm laborers, domestics, and skilled and semi-skilled workers. On the eve of the American Revolution, although free Indians labored in the region, from one-third to half of the native population in New England worked as slaves or indentured servants.

African slavery was not as widespread in New England as in other colonial regions, but it was ubiquitous nonetheless. Although some slaveholders possessed as many as 20 or 30 slaves, for the most part, slaves were dispersed in the countryside and towns in smaller numbers and thus worked in close contact with their masters. In New England seaports, African slaves were most clearly visible, as one-third of all Massachusetts slaves resided in Boston, and the same proportion of African slaves in New Hampshire lived in Portsmouth. Urban families employed slaves as domestics and symbols of status, while artisans purchased Africans to work alongside them in trades as blacksmiths, coopers, carpenters, masons, and shipyard workers. In these urban environments, African slaves socialized in taverns and back alleys with each other (and with Europeans and Indians), and they were not as isolated from other Africans as in rural areas.

The engagement of New Englanders in the African slave trade undoubtedly contributed to the growth of African slavery in New England. The region's merchants shipped most of their slave cargoes from Africa to the West Indies or the southern mainland colonies, but brought a small portion of those they transported to New England. By 1720, there were approximately 4,000 African slaves in New England—less than a quarter of the number of African slaves in Maryland, and about 70% of New York's total. Thirty years later, the number of African slaves in New England increased to nearly 10,000—almost as many as in New York, and more than a quarter of Maryland's slave population.

By the 1720s, many New England ministers began the call for conversion of their African slaves. In Boston, the leading Puritan cleric, Cotton Mather, a slaveholder, delivered and published sermons urging his co-religionists to baptize, conduct slave marriages, and otherwise include the African population in their churches. (Massachusetts became one of the only English colonies to legalize slave marriages—the Puritans wanted to prevent sinful sexual liaisons among their slaves.) When one of Mather's own slaves, Oneismus, taught his master inoculation as a method to prevent small pox, a raging debate spread through Boston and into the Atlantic world about not only inoculation, but the expediency of gaining practical information from Africans. Despite virulent opposition, particularly from the medical community, inoculation won the day and thousands, if not millions of lives were saved from small pox in the Atlantic world. In the aftermath, in America and Great Britain, more attention was paid to Africans by Europeans as not just potential slaves, but as humans who possessed valuable knowledge and souls. By the 1730s, growing efforts were made to convert Africans to Christianity as the English and other Europeans increasingly recognized their humanity.

## PURITAN–INDIAN WARFARE

No discussion of New England would be complete without an assessment of its militarism. Some historians have downplayed New England's military nature by arguing that the region lacked a warrior culture, as the Puritans did not highly value or reward military service. This assessment overlooks the military experience that key Puritan leaders attained in Europe and employed in the colonies. These historians also contend that New England's military activities were largely defensive, and mostly a response to threats posed by the French and allied Indians to the north. It is true that the Puritans did not create a substantial class of professional soldiers, but their militias—virtually all adult males aged 16 to 60 had to serve—and provisional armies raised and frequently used for specific military actions, insured that Puritan New England could not only protect itself, but greatly expand its land base against Indians and French and actively participate in the imperial wars of the late 17th and 18th centuries. Invasions of French Canada, for instance, were often wildly popular in New England and usually had no problem obtaining thousands of volunteers. Within the region, wars against Indians, though sometimes unwelcomed because of the danger they risked to lives and property, were prosecuted aggressively and lethally. The Puritans had few qualms about using military force to achieve their ends.

### King Philip's War (1675–1676)

As so often was the case in early America, trade disagreements, the European desire for Indian land, and cultural myopia precipitated wars between the natives and the newcomers. Enslavement of Indians, if not always a source of conflict, was certainly a frequent consequence. A case in point: in 1675 one of the bloodiest wars in American history broke out, King Philip's War, a watershed event that devastated the Indians of southern New England and lead to English dominance of the region. In its basic patterns, this conflict appears like so many others. Natives responded to long-term grievances and provocations by attacking the Europeans in a quest to preserve their families and land; Indians displayed great ability to resist and overpower Europeans, who often had to rely on other Indians to protect them. As with the almost simultaneous Virginia War with Indians initiated by Nathaniel Bacon, the New England English had little luck locating the enemy. Frustrated, they attacked Indians who had little or nothing to do with the conflict. Indian men, women, and children were mercilessly killed or turned into slaves. This violent venting of military impotence did nothing in the war against one's enemies—the English were forced to enlist other natives to do their bidding.

King Philip's War united the colonies of Massachusetts, Connecticut, Plymouth, and Rhode Island against many of the native peoples of southern New England. The war's background: Indian resentment of steady growth and expansion of colonial settlements. As English power grew, so did trade abuses and arrogance. The Wampanoag, who for more than a generation had been Plymouth's chief ally, found their complaints unheeded. They reminded the colonists that "when the English first came, the king's father [Massassoit] was a great man, and the English as a little child; he constrained other Indians from wronging the English, and gave them corn and showed them how to plant . . . and let them have a hundred times more land than now the king had for his own people." In the late 1660s, Massassoit's son Metacom (also known as King Philip) maneuvered to strengthen the Wampanoag position vis-à-vis other natives in the region, but he was humiliated by the English who forced him to pay heavy fines, which included the loss of land for disturbing the peace. Metacom tirelessly worked to effect an alliance against the English and, believing he had succeeded, attacked Plymouth in 1675. Though some natives joined him, others, notably the Mohegan, Niantic, and many Praying Indians, sided with the English. Although outnumbered by the English and their allies, the Wampanoag successfully fled and attracted additional natives to their side.

The war moved to the Connecticut River Valley in central Massachusetts, where Metacom's forces won a series of victories assaulting English towns with the English abandoning additional settlements. In early September, Northfield (Massachusetts) was taken and the Indians moved against Pocumtuck (later renamed Deerfield), which possessed more than 3,000 bushels of much-needed corn for feeding colonists desperately short of provisions. An English force of 50 soldiers and 15 "teamsters" was sent to retrieve the corn from Pocumtuck's fields. A combined force of Wampanoags, Pocumtucks, and Nipmucks annihilated the English, killing virtually every man, leading to further abandonment of the Connecticut River Valley by the English.

Unable to strike their enemies, the English raised a force of over 1,000, with Pequot and Mohegan allies, to strike against the powerful Narragansett, whom they accused of shielding Wampanoags. With the help of a Narragansett prisoner, they located a palisaded Narragansett fort in the Great Swamp (Rhode Island). Although the English suffered heavy casualties, about 20% of their force, they killed from 300 to 1,000 warriors and set fire to the wigwams burning to death hundreds of women and children. Surviving Narragansetts continued the war but eventually abandoned their ancient homes and migrated northward joining other native groups.

The war wound down as natives faced starvation from having their corn stocks burned, many fields having been left unplanted the previous year. Connecticut succeeded at maintaining peace with many of its native neighbors, allowing the Puritans to focus their efforts on Massachusetts, which bore the brunt of hostilities. Various Indian groups negotiated truces, but many were killed or enslaved. From the west, the Iroquois came to the Puritans' rescue and helped defeat the Wampanoag and allied peoples, the survivors forced to abandon their lands with many incorporated by the Iroquois. In the east, the English continued to capture Indians, many of whom they sold into slavery in the West Indies, though some remained slaves in New England. The war's end in 1676 meant nearly total English control of southern New England, the death and removal of most of the native inhabitants, and casualty estimates of from 10% to 25% of the total native population. The English had high losses as well. Dozens of towns had been abandoned, and an estimated one in ten adult English males lost their lives in the conflict. New England conflicts with Amerindians did not end: they moved to the northern frontier.

## Abenaki and Northern New England

The natives of Northern New England inhabited a dangerous frontier between the English and French. Referred to by the English as the "Eastern Indians," most were Abenaki, separate groups of people who occupied lands from modern-day Maine to Vermont, and north into Quebec. The Abenaki had contacts with Europeans (probably fishermen) even before the explorer Verrazano encountered them in 1524. The French in Canada then established good relations with the Abenaki prior to English settlement in North America; the English kidnapped some Abenaki during the period of first contact, and relations remained hostile through the colonial era.

The Abenaki separated French and English settlements in Acadia, an important area contested by the imperial powers. This large Atlantic coastal region included Nova Scotia, New Brunswick, the Prince Edward Islands, and portions of Quebec and Maine. England and France claimed overlapping portions of the region, which gave access to the rich fisheries of the northern Atlantic. Warfare in Acadia occurred sporadically, sometimes continuously, and often heavily as French and English struggled for control of the region beginning in the late 17th century.

French–Abenaki forces took the English fort at Pemaquid in 1689 on the Maine coast. New Englanders countered with an assault on French Port Royal, the following year, which netted much plunder but no change in the status quo. Another British attack by sea in 1707 ended disastrously, as did a subsequent assault in 1710. Finally, the English seized Port Royal in 1711 forcing a French surrender. France then ceded Acadia to the English at the Treaty of Utrecht (1713), but English power remained severely limited as the Abenakis and Micmacs had no reason to accept English claims. Even as England and France remained at peace, Abenaki conflicts persisted with New England, with the Abenaki receiving support from the French. The eastern Abenaki were buttressed by missionaries such as Sebastien Rale who converted Abenaki and maintained their alliance with the French. Rale had served in the Illinois Country and then at Quebec before receiving an assignment at the Abenaki settlement of Norridgewock on the Kennebec River in Maine. In 30 years among the Abenaki, he put together an Abenaki dictionary and was accused by the English of sending Indians against their settlements. In 1724, the English destroyed Norridgewock, killing Rale and about 80 Abenaki. Hostilities continued between the English and Abenaki, with many of the latter abandoning the region by moving west and north, where they remained allies of the French. Others stayed in Acadia and helped keep the English presence from expanding. Although a stalemate of sorts set in on the northern frontier between the English and French, who officially remained at peace until the 1740s, hostilities simmered as both powers and their native allies sought to secure themselves before the inevitable resumption of full-scale warfare.

## Conclusion

New England Indians faced many challenges in 1670. Although the impact of European diseases had declined, the population growth of settlers and the alteration of environmental conditions threatened their land base, especially hunting lands. Many native peoples in the southern portion of the region had been killed in King Philip's War, put into slavery, or otherwise removed or fled from the region. Attempts at assimilation through conversion to Christianity and the English way of life had also failed. Natives in northern New England found themselves on the front lines between the French and English. Though affected by the imperial and colonial wars that began at the end of the 17th century, they still retained much of their military power and their lands in 1730. The renewal of imperial warfare in the mid-1740s and 1750s would undermine their position, especially with the defeat of the French in the 1760s, as there would be no European power to check English pretensions in the area.

Most New England Puritans did not view themselves as aggressors against the native population, though some questioned the dominant ethos of racism and hostility towards Indians. Instead, the Puritans perceived themselves as victims of French-allied Indian raids and believed they must protect themselves from Indian cultural influences, which they associated with the devil. Half-hearted attempts to convert Indians were subsumed by racism, and the belief that Indians were not entitled to their land, which God had intended for his chosen people—themselves. The debasement of Indian peoples justified their enslavement. Even though some Puritans held qualms about slavery, especially Indian enslavement, and the institution of slavery never became the major form of labor that it did elsewhere in the colonial world, where plantation agricultural and intensive mining promoted reliance on unfree labor, the Puritans actively engaged in the regional and international slave trades and kept significant numbers of Indians and Africans as slaves. Local authorities disregarded their own laws to prevent Indian enslavement and sentenced large numbers of Indians to a life of slavery.

Despite their racism, the Puritans could not but be influenced by Indians. Though the Puritans condemned Indian child-rearing practices, mobility, and military tactics, they adapted these and other things from Indian peoples. The Puritans learned hundreds of medical treatments from New England natives, borrowed their technology, as in fishing, clearing land, and use of snowshoes, and even adapted from their language an array of nouns to describe their landscape. By the onset of the 18th century, Puritan parent–child relations reflected the more "affectionate" bond that was visible in Indian societies. Puritan house-holders rejected the restrictions that previously bound them to live in propin-quity to one another and celebrated the freedom to move out of town centers to their land, a freedom of movement in Indian society they earlier had con-demned. Puritans adopted the "skulking" way of war, practiced and promoted scalping, and otherwise incorporated Indian military tactics as their own.

The New England of 1730 was much different than that of 1670. The English had become the dominant force in the region, transforming the envi-ronment, building hundreds of towns, and vastly reducing the native presence in the more arable southern portion of the region. But the English themselves had changed. Demographic growth, the environment, and interactions with na-tive peoples had altered the culture of the English colonists. A century had passed since John Winthrop arrived in Massachusetts. If he had lived in 1730, Winthrop would have been amazed at the growth of Puritan settlements, both spatially and demographically.

Certainly there was no precedent in England for such rapid population growth. Demographic growth in England was roughly 8% to 10% from 1630 to 1730, while New England's population quadrupled from just 1670 to 1730, mostly owing to natural increase. We can also assume that Winthrop would have been greatly disappointed at the decline in religiosity as he understood it. The Puritans them-selves bewailed the loss. They called it declension—a decline in religious sensibilities and fervor. The vision of the founders to create a New Jerusalem had all but vanished. The churches had lost their dynamism. The people had become pre-occupied with worldly things. Winthrop would have rued that indeed they had forgotten his warning to not let themselves be "possessed" by the land. From his vantage point, he might very well have concluded that the devil had won, or was winning the bat-tle. Winthrop's people had become like the Indians—living freely and enjoying Eden's abundance with little thought as to God's purpose for them.

# DOCUMENTS

## 8.1. The Background for King Philip's War

*John Easton, a Rhode Island Quaker, published an account of the early stages of King Philip's War, in which he largely blamed the colonists for hostilities. Easton's view contrasts with the accounts produced by Puritans in Massachusetts, which blamed savage, self-interested Indians for the onset of the war. In the following excerpt, Easton reports on some of the background to the conflict, including Indian grievances against the colonists. What was the nature of Indian grievances against the English? (In text yᵗ altered to that, i to j, u to v, and f to oug when appropriate.)*

In the Winter in the Year 1674, an Indian was found dead, and by a Coroner's Inquest of Plimouth Colony judged murdered. He was found dead in a Hole thro Ice broken in a Pond with his Gun and sum Foulls by him.

*(Continued)*

Sum English suposed him thrown in, sum Indians that I judged intelegabell and impartiall in ye Case did think he fell in and was so drouned, and that the Ies did hurt his Throat, as the English said it was cut; but acnoledge that sumetimes naty Indians wold kill others but not as ever they herd to obscuer as if the dead Indian was not murdered. The dead Indian was caled Sansimun and a Christian that could read and write. Report was he was a bad Man, that King Philip got him to write his Will, and he made the Writing for a great Part of the Land to be his, but read as if it had bin as Philip wrote; But it came to be known, and then he run away from him.

Now one Indian informed that three Indians had murdered him, and sheued a Coat that he said thay gave him to conseall them. The Indians report that the Informer had playd away his Coate, and these Men sent him ye Coate, and after demanded Pay, and he not to pay, so acused them, and knoing that it wold pleas the English so to think him a beter Christian, and the Reporte came that the three Indians had confesed and acused Philip so to imploy them, and that ye English wold hang Philip; so the Indians wear afraid, and reported that the English had flatred them (or by threats) to bely Philip that thay might kill him to have his Land, and that if Philip had dun it, it was ther Law so to execute home there Kings judged deserved it, that he had no Case to hide it.

So Philip kept his Men in Armes. Plimoth Governer required him to disband his Men, and informed him his Jealousy was false. Philip answered he would do no Harm, and thanked the Governer for his Information.

The three Indians wer hunge, to the last denied the Fact; but one broke the Halter as it is reported, than desired to be sayed, and so was a littell while, then confessed they three had dun the Fact; and then he was hanged. And it was reported Sausimun before his death had informed of the Indian Plot, and that if the Indians knew it they wold kill him, and that the Hethen might destroy the English for their Wickedness, as God had permitted the Heathen to destroy the Israellites of olde. So the English wear afraid and Philip was afraid, and both incresed in Arems. But for four Yeares Time, Reports and Jealosys of War had bin veri frequent, that we did not think that now a War was breaking forth; but about a Week before it did, we had Case to think it wold. Then to indever to prevent it, we sent a Man to Philip, that if he wold cum to the Fery we wold cum over to speke with him. . . .

Thay said thay had bine the first in doing Good to the English, and the English the first in doing Rong; said when the English first came, their King's Father was as a great Man, and the English as a littell Child; he constrained other Indians from ronging the English, and gave them Corn and showed them how to plant, and was free to do them ani Good, and had let them have a 100 Times more Land than now the King had for his own Peopell. But ther King's Brother, when he was King, came miserably to dy by being forced to Court, as they judge poysoned. And another Greavance was, if 20 of there onest Indians testfied that a Englishman had dun them Rong, it was as nothing; and if but one of their worst Indians testified against any Indian or ther King, when it pleased the

English it was sufitiant. Another Grievance was, when their King sold Land, the English wold say, it was more than they agreed to, and a Writing must be prove against all them, and sum of their Kings had dun Rong to sell so much. He left his Peopell none, and sum being given to Drunknes the English made them drunk and then cheated them in Bargains. . . . Another Grievance, the English Catell and Horses still incresed; that when thay removed 30 Mill from where English had ani thing to do, thay could not kepe ther Corn from being spoyled, thay never being used to fence, and thought when the English bought Land of them thay wold have kept their Catell upon ther owne Land. . . .

After the English Army, without our Consent or informing us, came into our Colony, brought the Naroganset Indians to Articles of Agreement to them. Philip being flead, about a 150 Indians came in to a Plimouth Garrison volentarley. Plimouth Authority sould all for Slafes (but about six of them) to be carried out of the Country. It is true the Indians genaraly are very barbarous Peopell but in this War I have not heard of their tormenting ani, but

that the English Army cote an old Indian and tormented him. He was well knone to have bine a long Time a veri decrepid and harmless Indian. . . .

I having often informed the Indians that English Men wold not begin a War, otherwise it was brutish so to do. I am sorry so the Indians have Case to think me desaitfull, for the English thus began the War with the Narogansets. . . . The Army first take all those Prisoners then fell upon Indian Houses, burned them and killed sum Men. The War [began] without Proclamation, and sum of our Peopell did not kno the English had begun Mischief to Indians. . . .

But I am confident it wold be best for the English and Indians that a Peas wear made upone [h]onest Terems, for each to have a dew Propriety and to enjoy it without Opretion or usurpation by one to the other, but the English dear not trust the Indian's Promises, nether the Indians to the Englishes Promises; and each have gret Case therefor.

Source: John Easton, *A True Relation of What I kno & of Reports & My Understanding Concerning the Begining & Progress of the War Now Between the English and the Indians* (1675).

## 8.2. Mary Rowlandson's Captivity Among the Narragansett

*Mary Rowlandson was captured during King Philip's War and spent six weeks as a captive of the Narragansett. After she was redeemed, she wrote an account of her ordeal that became hugely famous, and a model for future accounts by redeemed captives: the captive must put their faith in God. How did the Indians treat Rowlandson during her captivity? How did she view her captors?*

On the tenth of February 1675, came the Indians with great numbers upon Lancaster: their first coming was about sunrising; hearing the noise of some

guns, we looked out; several houses were burning, and the smoke ascending to heaven. There were five persons taken in one house; the father, and the

*(Continued)*

mother and a sucking child, they knocked on the head; the other two they took and carried away alive. There were two others, who being out of their garrison upon some occasion were set upon; one was knocked on the head, the other escaped; another there was who running along was shot and wounded, and fell down; he begged of them his life, promising them money (as they told me) but they would not hearken to him but knocked him in head, and stripped him naked, and split open his bowels. Another, seeing many of the Indians about his barn, ventured and went out, but was quickly shot down. There were three others belonging to the same garrison who were killed; the Indians getting up upon the roof of the barn, had advantage to shoot down upon them over their fortification. Thus these murderous wretches went on, burning, and destroying before them.

At length they came and beset our own house, and quickly it was the dolefulest day that ever mine eyes saw. The house stood upon the edge of a hill; some of the Indians got behind the hill, others into the barn, and others behind anthathing that could shelter them; from all which places they shot against the house, so that the bullets seemed to fly like hail; and quickly they wounded one man among us, then another, and then a third. About two hours (according to my observation, in that amazing time) they had been about the house before they prevailed to fire it (which they did with flax and hemp, which they brought out of the barn, and there being no defense about the house, only two flankers at two opposite corners and one of them not finished); they fired it once and one

ventured out and quenched it, but they quickly fired it again, and that took. Now is the dreadful hour come, that I have often heard of (in time of war, as it was the case of others), but now mine eyes see it. Some in our house were fighting for their lives, others wallowing in their blood, the house on fire over our heads, and the bloody heathen ready to knock us on the head, if we stirred out. Now might we hear mothers and children crying out for themselves, and one another, "Lord, what shall we do?"...

I had often before this said that if the Indians should come, I should choose rather to be killed by them than taken alive, but when it came to the trial my mind changed; their glittering weapons so daunted my spirit, that I chose rather to go along with those (as I may say) ravenous beasts, than that moment to end my days; and that I may the better declare what happened to me during that grievous captivity, I shall particularly speak of the several removes we had up and down the wilderness.

**The First Remove**

Now away we must go with those barbarous creatures, with our bodies wounded and bleeding, and our hearts no less than our bodies. About a mile we went that night, up upon a hill within sight of the town, where they intended to lodge. There was hard by a vacant house (deserted by the English before, for fear of the Indians). I asked them whether I might not lodge in the house that night, to which they answered, "What, will you love English men still?" This was the dolefulest night that ever my eyes saw. Oh the roaring, and singing and dancing, and yelling of those black creatures in the night, which made the place a lively resemblance of hell. And as miserable was the waste that was there made of horses, cattle, sheep, swine, calves, lambs, roasting pigs, and fowl (which they had plundered in the town), some roasting, some lying and burning, and some boiling to feed our merciless enemies; who were joyful enough, though we were disconsolate. To add to the dolefulness of the former day, and the dismalness of the present night, my thoughts ran upon my losses and sad bereaved condition. All was gone, my husband gone (at least separated from me, he being in the Bay; and to add to my grief, the Indians told me they would kill him as he came homeward), my children gone, my relations and friends gone, our house and home and all our comforts—within door and without—all was gone (except my life), and I knew not but the next moment that might go too. There remained nothing to me but one poor wounded babe, and it seemed at present worse than death that it was in such a pitiful condition, bespeaking compassion, and I had no refreshing for it, nor suitable things to revive it. Little do many think what is the savageness and brutishness of this barbarous enemy, Ay, even those that seem to profess more than others among them, when the English have fallen into their hands.

But I was fain to go and look after something to satisfy my hunger, and going among the wigwams, I went into one and there found a squaw who showed herself very kind to me, and gave me a piece of bear. I put it into my pocket, and came home, but could not find an opportunity to broil it, for fear they would get it from me, and there it lay all that day and night in my stinking pocket. In the morning I went to the same squaw, who had a kettle of ground nuts boiling. I asked her to let me boil my piece of bear in her kettle, which she did, and gave me some ground nuts to eat with it: and I cannot but think how pleasant it was to me. I have sometime seen bear baked very handsomely among the English, and some like it, but the thought that it was bear made me tremble. But now that was savory to me that one would think was enough to turn the stomach of a brute creature.

One bitter cold day I could find no room to sit down before the fire. I went out, and could not tell what to do, but I went in to another wigwam, where they were also sitting round the fire, but the squaw laid a skin for me, and bid me sit down, and gave me some ground nuts, and bade me come again; and told me they would buy me, if they were able, and yet these were strangers to me that I never saw before.

**The Tenth Remove**

That day a small part of the company removed about three-quarters of a mile, intending further the next day. When they came to the place where they intended to lodge, and had pitched their wigwams, being hungry, I went again back to the place we were before at, to get something to eat, being encouraged by the squaw's kindness, who bade me come again. When I was there, there came an

*(Continued)*

Indian to look after me, who when he had found me, kicked me all along. I went home and found venison roasting that night, but they would not give me one bit of it. Sometimes I met with favor, and sometimes with nothing but frowns. . . .

### The Twelfth Remove

It was upon a Sabbath-day-morning, that they prepared for their travel. This morning I asked my master whether he would sell me to my husband. He answered me "Nux," which did much rejoice my spirit. My mistress, before we went, was gone to the burial of a papoose, and returning, she found me sitting and reading in my Bible; she snatched it hastily out of my hand, and threw it out of doors. I ran out and catched it up, and put it into my pocket, and never let her see it afterward. Then they packed up their things to be gone, and gave me my load. I complained it was too heavy, whereupon she gave me a slap in the face, and bade me go; I lifted up my heart to God, hoping the redemption was not far off; and the rather because their insolency grew worse and worse.

### The Thirteenth Remove

Instead of going toward the Bay, which was that I desired, I must go with them five or six miles down the river into a mighty thicket of brush; where we abode almost a fortnight. Here one asked me to make a shirt for her papoose, for which she gave me a mess of broth, which was thickened with meal made of the bark of a tree, and to make it the better, she had put into it about a handful of peas, and a few roasted ground nuts. I had not seen my son a pretty while, and here was an Indian of whom I made inquiry after him, and asked him when he saw him. He answered me that such a time his master roasted him, and that himself did eat a piece of him, as big as his two fingers, and that he was very good meat. But the Lord upheld my Spirit, under this discouragement; and I considered their horrible addictedness to lying, and that there is not one of them that makes the least conscience of speaking of truth. In this place, on a cold night, as I lay by the fire, I removed a stick that kept the heat from me. A squaw moved it down again, at which I looked up, and she threw a handful of ashes in mine eyes. I thought I should have been quite blinded, and have never seen more, but lying down, the water run out of my eyes, and carried the dirt with it, that by the morning I recovered my sight again. Yet upon this, and the like occasions, I hope it is not too much to say with Job, "Have pity upon me, O ye my Friends, for the Hand of the Lord has touched me." . . .

That night they bade me go out of the wigwam again. My mistress's papoose was sick, and it died that night, and there was one benefit in it—that there was more room. I went to a wigwam, and they bade me come in, and gave me a skin to lie upon, and a mess of venison and ground nuts, which was a choice dish among them. On the morrow they buried the papoose, and afterward, both morning and evening, there came a company to mourn and howl with her; though I confess I could not much condole with them. Many sorrowful days I had in this place, often getting alone. "Like a crane, or a swallow, so did I chatter; I did mourn as a dove, mine eyes ail with looking upward. Oh, Lord, I am oppressed; undertake for me" (Isaiah 38.14).

Source: Mary Rowlandson, *The sovereignty and goodness of GOD, together with the faithfulness of his promises displayed, being a narrative of the captivity and restoration of Mrs. Mary Rowlandson, commended by her, to all that desires to know the Lord's doings to, and dealings with her* (1682).

## Bibliography

Axtell, James. *The Invasion Within: The Contest of Cultures in Colonial North America* (1985).

Berlin, Ira. *Many Thousands Gone: The First Two Centuries of Slavery in North America* (1998).

Calloway, Colin G. *The Western Abenakis of Vermont, 1600–1800: War, Migration, and the Survival of an Indian People* (1990).

Cogley, Richard W. *John Eliot's Mission to the Indians Before King Philip's War* (1999).

Eccles, W. J. *The Canadian Frontier: 1534–1760* (1969).

Greene, Lorenzo Johnston. *The Negro in Colonial New England, 1620–1776* (1942).

Jennings, Francis. *The Invasion of America: Indians, Colonialism, and the Cant of Conquest* (1975).

Kawashima, Yasuhide. *Igniting King Philip's War: The John Sassamon Murder Trial* (2001).

Leach, Douglas E. *The Northern Colonial Frontier, 1607–1763* (1966).

Lepore, Jill. *The Name of War: King Philip's War and the Origins of American Identity* (1998).

Lockridge, Kenneth A. *A New England Town: The First Hundred Years, Dedham, Massachusetts, 1636–1736* (1970).

Morrison, Kenneth M. *The Embattled Northeast: The Elusive Ideal of Alliance in Abenaki-Euramerican Relations* (1984).

Pierson, William Dillon. *Black Yankees: The Development of an Afro-American Subculture in Eighteenth-Century New England* (1988).

Reid, John G. *Acadia, Maine, and New Scotland: Marginal Colonies in the Seventeenth Century* (1981).

Silverman, David J. *Faith and Boundaries: Colonists, Christianity, and Community Among the Wampanoag Indians of Martha's Vineyard, 1600–1871* (2005).

Vaughan, Alden. *New England Frontier, 1620–1675* (1965).

# 9

# The Middle Colonies and the Wars for Empire, 1670–1730

## INTRODUCTION

The "Middle Colonies" refers to the English colonies on the Atlantic Coast between the New England and Chesapeake colonies: the modern-day states of New York, New Jersey, Pennsylvania, and Delaware. The first European colonizers to this area were the Dutch and Swedes (see chapter four). English conquest of New Netherland (1664), later renamed New York, paved the way for English colonization throughout the region. Despite English ownership, the Middle Colonies maintained the ethnic diversity they enjoyed under the Dutch: English settlers never comprised a majority, a characteristic the entire region maintained through the centuries. Scots, Scots-Irish, Dutch, and particularly Germans were among the many Europeans who lived in and migrated to the region. Family farms typified the countryside, with greater prosperity per capita than in New England, as many produced surpluses of wheat for sale to the burgeoning cities of New York and Philadelphia, which engaged in world trade that fostered thriving merchant and artisan communities. These two cities displayed great entrepreneurship and cosmopolitanism, and by the end of the colonial period stood at the forefront of economic, social, scientific, and political advancement in colonial America.

If the urban areas of the Middle Colonies along the Atlantic Coast were largely secure from foreign hostilities, the same was not true of their backcountries, particularly New York's. French power extended in a northern and western arc around the Iroquois and the Middle Colonies. French and allied Indian settlements stretched from southern Canada through the Great Lakes, with heavy concentration along the St. Lawrence Seaway. French traders, missionaries, soldiers, and settlers could also be found deep in the interior of the continent, well beyond the Mississippi River, while they also descended the Mississippi and traversed adjacent waterways in Illinois Country, Arkansas, and south all the way to the Gulf of Mexico. The contest between the French and English for control over inland territory and influence among native peoples insured that their disputes frequently would be violent, but France and England's wars for empire, which began in the late 17th century, magnified the conflicts and increased the scale of warfare, as European ships, men, and weaponry were sent to America to tip the scales in favor of one or the other. Nonetheless, both French and English pretensions to empire were held in check by the Iroquois. Middlemen in the fur trade between Europeans and Indians, the Iroquois wielded great military, diplomatic, and political power. Their influence ranged throughout eastern America. Although based in New York, Iroquois could be found raiding the Chickasaw in Mississippi, at the council fires of the Creek Indians in Georgia, trading furs in Montreal, or visiting the English crown in London. In many ways, the axis of French Canada–Iroquoia–English New York was the most important diplomatic axis on the North American continent, as the repercussions of relationships there reverberated for thousands of miles. French and English both realized that their success in the interior continent depended on their relations with the Iroquois. They worked diligently to accommodate or intimidate the Iroquois. The Iroquois practiced a similar diplomacy with their European and Indian neighbors. But the stakes were much higher for the Iroquois and their Indian neighbors than for the French and English. The latter could return to their mother countries or go to other colonies if they lost their land in America; the Indians did not enjoy that luxury.

If New York with its powerful Iroquois was the focal point for French and English competition over the interior continent, a far different situation existed to the south in Pennsylvania. Founded by pacifist English Quakers intent on avoiding war, Pennsylvania usually maintained harmonious relations with native peoples. Pennsylvania was able to avoid direct participation in the early wars of empire because New York separated them from New France. (This changed in the 1750s when the French entered western Pennsylvania.) Nevertheless, Pennsylvania's history offers valuable points for comparison with other English colonies. It provides an example of a persecuted religious group establishing a colony and not persecuting non-members. It evinces how Europeans building a colony intent on good relations with Indians could have much success, albeit there would be failures as well. And the colony prospered. It quickly developed a balanced economy between rural and urban areas, a large middle class, and an active civil and intellectual life in Philadelphia. The dynamism of Philadelphia, supported by strong hinterlands, would make it the most important city in the English mainland colonies.

## FROM NEW NETHERLAND TO NEW YORK

The transfer of the Middle Colonies from the Dutch to the English occurred during the second of three Anglo-Dutch wars fought in the third quarter of the 17th century. For a century before then, the Dutch and English had been natural allies as Protestant nations mutually struggling against Catholic Spain's military power, and using their formidable navies and privateers to attack and reduce the Spanish and Portuguese empires. By the 1650s, Spanish power had greatly declined at sea and the English and Dutch turned their canon on each other. Although not entirely apparent at the time, English victory marked their steady ascendancy to becoming the leading naval power in Europe, and their growing eminence as one of the world's foremost trading and manufacturing nations in the world.

Even less apparent was the significance of the English conquest of New Netherland in 1664, a colony of relatively minor economic value to the Dutch. Conquest allowed an uninterrupted territorial connection for the English mainland colonies along the Atlantic seaboard and the elimination of a powerful competitor for the inland fur trade, thus strengthening the English position with many groups of American Indians, especially the Iroquois. The agricultural wealth of the region attracted many new European migrants, whose prosperity led them to purchase English manufactured goods, making the Middle Colonies a valuable asset of the English empire.

### The Dominion of New England

Upon conquest of New Netherland, King Charles II gave New York to his brother, James, Duke of York. Initially, James permitted the New Yorkers a legislature, but after his accession to the throne in 1685, when New York became a royal colony, he changed his mind. The colony would be the sole mainland English colony without a legislature until permitted in 1691. During James's brief reign as King of England (1685–1688), he sent Edmund Andros to govern New York, New Jersey, and all of New England, whose charters he revoked, combining them into one large colony, the Dominion of New England.

Andros was a military man, and the unification of the colonies was designed in part to better organize them to counter French power in Canada. But James and his advisors also hoped to extend greater imperial control over the colonists. With little concern for colonists' interests or desires, Andros alienated a large proportion of the population. In New England, he ended the Puritan monopoly over religious life, prohibited town meetings, and brought into question the legitimacy of land titles. New York's commercial interests became irate when Andros shipped all the pubic records to Boston.

Dutch New Yorkers not only lost power in the transfer to English rule, but had to adjust to a new legal system, laws, and business practices. The Dutch in Albany were permitted to continue their fur trade operations, but now had to sell the furs in New York City, whose merchants held exclusive rights to the colony's export trade. Farmers on Long Island could no longer ship their wheat across Long Island Sound to

Connecticut—it had to go to New York City first. And nothing could be shipped to the Netherlands—which almost entirely altered import and export patterns, as well as financing and insurance.

When Dutchman William of Orange invaded England at the behest of many English and forced King James to flee in 1688, colonists in many English colonies responded by revolting against local rule. William became King of England and jointly ruled with his wife Mary Stuart, daughter of the deposed James. Most English supported the accession of William and Mary to the throne, as they believed James had intended to restore England to Catholicism and they opposed his attempts to undermine Parliamentary power. In the colonies, news of James's overthrow led colonists to stage their own revolutions against imperial officials. For instance, in Massachusetts, Governor Andros was imprisoned for a year as the Puritans negotiated with their new monarchs for the return of their charters. (It was at this time that Plymouth, which never had a charter, was put into Massachusetts.) In May 1689, colonists in New York rose against Andros's officials in Leisler's Rebellion.

The German Jacob Leisler held close ties with the Dutch community. When he seized power, he received opposition from James's appointees, but gained much popular support when the French posed a threat from the north. After a bloody French assault on the northern New York community of Schenectady, Leisler ordered the repression of all Catholics and convened an intercolonial meeting in New York—the first of its kind—to deal with the French threat. As preparations were made for an assault upon Canada, rioting broke out over taxation to support the expedition, which in the event ended disastrously. Growing opposition to Leisler, particularly from Puritan colonists, led to revolts against his rule. When an English fleet arrived in New York sent by William and Mary, Leisler refused to step down until the newly appointed governor arrived. Violence exploded in the city between Leisler's supporters and opponents. The new governor, Henry Sloughter, arrived in March 1691, arrested Leisler, and quickly had him convicted of treason and hanged. New York was left in disarray, as the bitterness over Leisler's quick trial and execution disrupted the colony for years. Although the English Parliament in 1695 overrode the New York Court's sentence of treason, which allowed Leisler's heirs to inherit his property, bitter factionalism remained in the colony for over 20 years, as the anti-Leislerians controlled the government, vindictively excluding their opponents from political power and the plums of government contracts.

Despite near-constant political problems, New York's economy grew, led by merchants who improved their share of intercolonial trade. This commerce revolved around the export of furs from Albany and wheat from the prospering counties around New York City. One advantage lay in their ability to export more than they imported, and the New Yorkers developed a profitable trade for Virginia tobacco, which they carried to England. When the fur trade declined, the New Yorkers turned to the production of small-scale manufacturing, but their strength remained in the carrying trade of other colonies' products. Particularly helpful, however, was the outbreak of wars between France and England, for the New Yorkers actively engaged in, and benefited from, privateering against French ships in the West Indies.

## Slavery in New York

Africans comprised a significant portion of the population and labor in colonial New York. The foundation for their presence began with the Dutch, who imported

Africans in large numbers to New Netherland. Many of the early Africans obtained freedom in the Dutch period, leading to the development of a free black community near the bowery on the southern end of Manhattan Island. Some earned freedom through their labor, but masters also freed slaves who accepted baptism into the Dutch Reformed Church. Most masters, however, refused to allow their slaves to convert to Christianity, so they would have no expectation of freedom, but many slaves pursued conversion anyway in the hope that their owners would experience pangs of conscience from keeping fellow Christians in bondage.

With the English conquest of New Netherland, New York continued as a slave society. Colonists tried to prevent the growth of the free black class, and the English government had to step in to protect those already free from persecution. American Indians were also enslaved by the New Yorkers, who purchased them from ships bringing captives taken from Spanish colonies. Occasionally, these Indians were liberated by the English government to appease the Spanish.

The African population of New York almost doubled from the Dutch conquest of 1664 to the end of the century. Nearly half of all Dutch males possessed slaves in New York City, and close to 40% of English males. Slaves were less prevalent among the city's French Huguenot and Jewish populations, as only 13% of the former and 2% of the latter owned slaves. Female slaves far outnumbered male slaves in the city, by almost 2 to 1, a ratio reversed in the countryside, making it difficult for Africans to establish families.

New York enacted slave codes at the beginning of the century to restrict and control African behavior. This led to increasingly violent resistance. On New Year's Day, 1712, a revolt began that resulted in brutal reprisals, as Africans, guilty or not, were shot and stabbed in the streets, and 18 executed by the courts. The governor, supported by the British government, pardoned others who had been convicted on flimsy testimony. Another set of laws were enacted in 1712 to contain the slave community and to prevent slaves from receiving freedom through emancipation. Any master who freed a slave had to provide a £200 bond for the freeman's good behavior and £20 yearly for his or her support. Thus, in 1713, according to the will of George Norton, his slave Sam was supposed to receive his freedom, £30, a slave, and Norton's butcher shop, where he had worked for many years. The executor, however, refused to provide the necessary £200 bond or to fulfill the will's stipulations and forced Sam to work for him. In 1717, Sam petitioned for release. The Board of Trade in London threatened the colony of New York that it would repeal the entire 1712 law unless it was amended. The New York government promised thereafter that slaves could be freed without bond if the master ensured that the emancipated would not live in poverty requiring public assistance. Since Sam's master was already deceased, a local joiner and a merchant stood bond for him.

The 1712 slave revolt did not deter New Yorkers from importing more slaves. By 1723, nearly 20% of the population of Manhattan and Kings County (Brooklyn) was African or African American, with the surrounding counties including those of eastern New Jersey, having slave populations from 10% to 17%. These percentages generally grew in the coming decades, though only in Kings County did African Americans become more than one-third of the population. The figures signify that New York and East New Jersey indeed had become slave colonies, as bondpeople provided the major source of labor in both city and countryside. Whether working on farms or in trades, as domestics or unskilled laborers, free New Yorkers relied heavily on New York's slave population.

# PENNSYLVANIA: WILLIAM PENN AND THE SOCIETY OF FRIENDS

The removal of the Dutch from New Netherland prepared the way for settlement by the English to the east and south of the Hudson River. Land grants were made in East and West Jersey, later to come together as New Jersey, and these attracted members of the Society of Friends, known commonly as Quakers, among others, who fled persecution in England. Difficulties with the proprietors of these tracts led William Penn to seek another refuge for the Quakers, which he received by charter for the colony of Pennsylvania in 1681.

## The Quakers in England

Penn's father was a highly regarded naval captain who had served the deposed Stuarts faithfully during the English Civil War (1649–1660). Forced to flee to Ireland with his family, the young Penn was greatly moved by a Quaker preacher, Thomas Lee, whom he heard speak in Dublin. Though Penn did not yet become a Quaker, his spiritual yearning led him to seek out and study a wide range of religions outside the Church of England. Oxford University later expelled him for refusing to attend Anglican services, and his father sent him abroad to continue his education, hoping he would abandon his dissenter tendencies. But Penn spent two years studying theology, returned to England to study law for a year, and then went to Ireland to run his father's business affairs. In Ireland, he again encountered Lee. At age 21, he decided to become a Quaker.

The Quakers faced intense persecution in England. Over 15,000 were imprisoned during the Restoration of the Stuart monarchy. Penn himself was jailed four times. The Quakers felt bound to preach the word of God effusively, thus their nickname, as they appeared to their critics to quake uncontrollably when illegally preaching in the streets. Their radicalism was both religious and social. All people possessed, they believed, the "Inner Light" from God, placing everyone on an equal spiritual footing. This contrasted with the Puritan belief that only the chosen few would benefit from God's grace, and it differed from the established Church of England, which required membership in their communion and the fulfillment of religious rituals. Quaker emphasis on spiritual equality led them to disregard the laws and customs of England, which divided people in a social hierarchy. They addressed all by the informal "thee" and "thou" and would not remove their caps before social betters, like judges, which resulted in imprisonment for contempt of court. They also faced imprisonment for not attending Anglican services, and refusing to swear judicial oaths, which they believed against biblical law.

In 1666, George Fox organized the Quakers into a religious movement, the Society of Friends, and his followers moved from individual displays of religious effusion to group and self-discipline. Zealotry for conversion was replaced by moderation and toleration. Since all possessed the Inner Light, the Quakers tolerated all religions. Conversion would be by example—or quiet means—rather than public challenges of the unconverted. Penn led the charge in promoting religious toleration in England. He published prolifically throughout his life. Frequently incarcerated, from prison he penned, *The Great Case of Liberty of Conscience*, and later *England's Great Interest*, both calling for an end to religious persecution.

In 1681, Penn used his father's connections to the Stuarts to receive a patent for a Quaker refuge in the New World—Pennsylvania—a tract of land nearly as large as England. Undoubtedly, the king viewed the colony as a way to rid the realm of these troublemakers. Penn was given sole ownership of the land and could establish any sort of government he wished. The English government retained the right to veto laws and to reverse court judgments.

## The New Utopia

Penn spent much time planning his new colony, intending to establish a utopia. Informed by years of deep study of political systems, and influenced by the radical republicanism of his day, he hoped to construct a model form of government. His initial "Frame of Government" included the protection of religious liberty, but rigid maintenance of the Sabbath. All adult male property-holders could vote or serve in government. The property requirements were low enough to allow about half of the adult males to vote—a larger percentage of political participation than in most colonies and in England. Penn revised his frame of government almost 20 times, and its final form received criticism from those who felt it was not "republican" enough by keeping too much power in his own hands and those of the elite. He also had made compromises in the dispersal of land. Settlers would receive adequate shares, but to raise money to defray the costs of colonization, Penn sold large tracts to speculators and private companies.

Penn published promotional tracts and hired agents to recruit settlers in Britain and on the European continent. By 1685, 8,000 Quakers migrated to his colony. In Pennsylvania, Penn set about establishing good relations with the native inhabitants, mostly Lenni Lenape (Delawares). Like many of his contemporaries, Penn believed the American Indians to be descendants of the Ten Lost Tribes of Israel, which made them seem more familiar than in actuality. Penn gave the Indians generous presents and payment for land, and settlement proceeded on friendly terms. Penn then chose a spot to begin settlement, which he called Philadelphia, the City of Brotherly Love, the first planned city in the English colonies. Streets were laid out on a grid pattern with tracts reserved for parks—the city was to represent the orderliness that Quakers hoped to bring to their personal lives.

Penn returned to England to protect his proprietorship from jealous interests that wished the crown to take control of the colony. He faced a host of unforeseen problems, including disputes with the Calvert family over the border between his colony and Maryland, and discontent from the lower three counties, included in his patent but settled prior to Pennsylvania, which eventually became Delaware. Most irksome, however, was opposition from Quakers in Pennsylvania, who wished greater autonomy and chafed under his demands that settlers pay quitrents to him on their land. Penn compounded his problems with the settlers by using poor judgment in his choice of governors, including sending a military man who offended Quaker pacifist sensibilities.

The Quakers were never ones to quietly acquiesce to authority. Pennsylvania politics became marked by contentious debates and disputes over the future of the colony and the Society of Friends. The fiery George Keith sought to instill greater discipline in the Society only to be thrown out. He called his opponents, "Fools, idiots, silly souls, hypocrites, heathens, rotten ranters, Tyrants, Popes." His opponents unleashed similar invectives against him.

## Prosperity in Pennsylvania

If politics was contentions, and would remain so for decades, it did not prevent the colony from flourishing. The Quakers did not reject materialist aspirations. They shared with the Puritans a belief in work as a "calling" from God, and that the accumulation of goods from a diligent and able application of labor should result in prosperity. This prosperity would permit improvement in the material conditions of others and should not lead individuals to unseemly displays of self-worth. Nor should it detract individuals, both Quakers and Puritans hoped, from focus upon eternal rewards rather than earthly pleasures. Idleness rather than prosperity was the enemy, but frugality was heartily encouraged. Bankruptcy evinced poor character, not poor judgment—the bankrupt could be excluded from the Society of Friends.

Philadelphia and Pennsylvania both prospered. The sources of prosperity arose from a combination of factors. First, Quaker merchants steadily gained an increasing proportion of the coastal carrying trade from the merchants of New England and New York and did extremely well in international waters as well. Second, the rich agricultural lands of Pennsylvania became a breadbasket providing wheat and flour for export. Third, Philadelphia attracted a large number of skilled artisans who employed semi-skilled and unskilled laborers in a bustling construction industry and in local manufactures for the prospering hinterlands.

Quaker merchants established networks of trade with other Quaker merchants in the Atlantic world. They sent their sons as supercargoes aboard ships to dispose goods in West Indian and other colonial ports. Sometimes the sons remained in these ports for a period of years to learn local conditions as shopkeepers or as apprentices to substantial merchants. They gathered expertise before returning home to assist in or take over their father's businesses, making good use of their new connections and knowledge of other markets. At home, the Philadelphia merchants invested surplus capital in land, iron mines, and manufacturing. They also built grand homes and formed a local aristocracy that played a leading role in city and colony politics. Their houses, clothes, and carriages were simple but elegant, exhibiting the finest materials, but austere in decoration, as showiness remained frowned upon.

In retrospect, there is great irony in Quakers, most of whom arose from the lower class, doing so well economically in the New World as to form an economic and political elite. As outsiders, they had challenged the established order on religious, social, and political grounds. As insiders in Pennsylvania, they used political power to guarantee religious tolerance, while often employing personal wealth in charitable enterprises. Nevertheless, tension arose within the Society over the materialism that accompanied the accumulation of estates, and the belief that the individual should cultivate the "inner plantation" with piety, humility, and steadfast focus upon one's spiritual welfare. Some resolved the dilemma by leaving the Society—or being expelled—others redoubled their efforts by devoting themselves to the social welfare of the community. But not until late in the colonial period would Quakers, as a whole, have to contend with choosing between wielding political power and remaining faithful to Quaker ideals.

## FRANCE AND ENGLAND: IMPERIAL CONFLICTS IN AN AMERICAN CONTEXT

The lives of colonists and Indians revolved around their own locale and larger region, but historical forces from beyond the region had great impact on all. One of these forces was the imperial contest between England, France, and Spain. From 1689 to 1815, France and England fought a series of conflicts that historians term the "Wars for Empire"—which finally ended with Napoleon's defeat at Waterloo. These conflagrations between the two most powerful European states involved many nations and were fought not just in Europe, but in other parts of the world, including North America, the West Indies, Africa, and India. Spain's military power was in decline, but its empire was of central importance in the competition between France and England. Spain usually allied with France, while one of Britain's major goals was to earn trade rights in Spanish colonies, a long-term policy that eventually led to British economic dominance of much of Latin America. In North America, the colonies were greatly affected by these imperial European disputes, particularly on the long northern frontier that divided the French from the English, the scene of much military conflict during the entirety of the Anglo-French dispute.

Each imperial conflict in Europe had a North American component. Although at first appearance one might say that colonists were drawn into these disputes by their mother countries, in fact, many colonists welcomed the wars as an opportunity for expansion and booty. English, French, and Spanish colonists also fought with one another during times of official peace between the empires, sometimes against the mother country's wishes, and they played a key role in lighting the powder keg that began new conflicts, as in the French and Indian War (1754–1761). All the wars for empire also involved American Indians who allied with one European nation or another, or sought to retain neutrality between them.

### Canada and the Interior Continent: French, Iroquois, and Algonquins

The French empire in North America revolved around maintaining the strength of core settlements at Quebec and Montreal. Through diplomacy and fur trade, the royal government aimed to secure the alliance of inland Indians and earn profits. The fur trade was largely conducted by coureur de bois, woodsmen who traveled great distances through the Great Lakes, the Upper Mississippi River, and beyond. They carried European goods to distant Indians and returned with furs. The French crown initially opposed these men's activities, preferring Indians to bring their furs to Montreal. But with the threat of capture by Iroquois, who sought to monopolize the trade first with the Dutch and then with the English by forcing Indians to use them as middlemen, distant natives preferred not to go east and let the French to come to them.

Colonial officials in New France constantly pushed for extension of French settlements, and thus imperial claims, to the west despite opposition from the home government. The French crown worried that a western empire would be indefensible, and they opposed promoting immigration of French people to America, fearing the depopulation of France. Compromises were made, whereby the colony could build new posts in the Great Lakes and on the Mississippi River in the Illinois Country in the 1670s and 1680s. The crown hoped to maintain control of the Indian trade over private interests, but a flood of coureur de bois, perhaps 800, entered the interior continent to take advantage of the new posts and traded as far as the Missouri River with the Sioux, and perhaps reaching as far as modern-day Montana.

French expansion and economic alliance with Indians in the interior continent threatened the Iroquois economic and military position. The Iroquois responded by disrupting the trade at every chance. They attacked the native allies of the French, forcing Algonquins and other Indians of the Ohio Country (modern-day states of Ohio, Indiana, and Illinois) to abandon their lands. Many moved north to the Great Lakes region, forming new communities with extensive ties to the French to resist the Iroquois. The English supported Iroquois efforts, though not with soldiers, and a fluid situation existed in the commerce of the inland continent. Because the French economy could not absorb all the furs coming from Canada, a lively smuggling trade developed between the French and Albany, bypassing the Iroquois.

Not wanting to be cut out of the fur trade, and facing declining power as the Algonquin–French alliance strengthened, the Iroquois attacked Ft. St. Louis (Illinois) in 1684, just below where the Ohio River enters the Mississippi. The French government sent troops to bolster New France and removed English trading posts from Hudson Bay northwest of Quebec. They also captured two English trading expeditions from New York to the Great Lakes, which temporarily ended English commerce in the area. The French then destroyed Iroquois villages and fields in 1689, but not people, who had fled. The Iroquois countered with a successful assault on Lachine, near Montreal, and subsequent attacks that put the French on the defensive.

## King William's War and the End of the Iroquois Wars

On the northern frontier, the preferred English military strategy was naval invasions organized in New England. Royal navy ships carried English and colonial forces north against the maritime provinces of Canada, with the goal of entering the St. Lawrence Seaway and subduing Quebec—the heart of French power. In contrast, the French had neither the men nor the ships for a massive assault on the English colonies, and there was no single target that could be taken to effectively conquer the English colonies. Instead, the French and their Indian allies undertook guerilla operations along the long frontier that extended from Maine to New York, often in winter, when war ordinarily halted because of severe weather. These forays forced the English to defend their far-flung frontier communities with forts and troops. The French and their Indian allies would surprise towns, capturing many people, whom they brought home to be either ransomed or incorporated into French or Indian society.

The first of the wars for empire, the War of the League of Augsburg, broke out in Europe in 1688 and extended to North America in 1689, where English colonists termed it King William's War. The North American aspect of the conflict had been brewing for some time. At stake was dominance over the fur trade, and the continual competition between the Iroquois and English against the French and their Indian allies. Franco-Indian parties undertook a series of successful assaults against widely spread English settlements including Schenectady (New York), Salmon Falls (New Hampshire), and Falmouth (Maine). The English responded by attacking Indian villages in Maine. More ambitiously, the English raised a massive force against Acadia, Canada, from which they returned with enough booty to pay for the expedition. This success convinced the English colonists that they could mount huge expeditions against the center of French power in Quebec. From New York, the English invaded

Canada reaching almost to Montreal before failing. Much more effort was put into a fleet of 32 vessels with the goal of taking Quebec City. The French won a great victory, turning back the invaders, and the New Englanders lost interest in trying again when an English fleet arrived in Boston to make a second attempt. The war then became a matter of protecting frontier settlements from repeated raids. The Treaty of Ryswick ended King William's War in 1697. It provided for the return of all colonial gains, but by not settling the points of contention paved the way for the resumption of hostilities.

Indian allies of the French and English were the great losers in King William's War, as they bore the brunt of fighting. The Iroquois especially experienced grave losses. The French had adapted *la petite guerre* to reduce Iroquois power. Instead of large armies, they turned to small raiding parties to surprise Iroquois hunters—to make it dangerous for Iroquois to leave their villages. They followed these ambushes with destruction of villages. The Iroquois sued for peace, ending the 60-year "Iroquois Wars."

Despite settling their differences with the Iroquois, the French had no desire to mediate peace between the Iroquois and their own allies, who might then trade their pelts to the English through the Iroquois. Likewise, the Iroquois did not want English traders in the west, which would cut out their position as middlemen. They refused English desires to establish a trading post on Lake Ontario. But Iroquois losses led them to accede to Huron, Miami, and Ottawa demands to permit them to conduct a direct trade with the English at Albany in 1703. The French were in a difficult position. The glut of furs in France meant they could not purchase all, or even most of them, but they did not want to strengthen English influence by allowing their allies to trade with the English. They chose politics over economy deciding to buy their allies' furs even if it meant losing money. Maintaining the western empire was seen as crucial to the health of all French settlements. The French chose to erect a fort at Detroit in 1701 to attract the Ohio Valley Indians to trade, which led to the construction of more French outposts and larger government expenditures on presents to maintain alliances. It was this expansion, less for economic reasons and more for keeping the English out of the interior continent, that led to the extension of the French empire westward and ultimately south to the Gulf of Mexico.

## Queen Anne's War

As the Iroquois Wars ended, war again broke out in Europe—a conflict Anglo-Americans labeled Queen Anne's War (1702–1713), but was referred to in Europe as the War of the Spanish Succession. Spain played a more active role as France's ally, as both built mutually supportive settlements along the Gulf of Mexico at Pensacola (Florida) and Mobile (Alabama), while the French expanded their fort-building in the Great Lakes region. In this war, as in all the colonial conflicts on the northern mainland, a basic factor driving French and Spanish decision-making lay in the English possessing so many more colonists than themselves. English colonists, for instance, outnumbered the French by a factor of 20 in North America and had the chance to overwhelm them by sheer force of numbers.

The French again assaulted frontier communities to divert English forces. They sent a French-native force of 500 to reduce seven frontier communities in Maine, and in 1704, they had a spectacular success at Deerfield, Massachusetts, which netted over 100 civilian captives. Nevertheless, English creation of garrison towns formed a fairly effective protective ring in the north, so that colonists' terror obscured their overall success against invaders. In revenge, the English pursued their own guerilla war and prepared a massive invasion force against Quebec and Acadia. The English failed against the latter in 1709, but more than redoubled their efforts for the assault on Quebec. As in 1690, the 1711 invasion ended disastrously. Six thousand regular British troops, supported by 5,000 sailors and 1,500 colonists, entered the St. Lawrence Seaway in August. Fog dispersed the fleet and led to the loss of 800 men when a sloop struck breakers. Lacking pilots and unclear about the river ahead, the fleet returned home. This forced the abandonment of a complementary invasion of English colonials and Iroquois from New York, which was to attack Quebec from the west.

In the South, the Carolinians (see chapter ten for the English establishment of the Carolina colony) failed in their conquest of Spanish St. Augustine in 1702, but succeeded a few years later in smashing Spain's most important ally in Florida, the Apalachee, thousands of whom ended their lives in slavery. A Franco-Spanish-Indian force countered with a failed assault upon Charles Town (modern-day Charleston, South Carolina), in 1706. The captured Indians were enslaved, and the French and Spanish were imprisoned. Thereafter, the war in the South was mostly fought between the Indian allies of each side and included a large foray by the Creek, Chickasaw, and English against the Choctaw, France's most important ally in the region, yielding hundreds of slaves. But French power was little reduced on the Gulf of Mexico and along the Mississippi, as English-allied slaving strengthened the French by leading more Indians to seek their alliance.

When Queen Anne's War ended in 1713, France surrendered Acadia, Newfoundland, and Hudson Bay to the English. For three decades afterwards, France and England remained at peace in Europe, while their Indian allies intermittently fought with one another, and sometimes with the French or English. In other words, the imperial competition and conflicts continued in the colonies, even as France and England kept the peace in Europe. Moreover, Anglo-Spanish hostilities persisted, particularly in the West Indies and the American South.

During the peace between France and England, the French temporarily broke with their erstwhile Spanish ally. French forces in Louisiana captured Pensacola in 1719, only to have it recaptured the same year. The Spanish then attempted to eliminate the French at Mobile, which was a failure. In turn, the French again captured Pensacola in 1719, but in 1722 restored it to Spain, an action that helped lead the way to the two powers re-allying against England in future imperial wars.

## Conclusion

Located between the plantation colonies of the Chesapeake and the town-oriented farming colonies of Puritan New England, the Middle Colonies combined characteristics of both. The Middle Colonies relied on family farms as in New England, but had greater amounts of unfree labor, both indentured servants and slaves. Able to produce more surplus for Atlantic World trade, particularly wheat and flour, the merchants of the Middle Colonies competed successfully with the New Englanders, especially in capturing portions of the trade of the Chesapeake and West Indies. The Middle Colonies also displayed much more ethnic diversity among its European population, as the English settlers were not a majority in these colonies, unlike in New England

and the Chesapeake. Inter-ethnic hostilities contributed to political fractiousness in New York, but had little impact in Pennsylvania in this period. Quaker tolerance contributed to the colony's stability, where the biggest points of contention were among Quakers, and between the Quakers and Pennsylvania's proprietors.

The quickly growing prosperity of the Middle Colonies was not dependent on the fur trade of the interior continent, but that trade made New York especially important to English relations with Indians and to the relative power of the English vis-à-vis the French. Iroquois communities in modern-day upstate New York provided the English a buffer between them and the French, as well as a valuable trading partner. The English generally provided the Iroquois only weapons and not manpower, but Iroquois hostilities and competition with the French preoccupied the latter and forced them to expend precious resources on securing their allies and themselves, while attempting to lure the Iroquois into their own orbit. With the end of the Iroquois Wars in 1701, Algonquin Indians were able to move south and east onto their former lands in the Ohio country, and to conduct their own trade with the New Yorkers, though many retained trade and alliance with the French through the latter's trading post network that extended throughout the Great Lakes.

The early wars for empire between France and England had less negative impact on the Ohio country Indians than on the Iroquois and the Indians of Northern New England. English–French hostilities were focused on the New York and New England frontier, allowing the western Indians some respite. In general, these wars led to a stalemate between French and English, as the latter failed in repeated attempts to take Quebec, while French raids into the English colonies did little to alter the balance of power between the two.

# DOCUMENTS

## 9.1. William Penn on Religious Toleration

*William Penn, a leading member of the Society of Friends, and the proprietor of Pennsylvania, established the colony as a haven for Quakers. He wrote many tracts in England to promote religious toleration, including* The Great Case of Liberty of Conscience, *which he penned in Newgate jail in London in 1670. Penn's Pennsylvania became a model for religious toleration for other English colonies in America. The Puritans justified intolerance as stemming from their duty to God— how does Penn use his understanding of God to call for tolerance of diverse religions?*

THE Great CASE of Liberty of Conscience Once more briefly Debated and Defended, by the Authority of Reason, Scripture, and Antiquity: Which may serve the Place of a General Reply to such late Discourses; as have Oppos'd a *Toleration* (1670) The Author *W. P.*

*Whatsoever ye would that Men should do to you, do ye even so to them:* Mat. 7. 12.

*Render unto Caesar, the Things that are Caesar's; and to God, the Things that are God's. Mark 12. 17.*

To the Supream Authority of *England*.

TOLERATION (for these Ten Years past) has not been more the Cry of some, than PERSECUTION has been the Practice of others, though not on *Grounds equally Rational.*

The present Cause of this Address, is to solicite a Conversion of that Power to our Relief, which hitherto has been imploy'd to our Depression; that after this large Experience of our Innocency, and long since expir'd *Apprenticeship of Cruel Sufferings,* you will be pleas'd to cancel all our Bonds, and give us a Possession of those Freedoms, to which we are entituled by *English* Birthright.

This has been often promised to us, and we as earnestly have expected the Performance; but to this Time we labour under the unspeakable Pressure of Nasty Prisons, and daily Confiscation of our Goods, to the apparent Ruin of intire Families.

We would not attribute the whole of this Severity to Malice, since not a little share may justly be ascribed to Mis-intelligence.

For 'tis the Infelicity of Governours to see and hear by the Eyes and Ears of other Men; which is equally unhappy for the People.

And we are bold to say, that Suppositions and meer Conjectures, have been the best Measures, that most have taken of Us, and of our Principles; for whilst there have been none more inoffensive, we have been mark't for Capital Offenders.

'Tis hard that we should always lie under this undeserved Imputation; and which is worse, be Persecuted as such, without the Liberty of a just Defence.

In short, if you are apprehensive, that our Principles are inconsistent with the Civil Government, grant us a free Conference about the Points in Question, and let us know, what are those Laws, essential to Preservation, that our Opinions carry an Opposition to? And if upon a due enquiry we are found so Heterodox, as represented, it will be then but time enough to inflict these heavy Penalties upon us. . . .

*From a Prisoner for Conscience-Sake,*
> *Newgate,* the 7th of the 12th
> Month, call'd *February,* 1670.
> W. P.

## The PREFACE

WERE some as Christian, as they boast themselves to be, 'twould save us all the Labour we bestow in rendring *Persecution* so Unchristian, as it most truly is: Nay were they those Men of Reason they Character themselves, and what the *Civil Law* stiles good Citizens, it had been needless for us to tell them, that neither can any external Coercive Power convince the Understanding of the poorest Idiot, nor Fines and Prisons be judg'd fit and adequate Penalties for Faults purely intellectual; as well as

*(Continued)*

that they are destructive of all Civil Government....

Not that we are so ignorant, as to think it is within the Reach of Humane Power to fetter Conscience, or to restrain it's Liberty *strictly taken:* But that plain *English, of Liberty of Conscience,* we would be *understood* to mean, is this; namely, *The Free and Uninterrupted Exercise of our Consciences, in that Way of Worship, we are most clearly perswaded, God requires us to serve Him in (without endangering our undoubted Birthright of English Freedoms) which being Matter of FAITH; we Sin if we omit, and they can't do less, that shall endeavour it.* . . .

Let no man therefore think himself too big to be admonish'd, nor put too slight a Value upon the *Lives, Liberties,* and *Properties,* of so many Thousand Free-born *English* Families, Embark't in that one Concern of *Liberty of Conscience.* It will become him better to reflect upon his own Mortality, and not forget his Breath is in his Nostrils, and that every Action of his Life the Everlasting God will bring to Judgment, and him for them.

*That Imposition, Restraint, and Persecution for Conscience-Sake, highly Invade the Divine Prerogative, and Divest the Almighty of a Right, due to none beside Himself, and that in five eminent Particulars.*

THE great Case of *Liberty of Conscience* so often Debated and Defended (however dissatisfactorily to such *as have so little Conscience as to Persecute for it)* is once more brought to publick View, by a late Act against Dissenters, and Bill, or an additional one, that we all hop'd the Wisdom of our Rulers had long since laid aside, as what was fitter to be passed into an Act

of perpetual Oblivion. The Kingdoms are alarm'd at this Procedure, and Thousands greatly at a Stand, wondring what should be the Meaning of such hasty Resolutions, that seem as fatal as they were unexpected: *Some ask what Wrong they have done; others, what Peace they have broken; and all, what Plots they have form'd, to prejudice the present Government, or occasions given, to hatch new Jealousies of them and their Proceedings,* being not conscious to themselves of Guilt in any such Respect.

For mine own Part, I publickly confess my self to be a *very hearty Dissenter from the establish't Worship of these Nations,* as believing *Protestants* to have much degenerated from their first Principles, and as owning the *poor despised Quakers,* in Life and Doctrine, to have espoused the Cause of God, and to be the undoubted Followers of Jesus Christ, in his most Holy, Straight and Narrow Way that leads to the Eternal Rest. In all which I know no Treason, nor any Principle that would urge me to a Thought injurious to the Civil Peace. . . .

In short we say, there can be but two Ends in *Persecution,* the one to satisfie (which none can ever do) the *insatiable Appetites of a decimating Clergy (whose best Arguments are Fines and Imprisonments)* and the other, as thinking therein *they do God good Service;* but 'tis so hateful a Thing upon any Account, that we shall make it appear by this ensuing Discourse, to be a declared Enemy to *God, Religion,* and the *Good of humane Society.*

### The Terms explained, and the Question stated

First, By *Liberty of Conscience,* we understand not only a meer *Liberty of the*

*Mind,* in believing or disbelieving this or that Principle or Doctrine, *but the Exercise of our selves in a visible Way of Worship, upon our believing it to be indispensibly required at our Hands, that if we neglect it for Fear or Favour of any Mortal Man, we Sin, and incur Divine Wrath:* Yet we would be so understood to extend and justifie the Lawfulness of our so meeting to worship God, as not to contrive, or abet any Contrivance destructive of the Government and Laws of the Land, tending to Matters of an external Nature, directly, or indirectly; but so far only, as it may refer to religious Matters, and a Life to come, and consequently wholly independent of the secular Affairs of this, wherein we are suppos'd to Trangress.

*Secondly,* By Imposition, Restraint, and Persecution, we don't only mean, the strict Requiring of us to believe this to be true, or that to be false; and upon Refusal, to incur the Penalties enacted in such Cases; but by those Terms we mean thus much, any coercive Lett or Hindrance to us, from meeting together to perform those Religious Exercises which are according to our Faith and Perswasion.

**The Question stated**

For Proof of the aforesaid Terms thus given, we singly state the Question thus, Whether *Imposition, Restraint,* and *Persecution,* upon Persons for Exercising such a Liberty of Conscience, as is before expressed, and so circumstantiated, be not to impeach the Honour of God, the Meekness of the Christian Religion, the Authority of Scripture, the Priviledge of Nature, the Principles of common Reason, the Well-being of Government, and Apprehensions of the greatest Personages of former and latter Ages.

First, Then we say that *Imposition, Restraint,* and *Persecution, for Matters relating to Conscience, directly invade the Divine Prerogative, and Divest the Almighty of a Due, proper to none besides himself.* And this we prove by these five Particulars. . . .

Secondly. *Such magisterial Determinations carry an evident Claim to that Infallibility,* which *Protestants* have been hitherto so jealous of owning, that to avoid the *Papists,* they have denied it to all, but God himself. . . .

Thirdly, *It enthrones Man as King over Conscience, the alone just Claim and Priviledge of his Creator, whose Thoughts are not as Men's Thoughts but has reserv'd to himself, that Empire from all the Caesars on* Earth; for if Men in Reference to Souls, and Bodies, things appertaining to this and t'other World, shall be subject to their Fellow-Creatures, what follows? but that *Caesar* (however he got it) has all, God's Share, and his own too; and being Lord of both, Both are *Caesar's* and not *God's.*

Fourthly, *It defeats God's Work of Grace, and the invisible Operation of his Eternal Spirit, which can alone beget Faith, and is only to be obey'd, in and about Religion and Worship, and attributes* Men's Conformity *to outward Force and Corporal Punishments.* A Faith subject to as many Revolutions as the Powers that enact it.

Fifthly and Lastly, *Such Persons assume the Judgment of the great Tribunal unto* themselves; for to whomsoever Men are imposedly or restrictively subject and accountable in Matters of Faith, Worship and

*(Continued)*

Conscience; in them alone must the Power of Judgment reside; but it is equally true that God shall judge all by Jesus Christ, and that no Man is so accountable to his fellow Creatures, as to be imposed upon, restrain'd, or persecuted for any Matter of Conscience whatever.

Thus and in many more particulars are Men accustomed to intrench upon *Divine Property,* to gratifie particular Interests in the World (and at best) through a Misguided Apprehension to imagine *they do God good Service,* that where they cannot give Faith, *They will use Force,* which kind of Sacrifice is nothing less unreasonable *than the other is abominable:* God will not give his Honour to another, and to him only that searches the Heart and tries the Reins, it is our Duty to ascribe the Gifts of Understanding and Faith, without which none can please God.

Source: William Penn, *The Great Case of Liberty of Conscience* (1670).

## 9.2. The Aftermath of Jacob Leisler's Death

*In many of the colonies, the local government administration was overthrown when James II fled England and William and Mary came to power. In all these colonies, those who seized power awaited word from England on their new government's legitimacy. The royal government also took the occasion to re-issue colonial charters, which allowed for revision and amendment. In New York, Jacob Leisler seized power and faced strong opposition from a variety of colonial groups. When Leisler refused to turn over the government to newly arrived Captain Richard Ingoldsby, a showdown occurred, which ended with the hanging of Leisler and some of his supporters. This episode played a key role in further fractionalizing New York politics for over a generation. In the following documents, Leisler's son petitions William and Mary for the return of the confiscated estates of those who were hung. The monarch's response is also included. What was Leisler's son's view of his father's and Ingoldsby's dispute?*

### Petition of Jacob Leisler *to the King*

To the Kings most Excellt Majesty

The humble Petition of Jacob Leisler son of Capt" Jacob Leisler deceased, late Commander in Cheif of your Maty" Province of New York in America

Sheweth That upon the late happy Revolution, your Petitioners said Father was very instrumental in Securing the said Province for your Majesty, [and being of known integrity to your Majesties interest]' and the Protestant Religion, Capt" Francis Nicholson then Deputy Governor having withdrawn himself from the said Province, your PetTM said Father upon the 16th of August 1689 was by the Freeholders and Inhabitants elected and constituted Commander in Cheif untill your Majesties Royall Pleasure shod be declared concerning the said Province, accordingly he entered upon the Government, and was acknowledged as such by the people, and was in possession of the Fort and Garrison which till that time were ruinous and incapable of defence and did proclaim your Majesty and your Royall Consort to be our Soveraigne Lord and Lady King and Queen, and caused the same to be done in other Provinces.

That on the 10th of December 1689. Your Matys gracious letter dated the 30th July before, arrived there, the same being directed to the said Capt" Nicolson and in his absence to such as for the time being, took care for preserving the Peace and administring the lawes within the said Province, whereby your Majesty was graciously pleased to authorize the Person then Commanding in Cheif as aforesaid to take upon him the Government, calling to his Assistance in the administracon thereof, the Principal Inhabitants or as many of them as he should think fitt willing and requiring him to do and perform all things which to the Place and Office of Lieutenant Governor and Commander in Chief did appertain, as he should find necessary for your Majestys Service, and the good of your Subjects there, untill further order from your Majesty. That your Petitioners said father being so confirmed in the said government, by your Majesty said Royall Letter, did faithfully observe your Majesty commands thereby declared and did in all respects Provide for the Security of the said Province as well against all attempts of the French, who are very powerful in these Parts, as Papists and other disaffected persons of which there were many resident in the said Province.

That on the 28th of January last past, Capt" Richard Ingoldsby arrived at New York with some Soldiers from England, to whom your Petitioner's said Father offered all sort of accomodation, but the said Ingoldsby required the Possession of the said Fort, and Government for which your Petitioner's said Father desired to see his orders being ready to obey the same if he had any such from your Majesty, or from Coll Sloughter whom your Majesty had been pleased to make Governor; but the said Ingoldsby had no such orders or would not produce the same, whereupon your Petitioners said Father having advised with the Principall Inhabitants was councill'd and directed by them to keep and maintain the Possession of the Fort and Goverment (in regard the said Ingoldsby would not shew his orders to receive the same) until the Governor arrived and your Maty" pleasure was known, That Ingoldsby thereupon joyning himself to the Papists and other disaffected Persons, did by many indirect means to the great Terror of your Majestys Lieige Subjects in a hostile and dreadfull manner assemble great numbers of French and other persons, and beseiged the said Fort, and raised divers batteries against the same, and so continued in Arms about six Weeks, that on the 19th of March last Coll Sloughter did arrive, and as soon as your Petitioners said Father had certain knowledge thereof, which was not till eleven oclock that night, He did send the Mayor of the Citty and Mr Milbourne his Secretary from the said Fort to wayt upon him, and to offer him the Possession thereof, but the said Coll Sloughter without hearing them speak, committed them all close Prisoners, who not returning as your Petitioners Father expected, he did very early

*(Continued)*

next morning, write to the said Coll Sloughter desiring him to come and receive the Fort, and accordingly he came and took possession thereof on the 20th March, but presently after caused all the Soldiers and Inhabitants in the said Fort and Citty to be disarmed, and contrary to all Law and Justice, committed your Petitioner and his sd Father and 26 other persons to Prison pretend^ they were Guilty of High Treason against your Maty" for keeping the said Fort as aforesaid, and the said Coll Sloughter and Ingoldsby confederating with divers others disaffected Persons to your Majesties, to put your Petitioners said father and others to death did in a most arbitrary and illegal manner cause him and seven others to be tryed Judged and Condemned to Death for some Pretended High Treason, and have since most barbarously caused your Petitioners said Father and your petitioners brother in Law (the said Milbourne) to be hanged and afterwards butchered, the said other six persons (if not since put to death) remaining in Prison under the same unjust Sentence of Condemnation, and have seized their Estates and Goods, and have also most unjustly prosecuted your Petitioner and many other of your Majestys good Subjects, confiscating their Estates, who for Preservation of their lives, have been forced to leave the said Province, by which cruell and barbarous practices great numbers of your Majestys Subjects are in danger of utter Ruine, and the said Country is like to be depopulated and made desolate, the said Coll Sloughter being dead, and the said Capt" Ingoldsby (since his death) commanding in Cheif in the said Province, who doth continue to exercise great Violence and barbarity against your Maty" loyal Subjects there.

Your Petitioner therefore humbly implores your most sacred Majesty, to take the Premises into your Princely consideration and to give such Orders therein as well for the preservation of the said Six Condemned Persons, and the Releif of your Petitioners and other Poor Sufferers as also for the Preservation and future good establishment of the said Province as to your Royall goodness & wisdom shall seem meet.

And your Petitioner as in
Duty bound shall ever Pray &c
JACOB LEISLER

*Order of Council in Case of* Leisler *and* Milbourne.

At the Court at Whitehall the 11th March 1691

PRESENT— The Queens most Excellent Maty in Councill

WHEREAS, The Right Honorable the Lords of the Committee for Trade and Plantations have by their Report dated the 11th Instt Represented to her Majesty that they have examined the matter of the Petition of Jacob Leisler the son of Jacob Leisler of New York, deceased, referred to the Committee by his Majesties order in Councill of the 7th of January last complaining of Proceedings against his father and Jacob Milbourne by Col! Sloughter at New York, who were thereupon condemned and put to Death, and their Estates confiscated, and their

Lordshipps having fully heard the said Jacob Leisler the P" by his Council Learned, upon the whole matter are humbly of opinion, that the said Jacob Leisler and Jacob Milbourn deceased were condemned and have suffered according to Law. But their Lordships do humbly offer their Intercession to her Majesty in behalf of their Families as fit objects of their Majestys Mercy, That the Estates of the said Jacob Leisler and Jacob Milbourne deceased may be restored to them upon their humble application to their Majestys by Petition for the same, Her Majesty in Council is this day pleased to approve the said Report, and to declare that upon the Humble application of the relations of the said Jacob Leisler and Jacob Milbourn deceased, Her Majesty will order the estates of the said Jacob Leisler and Jacob Milburn to be restored to their Families as objects of her Majestys mercy.

Source: *Documents Relative to the Colonial History of the State of New York*. Vol. 3. Edited by John R. Brodhead, Berthold Fernow, and Edmund B. O'Callaghan (1857), 825–827.

# Bibliography

Bonomi, Patricia. *A Factious People: Politics and Society in Colonial New York* (1971).

Calloway, Colin G. *The Western Abenakis of Vermont, 1600–1800: War, Migration, and the Survival of an Indian People* (1990).

Eccles, W. J. *The Canadian Frontier: 1534–1760* (1969).

Hodges, Graham Russell. *Root and Branches: African Americans in New York and East Jersey, 1613–1863* (1999).

Illick, Joseph E. *Colonial Pennsylvania: A History* (1976).

Jaenen, Cornelius J. *The French Relationship with the Native Peoples of New France* (1974).

Jaenen, Cornelius J. *Friend and Foe: Aspects of French-Amerindian Cultural Contacts in the Sixteenth and Seventeenth Centuries* (1976).

Kammen, Michael. *Colonial New York: A History* (1975).

Leach, Douglas E. *The Northern Colonial Frontier, 1607–1763* (1966).

Merritt, Jane T. *At the Crossroads: Indians and Empires on a Mid-Atlantic Frontier, 1700–1763* (2007).

Merwick, Donna. *Death of a Notary: Conquest and Change in Colonial New York* (1999).

Morrison, Kenneth M. *The Embattled Northeast: The Elusive Ideal of Alliance in Abenaki-Euramerican Relations* (1984).

Reid, John G. *Acadia, Maine, and New Scotland: Marginal Colonies in the Seventeenth Century* (1981).

Smolenski, John. *Friends and Strangers: The Making of a Creole Culture in Colonial Pennsylvania* (2010).

Tolles, Frederick Barnes. *Meeting House and Counting House: The Quaker Merchants of Colonial Philadelphia, 1682–1763* (1948).

White, Richard. *The Middle Ground: Indians, Empires and Republics in the Great Lakes Region, 1650–1815* (1991).

# 10

# On the Periphery of Empires: The Southeast and the Southwest, 1670–1730

## INTRODUCTION

European settlement on the broad swath of land in the South that extended 3,000 miles from the Atlantic to the Pacific on the southern reaches of the future United States fell on the periphery of existing empires. In the 17th century, Florida, the oldest established permanent European settlement in the future United States, had expanded north from St. Augustine onto the sea islands of Georgia; it remained one of the remotest colonies in

Spain's Atlantic empire and its northernmost outpost. Over 2,000 miles to the west, sparsely populated Spanish New Mexico paled in insignificance compared to Mexico and other Spanish colonies to the south. By the last quarter of the 17th century, France had explored and then colonized in the interior of the South, sending missionaries, soldiers, and a few colonists to the Mississippi Valley, establishing the vast Louisiana colony that included the area of future states such as Alabama, Mississippi, Louisiana, Arkansas, Illinois, and Missouri. Tucked between the Spanish Southwest and Southeast, French settlements were relatively small and diffuse, mostly trading posts. Their remoteness from other European settlements provided some security, but their distance from French Canada, France, and the French Caribbean left them economically isolated as well. The French had to negotiate with neighboring native peoples to secure economic and military survival.

On the northeastern portion of the southern region, the English settled Carolina in 1670. Although more successful than the Spanish and French in attracting European settlers, the colonial population was significantly less than in the English colonies to the north. Though militarily vulnerable, the southern portion of Carolina, later to become South Carolina, connected easily by sea to other English colonies, especially in the Caribbean, with which the colony quickly established commercial ties. The northern portion of Carolina, later to become North Carolina, remained more isolated as it lacked good ports and commodities to attract ships from elsewhere in the Atlantic world.

Despite the sparse population of European settlements in the Southeast and Southwest, the native peoples were greatly affected by the new colonies. The Europeans brought new diseases that spread through Indian towns and villages. The Spanish continued their active quest to alter Indian cultures by placing Indians on missions. The Europeans, particularly the English, also introduced a massive trade in Indian slaves that disrupted life for all, and the imperial wars and colonial competition engaged Indians in bloody conflicts. The period 1670–1730 saw the introduction of the Atlantic world economy to many, if not most, southeastern and southwestern Indian peoples, introducing an array of European trade goods, while luring them into providing commodities for distant markets, including Indian slaves. Indians adopted to the inroads of the Europeans and the new market forces by creating new polities and strategies for coping with a rapidly changing world.

## THE SOUTHEAST: THE ENGLISH IN CAROLINA

English colonial expansion into the South began with settlement of Carolina in 1670. The colony had been granted in 1660 to a group of seven men known as the Lords Proprietors, who could design the colony in any way they wished as long as they did not enact laws repugnant to those of England. Philosopher John Locke, who served as secretary to one of the proprietors, helped draw up some of the many drafts known as the "Fundamental Constitutions" to govern the colony. These determined the distribution of land and religious policies, and distinguished proprietary and settler rights. The proprietors originally intended to establish a class system akin to England's by which elites would receive baronies of 12,000 acres, and lesser men would have smaller tracts according to their social status. The proprietors intended to garner an income from quitrents that landowners paid as an annual tax on their land, and by monopoly control over the Indian trade.

Unfortunately for the proprietors, they never received much income from the colony. Colonists generally refused to pay the quitrents and disregarded the strictures against trading with Indians. Moreover, the men sent to rule the colony as governors, judges, councilors, and other administrators also disregarded proprietary directives and engaged in illegal money-making activities. These men went to America to get rich.

Most of Carolina's early free settlers emigrated from England or Barbados. The latter brought African slaves with them, who provided most of the labor for building the colony. They cut wood, erected buildings, and performed many of the crucial economic functions for survival: fishing, hunting, planting, piloting boats, serving as soldiers to protect the settlement, and experimenting with a variety of economic enterprises to produce profits from trade with Indians and the island of Barbados. In the words of one historian, Carolina became "a colony of a colony," as the Barbados trade became crucial to the colony's economic development. Carolina shipped lumber, cattle, vegetables, and shingles, all produced by slave labor, and in exchange received manufactured goods that the Barbadians had purchased from England and more African slaves. But the Carolinians also accumulated much of their capital through avid participation in an Indian slave trade.

## The Indian Slave Trade

The trade in Indian slaves preceded Carolina's settlement. Westo Indians, who had moved south from New York, stopped in Virginia, where they established links with Virginia traders, before moving further south and raiding the Spanish Indian missions along the Georgia coast in the 1650s. They sold their victims to Virginia traders. The decimated missions crumbled under their assaults, and the attacks of European pirates seeking slaves and booty. The Westo then turned their attention to the west and south, assaulting many groups of Indians on the mainland in southern Georgia and northern Florida. With Carolina's settlement, the Carolinians replaced the Virginians as the Westos' partners, their closer location made them much more convenient for conducting the Indian slave trade.

For the Carolina settlers, it was as if one could create capital out of thin air. A settler merely had to capture Indians or purchase them from Indians whom they convinced to go slaving. Captives were easily moved—they could be marched hundreds of miles to Charles Town and put aboard ships for sale elsewhere in the Atlantic world. Some remained in Carolina to labor, but owners feared they could run away to rejoin their people, so most were transported to the West Indies or mainland ports in New England, New York, and Virginia.

By the last decade of the 17th century, the Indian slave trade in the south had expanded by leaps and bounds. Carolina traders traveled all the way to the Mississippi River, where they employed the Chickasaw and others to prey across the river into Arkansas, and south to the Gulf of Mexico. In the east, the Carolinians turned on their Westo partners and enslaved them, and then recruited first the Savannah (a Shawnee people) and then the Yamasee to prey on other Indian peoples. By 1702, the Carolinians had joined with many of the Indian peoples of Georgia and Alabama, then coalescing into a great new confederacy, the Creeks, to begin a series of massive assaults upon the Florida Indians, many of whom were allied with the Spanish. English troops heavily participated in these invasions against St. Augustine (1702) and

Apalachee (1704). In the coming decade, mostly Indian armies of Creeks and Yamasee proceeded south all the way to the Florida Keys and captured Timucuas, Calusas, and other Indians and sold them to the Carolinians. The Florida peninsula was nearly depopulated of its indigenous people.

The frenzy of slaving extended northward as well. In 1711, the Tuscarora War broke out in North Carolina, as Indians attacked settlers encroaching on their land and stealing their people. The war is misnamed because most of those fighting against the colony were not Tuscarora and many Tuscarora remained at peace with the English. South Carolina came to North Carolina's aid by raising an army of colonists and mostly Indians, both of whom were more concerned with capturing Indians to enslave than rescuing the colony. They concluded a dubious peace with North Carolina's native enemies and returned home with their booty. The war resumed and South Carolina sent another army northward. This army concluded a more enduring peace. Captured enemies were again shipped as slaves to the West Indies, and many of the surviving Tuscarora migrated to New York, where they joined the Iroquois.

Although the alliance of South Carolina and its Indian neighbors had been a great success in the Tuscarora War, discontent brewed among the latter. This discontent arose from numerous sources, not the least of which was the more than 100 traders who lived in Indian towns. Many traders swindled the Indians, enslaved friendly Indians, and arrogantly made demands of sundry sorts. The South Carolina government had long recognized the discontent and tried to rectify abuses by assigning agents to overlook the trade. They also created a commission to regularly meet and hear charges brought by Indians against guilty traders. But the trade was beyond their control—many Indian towns were too distant and too many for the few agents to maintain order and justice. The commission's power was undermined by their own government's refusal to punish notorious traders, and the agents corruptly competed with one another to conduct illegal trade. How could traders be expected to obey the laws when those responsible for compliance only enforced measures against competitors.

In the spring of 1715, Indian despair at achieving justice exploded in the Yamasee War. The Yamasee, Creek, Cherokee, Chickasaw, and others killed over 100 traders in their towns. Those Indians living close to the colonists assaulted the colony. For distant Indians like the Creek, Cherokee, and Chickasaw, the killing of the traders was a political statement, whereby they asserted the necessity of negotiating a new relationship with Carolina. For the Yamasee and the dozen or so groups that lived next to and among the colonists, the war comprised an attempt to keep their lives and lands from enslavers and encroaching colonists.

The war was a disaster for the colony as it faced annihilation. Hundreds of colonists were killed and the colony reduced to the environs of Charles Town. But after negotiating settlements with the Cherokee, and then the Chickasaw and Creek, South Carolina focused its attention on the Yamasee and their allies, many of whom fled to Florida and allied with the Spanish. Other Indians simply laid low in the Carolina Piedmont, where they would live for a hundred years and more but no longer as a direct threat to Carolina. Nevertheless, the colony had lost its best ally, the Yamasee, who previously had protected South Carolina from Spanish Florida. The Yamasee liberated many African slaves from Carolina plantations and brought them to Florida. The Africans formed a free black community, Fort Mosa, established by the Spanish outside St. Augustine. Future runaways from South Carolina enlarged the community.

The freed Africans became a valuable militia for the Spanish. When Spain abandoned Florida in 1763, this militia moved to Cuba and the Bahamas, where their descendants live to this day.

## Impact of the Slave Trade on Native Peoples

All told, in the 50 years after the founding of Carolina in 1670, somewhere between 30,000 and 50,000 natives in the Southeast, perhaps more, were transported as slaves from the region by the English. (The French also enslaved Indians in Louisiana, but not in the same numbers.) Much of Georgia, Florida, Arkansas, and South Carolina were depopulated of its native population. The South, like much of the colonial world, became a land of warfare and suspicion—and remained so. Many survivors of the decimated native groups joined the big confederacies such as the Creek, Cherokee, and Choctaw. These held substantial military power over the next 100 years. But out of the slaving and the Yamasee War, the confederacies also developed long-term enmities with one another. The Choctaw never forgave the Chickasaw for their slaving, and the two periodically warred with one another through the 18th century. The Creek would not forgive the Cherokee for turning on them during the Yamasee War. They warred with one another for decades, as did the Creek and Choctaw. Nevertheless, these large confederacies were strong enough to withstand the power of the English, Spanish, and French in the South.

Indian power in the South was further strengthened by potential alliance with African slaves in English and French colonies. The French and English feared their African slaves combining with Indians to overthrow them and did all they could to create mutual hostility. The English enacted laws barring Africans from working in the Indian trade, but to little avail, as the English, French, and Spanish governments all employed linguistically skilled Africans as interpreters, messengers, and diplomats to Indian peoples. Many Indians who lived close to French communities along the Gulf Coast (termed Les Petite Nations) and those residing near the English plantations (termed Settlement Indians) gained employment as slave catchers. African runaways who escaped the clutches of these slave catchers sometimes found sanctuary among the native confederacies that could resist the near constant pressure placed upon them by Europeans to return their bondpeople. Runaway Africans provided these Indians with valuable assistance. They became cultural mediators who transferred not only their own culture, but that of Europeans to Indians. The runaways provided information about practical matters such as European fort construction, diplomacy, politics, and demography. Eventually, many southern Indians would adopt European plantation agriculture and purchase their own African slaves, but that did not prevent African runaways from assimilating as free people in Indian societies. One product of the close association of Africans and Indians was a sharing and blending of folklore. Another was the creation of maroon communities—mixed of Indian, African, and European peoples who lived in areas of difficult access, such as the Great Dismal Swamp of North Carolina and Virginia. These communities provided refuge from, and its inhabitants traded with and sometimes robbed, Indian and European communities.

The Yamasee War was a watershed in Southern history. The Indian slave trade went into a precipitous decline. Not that enslavement of Indians ceased, but whole-sale wars to capture Indians ended in the region. Indians generally refused to undertake slaving wars and raids to gain captives for sale to the English. They also refused to closely ally with the English, literally keeping their distance from them. The Creek and Chickasaw, and to a lesser extent the Cherokee, adopted a policy of trading with all Europeans and playing them against one another. This ensured that European trade goods would flow from several sources, and that the Europeans could not close off trade as a means to force Indians to do their bidding. Indians also recognized their own military power. The large confederacies could not be conquered by the Europeans, but only by a coalescence of forces against them. The Indians occasionally provided military assistance to colonies, but rarely entire armies, so that the English, French, and Spanish were largely left to their own devices in the disputes between them, save for Indian scouts and auxiliaries.

## African Slavery

After the Yamasee War, English attention shifted from the profits to be gained through trade with Indians to development of agriculture. The discovery of rice as a profitable staple crop led to a society whose economy, politics, and social system revolved around African slavery. Rice was introduced to Carolina by African slaves familiar with the crop in their homeland. The crop's value lay in it being a relatively inexpensive food source for slaves in the West Indies, where land was put to sugar cultivation for export rather than subsistence agriculture. Low country South Carolina possessed a perfect environment for rice. Land had to be periodically flooded, and the saltwater tides pushed freshwater rivers over land that was diked to allow flooding when needed. The building of sluices, the flooding of fields, and the cultivation of the crop were all labor intensive. Only those who commanded large numbers of slaves could afford to establish rice plantations.

As South Carolina planters stepped up importation of Africans, who outnumbered the European settlers by 1708, tension grew apace. Rice production increasingly confined slaves to the plantations, creating resentment among bondpeople who previously had greater mobility, less outside control over their social lives, and more varied work routines. Moreover, the rice fields were unhealthy, as the mosquitoes that spread malaria flourished in the standing freshwater. Although some Africans had greater resistance than Europeans due to previous exposure to malarial conditions and possession of the sickle cell trait, which provides some resistance to malaria, the environment was unhealthy for all. European masters left the plantations in their overseers' hands during the hot summer months, and in many rice areas, the slave population approached 90%. Enjoying only limited contact with Europeans, Gullah culture thrived. Gullah refers to both a language—a lingua franca—by which slaves from different African cultures communicated with one another and their masters and overseers, and a range of traditions and folkways practiced in the rice areas along the Atlantic Coast and on the sea islands. From basket weaving to music, and from agricultural techniques to forms of worship, Gullah tied together much of the African American community of the low country and sea islands until well into the 20th century.

## North Carolina and the Spirit of Leveling

The area that evolved into North Carolina was unusual in that European settlers migrated to the area before it became a colony. Many of these first settlers were indentured servants fleeing Virginia, or free people unable to compete with unfree labor in that colony. After the region was included in the grant of land to the proprietors of Carolina, North Carolina attracted individuals known in England as "levelers," people who disdained political, social, and economic hierarchy.

Distant from the southern portion of the proprietary grant, the northern half of Carolina operated independently, the two eventually splitting into the separate colonies of North Carolina and South Carolina. Whereas South Carolina developed into the most hierarchical of all English mainland colonies, with an elite that secured a political dominance that lasted nearly two centuries, North Carolina became one of the most "democratic" of colonies, retaining much of its leveling spirit, contributed to by the immigration of a significant number of Quakers. Most settlers opposed all governmental attempts—imperial, proprietary, and local—to interfere with their way of life.

With the rise of a small local elite of merchants and planters, the common folk continued to challenge the attempts of elites to extend control over their lives, especially by resisting the establishment of a state church, the payment of what they believed were unfair taxes, and the authority of administrators they deemed corrupt. One reason that those who wished to assert their authority were often not able to do so was demographic: the number of elites remained small. Despite rich agricultural lands, North Carolina did not possess good ports like neighboring South Carolina and Virginia: it was difficult for North Carolinians to get their commodities to world markets and the plantation districts remained relatively small. Elite outsiders who visited North Carolina, like the Virginian William Byrd, described the colony disdainfully. Byrd termed the colony "Lubberland," where men did little work, satisfied with the abundance that was easily harnessed for subsistence. Possessing little apparent economic value compared to other colonies, the proprietary and imperial governments paid scant attention to North Carolina and extended little effort to help local elites gain control over a largely disaffected and independent-minded populace. In many ways, North Carolina remained one of the remotest of English colonies from the rest of the empire, including from its near neighbors Virginia and South Carolina.

## FRANCE IN THE MISSISSIPPI VALLEY

France was the only European nation to establish significant settlements in the center of the future United States. Whereas English settlements hugged the Atlantic Coast, and the Spanish occupied the southern periphery in Florida and New Mexico, the French used the St. Lawrence Seaway in Canada as a springboard to the Great Lakes region, with numbers of traders heading much further to the distant west. By the last quarter of the 17th century, French traders, missionaries, and then soldiers had descended the Mississippi River and traversed the Arkansas, Missouri, and other rivers that fed into the Mississippi. Hundreds of young French males established trading relations and kin connections through marriage with dozens of native groups. As a result, the French built numerous trading posts and forts extending from Hudson Bay in Canada, south through the Great Lakes into the Missouri and Illinois country, eventually reaching the Gulf of Mexico. France was never sure what to make of its inland empire. From an imperial perspective, there was hope that their colonists would discover mines, and in the southern reaches pursue plantation agriculture. However things turned out, they hoped to keep the English out of the huge domain they claimed and to develop their own great empire on the American mainland.

## French Establishment of Louisiana

French entry into the Southeast began with the explorer La Salle's descent of the Mississippi in 1683, which proved that the Mississippi River fed into the Gulf of Mexico. La Salle convinced the French king to sponsor his return with a fleet of ships, but on his return he could not relocate the mouth of the Mississippi and got lost to the west, making his expedition an utter failure. In his wake, France attempted a two-pronged approach to expanding its empire in the interior of the American continent. Missionaries descended the Mississippi from Canada to convert Indians to Christianity, while soldiers, led by the French Canadian Pierre Le Moyne d'Iberville, arrived from the south by sea and settled the Gulf Coast establishing French power at Mobile (Alabama) in 1699.

Iberville visited many native peoples in the region, whom the French found on the defensive from the slave-raiding of the Chickasaw and their allies. French diplomacy hinged on their ability to organize Indians against the English and their slaving allies. Many smaller groups moved near French settlements and aided the French immeasurably—as military allies and trading partners. But the most important French ally was the Choctaw, the largest and most powerful confederacy in the area, who lived in central Mississippi. Although heavily victimized by the slavers, the Choctaw stoutly maintained their power through military skill and diplomacy. While the French tirelessly sought to separate the Chickasaw from the English and have them make peace with the Choctaw, the Choctaw would not forgive the Chickasaw for their slaving and invariably prevented a French rapprochement with the Chickasaw.

In the Illinois and Arkansas country, the French established several important forts to secure trade and the local European and Indian population against the military encroachments of the Iroquois, who had been pushing Algonquins westward into French alliance. As noted in the last chapter, Iroquois raiding parties traveled over 1,000 miles to secure booty and attempt to control the fur trade west of the Appalachians. By the end of the 17th century, the Iroquois largely ended their forays to the Mississippi and increasingly confined themselves to the trans-Appalachian region from southern Canada to the Carolinas, and particularly to New York, Pennsylvania, the Ohio Country, and along the eastern Great Lakes. This provided some respite for French settlements in the Mississippi Valley, particularly in the Illinois and Arkansas Country, but France expended relatively little resources on developing these regions. As in the English empire, the French were far more concerned with their islands in the West Indies, since these yielded great wealth through the valuable sugar crop, than investment in mainland colonies that provided limited short-term economic gain.

## French and Indians

In Louisiana, French settlement remained tenuous. Relatively few French emigrated and rarely did France send enough supplies to meet colonists' needs or fulfill Indians' desire for trade. French settlement of the Illinois Country helped the more southern settlements somewhat, as farmers shipped wheat south to fill hungry mouths, but it was not unusual for French commanders to send their soldiers to live with Indians during periodic food shortages. Dependent on Indians for a host of needs, the French developed great intimacy by crossing cultural boundaries. As in the Great Lakes region, French soldiers manned small posts in dispersed locales, living in close contact with Indian peoples, which lead to many marriages of French men and Indian women. The Church and the home government debated the efficacy of these marriages and decided they would be acceptable as long as the women converted to Catholicism.

In Louisiana and Canada, the French had a broader array of interactions with native peoples than the English and Spanish colonists generally had with their native neighbors. Europeans generally believed their own cultures much superior to the Indians', but the French were more at ease and curious about Indians. The nature of French settlement called for intimacy. French traders carved out lives living in Indian villages. French priests lived in Indian towns, rather than moving them to missions like the Spanish. French political leaders often learned native languages, unlike some Spanish and most English leaders. In this regard, it is worthwhile to compare Spanish, English, and French first-hand accounts of American Indians written by colonists and officials. Spanish reports tended to be detailed (often statistical) reckonings of Spanish success, or lack thereof, among Indians. The question for the Spaniard: How well are we accomplishing our objectives of converting Indians? English observers focused on political machinations: How might groups of Indians be manipulated, and who were their friends and enemies? In contrast, French accounts lacked the precise bureaucratic renderings of the Spanish, and though they discussed Indian politics like the English, they displayed greater interest in Indian culture and mores such as dance, dress, sexual behavior, and ceremonial rites. This curiosity, however, should not be confused with notions of equality with indigenous peoples.

The intimacy and exchange of culture among French and Indians in Louisiana also included Africans imported as slaves. Although slaves and masters often lived in antagonistic, if not violent relationships, the fluidity of the frontier forced creative adaptations by all parties. Africans, Indians, and Europeans in Louisiana influenced one another greatly as goods, foodways, music, folklore, skills, technology, architecture, and religion all were readily exchanged and adapted. New French arrivals expressed shock at the intimacy and cultural practices of French settlers who lived with Indian wives and worked closely with Africans. Even those who resided in French towns such as New Orleans (established 1718) adapted many characteristics of Indians and Africans. The Creole culture that developed continued to shape the region in the coming centuries, with the result that racial lines were more nuanced and seemingly haphazard than the much stricter racial divides that existed in Spanish and especially English settlements.

## French Problems in Louisiana

Despite the cross-cultural intimacy of many individuals and the creolization of cultures, the French had no intention of ceding their political dominance. When the French did desire Indian land, their behavior mirrored the English. In 1729, French land hunger led to war with the powerful Natchez, who inhabited rich lands on the Mississippi River in modern-day Mississippi. The Natchez were one of the few chiefdoms surviving from the Mississippian Era. They still built great mounds and temples, worshipped the Sun, and lived in a highly hierarchical society. Many French admired their culture, but those who desired their land had the means to provoke the Natchez to war.

Fearing that an alliance of Indians with Africans in the Natchez War (1729–1733) would destroy the colony—hundreds of African slaves had joined the Natchez at the outbreak of war—the French commandant, Etienne Périer, purposefully had a group of African slaves murder a party of Chaöucha Indians below New Orleans, whom he knew innocent of any wrongdoing against the colony. He did this solely to create hostilities between Africans and Indians in the region. The Choctaw also agreed to help the French by attacking the Natchez. They recaptured the Africans who had joined the Natchez, but refused to turn them over to the French, using them as pawns to gain concessions in their trade relations with the French. Ultimately they returned the slaves. Choctaw defeat of the Natchez was an unmitigated disaster for the latter. The Natchez lost their homeland. Many refugees joined the Chickasaw and then the Creek and Cherokee, while the French shipped Natchez captives as slaves to the West Indies. Former governor Jean-Baptiste Le Moyne de Bienville, who had known the Natchez for 30 years, on his return to assume the governorship of Louisiana, encountered Natchez chiefs shortly after their enslavement in Santo Domingo. The chiefs begged Bienville to take them with him to their homeland promising to restore the peace that once existed between their peoples. There is no record that Bienville did so.

The French held onto Louisiana not because of any inherent strength of the colony, but because many Southern Indians saw the French as a useful counterweight to the English and bolstered the colony. In 1717, for instance, the Creek had invited the French to build a fort among them (Fort Toulouse, Alabama) to receive easier access to trade goods, but also to show the English their independence and that they would continue a line of neutrality between the Europeans. Although French trade goods were generally more expensive and of poorer quality than English goods, the French had the advantage of being able to supply plenty of gunpowder at reasonable prices and to place gunsmiths in native villages to repair guns. With widely dispersed posts and few population centers, Louisiana never fulfilled French hopes for becoming an economically valuable colony. But from an imperial standpoint, it displayed great potential, as the French were well placed, particularly through alliances with Indians, for building a substantial empire in the interior of North America.

## SPANISH AND INDIANS IN THE SOUTHWEST

When the French established Louisiana, there was but one European colony to the west in what is now the United States. A century earlier, Spain had extended its Mexican empire north with the conquest of New Mexico in 1598 by Juan Oñate. Oñate had sought an easy route to the Atlantic, but he and other Spanish officials mistakenly gauged the width of the North American continent, and also how far south they were in relation to places like Roanoke. From New Mexico, Oñate led expeditions northeast all the way to Kansas before returning to New Mexico and setting out to locate the Pacific Ocean, which he reached in 1605. This piqued Spanish interest in California. But Spanish officials forestalled building a base on the California coast, which would have been useful for trade with the Philippines, out of fear it would attract English and Dutch interlopers, thus undermining Spanish security in Acapulco, Mexico. This delayed Spanish settlement of California until 1769.

### Missions in New Mexico

As with Florida, New Mexico drained imperial resources, as it did not possess the precious metals nor rich agricultural environment that could make it self-supportive. The Spanish maintained the colony for strategic and religious purposes. Missionaries, soldiers, and a smattering of colonists immigrated to the colony—no more than

3,000 Spanish at any time lived in 17th-century New Mexico. Santa Fe served as the province's capital, while Franciscan missionaries sought to convert the Pueblo, Apache, and Navajo, enjoying great success in the 1620s. The missionaries brought an array of gifts—European-manufactured goods—and the Indians erected churches and other buildings for the missions. A few missionaries learned native languages and put special effort into the teaching and conversion of children. Later they taught Spanish to the Indians. Priests learned native customs so they could more effectively alter them. As in French Canada, one of the missionaries' biggest challenges lay in keeping their charges from learning European vices. The missionaries tried to segregate Indian communities by controlling when Indians could leave the missions and by barring non-Indians from living there.

Indians remained on the missions as a means to secure their lands against the encroachments of colonists, and to obtain Spanish assistance against enemy Indians. The Pueblos and Spanish mutually supported each other against the Apache; later the Apache invited missionaries to obtain support against the Comanches. There were other benefits as well. Many Indians believed the priests' spiritual power helped them contend with the natural elements, such as rain and drought, and to insure good harvests. The missionaries were much more successful among sedentary agriculturalists like the Pueblos than roaming hunters like the Apaches. The agriculturalists welcomed the domestic animals the Spanish introduced, particularly cattle. As was so often the case in New World conversion, New Mexican Indians grafted Christian beliefs onto their own, refusing to discard one spiritual world for another.

Conflicts occurred over native labor to support the missions and from efforts of Spanish officials, soldiers, and settlers to extract native labor. Pueblos were forced to labor for Spanish profits—gathering nuts and salt, manufacturing leather goods, working in the fields, and transporting goods to market, sometimes over 500 miles. Brutal and humiliating punishments were inflicted on those who refused to do Spanish bidding or continued to practice aspects of their religion banned by the missionaries.

Nor could the Spanish protect the Pueblo from disease, enemies, and drought. The Pueblo population declined nearly 80% in the first 80 years after Spanish settlement to between 20,000 and 25,000. Some of this resulted not only from disease, but also from warfare. Pueblo-Spanish attacks on the Navajo in the mid-17th century led to Navajo counterattacks that devastated several settlements. The Spanish paid ransoms to the Navajo, Kiowa, and Comanche to redeem Pueblo prisoners, who then had to work 10 to 20 years to pay back the Spanish, effectively making them slaves.

The Spanish introduced another form of slavery in New Mexico by creating a large caste of *genizaros*. These were Indians captured from "alien" groups and forced to become slave-soldiers. The Spanish modeled the genizaros on the Ottoman practice of capturing Christians in the Balkans and using them as slave-soldiers and administrators. The genizaros would not have ties to local Indians and could be expected to retain loyalty to the Spanish. They received land for themselves and their families but remained slaves performing military service for the colony. Thousands of genizaros were kept during the Spanish period.

## The Pueblo Revolts

The combination of forced labor and drought; the failure of the Spanish to protect the Pueblo from external enemies; the abuses of priests, soldiers, and settlers; and the exaction of heavy tribute led to a revolt carefully organized by chiefs and medicine men. On August 15, 1680, Pueblo led by Papé sieged Santa Fe, the center of Spanish power in New Mexico, which fell nine days later. Twenty-one Franciscans and 380 colonists were killed, and the survivors fled to El Paso.

The torture of the missionaries illustrated the blame and hostilities many Pueblo felt towards them. Pueblo military and religious leaders forced their followers to discard all remnants of Catholicism. Crosses were removed from around necks, church iconography destroyed or put to new uses, and all were barred from mentioning Christ, the Virgin Mary, and the saints. Use of the Spanish language was prohibited.

The Spanish made several attempts to retake the province. All failed. But a decade later, the unity of the Pueblo gave way to internal factionalism and warfare. This prepared the way for the Spanish to re-conquer the province with relative ease in 1692, many Pueblo seemingly accepting Spanish rule. When new colonists arrived in 1693 from Mexico and El Paso, the Spanish found they were mistaken about Pueblo sentiment as many opposed their re-entry. Bitter fighting eradicated the armed resistance of the Indians, and the Spanish re-established 11 missions near Santa Fe.

A few years later, in 1696, the Pueblo again planned to overthrow the Spanish. Five missionaries and a couple dozen other Spanish were killed. But this revolt lacked the unity of the 1680 rebellion, and after six months, the Spanish prevailed. Once again they re-established the missions, but fearing future rebellions, the Spanish employed great restraint in seeking to control Indian spiritual and material lives, holding only loose reins over the Pueblo.

## The Texas Missions

During their eviction from New Mexico, the Spanish grew extremely interested in the lands to the east—modern-day Texas—though their reasons had nothing to do with New Mexico. Learning of La Salle's discovery of the mouth of the Mississippi, and of his subsequent return to establish a colony, the Spanish sent 11 expeditions in a four-year period to remove the French. Thus Spanish interest in Texas arose only to keep another European power from its occupation, as a French presence on the Gulf of Mexico would threaten Florida and Mexico.

Once they learned of La Salle's failure to establish a colony, the Spanish imperative for settlement declined but they decided to establish missions in Texas against an expected French return. Missions had the advantage of being the least expensive form of occupation, as they were cheaper than supporting large contingents of soldiers at military outposts and could become self-supporting. The Spanish selected the sedentary Caddoes of East Texas, who initially welcomed the Spanish in the early 1690s. But the Spanish also brought small pox with them, and in the midst of a terrible epidemic, the Caddoes evicted the missionaries.

After French settlement at Mobile in 1699, the Spanish kept a close eye on the intruders. When Frenchmen from Louisiana entered New Spain in 1714, the Spanish once again undertook the building of missions in Texas. Five presidios with missions were established from 1716 to 1733, but only three were long-lived: San Antonio (1718–1821), Matagorda Bay (1721–1821), and western Louisiana (1721–1772). Three additional missions were built in the 1750s.

One reason Texas Indians accepted the missions was for help in resisting the raids of Spanish and Indians to obtain slaves. In the 1720s, the Lipsan Apache of central Texas raided the missions for horses. The Spanish responded with their own raids. The Apache tried to make peace, but the raids continued—for the Spanish found profits in enslaving Apaches. The missionaries pressured their government to halt the raids and bring peace to the region, but to little avail. By the 1740s, warfare increased with Apache attempting to remove the Spanish from San Antonio to end the slaving, and the Spanish were forced to accept peace. The two then united against the aggressive inroads of Wichitas and Comanches, who with other allied Indians battered the Spanish in Texas and the Apaches in the coming decades, selling their captives in Spanish New Mexico and French Louisiana. As in most other colonial regions, the enslavement of Indian peoples played a central role in Texas's early history—and in the lives of its peoples.

## Conclusion

By the early 1730s, clear patterns had developed in early America that mostly remained unseen and unknowable to those who lived at the time. In hindsight, the English colonies were far more secure and powerful vis-à-vis French, Spanish, and native enemies than all the powers realized. The English colonies were also extremely well integrated into the international economy, which contributed to their ability to attract large numbers of immigrants, including indentured servants. Their military weakness lay in their prosperity. Far-flung plantations and frontier communities were difficult to defend from invaders. But older settled areas generally lay free from invasion by land and sea.

The French position in North America looked extremely promising. French expansion to the Mississippi and the Gulf of Mexico gave them a huge presence in the interior continent diplomatically and politically. The economic benefits were scarce to be seen, however, as few French went to North America to develop plantations or extractive industries, and the pelt trade had only limited economic value. But the foundation had been laid and the French would build upon it in the next generation.

For Spain, the present and future did not look so promising in North America. Spanish power rapidly declined in Florida from the crumbling of the mission system under the onslaught of the English-allied slavers. The Spanish barely held on in Florida. In the Southwest, the Spanish remained largely unchallenged by other Europeans. But the story was largely the same in both regions. The Spanish attracted few colonists to their settlements and had to devote their resources to the missions and soldiers to secure their domain. The lack of profitability of the missions, the inability of colonists to reap great economic rewards, and the strength of neighboring Indians limited the growth of Spain's American empire in the Southeast and Southwest. The strategic importance of these colonies to Spain lay in their protecting more valuable areas of the empire, particularly Mexico, from the French and English.

In 1730, few, if any, American Indians east of the Mississippi River had no contacts with Europeans, but most of the land remained in native hands. The French in Louisiana occupied relatively small parcels. Both Carolina colonies were sparsely populated, a situation that would change after 1730. South Carolina thereafter enjoyed a rapid expansion of their plantation system bolstered by the importation of large numbers of African slaves and precipitated by a parliamentary law in 1729 that allowed rice producers to ship their crop directly to many more places in the Atlantic world. North Carolina would attract large numbers of European immigrants, many of whom took up subsistence farming. And the English shortly expanded southward by founding the new colony of Georgia. But this demographic and territorial expansion had relatively little impact on the Indians of the southeast for a generation. Not until the 1760s, and even later in most places, was pressure placed on Indians for their land in the South. English settlements remained east of the Appalachians and tended to hug the Atlantic Coast below Virginia. This is not to say that the English had no impact on the southern Indians, only that outside of the low country that impact did not concern Indian land. Slaving, trade, warfare, and disease emanating from the Europeans forced the Southern Indians to adapt to rapidly changing circumstances. One of the most notable and important adaptations was the creation of powerful confederacies. The Creek,

Choctaw, Cherokee, and Chickasaw all faced numerous internal problems, and were hostile towards each other, but they were powerful enough to resist European encroachments and participate in Atlantic world trade. Not until the 19th century would there be a precipitous decline in their power.

For the African peoples of the Southeast, most of whom were slaves, their lives were shaped by a confluence of circumstances that to some degree depended on where they lived. Unlike Africans in the rural North who had less opportunity for forming family and communal bonds with other Africans because of their dispersal through the countryside and the unbalanced gender ratios of urban areas, slave life slowly gained some stability in the Carolinas, as it did in Virginia and Maryland. Africans wrested into slavery in those colonies could at least find solace in forming family and community ties with others of similar cultures and condition. Nevertheless, work conditions and diet were likely much better in the north than on the rice plantations of South Carolina, where a brutal work regimen was in place by 1730. Slave discontent rose in that decade and would explode in rebellion (see chapter eleven).

# DOCUMENTS

## 10.1. The Pueblo Revolt of 1696

*The 1696 revolt of the Pueblo against the Spanish in New Mexico has not received as much attention from scholars as the earlier uprising of 1680. The second revolt was not as widespread, nor did it result in Spain's abandonment of New Mexico, as occurred in 1680. But the second revolt led to many adjustments in Spanish relations with the Pueblo to prevent a reoccurrence. The following excerpts, from two letters by a Franciscan friar, Francisco de Vargas, provide a Spanish perspective on the*

*(Continued)*

*martyred deaths of his co-religious and countrymen, the assistance he received from Christian Indians against the apostates, and his skepticism about ever bringing the latter to "true" religion. On what grounds did Vargas believe the Indians could never become true Christians?*

*Fray Francisco de Vargas to the Commissary General, Santa Fe, July 21, 1696.*

OUR most reverend father commissary general, Fray Manuel de Monzabal, my father and lord.

Our most reverend father commissary general, I have written to Your Most Reverend Paternity on May 17 of this year, in which I reported to Your Most Reverend Paternity the state in which this holy custody found itself, and now, on July 21 of this present year, I write to report to you, with sorrow in my heart, the sad and unfortunate death of five religious of this holy custody who passed away at the hands of the apostate Indians of our faith. The deceased are: father preacher Fray Jose Arbizu, secretary general of this custody and minister president of the pueblo of San Cristóbal, and in his company they killed the father preacher and *definidor* [elected representative of the friars of the province] of this custody Fray Antonio Carbonel, of the province of Valencia, and in the pueblo of San Ildefonso the father preacher Fray Francisco Corbera, minister president of the said pueblo, died along with some Spanish men, women, and children who took refuge in the convent, which was surrounded by the Indians and set afire on all sides, and not being able to escape, they huddled in a small cell, but it was to no avail because of the fierce flames, and they were suffocated by the smoke and all of them died. In their company was the father preacher Fray Antonio Moreno, who that day had gone to the convent for spiritual consolation. The said father was the minister president of the pueblo of Nambé, in which pueblo the Indians killed some other Spaniards and one woman. In the pueblo of San Diego de Jémez they killed the apostolic father preacher Fray Francisco de Jesus, son of the holy province of Catalonia, and in the said pueblo they killed a soldier who had the rank of captain, three Spaniards, and three children. And in the pueblo of San Juan de los Jémez, they killed the *alcalde mayor* and two of his servants. So that of all of the Spaniards who died in different places there were about thirty persons.

The other religious who were at their missions miraculously escaped with their lives. There are no words to magnify the outrages they committed with regard to the objects of divine worship, profaning the sacred vessels; inspired by the devil, they pulled off even the crosses and rosaries that they had hanging from their necks and threw them to the ground. With such diabolical actions we cannot have much hope that there will be any emendation of these missions, for they have relapsed so many times in their apostasy, and it is known that they acted in *odiu fide* [hatred of the faith] in carrying out the above outrage, and the said Indians prefer to die in rebellion and apostasy rather than to yield or subject themselves to the yoke of the church. . . .

May God our Lord keep Your Most Reverend Paternity many happy years for my protection and that of this holy custody.

The convent of our father Saint Francis, Villa of Santa Fe, July 21, the year 1696. Your Most Reverend Paternity's son and humble servant, who kisses the feet of Your Most Reverend Paternity.

Fray Francisco de Vargas.

*Fray Francisco de Vargas to the Provincial, Santa Fe, July 21, 1696.*

OUR very reverend father minister provincial Clemente de Ledesma, my father and lord.

[S]eeing that Father Fray Francisco de Jesús was late in replying to the letter I sent him telling him to come to the mission of Santa Ana, I presumed that he was with the *alcalde mayor* of his pueblo and two other Spaniards, locked up in the convent and defending themselves from the multitude of hostile Indians, and I judged that they had not come in answer to my call, even though there still was time, because they had no horses to do so.

Therefore, I decided to go and rescue them, taking with me the servants who accompanied me, who are experienced and brave, and these were joined by some Indians of the pueblo of Santa Ana and others of the pueblo of Zia, and so from all of them I had some consolation in seeing that they offered to accompany me even without my asking them to do so. All together, some forty persons were gathered, and I exhorted them to take heed that they were Christians and that they should realize that they were pursuing the cause of God our Lord,

because it was my intention to go and rescue Father Jesús and the Spaniards and the sacred vessels, for I had no other motive. To this they displayed great bravery and said that they would follow me, as they did with their arms and horses. But despite all of these demonstrations I did not fully trust the said Indians, and I ordered the domestic servants who accompanied me personally not to leave me but rather to be always at my side, to be sure that I would not be taken by surprise by some treacherous act.

And having traveled about six leagues, we arrived at the pueblo of San Juan de los Jémez, where the minister was the apostolic father preacher Fray Miguel de Trizio, who a few days earlier I had granted permission to go to the pueblo of Pecos at the request and for the consolation of the father who was stationed there. And on coming in view of the said pueblo of San Juan, the Indians who accompanied me decided, themselves, to lay siege to the pueblo to see if they could capture an Indian from whom they could find out if Father Fray Francisco de Jesús was alive or dead, because the pueblo of San Juan is only one league from that of San Diego, where he resided. And having placed this plan in operation, the advance to the pueblo was made, and eleven persons, children, men, and women, were captured, and these later stated that Father Jesús and the Spaniards had been killed with the help of other nations.

But the said Indians who accompanied me were not satisfied with the eleven persons taken prisoners, and some of them went out to explore

*(Continued)*

the roads, where they found many Indians who were fleeing to the mountains loaded with food supplies and clothing, and when they were seen, they opened battle and killed five of them, and of the Indians who accompanied me, only five were wounded, but not dangerously. And they took from the apostates many horses, clothing, and corn. And during the time that they were engaged in this activity, with the few Indians who remained with me I ventured to the convent to remove what I could of what pertained to our divine religion, and what I found was the images of the saints destroyed and in pieces and the crosses broken. And in the church it was the same, the rosaries thrown on the ground and covered with feathers, ashes, and some rabbit skins, leaving no trace of anything Christian, a mockery which caused very much affliction in my heart and which would cause the same to any Catholic on seeing the little benefit that had been derived from these souls. And passing on to their houses and dwellings, I searched them and removed many articles of divine worship, some of which they had buried and others hidden. And while we were engaged in this activity, we were already noticed by the pueblo above, from which many Indians came on foot and on horseback, some armed with harquebuses and leather jackets, but it was the will of our Lord God that on reaching about four squares from the pueblo, where we were, seeing the large number of their adversaries and judging that all those who were accompanying me were Spaniards, they returned in flight to their pueblos, for which I give many

thanks to His Divine Majesty, because the removal of the articles of divine worship, which I have referred to, was accomplished. Women and children were captured besides the men, who were five. Three of the Indians had an untimely end for their little heed, because the governors and captains of the two pueblos of Santa Ana and Zia together decided to send them to the lord governor, and that night one of them escaped from the *estufa* [steam house] where they had been imprisoned, and in the morning when they were inspected two were found who had hanged themselves by their own hands. They are so obstinate that they prefer to die in despair rather than live under the yoke of our holy religion. . . .

As for any prospect of winning over the rebellious Indians in the mountains, there is no hope that they will submit to our holy faith. And although the governor of this kingdom, in the campaigns he has made with his soldiers and Indian allies, having punished and killed up to eighty Indians, having captured some women and children, and having seized their food, even with all of this[,] it is evident that the enemy is very rebellious and contumacious in their relapse to apostasy. And they are well aware of the little military strength of the Spaniards and that the rigors of winter are near at hand, at which time the Indians can make war against the Spaniards in full safety without any harm being done to them. And what is most regrettable is that the governor, seeing the wickedness that they have carried out up to now, is sending a mission of peace, as he has done with three Indian women of those taken captive, whom he sent to the mountains with some crosses to negotiate peace with them, as though the said apostates, being enemies of our holy faith, would venerate or adore the holy cross, especially when they have just completed the outrage that they committed on the priests. And I recognize that if they should come down peacefully, what minister will want to assist them, when it is seen how little progress is gained in the attempt to win their souls, and what can be expected in living with them in the future? And if the governor aspires to pacify them only by his point of honor and standing, and if this peace is only to be a pretense to cover up their wickedness, as bloodthirsty wolves in sheep's clothing, we ministers of the gospel cannot profit from such evilness. And now that God our Lord has been served, with only five religious and approximately thirty Spaniards having perished, with the women captives who have remained with them, we cannot place ourselves under the risk of having all of the priestly ministers perish.

Convent of Our Father Saint Francis of Your Most Reverent Paternity. Villa of Santa Fe, July 21, the year 1696. Your son and humble servant, who kisses the feet of Your Most Reverent Paternity.

Fray Francisco de Vargas.

---

Source: *The Pueblo Indian Revolt of 1696 and the Franciscan Missions in New Mexico: Letters of the Missionaries and Related Documents.* Translated and edited by J. Manuel Espinosa (1988), 243–246, 249–257.

## 10.2. Andre Pénicaut's Adventures in Louisiana

*Andre Pénicaut's account is an invaluable source on the early years of French Louisiana. A master carpenter, Pénicaut provides a "common man's" view of the Indians and his fellow Frenchmen during his life in America from 1698 to 1721. On several occasions, Pénicaut took the opportunity to live with Indians, and recorded their habits, customs, and beliefs. A food shortage among the French led the French governor to permit many of his men "to go into the woods and live from hunting or live among the savage nations friendly to [the French]," until relief supplies arrived from France. Pénicaut and several others took advantage of the situation and spent many enjoyable months among the Natchez Indians. Why did Pénicaut so enjoy his time living with Indians?*

### The Year 1704

As I was young and passionately fond of rambling, I went with the group. We went in several row boats, all keeping together, as far as the Baye de St. Louis, where we had very good hunting and fishing, off which we lived. After a few days I proposed to twenty of my comrades, the youngest ones, that we go back up the Missicipy together and visit some of the nations along the bank of the river. I was acquainted with all these nations because on my

*(Continued)*

own account I had ascended it three times already . . . and because, too, I had learned their languages tolerably well during the five years I had been in Louisiana, especially Mobilien, the principal one, which is understood in all the nations. So, without saying anything to our other comrades, some twenty of us set out with three boats and one kettle. We ascended as high as the Soupnatcha, where we found the Biloxis, a small nation that earlier lived close to the first fort we had after we arrived in the country. M. de St. Denis had since made them come to that place and settle because, by having them nearer to his fort, he would sometimes get food from them with which to subsist the more easily in his establishment. After spending the night in their huts, we set out again next morning. We took some small supplies of food stuffs that they gave us and carried our boats overland to a point half a league from there, where the Missicipy is, and embarked upon it.

When we got to Baton Rouge, we went ashore to hunt. We entered a forest, some ten of us who were together, the others staying with the boats to watch them and to keep fire burning. Beyond the forest into which we had entered we found a prairie. Never in my life have I seen such great numbers of buffalo, harts, and roes as there were on that prairie. We killed five buffaloes, which we skinned and cut up in order to carry some to our comrades who had stayed with the boats; and as there was fire burning we broiled some of it on spits and boiled some, too, in our kettle. Our comrades made some shelters on the bank of the Missicipy while we went

for the rest of our buffaloes, which we transported in our boats. We felt so well off at that place that we remained more than ten days. Some of us went hunting every day, especially during the evening, in the woods where one commonly finds bustards and turkeys coming to roost in the trees; so we changed our menu from time to time.

Time did not drag for us except at night; for, young as we were, we had in our own group elected a leader whom we obeyed and who made us stand sentry duty two at a time when night came. One of these sentries was given a position half a gunshot beyond the other, who watched over those asleep under the shelters. Each man took his turn of an hour at sentry duty. Furthermore, prayers were strictly held morning and night.

When ten days had passed, we cooked what we had left of the meat, put it in our boats, and set out for the Oumas, who are another savage nation friendly to the French, dwelling on the bank of the Missicipy thirty leagues from Baton Rouge. They received us very well indeed, giving us abundantly of their food supplies. Here we remained only six days, after which we left to go to the Natchez, who are the nation that has seemed to me the most courteous and civil along the banks of the Missicipy.

At noon three days later we got there and were received with every possible mark of cordiality and affection. Everybody in the village was happy because it was the opening of a dance festival, a description of which I shall give. We remained for a very long time in their villages, where we all but forgot M. de Bienville's instructions because of the amusements we had.

The village of the Natchez is the most beautiful that could be found in Louisiana. It is located one league away from the bank of the Missicipy. It is beautified by very pretty walks which nature, and not artifice, has formed there. Around it are flower-adorned prairies, broken by little hills upon which there are thickets of all kinds of fragrant trees. Several little streams of very clear water issue from beneath a mountain visible for two leagues across the prairies and, after watering them in many places, they gather up into two big creeks which encircle the village, beyond which they unite in the form of a small river which flows over very fine gravel and passes on by three villages separated one from the other by half a league and then, two leagues away, flows into the Missicipy. The water in it is very pleasant to drink, being cold as ice in summer and tepid in winter. . . .

In this village one finds every amenity conducive to association with this nation, which does not at all have the fierce manners of the other savages. All the necessaries of life are here, such as buffaloes, cows, hinds, harts, roes, chickens and turkeys and an abundance of geese. There are also fish in abundance, all kinds of them; there are carp weighing more than twenty pounds, which are of an exquisite taste. As for fruit, there is more than in any other place in Louisiana. They have many cherries, which grow in bunches like our grapes in France; they are black and have a touch of bitterness, but are excellent in brandy, in which they put many of them. In their woods everywhere are many peach trees, plum trees, mulberries, and walnuts. They have three kinds of walnut trees: there are some that bear nuts as big as one's fist; from these they make bread for their soup. But the best are scarcely bigger than one's thumb; these they call pacanes.

Beginning with the first of May, their prairies are flecked with every sort of flower and fragrant grass. Here grow multitudes of strawberries as big as one's thumb and of an exquisite flavor. In their woods they have a grape that grows as a vine arbor; the stem clings to trees and grows round and round them. This grape is small and a little sour; a wine is made from it that will not keep more than a week or ten days.

This nation owns nine settlements, or villages; but the village where we were is foremost of them all and the most substantial because it is the residence of the Grand Chief; he is named Sun, which means noble. They are much more decently housed than any other savage nation. In front of their houses they have peach trees right in the open, which bear excellent peaches and make a pleasant shade for their houses.

Natchez men and women are very handsome and quite decently clothed. The women wear white linen dresses that hang from the neck to the feet, made almost like our Andriennes of the ladies of France. They make this linen cloth from nettle bark and mulberry bark. They prepare the bark in the following manner: they soak it in water for a week; they put it out to dry in the sun for a long time; and when the bark is quite dry, they beat it until it becomes tow; then they put it through the laundering process and wash it three or four times until it is white. Then they spin it and make it

*(Continued)*

into linen cloth, which they use according to their needs.

The men wear deer skins made like our jackets, which hang halfway down their thighs. They have *braguets* and leggings under them, which cover them from the feet to the hips. They have rather handsome faces, and so do their wives. Their speaking voices are quite pleasing, as they do not speak so strongly from the throat as the other savages. The dress of the girls is different from that of the women: girls wear only *braguets*, which are made like those little taffeta aprons that the young ladies in France wear over their skirts. The *braguets* worn by the girls, which are commonly made from a fabric of white thread, cover only the forepart of their nakedness, from the waist to the knees. They tie them at the back with two pieces of tape, to the ends of which they hang tassels that drop down behind. In front, fringes are sewed to the hem of the *braguets* until the girls reach puberty, when they take the dress of a woman. The girls are courteous and love the French very much. We found it fascinating to watch them dancing during their festivals, when they put on their most beautiful *braguets*, and the women their pretty white dresses, all of them bareheaded, their long black hair hanging to their knees and as low as the heels of many of them.

Here is how their dances are arranged: women dance with men, and boys with girls. They always dance twenty or thirty together, as many boys as girls. A married man is not permitted to dance with the girls nor boys to dance with the women. After they have lighted a great flambeau, which is commonly the dry trunk of an old pine tree, which blazes up, lighting the public square of the village, and another in front of the house of the Grand Chief, the master of the dance, at the head of some thirty men and women, commences the dance at sunset to the sound of a little drum and the cries of spectators; and each one dances in turn till midnight, when the men go to their homes with their wives, turning the area over to the boys and the girls, who dance from midnight till broad daylight. The dances are repeated time and again, each one dancing in turn; they are danced just about like the new cotillion in France. With this difference: when a boy has danced in that region with the girl at his side or in front of him, he is permitted to escort her beyond the village and into one of the thickets out on the prairie, where he dances with her another cotillion a la Missicipyene. Afterwards they go back to the village square and take their turn dancing as before. Thus they continue their dances till broad-open daylight, so that in the morning the boys in particular are like disinterred corpses, on account of the loss of sleep as well as the exhaustion caused by dancing with the girls.

I should not be at all surprised if these girls are lustful and devoid of restraint because their fathers and their mothers and their religion teach them that, when they leave this world, they have to cross over a narrow and difficult plank before they can enter their Grand Village, where they claim they go after death, and that in the Grand

Village will be only those who will have made merry indeed with the boys-they will pass easily across this plank.

From the tenderest age, what detestable lessons are instilled in them-sup-ported by the liberty and the idleness in which they are maintained! For until they are twenty or twenty-five, girls do nothing else, their fathers and mothers being obliged to keep their food always ready for them and, furthermore, according to their tastes and their demands, up until the time they are married.

If by these wretched prostitutions they become pregnant and give birth to children, their fathers and mothers ask them whether they wish to keep their babies. If they answer that they do not and that they cannot suckle them, the poor little unfortunate newborns are strangled outside the huts and buried, without the slightest stir. But if a girl wishes to keep her baby, it is given to her and she suckles it. . . .

Nobility among them is quite different from nobility among our Europeans, for in France the more ancient it is, the more it is esteemed. Their lineage, on the contrary, is considered noble only up to the seventh generation; furthermore, they derive their nobility from the woman and not from the man. When I asked them the reason for this, they answered me that nobility can come only from the woman, because the woman is more certain than the man about whom the children belong to.

Source: *Fleur de Lys and Calumet: Being the Pénicaut Narrative of French Adventure in Louisiana.* Translated and edited by Richebourg Gaillard McWilliams (1953), 80–90.

# Bibliography

Barr, Juliana. *Peace Came in the Form of a Woman: Indians and Spaniards in the Texas Borderlands* (2007).

Braund, Kathryn E. Holland. *Deerskins and Duffels: Creek Indian Trade with Anglo-America, 1685–1815* (1993).

Brooks, James F. *Captives and Cousins: Slavery, Kinship and Community in the Southwest Borderlands* (2002).

Chipman, Donald E. *Spanish Texas, 1519–1821* (1992).

Crane, Verner W. *The Southern Frontier, 1670–1732* (1928).

Gallay, Alan. *The Indian Slave Trade: The Rise of the English Empire in the American South, 1670–1717* (2002).

Giraud, Marcel. *A History of French Louisiana: Volume Five, The Company of the Indies, 1723–1731* (1987).

Hall, Gwendolyn Midlo. *Africans in Colonial Louisiana: The Development of Afro-Creole Culture in the Eighteenth Century* (1992).

Hann, John H. *Apalachee: The Land Between the Rivers* (1988).

John, Elizabeth A. H. *Storms Brewed in Other Men's Worlds: The Confrontation of Indians, Spanish, and French in the Southwest, 1540–1795* (1975).

Kelton, Paul. *Epidemics and Enslavement: Biological Catastrophe in the Native Southeast, 1492–1715* (2007).

Knaut, Andrew L. *The Pueblo Revolt: Conquest and Resistance in Seventeenth-Century New Mexico* (1995).

Mcilvenna, Noeleen. *A Very Mutinous People: The Struggle for North Carolina, 1660–1713* (2009).

Ramsey, William L. *The Yamasee War: A Study of Culture, Economy, and Conflict in the Colonial South* (2008).

Spicer, Edward. *Cycles of Conquest: The Impact of Spain, Mexico, and the United States on the Indians of the Southwest, 1533–1960* (1962).

Usner, Daniel H., Jr. *Indians, Settlers and Slaves in a Frontier Exchange Economy: The Lower Mississippi Valley Before 1783* (1992).

Weber, David J. *The Spanish Frontier in North America* (1992).

Wood, Peter H. *Black Majority: Negroes in South Carolina from 1670 Through the Stono Rebellion* (1974).

PART **3**

# Colonies, Empires, and Peoples in a Transfomative Age, 1730–1783

# 11

# Problems and Solutions in an Era of Growth, 1730–1770

## INTRODUCTION

From 1730 to 1770, the British colonies emerged as the dominant power east of the Mississippi River. But in 1730, let alone 1750, it was not entirely clear that things would turn out this way. The power of Indian confederacies in the South, and the Iroquois in the north, meant that most land in the region was in Indian hands, and remained so in 1770. Moreover, the French not only posed a threat to the British from Canada but, actively and more successfully than the British, were expanding through the interior continent.

The strength of the British colonies lay in their demographic and economic growth. The British colonies' rapid, if not phenomenal, expansion of population made conquest by French or Indians all but impossible. French and Indians could limit British territorial expansion and harass and destroy British colonial communities, but they could not effectively strike to reduce the British colonies. All they could hope for was to keep the British colonials east of the Appalachians and south of Canada.

The demographic expansion of the British colonies owed in large measure to the economic opportunities available in the British colonies, the relatively healthy environment that prompted natural increase, the availability of food to support large populations, the lack of imperial restrictions on European immigration, the inexpensive passage on ships to America for those who had a bit of capital, the prosperity of planters who could afford to import large numbers of Africans, and the membership in the British empire. Population growth fostered prosperity, and prosperity fostered population growth. Not that the two did not create problems as well. The massively growing slave population produced great wealth for the master class but threatened the colonies from within. Hostility between the older more prosperous areas that controlled the colonial legislatures and the newly colonized backcountry areas festered and broke into violence. Some of these hostilities persisted for over a century.

Free people in the British colonies in 1730 or 1750 could not predict the British colonies' eventual dominance in the east. The power of French and Indians was real and feared. The Spanish remained a force to be reckoned with in Florida. In fact, many British colonials were filled with dread about their present and future. These anxieties paved the way for the spread of evangelical Christianity in the first intercolonial movement in the British colonies: the Great Awakening. Evangelicals offered solutions to many of the problems that seemed to plague colonial America. But they were not the only voices heard. The spread of rationalism in the Enlightenment offered other methods and solutions to societal problems. This was an era of experimentation. Some of the experiments had their sources in religion, political economy, and the desire to improve the world. On the southern frontier of the British empire, a bold utopian experiment was attempted through establishment of a new colony, Georgia. In Philadelphia, public spiritedness, philanthropy, and theorizing about poverty led to the creation of new institutions to take care of the elderly and disabled, while providing employment for the working poor. Although much of the experimentation of this period failed, the emergence of self-confidence, and confidence in the future, characterized many free people in the British colonies: this trait came to define many colonial Americans and their descendants in the coming centuries.

## POPULATION GROWTH AND PROSPERITY IN THE AMERICAN COLONIES

The territorial expansion of British America owed to the tens of thousands of Europeans migrating to the colonies in the mid-18th century. The British colonies were viewed in Europe as a land of opportunity. The colonies were well integrated into British trade networks and with other Atlantic world markets in southern Europe, South America, Africa, and the West Indies. Northern merchants acquired large estates carrying the goods of their own regions, as well as from the plantation colonies of the South and the West Indies, and they transported African slaves to many colonies.

Northern farmers expanded wheat production for export, creating prosperous hinterlands around cities. The burgeoning plantation system of the South continued to provide agricultural goods to world markets, leading to a wealthy and cosmopolitan class of planters who increased production by importing ever larger numbers of African slaves. The steady increase in export commodities was matched by the growth of imports and the rise in per capita income for free people. Although there is no way to gauge per capita income for American Indians, it is clear that native peoples east of the Mississippi became more actively engaged in the market economy of the Atlantic world, assimilating European-manufactured goods into their daily lives and producing commodities for exchange. Slaves became an even more important group of commodity producers for export, but there is little data on their consumption of goods in the colonial period. (There is more data on slave consumption in the 19th century.) We do know, however, that by the 1730s the material culture of slaves altered, somewhat for the better, as family cabins replaced barracks-style shelters. Also, as the plantation system stabilized, masters increasingly used material rewards (i.e., money, items of clothing) to obtain compliant labor and allowed slaves to earn money through extra work, which led them to greater participation in the market economy as purchasers of personal items.

## Emigration and Population Growth

Emigration to the mainland British colonies exploded in the 1730s. The number of new arrivals, over 75,000, exceeded the total number of combined arrivals of the previous three decades. Although the percentage increase declined in the next three decades, the number of emigrants rose to above 100,000 in the 1740s, 120,000 in the 1750s, and approached 160,000 in the 1760s. Almost half of the new arrivals from 1730 to 1770 were Africans. The number of Africans brought forcefully to the mainland colonies quadrupled from the 1720s to the 1730s, increased again by almost 50% in the 1740s, declined by about one-sixth in the 1750s (probably owing to the Seven Years' War), and then exploded in the 1760s to over 82,000, more than double the number imported in the 1730s. The large number of African slaves imported from the 1730s through the 1770s reflects the prosperity of plantation agriculture, which provided colonial slaveholders with the capital or access to credit to make such substantial purchases. Colonial prosperity also contributed to the migration of Europeans. The number of European migrants almost tripled from the decade of the 1720s to the 1730s, and more than doubled again in the 1760s. The largest portion of European migrants in the English colonies from 1730 to 1770 comprised Germans (73,000). Scots-Irish, Catholic Irish, and English migrants each numbered about 33,000, and Scots from Scotland about 20,000. Approximately 5,000 emigrants hailed from other parts of Europe, mostly the Netherlands, France, and Sweden.

Relatively inexpensive passage across the Atlantic and the opportunity to own land drew many Europeans to the British mainland colonies. Although the rate of economic growth had declined in the British colonies from the 17th century to the 18th century, it remained substantial at approximately 1% per year. Economic growth owed both to the export sector and to the massive influx of migrants who required supplies. Although some of the free migrants took jobs rather than immediately settle on land and become farmers, many of the available jobs were filled by the large numbers of indentured servants, redemptioners, prison laborers, and enslaved Africans. Nevertheless, free skilled and semi-skilled laborers could find employment in the coastal towns by working in the shipping and construction industries and in the metal trades.

Population growth, prompted by both migration and natural increase, was one of the most significant factors shaping life and economic development in the British colonies, as all regions expanded dramatically from 1730 to 1770. The slowest growing region was the West Indies. Population expansion in the British West Indies lagged behind the mainland colonies, probably due to the high death rate. The total population in the British West Indies grew 28% from 1730 to 1750, wholly owing to the increasing numbers of African slaves, most of whom were recent arrivals—the European population actually declined. The European population did increase from 1750 to 1770 as the total population grew by 45%, with slaves accounting for over 90% of the growth. The New England colonies, the Chesapeake colonies, and the Middle Colonies, all experienced roughly the same population growth in Europeans from the 1730s through the 1750s, roughly 150,000 in each region, but the percentage increase was much greater in the Middle Colonies, where Pennsylvania attracted so many emigrants that the entire region's numbers doubled. New England grew by 65% in that 20-year period, almost wholly owing to natural increase, and the Chesapeake by 69%, of which two-thirds of the growth owed to the importation of slaves. From 1730 to 1740, for instance, the Chesapeake's white population increased only 7%. In that same decade, the Middle Colonies white population grew by 60%, illustrating that Europeans preferred emigrating there than to the Chesapeake or New England. The impact of emigration on the Lower South was even greater than in the Middle Colonies, as the total population of the region increased 120% from 1730 to 1750, with the European portion totaling 140%. The general demographic pattern of each region continued in the next 20 years as well, from 1750 to 1770, except that the growth of the white population picked up substantially in the Chesapeake, which increased by over 75%. In fact, we should now refer to the Chesapeake colonies as the Upper South, since so much of the population then lived far west of Chesapeake Bay, for at the end of the Seven Years' War many people began moving through the gaps in the Appalachian Mountains. The availability of this land attracted not only European migrants, but whites from the more northerly colonies. Overall, the population of the British mainland colonies (excluding American Indians) increased from 649,000 in 1730, to 1,180,000 in 1750, and 2,150,000 in 1770, with the African and African American portion of that total going from 97,000, to 243,000, to 456,000, and comprising 18.6% of the total population in 1770.

French and Spanish colonies above Mexico experienced population growth, but could not keep up with the British colonies. New France grew from 34,000 to 65,000 from 1730 to 1760, just more than half of the European population of Maryland. To the south, the Louisiana colony reached just over 30,000 people of African and European descent only in the mid-1780s, many fewer people than could be found in Delaware, the smallest state of the new United States. The Spanish mainland colonial population also paled beside the British colonies. Only 3,124 Spanish and their slaves inhabited Florida in 1763, less than 1,200 in Texas, and fewer than 10,000 in New Mexico.

## Prosperity and Material Culture

Great disparity existed from one region to the next in terms of per capita wealth. Free Europeans in the British West Indies were just under 10 times richer per capita than those of the Upper South and Lower South, while those of the latter possessed per capita wealth at a rate 2.5 times greater than their peers in the Middle Colonies, and 4 times greater than in New England. The wealth of the plantation colonies continued to be driven by ownership of African slaves producing staple crops. Tobacco maintained its dominance in the Upper South colonies, where planters and farmers also began producing enough food to fulfill most of their needs. In the Lower South, the export economy was more diversified. Rice retained prominence as the most important staple for export and home consumption, but was supplemented by indigo, wood products, and naval stores, the latter of which held special importance to North Carolina. Wheat and milled flour dominated the Middle Colonies, which enjoyed increased trade with the West Indies and Britain. Family farms, fishing, the carrying trade between colonies, ship building, and wood products continued to characterize New England. If we subtract the new backcountry emigrants from the per capita wealth figures for the South, we would find an even greater disparity between the southern and northern colonies. Although there were instances in the north of merchants becoming rich, there was no parallel to the large number of wealthy Virginia tobacco planters and South Carolina rice planters. Valuable rice land in South Carolina and Georgia, for instance, was more valuable per acre in 1770 than any other agricultural land in the colonies, and probably would have brought more through sale than the most valuable acreage in Boston, Philadelphia, and New York. For most planters, however, slaves were their most valuable property, comprising over two-thirds of their estate's value. And not only did slaves produce wealth for their master through their labor, but also by reproduction.

Much of the wealth of the colonies was driven by the export economy. Exports from New England totaled about £439,000 in 1770. New England's main export commodity was fish, accounting for about one-third of the total, almost two-thirds of which went to the West Indies and the other one-third to southern Europe. Livestock and wood products were also shipped to the West Indies, together making up over one-third of the region's exports. But as noted earlier, much of New England's income arose from the carrying trade, whereby New England transported and sold other regions' commodities. The value of this trade was about £330,000 in 1770. New England also produced commodities for consumption within New England, which reduced dependence on imports. These commodities included shoes, rum, flour, textiles, and lumber.

The exports of the Middle Colonies exceeded New England's in 1770 by about one-fifth in value. Likewise, the Middle Colonies had grabbed a larger share of the shipping trade, with Philadelphia becoming the major port of the mainland colonies. Grain was by far the single most important export from the Middle Colonies with almost half going to the West Indies and the other half to southern Europe.

The Upper South colonies exported twice as much as the Middle Colonies with three-fourths of the total comprising tobacco shipped to Great Britain. Grain totaled four-fifths of the remainder, half of which went to southern Europe. The other important export items from the region were iron and wood products.

The British Lower South exported a bit more than half of the exports of the Upper South in 1770. In terms of exports, its economy was more diversified. The chief item of export was rice, which comprised close to 55% of the total. But the region also exported indigo, deerskins, naval stores, wood products, and other items. Less than 20% of the region's exports went to the West Indies, and almost 10% to southern Europe. Most of the rest went to Great Britain.

How did the British mainland colonies compare to the British West Indies in terms of exports? In 1770, the value of Muscavado sugar exported from these islands exceeded the combined value of all mainland English colonial exports. When we add in the value of the islands' rum and white sugar trade, the total value of the mainland colonies' exports was less than two-thirds that of the British West Indies.

England economically benefitted from its colonies in a variety of ways. One way was through the re-export trade. This included items like tobacco, which colonists had to ship to England before sale outside the empire. Other unrestricted commodities were also shipped to England and then exported. From 1700 to 1770, the re-export trade grew by an average of about 1.5% per year. (Imports and exports with the colonies averaged an increase of about 1% per year.) The re-exported goods constituted a significant portion of England's total exports. Not all re-exported goods came from the American colonies, but much of it did. In 1750, re-exported goods accounted for about 30% of England's total exports. By 1770 that figure rose to 37%, while increasing in value by around 60%. Imports from the colonies that remained in Britain, some of which were then processed and manufactured, and a portion of which were then re-exported, increased at an even greater rate. The colonies also became a greater market for English manufactures, receiving over a third of English exports by 1770. About 80% of these exports were manufactured goods, especially ceramics, glassware, iron, and textiles. Almost 80% of English exported linens; 75% of the iron nails and 60% of wrought iron went to the English colonies. Britain and its colonies existed in a mutually beneficial economic relationship.

## Indian Population and Material Culture

Gauging numbers of American Indians is a difficult task. In the American Southeast, there were approximately 55,000 to 60,000 Indians from the mid- to late 18th century, a decline of two-thirds to three-fourths from the previous century that owed to disease, warfare, out-migration, and perhaps a declining birth rate. From 50,000 to 100,000 indigenous peoples likely lived to the north, below Canada and east of the Mississippi. West of the Mississippi numbers are nearly impossible to estimate, as few Europeans visited native peoples outside of the Spanish Southwest and a few French trading posts, and not enough native inhabitants passed on census information to their descendants. Overall, however, there was relative stability in numbers of American Indians during the last half of the 18th century, especially compared to the massive decline over the previous two centuries, and the great reduction that would occur in the 19th century.

In terms of material culture, American Indians obtained many labor-saving devices and new textiles from European trade. Knives and axes made it easier and quicker to work wood, especially to build piraguas and canoes, cut firewood, and clean animal pelts. Knives, scissors, and pins allowed Indians to furnish clothing from

European cloth and to cobble moccasins from deerskins. Europeans also sold to Indians finished clothing, especially jackets and shirts. European textiles included an array of blankets, which supplemented and replaced animal skins. Other European goods widely integrated into Indian life included brass pots, beads, guns, toys, weaponry, and alcohol. How much many of these items "improved" Indian life is subject to question, but Indians pursued these items as desirable. To obtain them, Indians exchanged animal pelts that they trapped or hunted, and then processed. They also offered their services as warriors, and Indians provided Europeans with a variety of foodstuffs, such as venison, vegetables, and grain. Many Indians became dependent on European goods, particularly the metal tools, guns, and alcohol.

Indians had to keep producing commodities or offering services in order to obtain more European goods. The same could be said for colonists: they too had to keep producing to obtain goods. The difference was diplomatic—Indians had to obtain goods from Europeans, making trade a diplomatic issue. Europeans could threaten to close off trade if Indians did not follow their directives. Fortunately for many Indians, if the French, Spanish, or British closed off trade, then Indians could go to one of their European competitors or obtain items from European traders who refused to follow the directive of their government. After the 1750s, when the French empire was removed from North America, the British colonies were better able to wield the closing of trade as a weapon. Nonetheless, Indians often found ways to bypass the British colonies' threat to close off trade as a weapon to make them cede land or to do other things they demanded.

Accumulation of European goods had impact on authority within Indian communities. Some Indians who succeeded in obtaining significant amounts of goods from the Europeans gained prestige as well as items to distribute to followers, and then challenged traditional chiefs for leadership positions. Alcohol dependency also undermined communities and debilitated individuals. Sometimes Indian leaders worked with colonial officials to effect prohibition of the alcohol trade, but unscrupulous traders ignored the restrictions. As a result of a host of challenges, many Indian peoples creatively adopted their communities to secure trade and strengthen themselves against the European colonies and other Indian peoples. In the Ohio Country, for instance, numerous Indians formed new inter-ethnic communities, thus evincing the ability to break down ethnic barriers that previously divided them. The evolution of Indian polities, social systems, and economies would continue as Indians, like Europeans and Africans, were forced to contend with a rapidly altering world.

## GEORGIA: SOCIAL EXPERIMENTATION AND FAILURE

After the Yamasee War, South Carolina lay exposed to the raiding of hostile Indian peoples and Spanish. Natives who previously had provided a ring of towns to protect the colony had moved away, and none would take their place given the colony's history of turning on its allies. Carolinian John Barnwell came up with the idea of settling ten fortress communities of poor Protestants from Europe, and the legislature provided money towards that end, but only two were established. Barnwell then went to England, and along with Scotsman Robert Montgomery, promoted the settlement of land far to the south of the colony on Spanish territory as a way to protect Carolina.

On Barnwell's return, with Carolina's approval, he built a fort on the Altamaha River—a direct threat to Spanish Florida, but the fort only lasted a few years. Still, Barnwell's activities brought to the British government's attention the need for defense of Carolina's valuable rice plantations and of Spain's inability to settle and control the area north of St. Augustine.

In England, a group of philanthropists, wealthy men interested in charitable enterprise and the promotion of Protestantism, convinced King George II to grant them a colony that would fulfill the need to protect Carolina, while providing a refuge for poor Protestants. The king was German, so they promised to promote the settlement of his Protestant countrymen persecuted for their religion by Catholic German princes. In 1732, they received a charter for the creation of Georgia (named for the king).

## The Utopian Experiment

The proprietors of Georgia, called the Trustees, created a colony unlike any other. In addition to poor European Protestants, they provided a refuge for debtors languishing in English jails. The Trustees agreed to pay the emigrants' passage and provide tools, seed, and other forms of assistance, as well as free land. They intended to create a utopia, where none would be poor or rich. Landholding was limited: no one could increase their estates to larger than 500 acres by purchase, inheritance, or grants. Originally, women could not own land, but this provision soon ended.

The Trustees foresaw a society of middling farmers, who through hard work and Christian fellowship would live in harmony. They prohibited alcohol for its debilitating affects, barred Catholics and Jews to keep the colony solely for Protestants, promoted good relations with Indians, and refused to allow slavery. The prohibition against slavery had numerous sources—and was the only prohibition against African slavery in the British colonies. The Trustees feared that slaves could become a "fifth column" by uniting with the Spanish in Florida to destroy the colony. There were other reasons as well. The Trustees believed that the free people of neighboring South Carolina lived profligate lives. Interestingly, they partly blamed the Africans for this profligacy, believing that the heathens influenced the Europeans to follow their own sinful behavior, especially in sexual relations. But most importantly, the Trustees affirmed that the Carolinians sunk into depravity because they did not have to work hard, as they had slaves perform all the difficult labor; the Trustees believed that a good work ethic was necessary for becoming a good Christian and free Carolinians had grown used to living in the lap of luxury.

One Trustee, James Oglethorpe, led the colonists to Georgia and became their governor. A former member of Parliament, Oglethorpe had championed debtor rights in England and promoted their release from prisons and settlement in Georgia. He held the new colony together with able leadership and diplomatic and military skills. Oglethorpe possessed a rare flexibility in interacting with people of varied walks of life. He developed an excellent relationship with southern Native Americans, who could easily have destroyed the colony at any time. Oglethorpe's most important partner was Tomochichi, a Yamacraw Indian leader who paved the way for Georgia's peaceful relations with the powerful Creek Indians, to whom the Yamacraw were related. This insured that the Creek would not destroy the colony, and the Indians provided invaluable military assistance against the Spanish. Oglethorpe took several Yamacraw, including Tomochichi, to England to promote the colony, and they enjoyed a celebrated visit at the royal court that helped win English support for Georgia over the coming years. Tomochichi became nearly as much a "founder" of Georgia as Oglethorpe.

Oglethorpe ably worked with a variety of non-English Europeans to strengthen the colony. On the southern reaches, he settled Scots Highlanders, many of whom had military experience, as a first line of defense against the Spanish. Up the Savannah River, he placed poor German Salzburgers to protect the colony's northwest flank. When Savannah was beset by an unknown illness, and a boatload of Sephardic Jews arrived seeking sanctuary, he allowed a Jewish physician to land and treat the colonists. The physician had great success ending the illness. Oglethorpe allowed the Jews to settle in opposition to the wishes of his fellow Trustees, and adamantly refused to reverse his decision. Oglethorpe also gained assistance from the Carolina government, which appreciated having the Georgia buffer to secure their colony, and that Georgia's barring of slavery meant the new colony would not compete economically with South Carolina by producing plantation crops. He also received help from private citizens in South Carolina, who ran cattle to Georgia and provided food stuffs inexpensively to the colonists. Georgia held great promise as a multi-cultural enclave offering refuge and hope to a variety of distressed Europeans who could live in relative harmony with their native neighbors.

## Difficulties in Utopia

Georgia became a cause célèbre in England, eventually receiving hefty parliamentary funding for the colony's defense. To promote the colony, on her birthday in 1735 Queen Caroline wore a dress made of Georgia silk. Nevertheless, there were difficulties in utopia. A group arose known as the Malcontents, who sought to overthrow the proprietorship and turn Georgia into a royal colony. The Malcontents chafed at the absence of representative government, claiming that the distant Trustees did not understand local problems, and with Oglethorpe frequently away, they asserted the need to control their own affairs. Their main complaint or charge, however, was that the colony could never achieve a secure footing, let alone prosper, without allowing free men to own slaves.

In England, the Malcontents published pamphlets to convince king and Parliament to look into their plight. The basis of their argument, which became standard in the history of African slavery in the Americas: Europeans were unfit to perform hard labor in hot countries, while Africans were particularly suited to the task. Without African labor, they asserted, Georgia could never produce the staple crops necessary to earn profits in the New World, as neighboring South Carolina could always undersell Georgia through use of cheaper labor. The Trustees countered with their own pamphlets, pointing to the German Salzburgers as proof that hard-working Europeans could flourish in the Georgia climate. They also asserted that the poor colonists could not afford slaves and the Trustees could not afford to provide them.

Georgia's weakness arose not from whether it had slavery, but to the colony's precarious position in the empire. In 1739, war had broken out between Spain and Britain. Oglethorpe returned from England with troops to undertake an invasion of Florida, for which he also enlisted recruits from South Carolina and Georgia, and naval help from the British West Indies. In June 1740, these forces unsuccessfully assaulted St. Augustine. The walls of the great fort, the Castillo de San Marcos, absorbed the ships' cannon balls and the land troops could not gain entry. In a daring foray, Spanish troops left the fort and captured and killed about 200 men, including many of the Scots Highlanders who had occupied Fort Mosa, the free black fort of runaway slaves from South Carolina that had been abandoned during the invasion. The Trustee colony never fully recovered from the military fiasco. The Scots Highland community had been decimated and forced to abandon their outpost. Expecting a Spanish counter-invasion, many of the Jews fled to South Carolina fearing the arrival of the Spanish Inquisition. And when Georgia forced all its male citizens to bear arms, the hard-working pacifist German Moravians left the colony and settled in North Carolina. Laws barred colonists from leaving, but people slipped away in the night. Oglethorpe did turn back the Spanish invaders in 1742, but Georgia remained too dangerous a place to attract new settlers.

By the late 1740s, the Anglo-Spanish War had ended but the colony still failed to draw immigrants. Worn down by the Malcontents, and rapidly losing interest in the colony, the Trustees agreed to permit a limited form of slavery in 1750, and soon thereafter turned the colony over to the king. As soon as it became a royal colony in 1755, the new Georgia government ended the laws restricting land ownership and permitted full-scale slavery. The new government gave out land at the rate of 50 acres per person, with free people receiving an additional 50 acres for each dependent they brought to the colony. A married slaveholder with 5 children and 50 slaves automatically received 2,850 acres—enough to start a substantial plantation. On the very first day of land granting, slaveholders from South Carolina lined up at the land office for their portions, receiving the very best parcels for producing rice. In the following years, many slaveholders with their workers moved to the colony from South Carolina and the West Indies. These planters turned Georgia into a colony akin to South Carolina: dominated by a planter elite whose wealth revolved around slaveholding and rice production. The utopian experiment at creating a classless society had lasted less than 20 years.

## GROWTH AND SOCIETAL PROBLEMS IN THE CAROLINAS

To the north of Georgia, the phenomenal population growth of the Carolinas in the period 1730–1770 created severe social problems. In lowcountry South Carolina, the population became overwhelmingly African—in some areas approaching 90%. The Africans were forced to work in unhealthy conditions, standing in swamps to cultivate rice, building sluices to control the flooding of fields, and were subject to an array of diseases. The work regimen was brutal and the Africans were treated as sub-humans. Many of the workers were recent arrivals from Africa who resented their condition and practiced all sorts of resistance, some of which threatened the existence of the colony.

Inland, in what was called the backcountry, immigrants flocked from Europe and practiced subsistence agriculture. The backcountry of both South Carolina and North Carolina attracted so many Europeans that it out-populated the lowcountry by the 1760s. Societal discord reared its head in the backcountry and exploded in violence in what became known as the Regulator Movements. The Regulator Movement in

South Carolina and then in North Carolina illustrated a pattern that was repeated in other colonies (and later states) in American history, such as in the land riots in New York and New Jersey in the 1760s and 1770s, Shays Rebellion in New England in the 1780s, and the Whiskey Rebellion in Pennsylvania in the 1790s. All these uprisings involved resentments of the older settled areas and their exploitative government policies. Backcountry farmers resorted to arms when their property was seized through the action of elite controlled courts to address inequitable taxation policies, and to redress their lack of representation and power in government. In the case of South Carolina, the backcountry was denied equal representation in the colonial government and proper government services. In North Carolina, elite control of the court system led to corrupt seizures of farmers' property. Although frontier areas often attracted lawless elements, they also filled with small property-holders, and it was the latter who typically rose in rebellion to protect their interests.

## Slave Resistance in the South Carolina Lowcountry

The South Carolina slaveholding regime was the most brutal on the North American mainland. Largely influenced by the brutal slaveholding regime of the West Indies, typical masters of the 1730s believed they must employ excessive force to discipline their workers to obtain profits and maintain control over a dangerous population that far outnumbered them. Only slowly would slaveholders learn how to earn profits through less violent means, such as the creation of the task system, and by instituting more effective policing policies to regulate slaves' behavior, as well as the use of rewards and other measures to try to minimize the slaves' desire to rebel.

Much slave resistance took subtle forms. Bondpeople pretended ignorance when purposefully breaking tools or sabotaging crops. They cursed masters in their native languages, feigned illness, and robbed the larder. Secretly they practiced religion (African traditional, Muslim, and Christian) and surreptitiously left the plantation at night to visit friends and relatives. More hostile acts included burning crops and plantations. When much of Charles Town burned to the ground in 1740, slave arson was suspected. Some masters were poisoned or killed by other means. Running away was prevalent. Most slaves who fled did not leave permanently, but took extended "vacations" to visit family and avoid work, especially at harvest time. Masters responded to resistance through increased whipping, chaining, torture, and maiming. Advertisements for runaways in the colony's newspaper, the *Gazette*, are filled with physical descriptions of slaves that make evident the brutality of punishment, and the frequency with which runaways became repeat offenders.

Especially irksome to the planters was a long-standing offer from Spanish St. Augustine, who promised freedom to South Carolina slave runaways. The Spanish were not opposed to slavery, but resentful of English settlement on their land, particularly through settlement of Georgia, and saw the offer as a way to undermine their enemy. News of these pronouncements was carried by Indians who freely visited both colonies. English representations to the Spanish to end the offer of freedom fell on deaf ears.

In September 1739, the Spanish invitation of freedom and slave discontent fomented into the Stono Rebellion. A group of 20 Kongolese slaves, who later attracted to their cause upwards of 80 or more, killed over 20 Europeans. The rebels met on the southern reaches of the colony to celebrate their actions and perhaps to wait for more to join them. But instead of continuing to St. Augustine and freedom, they stayed put, perhaps seeing their strength and believing they could conquer the colony. But the militia defeated the rebels, and in the aftermath, dozens of slaves were killed, their heads placed on poles at crossroads to warn others of the deadly consequences of rebellion.

South Carolina enacted slave codes to secure colonists against their bondpeople. These codes became the model for future plantation regimes in the Lower South. They barred slaves from handling weapons and owning drums (which had been used by the rebels to signal one another). Meetings of slaves from different plantations were prohibited. Slaves had to carry passes when off the plantation and teaching a slave to read was outlawed, so they could not forge passes. The colony organized patrols to keep slaves on the plantation, and shored up the "watch" to prevent slaves from being out after dark in Charles Town. The legislature enacted laws to ensure that masters properly fed and clothed their servants, believing slaves were less likely to rebel if they received proper physical care. And since the Stono rebels had risen on a Sunday, while many whites attended church, white males were required to bring arms to church in case of another rebellion.

As with future slave uprisings, when the threat died down, whites tended to disregard many of the strictures on slaves. Slaves frequently were lent guns to hunt, and they continued to meet for religious and social purposes and left the plantations at night without passes. Masters could not live in a constant state of siege overseeing every movement of bondpeople, and thus ignored much of slaves' personal lives and behavior. The slaves themselves accommodated to their condition—rather than rebel and face near-certain death. They carved out lives within slavery by establishing families—masters steadily replaced barracks housing in favor of cottages to house family units, forging community bonds, and on an individual level, accumulating small amounts of property through work after hours and by theft. The slaves' work regimen, to a large degree, fell under their own control in Carolina. Many of the rice plantations switched to the task system, whereby slaves were given tasks to perform each day, often unsupervised, and when work was completed their time became their own. As long as a plantation produced profits, and the workers did not get in trouble with the law, many Carolina masters would not contest a range of slave assertions of autonomy.

## The Regulator Movements

Whereas most Africans in the South lived on lowcountry plantations near the Atlantic Coast, the European migrants of the 1730s through 1760s largely settled in the southern backcountry. Many initially arrived in Philadelphia, then traveled south through the backcountry of Maryland, Virginia, the Carolinas, and Georgia. The massive influx created problems with the native population, as disputes arose over land, trade, and thievery, beginning a push of Indian peoples to west of the Appalachians. The colonial governments, and the lowcountry elites who controlled these governments, had some sympathy for Indian peoples and held hostility to the relatively poor European immigrants whom they viewed as savages. The governments hoped to prevent war on the frontier, which would be expensive and threaten to spread to the older settled areas, but government leaders lacked the will to effectively regulate backcountry settlement to maintain good relations between Europeans and Indians. As a corollary, the eastern elite generally ignored the needs of the new settlers. They refused to extend political power to the backcountry by creating new counties and permitting fair representation in government. They also refused to extend institutions to the backcountry, such as courts, which forced people to travel 100 miles or more to try civil suits and to vote. In many colonies, the provincial governments would not undertake costly internal improvements, such as road-building, expecting westerners to improve their economic infrastructure without tax dollars. This sectionalism characterized America's expansionistic development through the next century and a half on colonial, and then state and national, levels as older settled areas assumed they had no obligation to help newer areas with public funding. In the case of the South, the colonial (and later state) governments feared sharing power with non-slaveholders, believing if the latter held political power, they would raise taxes on the slaveholders' most valuable property, their slaves.

Despite frustration at their lack of representation in colonial government and the economic benefits that would accrue, and their desire for colonial governments to play a more active role against their native neighbors, backcountry farmers saw advantages in their distance from "settled" society and government institutions, which allowed them to maintain a modicum of control over their lives and communities. Many of the newcomers had fled Europe to escape elite control. They resented the wealthy and their dominance of political and religious institutions. Churches were few in the backcountry, as they represented engines of oppression to many immigrants, who had been forced in their mother countries to pay tithes in support, so that religious life remained informal on the frontier, when practiced at all. With their distance from markets, the backcountry settlers became subsistence farmers trading with one another and with native peoples.

By the late 1760s, two societies had developed in the South Carolina backcountry, one engaged in farming and the other in hunting. The former wished to build orderly communities, develop their tracts of land, and engage in the market economy by providing food crops for the lowcountry plantations. The latter lived "roughly," obtaining subsistence through fishing and hunting, cultivation of maize, and petty trade. The Cherokee War (1759–1761), as well as droughts in 1759 and 1766, had pushed many farmers into becoming hunters and their numbers were growing. Some turned to crime against both Indians and settlers, and it was their activities that spurred the creation of the Regulator movement in South Carolina. Without courts, jails, sheriffs, and judges, the Regulators took the law into their own hands. At first they transported accused criminals for trial to distant Charles Town. They watched in astonishment as officials released alleged perpetrators, perhaps because the government did not want to bear the cost of incarceration. The Regulators banded together to punish suspected criminals on their own by beatings, whippings, and burning them out of their houses.

Thousands of Regulators remonstrated against the South Carolina government and high lawyer fees and for a cheaper, streamlined process for issuing deeds for land. Denied representation in the colonial assembly, they traveled en masse into the lowcountry to vote. Although prevented from voting in some districts, in others they could and carried elections for their candidates. The Regulators sought to bring order to the backcountry by eliminating or reducing the large numbers of people who lived off of hunting—and in their eyes, by extension, off of thievery: stealing livestock, stealing horses, attacking travelers, and robbing small businesses. They wanted schools to transform wild youth into agriculturists and vagrancy laws to force adults to take up farming. Their "Plan of Regulation" in 1768 called for "respectable people" to work "every day excepting Sundays." Those who refused would be whipped and evicted from the area.

The South Carolina government was slow to meet the Regulator demands. Violence broke out between Regulator and lowcountry militias in 1768 and continued for over a year. Finally, in 1769 a Circuit Court Act was passed that provided for erection of courts and jails in the backcountry, the appointment of sheriffs, and the creation of two new election districts. To restrict the hunting population, An Act for the Preservation of Deer was passed. A series of pardons for the Regulators followed over the next few years. Resentments between backcountry and lowcountry people did not end, but certainly the lowcountry had recognized the needs of the backcountry and paved the way for future cooperation.

The Regulator Movement in North Carolina emerged in 1768 as backcountry farmers began losing their farms when charged exorbitant fees and taxes by county officials. The farmers were losing their land to pay these debts—their property was sold at one-tenth of its value. The farmers hoped to gain control over local government, rid themselves of the corrupt officials, gain a say in the colonial government, and redraw the tax system: Governor Tryon promised to redress their grievances and get rid of the corrupt officials. But little was done and the farmers grew increasingly irritated as the government spent tax money on building "Tryon Palace" as a home for the governor.

In 1770, the Regulators turned violent. They attacked lawyers and merchants and destroyed their homes; they closed the courts so their property could not be condemned to pay debts. New laws were enacted to appease the people, but a Riot Act was passed to quell disturbances—the act was later repealed by the British government. The Regulators refused to stand down and the governor led troops to the backcountry. Only a few died at the Battle of Alamance, but it effectively ended the movement, and the governor pardoned most of the Regulators. Some of the ex-Regulators moved westward through the gaps in the Appalachian Mountains to what became Tennessee. Many stayed in North Carolina and retained their lands, as court officials became afraid to continue their gross exploitation of the farmers, who showed they would fight for their land. North Carolina remained a place with strong "leveling" tendencies with much popular suspicion of government as an engine of oppression.

## FIXING SOCIETAL PROBLEMS: AWAKENING AND ENLIGHTENMENT

In terms of population growth and economic development, the British American colonies were a great success story, but significant problems arrived in their wake. The flood of new immigrants led to tensions and warfare with native peoples who had to cope with the teeming European populace who desired their land. The French and Spanish also warily eyed British imperial and settler aggressiveness as threatening the existence of their settlements. The dependence of British colonials on slave-produced goods meant reliance on a large and dangerous slave population that might overthrow society from within or by joining with the Spanish or French or Indians.

British colonials sought answers from many quarters. Elimination of security threats by conquest of Spanish and French colonies and new policing measures could secure the British colonies. But colonists also considered looking elsewhere to solving problems that affected their society and themselves as individuals. Many thousands in this period turned to the new "revitalizing" religion, evangelical Christianity, as a way to transform themselves and their neighbors. In a great mass movement that crossed the Atlantic, evangelicals proposed a host of solutions including reform of slavery and the conversion of African Americans to Christianity, while also spreading their religion to the new European immigrants who lacked churches and ministers in the backcountry. Other Americans, particularly in urban areas and in the plantation districts, welcomed the rationalism of the European Enlightenment, which sought to apply reason to the problems of life. They emphasized a "rational" ordering of society, though differing on where that ordering should come from. Many turned to the past for solutions, while others welcomed experimentation, including the application of scientific methods to problems, both small and large, that would better the condition of mankind. The rationalists who continued to embrace Christianity, but put more stock in its ethics than its mystical qualities, tended to distrust and condemn the perceived "enthusiastic" excesses of the evangelicals, preferring a sober practice of religion.

## One Solution: The Great Awakening

Although an insignificant colony in the 1730s, Georgia helped give birth to the evangelical religious movement that swept through England and its colonies: the Great Awakening. Evangelical Christians introduced new forms of religious expression and a religious life that challenged the established churches and ministry, as well as civil authorities. Anglicans, Presbyterians, Congregationalists—in fact, most of the Protestant denominations—divided into evangelical (new light) and non-evangelical (old light) factions and churches. Throughout the British colonies and in Britain, new lights and old lights denounced each other as practicing false Christianity.

In Connecticut, Jonathan Edwards helped lay the groundwork for the Awakening through preaching that stressed Christians' need to become "convicted of sin." To many New Englanders, Christianity, as practiced, failed to move adherents to the necessity of looking after the state of their own souls. Edwards tapped into this religious malaise by re-emphasizing the old Puritan belief in the centrality of salvation to each person's life. He preached on the miserable nature of humanity in sermons like "Sinners in the Hands of an Angry God." The adamant proclamation that each Christian stood condemned before God, and had to acknowledge his or her sinful nature, appealed to many. Edwards had shifted religious experience from an institutional to individual level, much like Roger Williams before him, though Edwards and his followers recognized the importance of a community of believers to reinforce one another, as each explored the state of their soul individually. Although an intellectual concerned with the nuances of theology, Edwards's success was in reaching the hearts of many through sermons that moved the spirit as much as stimulated the mind.

It fell to two ministers of the Church of England to play the key role in spreading the new ideas to hundreds of thousands of people on both sides of the Atlantic. Their emphasis on the individual's need for salvation developed separately from Edwards, who nonetheless laid the groundwork for the popular reception of these ideas in New England. The two men, John Wesley and George Whitefield, became the most famous English-speaking ministers of the 18th century. Fellow students at Oxford, the idealistic Wesley emigrated to Georgia in 1736, where there was a shortage of ministers, in hopes of missionizing American Indians. The Indians were too distant from the colony; instead for almost two years, he saw to the needs of the settlers. Wesley fell into trouble over a woman he courted, refused to marry, then rejected giving communion. With lawsuits against him, the young minister fled home to England. Whitefield, unaware of Wesley abandoning his post, had followed his friend to Georgia to convert Indians. Whitefield traveled aboard a ship filled with German Moravians, pietists whose religiosity and emotionalism, particularly their expressions of joy for Christianity, touched him deeply. Once ashore, Whitefield adjusted his preaching style to appeal to Christian hearts. Previously, English ministers read prepared sermons that elucidated biblical texts in an academic manner. Whitefield still drew on the Bible, but let the spirit move him to explore his subject extemporaneously. Evangelicals thereafter refused to listen to prepared sermons.

Like Edwards, Whitefield underscored the need for people to become convinced of their sins, that the only path to redemption lay through God's saving grace. Grace, Whitefield argued, was an instantaneous transformation of the soul by God. Evangelicals to the present day emphasize grace as the central experience in a Christian's life, but disagree as to how grace occurs. For instance, 18th-century evangelicals disputed with one another whether grace was pre-ordained or humans could play a role with God in achieving salvation. Those receiving grace received a "new birth" in Christ—the promise of eternal life.

## George Whitefield in America

With a booming and sonorous voice, Whitefield stressed the sinfulness of humans. Congregants "melted" before Whitefield, tears rolling down their cheeks as he recounted humans' lowly condition. Some fell out of their seats, lost control of their bodies, struck with what evangelicals believed was new awareness of their abject lives. In Georgia and South Carolina, crowds flocked to hear Whitefield speak, but many ministers, after initially welcoming him and the accompanying throngs, closed their church doors. They disapproved of the emotional enthusiasm of evangelicals, and chafed under attacks on their own ministries. Evangelicals publicly castigated ministers who did not preach the new birth in Christ—or had not experienced grace as they defined it. They also called for a new morality, expecting ministers to condemn secular amusements, such as dancing, drinking, and living in material excess. Christians, they affirmed, should devote themselves to the glory of God.

Whitefield briefly returned to England where he showed his friend Wesley the power of preaching the new birth in Christ. Although soft-spoken, Wesley, too, found the people "melting" before him when hearing the evangelical message. As Wesley traveled through England gaining followers (who eventually created the Methodist Church, named for the "new method" for reaching Christ), Whitefield returned to America as the Anglican minister assigned to Georgia. But Whitefield could not be confined to one place, nor to one side of the Atlantic. He undertook numerous speaking tours—in all, 13 through the American colonies over a 30-year period.

Whitefield's message and style drew in thousands of people, north and south. Crowds grew so large that he took religion out of doors, which was illegal, giving birth to open-air preaching—or tent revivalism. Ben Franklin calculated that Whitefield's preaching could be heard by 30,000 at a single sermon. With growing numbers of supporters, the youthful Whitefield (he was only 25 in 1740) grew emboldened to challenge slavery. He published a lengthy public letter to the slaveholders of the mainland southern colonies, entreating them to reform the institution of slavery. Stating that he could not pass judgment on the morality of holding slaves, though he questioned it anyway, Whitefield condemned their barbarous treatment. In graphic detail, he described slaves being tortured, asserting that slaveholders treated their dogs and livestock better than their African slaves. The slaveholders' greatest sin, however, was denying Christianity to their slaves. After all, for evangelicals, life was of little consequence compared to eternity with God.

Many slaves flocked to hear the minister, and Whitefield's followers began preaching to slaves as well. Moreover, evangelicals believed that preaching should not be confined to university-educated and ordained ministers: any Christian moved by the spirit should preach. Converted slaves, women, poor folks in general, began to publicly espouse the word. In South Carolina, several of Whitefield's followers, slaveholders themselves, were arrested for ministering to slaves and allegedly promoting insurrection. Church and governmental authorities condemned the evangelicals for making emotional arguments that filled individuals with an undue sense of their own self-importance, while not actually teaching them true Christianity. Critics emphasized the "reasonableness" of Christianity, that conversion was a slow process evinced after leading a proper Christian life, and that it was dangerous to rouse slaves and poor whites with thinking they could instantly become Christians—and redeemed—without proper obedience to their social superiors. Would not religious enthusiasm and emotional excess lead the dispossessed to violently seek to change their condition? Had not religious enthusiasm led England to civil war in the previous century?

## Evangelicals and Slavery

Faced with the power of the state, evangelicals adjusted their method and message in the South. To convince authorities they were not opposed to slavery, only to brutal treatment of slaves and to denying them access to Christianity, several South Carolina slaveholders, including Hugh and Jonathan Bryan, gave Whitefield a plantation and slaves, operating it for him. The proceeds would be used to help feed Georgia orphans, for whom Whitefield established an orphanage. (Eventually 78 slaves worked to support a mere dozen or so orphans.) Whitefield, by becoming a slaveholder, hoped to convince established society that evangelicals did not oppose the basic social structure. Whitefield even agreed to lobby the Trustees of Georgia to legalize slavery in their colony, for "hot countries cannot be cultivated without Negroes," explaining to his evangelical friends that expansion of slavery would provide more opportunities for conversion. One of Whitefield's Christian allies in Georgia, the Salzburger minister, John Martin Bolzius, satirically complained to his friend for his about-face on slavery. He told Whitefield that, instead of spreading slavery to new areas, if he wanted "to imploy his Strength & time to Convert Negroes, he has in Carolina a Large Field." But Whitefield and his followers had decided to compromise their beliefs for the greater message—to preach the new birth in Christ. Evangelicals agreed to cease harassing ministers and criticizing treatment of slaves. Instead, they decided to make their own "model" Christian plantations, where ideally slaves would be converted to Christianity and receive more humane treatment. Evangelicals hoped to show their neighbors that Christian slaves would make better workers.

From these beginnings, the ideology of paternalism took root in the South. Although it took several decades to spread, many masters, evangelical and otherwise, began perceiving themselves as fathers to their slaves, whom they described as members of their family in legal documents. Paternalist masters saw themselves as possessing a duty to care for their slave children; that slaveholders performed a great social good—bringing Christianity to their heathen charges, now presented with the opportunity to receive heavenly rewards. Whether the slaves actually received better treatment is open to question, for later slaves noted the hypocrisy and cruel treatment of many self-described "Christian" masters, but there is no doubt that Christianity spread through the slave quarters. The slaves appropriated Christianity to their own advantage. While masters and white preachers instilled in them Christian lessons of proper behavior, acceptance of their place in society, and the need to obey their masters, slave preachers arose with their own message: they were the modern-day Hebrews whom God would eventually liberate from Egyptian taskmasters. There were also tangible benefits. The practice of permitting slaves release from work on Sundays spread through the South. Slavery altered in other ways as well. Barracks gave way to small cottages, as slaves began living in family units. Masters recognized that slaves were less likely to run away if they had to leave family members behind. Many slaves received small plots of land to produce their own vegetables and keep poultry. Slaves then assumed these privileges as rights and could hold masters to their own self-perceptions as paternalists. Hugh Bryan, for instance, after alienating his slaves with his behavior, found them disobedient for two weeks. Bryan rued, "my servants were called to prayers, but none came." Christianity became a matter of negotiation between master and slave. Survival as slaves meant manipulating the slaveholders' psychological need to see themselves as good masters and good Christians.

Although not nearly as threatening to the social order in the North as in the South, the evangelicals there too disputed society and brought about great changes. In communities throughout New England and the Middle Colonies, churches experienced bitter splits between Old Lights and New Lights. In forming their own churches, and raising to the ministry non-college educated, non-ordained ministers, common people took control of their religious lives and gained valuable skills in organizing and running their own churches. This experience proved invaluable. Some historians believe that the overthrow of established churches and the creation of new institutions contributed to later success against the British government in the American Revolution and the formation of a new nation.

## Another Solution: The Enlightenment in America

The rise of evangelical Christianity coincided with a very different intellectual movement, one that emphasized the importance of applying reason to govern life rather than a personal relationship with God. Since the 16th century, advances in mathematics, physics, botany, and astronomy had led many to believe that humans could uncover the mysteries of a universe that operated according to physical laws. Many Christians initially attacked these studies as tending towards atheism, for God had created an unknowable universe that operated according to his power, and not to any laws that humans could discover. Not all Christians opposed these endeavors. Some believed that scientific advances shed light on God's creation and helped people appreciate his glory. But by the mid-18th century, many Christians again saw danger in science, fearing it would lead to atheism or deism. Deism, which was prominent among some of the Founding Forefathers, posited God as the creator of the universe, who then allowed the universe to operate according to laws. Miracles, if they had ever existed, no longer occurred after the end of biblical times. God remained outside of his creation. They employed the metaphor of God as the great clock maker—he wound up the clock and let it go. Atheists, on the other hand, discounted the existence of God, believing reason against creation, and that the stories of Noah and the Flood, Moses parting the Red Sea, and the Resurrection of Christ were impossibilities. They ridiculed the Bible as a collection of stories that at best provided moral precepts for proper living.

Attacks on Christianity were muted in the colonies in the mid-18th century, but Americans, particularly in the urban areas of Boston, Philadelphia, Charles Town, and New York, and many elite planters in Virginia and South Carolina incorporated Enlightenment thinking into their world view. Intellectuals, including many artisans who held skeptical beliefs towards a religious understanding of the universe, combined scientific inquiry with practical needs to improve society. Franklin invented a new wood stove and the lightening rod, while steamboats were simultaneously invented in Virginia and Pennsylvania (years before Robert Fulton gained fame for his invention). Philadelphia goldsmith David Rittenhouse created an orrery, a mechanical device that plotted the paths of the planets around the Sun. (The original can still be seen at the University of Pennsylvania). In medicine, experimentation led to small pox inoculation becoming common beginning in the 1730s, and John and William Bartram, father and son, undertook the collection and identification of plants, sharing their information with European scholars to better understand the natural world through classification. American astronomers joined with Europeans in plotting the path of Venus, observing comets and other astral matter, and improving astronomical and navigational knowledge. Philadelphia became the British colonies' center for scientific inquiry with the formation of the American Philosophical Society to collect and distribute scientific information. The first medical school in the British colonies opened in Philadelphia in 1765.

The new science had far-reaching ramifications in colonial America. As people came to believe that the universe operated according to laws, they assumed that society itself would improve with the discovery of the "natural" laws governing economy and politics. On their own, or at universities, people actively engaged in the study of classical societies and the law, hoping to improve the human condition—a new idea in itself. Christianity always had emphasized improvement on an individual level, while Enlightenment thinking looked to the improvement of entire societies by applying reason to the governance of human institutions. Scientific advances gave people confidence—they believed that the world was getting better, and would continue to get better, if humans rid themselves of the binders of blind allegiance to illogical and unsubstantiated ideas, and replaced corrupt institutions with new ones based upon the social good.

By the 1750s and 1760s, the implications were seen only vaguely, but incipiently, as a few began to question the efficacy of mercantilism, colonial treatment of native peoples, and the social and political sources of poverty (which previously had been assumed to be individual). Mercantilism, many thought, unnecessarily created armed competition between states, while restricting trade and hampering economic development. Native peoples, many Europeans asserted, not only were entitled to their land, but might prove to be a valuable model for modern society. The mythology of the "noble savage" posited that Indian peoples lived uncorrupted by the archaic institutions that prevented Europe from achieving social, political, and economic betterment: thus Indians were worthy of study and emulation. In particular, American Indians were celebrated for their strong social bonds, which promoted unity of purpose and care for all members of society, hence no poverty. Interest in the connections between government policies and social welfare, in part, arose from concern for growing poverty in both Europe and America. Imperialism, mercantilism, and colonialism created great riches, and economic opportunities for many, but urban areas, in particular, became scenes of squalor, with impoverishment of widows and children of deceased soldiers—the unfortunate victims of imperial wars. Those hoping to solve societal problems looked to reform social policy. For instance, linen manufactories were established for poor women to earn their bread in Boston (1751), Philadelphia (1764), and New York (1765). They all failed, but they reflected a new experimental way for improving the conditions of the poor. The Pennsylvania Hospital for the Sick Poor opened in 1751 "to care for the sick-poor and insane who were wandering the streets of Philadelphia." In 1766, Quaker merchants raised money to fund "The Bettering House," which took in the impoverished elderly and disabled, while also functioning as a workhouse for the poor who could work. Almost 300 people lived there shortly after it opened. These practical and philanthropic measures extended to, and grew out of, theorizing about improving the human condition, some of which took its foundation from a new natural rights philosophy. This philosophy emphasized freedom and equality, and led to interrogation of the morality of slavery and the social distinctions that divided humans by birth. In other words, thinkers probed the artificial divides of class and race, considering "humans" in universal terms—a revolutionary ideology beginning to gain currency in the Atlantic world.

It is important to note that not all the challenges to mercantilism, imperialism, and racism arose from intellectuals. The leveling tradition of the English Civil War could be found throughout the Atlantic world, including in the American colonies. Many sailors, farmers, ex-indentured servants, and slaves subscribed to a worldview that neither accepted hierarchy nor human oppression. These people refused to defer to their social betters, committed piracy, publicly demonstrated against food shortages, opposed slavery, and promoted democratization of society and a more equitable distribution of property.

Warfare, itself, was challenged by religious pacifism, and among plebian culture could be found strains of internationalism and class identification against aristocracy and privilege. These political and social currents did not lead to organized political movements. Instead, they generally emerged as occasions warranted, as when women held bread riots three times in Boston from 1710 to 1713; urbanites protested against impressments of sailors in Boston in 1747 and New York in 1760 and 1764; and New York slaves and poor whites united in rebellion in 1741. Inter-racial maroon communities subsisted in the Great Swamp of North Carolina and Virginia, posing a threat to plantation society and to prevalent racial views. The mid-18th century saw some of these challenges enter print culture and reach a wide audience, as John Woolman, a Pennsylvania Quaker, promoted his anti-slavery, pacifist views in published journals and pamphlets that addressed numerous other social problems, including poverty, while attacking the morality of imperial warfare. Woolman's anti-slavery views were highly influential, forcing opponents to respond in print with a defense of slavery.

## Conclusion

The mid-18th century witnessed impressive population growth and prosperity in the British American colonies. Although New England received few migrants, the population increased rapidly due to a healthy environment, and expanded onto new lands to the north and west in the region. The New England environment could not support plantation agriculture but family farming did quite well, while entrepreneurs diversified the economy through active participation in Atlantic trade and small-scale manufacturing enterprises supplemented by household production of a variety of goods by women. In this period, the Middle Colonies surpassed New England in terms of Atlantic trade, and buttressed by a prosperous agricultural sector producing wheat and flour, developed a substantial artisanal class in Philadelphia and New York that helped create cosmopolitan cities that offered a variety of services and initiated new social services.

The success of tobacco fueled continued immigration of indentured servants to the Chesapeake colonies, and provided planters with enough capital to heavily invest in slaves. An elite class of planters emerged who built great plantation houses, purchased luxury items from Great Britain, and modeled themselves on the British country gentleman.

Many new European migrants entered Virginia and Maryland towards the end of the period, peopling the western areas of these colonies and beginning the move across the Appalachians into the area that later became West Virginia and Kentucky.

The British Lower South experienced the greatest percentage growth of population, almost entirely due to the influx of African slaves into the lowcountry and Europeans into the backcountry. The South Carolina planter elite accumulated wealth from slave-produced rice, and like tobacco planters built great plantation homes, purchased luxury goods, and styled themselves as British country planters. In Georgia, the Trustees experimented by colony-building without slavery, but when the experiment failed, Georgia copied its northern neighbor and developed a profitable plantation system based on rice production. While a wealthy plantation society characterized the lowcountry of the Lower South colonies of Georgia and both Carolinas, the backcountry was filled with subsistence farmers hostile to elite pretensions and their control of the colonial governments.

The lowcountry slaves were hostile to the planters as well. But with so many Europeans settling the backcountry, it became more difficult for the Africans to escape slavery. The Europeans became more efficient policing their slaves and securing their plantations. An accommodation of sorts was reached between masters and slaves. The latter received better working conditions—Sundays off, work under the task system, family unit housing, and financial rewards. Nonetheless, slaves did not give up their hope for freedom. Many became Christians and expected that God would liberate them as he did the Hebrews in the Old Testament. But this did not preclude self-help. When the American Revolution came, thousands of slaves took the opportunity to liberate themselves (see chapters fourteen and fifteen).

The prosperity of the British colonies offended the sensibilities of some colonists, who condemned the luxurious lifestyles of planters and merchants. The evangelicals, in particular, in no uncertain terms preached that people should look to God and consider the state of their soul, and reject the material excesses and secular amusements with which they filled their lives. Initially, the evangelicals posed a grave threat to elite society by their calls for the reform of slavery and their break with established churches. But they did not seek to overthrow society but to transform it from within, and many turned inward to look after the state of their own soul and reform both their lives and their communities.

The evangelicals were not the only ones seeking to improve themselves and their communities. Inspired by the rationalism of the Enlightenment, many American colonials applied reason to a host of problems and believed that science would lead to a better world. Enlightenment thinking was most evident in the cities and on plantations. In the urban areas, a wealth of scientific experiments and community projects were undertaken. On the plantations could be found planters who collected botanical specimens that they sent to Europe for study, experimentation in agricultural improvements, and study of law, history, and political economy. Enlightenment thinking and community projects gave many colonial Americans confidence in their futures. People in the mother country often viewed colonials as second-class citizens who were inherently inferior by living in colonies. But colonials had a far different perspective. By the end of the period, some had grown so boastful as to suggest that one day the British monarch would move to the colonies, which were on their way to becoming the center of the empire.

# DOCUMENTS

## 11.1. George Whitefield on Slavery

*George Whitefield's public letter to the Southern British colonists was the most significant public admonishment of slaveholding practices by a public figure in the first half of the 18th century. Whitefield condemned the treatment of bondpeople, including their refusal to allow slaves access to Christianity. Besides his own witnessing of cruelty and others' testimony of slaveholder barbarism, Whitefield assured his readers that God's punishments of South Carolina through disease and slave rebellion provided all the evidence needed that drastic reform must be undertaken or worse would befall the colonists. Yet Whitefield and his evangelical followers soon beat a retreat after publication of the letter: slaveholding society would not tolerate public attacks upon it; Whitefield would become both a slaveholder and an apologist for slavery so that evangelical Christianity could survive in the South. Why did Whitefield believe it necessary to convert the slaves to Christianity? What benefits would masters' receive from having Christian, rather than heathen, slaves?*

As I lately passed through your provinces, in my way hither, I was sensibly touched with a fellow-feeling of the miseries of the poor negroes. Could I have preached more frequently among you, I should have delivered my thoughts to you in my public discourses: but, as business here required me to stop as little as possible on the road, I have no other way to discharge the concern which at present lies upon my heart, than by sending you this letter. How will you receive it, I know not; but whatever be the event, I must inform you, in the meekness and gentleness of Christ, that I think God has a quarrel with you, for your abuse and cruelty to the poor negroes. Whether it be lawful for Christians to buy slaves, and thereby encourage the nations from whence they are brought to be at perpetual war with each other, I shall not take upon me to determine; but sure I am it is sinful, when bought, to use them as bad as, nay worse than brutes: and whatever particular exceptions there may be, (as I would charitably hope there are some) I fear the generality of you that own negroes, are liable to such a charge; for your slaves, I believe, work as hard, if not harder, than the horses whereon you ride.

These, after they have done their work, are fed and taken proper care of; but many negroes, when wearied with labour in your plantations, have been obliged to grind their own corn after they return home.

Your dogs are caressed and fondled at your tables; but your slaves, who are frequently stiled dogs or beasts, have not an equal privilege: they are scarce permitted to pick up the crumbs which fall from their masters tables; nay, some, as I have been informed by an eye-witness, have been, upon the most trifling provocation, cut with knives, and have had forks thrown into their flesh: not to mention what numbers have been given up to the inhuman usage of cruel taskmasters, who by their unrelenting scourges have ploughed upon their backs, and made long furrows, and at length brought them even to death itself.

'Tis true, I hope, there are but few such monsters of barbarity suffered to subsist among you: some, I hear, have been lately executed in Virginia for killing slaves; and the laws are very severe against such who at any time murder them.

And perhaps it might be better for the poor creatures themselves, to be hurried out of life, than to be made so miserable as they generally are in it. And indeed, considering what usage they commonly meet with, I have wondered, that we have not more instances of self-murder among negroes, or that they have not more frequently risen up in arms against their owners. Virginia has been once, and Charles-town more than once, threatened in this way.

*(Continued)*

And though I heartily pray God, they may never be permitted to get the upper hand; yet, should such a thing be permitted by providence, all good men must acknowledge the judgment would be just. For is it not the highest ingratitude, as well as cruelty, not to let your poor slaves enjoy some fruits of labour?

When passing along, whilst I have viewed your plantations cleared and cultivated, many spacious houses built, and the owners of them faring sumptuously every day, my blood has frequently almost run cold within me, to consider how many of your slaves had neither convenient food to eat, nor proper raiment to put on, notwithstanding most of the comforts you enjoy, were solely owning to their indefatigable labours. The scripture says, "Thou shalt not muzzle the oxen that treadeth out the corn." . . . He does not reject the prayer of the poor and destitute, nor disregard the cry of the meanest negroes: their blood which has been spilt, for these many years in your respective provinces, will ascend up to heaven against you; I wish I could say, it would speak better things than the blood of Abel. But this is not all. Enslaving or misusing their bodies, comparatively speaking, would be an inconsiderable evil, was proper care taken of their souls: but I have great reason to believe, that most of you on purpose keep your negroes ignorant of christianity; or otherwise, why are they permitted through your provinces openly to profane the Lord's day, by their dancing, piping, and such like? I know the general pretence for this neglect of their souls, is, that teaching them christianity would make them proud, and consequently unwilling to submit to slavery. But what a dreadful reflection is this upon your holy region? What blasphemous notions must those have, that make such an objection, of the precepts of christianity! Do you find any one command in the gospel, that has the least tendency to make people forget their relative duties? Do you not read, that servants, and as many as are under the yoke of bondage, are required to be subject in all lawful things to their masters, and that not only to the good and gentle, but also to the froward? Nay, may not I appeal to your own hearts, whether deviating from the laws of Jesus Christ, is not the cause of all the evils and miseries mankind now universally groan under, and of all the vices we find both in ourselves and others? Certainly it is. And therefore the reason why servants generally prove so bad is, because so little care is taken to breed them up in the nurture and admonition of the Lord. But some will be so bold perhaps as to reply, "That a few of the negroes have been taught christianity, and notwithstanding have been remarkably worse than others." But what christianity were they taught? They were baptized, and taught to read and write: and this they may do, and much more, and yet be far from the kingdom of God; for there is a vast difference between civilizing and christianizing a negroe. A black as well as a white man, may be civilized by outward restraints, and afterwards break through those restraints again; but I challenge the world to produce a single instance of a negroe's being made a thorough christian, and thereby made a worse servant: it cannot be. But further, if the teaching of slaves christianity has such a bad influence on their lives, why are you generally desirous of having your children taught? Think you, they are any way better by nature than the poor negroes? No, in nowise. Blacks are just as much, and no more, conceived and born in sin, as white men are: both, if born and bred up here, I am persuaded are naturally capable of the same improvement.

That you yourselves are not effectually convinced of this, I think is too notorious to want evidence. A general dreadness as to divine things, and not to say a general profaneness, is discernible both in pastors and people.

Most of you are without any teaching priest. And whatever quantity of rum there may be, yet I fear but very few bibles are annually imported into your different provinces. God has already begun to visit for this, as well as for other wicked things. For near two years past, he has been in a remarkable manner contending with the people of South-Carolina: their houses have been depopulated with the small pox and fever, and their own slaves have risen up in arms against them. These judgments are undoubtedly sent abroad, not only that the inhabitants of that, but of other provinces, should learn righteousness: and unless you all repent, you all must in like manner expect to perish. God first generally corrects us with whips: if that will not do, he must chastise us with scorpions. A foreign enemy [Spain] is now threatening to invade you; and nothing will more provoke God, to give you up as a prey into their teeth, than impenitence and unbelief. Let these be removed, and the sons of violence shall not be able to hurt you; no; your oxen shall be strong to labour; there shall be no decay of your people by epidemical sickness; no leading away into captivity from abroad; and no complaining in your streets at home. Your sons shall grow up as young plants, and your daughters be as the polished corners of the temple: and, to sum up all blessings in one, "Then shall the Lord be your God." That you may be the people who are in such a happy case, is the earnest prayer of,

Your sincere well-wisher and servant in Christ, G. W.

———

Source: "A Letter to the Inhabitants of Maryland, Virginia, North and South Carolina" (1740).

## 11.2. An Anonymous Supporter of the Ban on Slavery in Georgia

*Of the original 13 colonies, only Georgia prohibited slavery. Some colonists opposed this policy of the Trustees of Georgia. These men, known as the Malcontents, published in England several tracts calling for an end to the ban, requesting the king and Parliament take Georgia away from the Trustees and make it a royal colony. The anonymously authored An Account Shewing the Progress of the Colony of Georgia in America from Its First Establishment lays out many of the reasons why the Trustees had prohibited slavery, including its danger to the white inhabitants; the proximity of the colony to St. Augustine, to which slaves could easily escape; its devaluation of free labor; and its lack of necessity. Why was the use of free labor so important to the Trustees of Georgia? What thread did slave labor pose to free laborers?*

*(Continued)*

The Trustees were induced to prohibit the Use of Negroes within Georgia; the Intention of his Majesty's Charter being to provide for poor People incapable of subsisting themselves at home, and to settle a Frontier for South Carolina, which was much exposed by the small Number of its white Inhabitants. It was impossible that the Poor, who should be sent from hence, and the Foreign persecuted Protestants, who must go in a manner naked into the Colony, could be able to purchase or subsist them, if they had them; and it would be a Charge too great for the Trustees to undertake; and they would be thereby disabled from sending white People. The first Cost of a Negro is about Thirty Pounds; and this Thirty Pounds would pay the Passage over, provide Tools and other Necessaries, and defray the Charge of Subsistence of a white Man for a Year; in which Time it might be hoped that the Planter's own Labour would gain him some Subsistence; consequently the Purchase-money of every Negro, (abstracting the Expence of subsisting him, as well as his Master) by being applied that way, would prevent the sending over a white Man, who would be of Security to the Province; whereas the Negro would render that Security precarious.

It was thought, that the white Man, by having a Negro Slave, would be less disposed to labour himself~ and that his whole Time must be employed in keeping the Negro to Work, and in watching against any Danger he or his Family might apprehend from the Slave; and that the Planter's Wife and Children would by the Death, or even the Absence of the Planter, be in a manner at the Mercy of the Negro.

It was also apprehended, that the Spaniards at St. Augustine would be continually inticing away the Negroes, or encouraging them to Insurrections; that the first might easily be accomplished, since a single Negro could run away thither without Companions, and would only have a River or two to swim over; and this Opinion has been confirmed and justified by the Practices of the Spaniards, even in Time of profound Peace, amongst the Negroes in South Carolina; where, tho' at a greater Distance from Augustine, some have fled in Perriaguas and little Boats to the Spaniards, and been protected, and others in large Bodies have been incited to Insurrections, to the great Tenor, and even endangering the Loss of that Province; which, though it has been established above Seventy Years, has scarce white People enough to secure her against her own Slaves.

It was also considered, that the Produces designed to be raised in the Colony would not require such Labour as to make Negroes necessary for carrying them on; for the Province of Carolina produces chiefly Rice, which is a Work of Hardship proper for Negroes; whereas the Silk and other Produces which the Trustees proposed to have the People employed on in Georgia, were such as Women and Children might be of as much Use in as Negroes.

It was likewise apprehended, that if the Persons who should go over to Georgia at their own Expence, should be permitted the Use of Negroes, it would dispirit and win the poor Planters who could not get them, and who by their Numbers were designed to be the Strength of the Province; it would make them clamorous to have Negroes given them; and on the Refusal, would drive them from the Province, or at least make them negligent of their Plantations; where they would be unwilling, nay would certainly disdain to work like Negroes; and would rather let themselves out to the wealthy Planters as Overseers of their Negroes.

It was further thought, That upon the Admission of Negroes the wealthy Planters would, as in all other Colonies, be more induced to absent themselves, and live in other Places, leaving the Care of their Plantations and their Negroes to Overseers.

It was likewise thought, that the poor Planter sent on Charity from his Desire to have Negroes, as well as the Planter who should settle at his own Expence, would (if he had Leave to alienate) mortgage his Land to the Negro Merchant for them, or at least become a Debtor for the Purchase of such Negroes; and under these Weights and Discouragements would be induced to sell his Slaves again upon any Necessity, and would leave the Province and his Lot to the Negro Merchant; in Consequence of which, all the small Properties would be swallowed up, as they have been in other Places, by the more wealthy Planters.

It was likewise considered, that the admitting of Negroes in Georgia would naturally facilitate the Desertion of the Carolina Negroes, thro' the Province of Georgia; and consequently this Colony, instead of proving a Frontier, and adding a Strength to the Province of South Carolina, would be a Means of drawing off the Slaves of Carolina, and adding thereby a Strength to Augustine.

From these several Considerations, as the Produces to be raised in the Colony did not make Negro Slaves necessary, as the Introduction of them so near to a Garison of the Spaniards would weaken rather than strengthen the Barrier, and as they would introduce with them a greater Propensity to Idleness among the poor Planters, and too great an Inequality among the People, it was thought proper to make the Prohibition of them a Fundamental of the Constitution.

---

Source: An Account Shewing the Progress of the Colony of Georgia in America from Its First Establishment (1741), 8–10.

# Bibliography

Bonomi, Patricia. *Under the Cope of Heaven: Religion, Society, and Politics in Colonial America* (1986).

Braund, Kathryn E. Holland. *Deerskins & Duffels: The Creek Indian Trade with Anglo-America, 1685–1815* (1993).

Butler, Jon. *Awash in a Sea of Faith: Christianizing the American People* (1990).

Carney, Judith. *Black Rice: The Origins of Rice Cultivation in the Americas* (2001).

Gallay, Alan. *The Formation of a Planter Elite: Jonathan Bryan and the Southern Colonial Frontier* (1989).

Greene, Jack P. *Pursuits of Happiness: The Social Development of Early Modern British Colonies and the Formation of American Culture* (1988).

Gura, Philip F. *Jonathan Edwards: America's Evangelical* (2005).

Haines, Michael R., and Richard H. Steckel, eds. *A Population History of North America* (2000).

Hinderaker, Eric. *Elusive Empires: Constructing Colonialism in the Ohio Valley, 1673–1800* (1997).

Hindle, Brooke. *The Pursuit of Science in Revolutionary America, 1735–1789* (1956).

Lambert, Frank. *"Pedlar in Divinity": George Whitefield and the Transatlantic Revivals, 1737–1770* (1994).

Lefler, Hugh T., and William S. Powell. *Colonial North Carolina: A History* (1973).

Littlefield, Daniel C. *Rice and Slaves: Ethnicity and the Slave Trade in Colonial South Carolina* (1981).

Marsden, George. *Jonathan Edwards: A Life* (2004).

May, Henry F. *The Enlightenment in America* (1976).

McCusker, John J., and Russell R. Menard. *The Economy of British America, 1607–1789* (1991).

Mercantini, Jonathan. *Who Should Rule at Home?: The Evolution of South Carolina Political Culture, 1748–1766* (2006).

Morgan, Philip D. *Slave Counterpoint: Black Culture in the Eighteenth-Century Chesapeake and Lowcountry* (1998).

Spalding, Phinizy. *Oglethorpe in America* (1977).

Sweet, Julie Anne. *Negotiating for Georgia: British Creek Relations in the Trustee Era, 1733–1752* (2005).

Wood, Betty. *Slavery in Colonial Georgia, 1730–1775* (1984).

Wood, Bradford J. *This Remote Part of the World: Regional Formation in Lower Cape Fear, North Carolina, 1725–1775* (2004).

Wood, Peter H. *Black Majority: Negroes in Colonial South Carolina from 1670 Through the Stono Rebellion* (1974).

# 12

# Colonists, Indians, and the Contests for Empire, 1730–1763

## INTRODUCTION

Americans have always held the idea that they are not a militaristic people; that wars have been relatively few and always justified; that no better evidence for this tradition exists than in the small size of the American Army during peacetime from the American Revolution to World War II. The pervasiveness of colonial wars is blamed on the imperial connection—colonists unable to avoid the wars of their mother country.

Evangelical religion and Enlightenment rationalism altered how many Euro-Americans viewed their world and its problems, but neither trumped the ability of war to transform the landscape of colonial America. Almost all colonial enterprises were military by nature, as colonists took up arms to secure and settle land, capture booty, and enslave native peoples. They employed force—provincial soldiers, militia, or Indian warriors—to keep slaves and servants from running away or rebelling, and even to prevent their own people from leaving to join Indians, live on their own, or remove to other colonies. Many colonists welcomed imperial conflicts and fought with imperial enemies in periods of official peace (often against their mother country's wishes). American colonists may have been no more militant than the colonists of any other empire, nor more engaged in military activity than their native neighbors—but certainly they were no less engaged. However, from the French perspective in Canada, the Spanish perspective in Florida, and in the view of many American Indians, the colonists of British North America were *the* most warlike, militarily aggressive people they knew. If we measure a society's militarism by its propensity to undertake wars of aggression, and to recruit others to undertake wars for them, most of the British mainland colonies can be described as militaristic societies. The Anglo-American colonies did not need regular armies to be militarized, for the male populace was easily organized and armed, and many local government officials were quite adept at recruiting native soldiers to assist them. Moreover, local communities often proved capable of organizing military forays. This peculiar nature of American militarism continued through the 19th century: military expeditions were organized on an ad hoc basis against native peoples and neighboring Europeans; colonists and their descendants tended to be the aggressors in military action, rather than on the defensive or as victims. British Americans were not preoccupied with militarism or organized into warrior societies. Instead American militarism involved the easy resort to arms to effect economic, political, and social ends.

## IMPERIAL WARS AND NATIVE AMERICA, 1739–1755

War in mid-18th-century Anglo-America was a tool for territorial and commercial expansion. Anglo-Americans hoped to forestall French commercial and territorial expansion and influence over the inland continent between the Appalachian Mountains and the Mississippi River, and to reduce French power in Canada. In the South, Anglo-Americans maintained their intention to conquer Spanish Florida, part and parcel of the overall British attempt to penetrate and reduce the Spanish empire throughout the globe. Both Spanish and French increasingly perceived shared interests in holding back British expansion, and if they had possessed the military power would have been even more aggressive towards the British in the New World. As it stood, French military and economic power was growing, and they asserted themselves on land and sea against Britain. Given the aggressive competition of France and Britain, conflicts between the two were inevitable. The eruption came first between Britain and Spain, and then between Britain and France.

Caught in the maelstrom of European imperial rivalries, American Indians forged political and diplomatic strategies in pursuit of their own interests. In the 1720s and 1730s, much of the native population east of the Mississippi largely gained respite from European land encroachment and large scale wars with colonies and imperial armies. The period of slaving wars largely had ended; Indian peoples were still victimized by slaving but on a much smaller scale. In the American South, the creation of native confederacies secured many against the Europeans, though warfare remained endemic between the confederacies—raids and counter-raids characterized relations among the Cherokee, Creek, Choctaw, and Chickasaw. The Choctaw also succumbed to a brutal civil war (1746–1750), as some Choctaw wished to move away from the traditional alliance with the French, and draw closer to the English, consciously copying their neighboring confederacies' policy of playing French and English against one another. The Creek proved most adept at this policy, and even succeeded playing one English colony against another.

In the north, the Abenaki of Northern New England and Atlantic Canada occupied a perilous position between the French and English, but to the west, declining Iroquois power, and the French and English competition, worked to increase the standing of a great variety of Algonquin peoples from New York through Pennsylvania, and into the Ohio Country. Indians' land to the west was secured from European encroachment by the Appalachian Mountains, for European traders, rather than settlers, crossed the eastern continent's great divide. East of the mountains Indian life was less secure from settler encroachment, but colonial expansion had slowed until the new wave of immigration that filled the backcountries of Pennsylvania and the colonies to the south in the 1750s.

Diplomacy, trade, military power, demography, and a rough balance of power between France and England all contributed to relative stability in Indian life, at least compared to the periods before and after the second quarter of the 18th century. Perhaps contributing to the stability was the preoccupation of colonists in the English colonies with their own economic lives. In the North, commercial growth in the urban areas meant that coastal communities engaged in a lively export trade, as well as supplying goods for recently established inland farming communities. In the southern plantation colonies, this period saw a large importation of African slaves, who were assimilated into the production of crops for foreign markets. Native communities remained important to the colonies as a defensive bulwark or threat, and as trade partners, and increasingly diplomacy was conducted along more rational lines by colonial governments and imperial officials. Periodic diplomatic meetings were held in places like Albany, New York, and Charles Town, South Carolina, and by officials sent to Indian communities. The English and French sought to regulate trade to avoid the abuses that could lead to a breakdown in relations with Indians; they feared their trading partners allying with the other side. In the 1750s, however, the stability that existed crumbled, owing to a new period of expansion by British colonists, and the heated competition between France and Britain. At stake was control of the land west of the Appalachian mountains: the Ohio Country

## Anglo-Spanish War (1739–1744) and King George's War (1744–1748)

The renewal of wide-scale imperial warfare began with the breakdown in relations between Britain and Spain. Anglo-Spanish relations hinged on England's attempt to break open the Spanish empire—to force Spain's colonies to trade with them. Britain desired these colonies' raw materials, such as brasilwood (used for dyeing), and the gold and silver of Latin American mines. The British possessed a surfeit of manufactured goods they hoped to sell to Spanish colonists. Illicit trade occurred frequently, which the Spanish Navy tried to stop. At the close of the War of the Spanish Succession in 1713, Britain wrested from Spain exclusive rights for 30 years to supply Spanish colonies with African slaves, and permission to send a very limited number of ships to trade at Porto Bello and Vera Cruz. But British smuggling in the late 1730s led to a deterioration in imperial relations—the Spanish resented British smuggling with its colonists, and the British resented Spanish attempts to stop their smuggling. The British mistakenly believed that Spanish colonials wanted so much to trade with them that with a bit of military support they would rebel from Spain. As a result, the British looked to a military solution to further their interests. In 1739, the British attacked Porto Bello, on the Isthmus of Panama, because it was a base for the *guarda costas*, the ships that protected Spanish colonies from British smuggling. The "revolution" of Spanish colonials did not materialize—but Britain maintained its intent to militarily intimidate the Spanish into making concessions—a process in which their American colonists assisted (and a policy of aggression against Spain that continued under the United States government, which later used military force to wrest from Spain parts of its empire, notably Florida, the Philippines, and Puerto Rico).

In 1741, for the first time, American colonial forces played a major military role alongside British regulars and naval personnel *outside* of mainland North America. Shipped to the Caribbean, they supported British regulars in an offensive against Cartagena, Columbia. Admiral Edward Vernon led the British forces, which included 3,000 Americans. Among those serving under Vernon was Lawrence Washington, George Washington's elder half-brother. Captain Washington led 200 Americans in assaults on a few outposts, the only success the British enjoyed at Cartagena. The British followed with half-hearted attempts against Cuba, Santiago, and Panama City; all included American colonial troops. By 1742, British forces had withered under bullets and disease. Only about 300 Americans—10% of the original contingent—made it home. The survivors received lifetime half-pay pensions. Indicative of American pride in participating in Britain's imperial wars, Lawrence Washington named one of his plantations, Mount Vernon, after his commander—brother George later inherited this estate that would become the most famous home in America.

Despite British losses in the Caribbean, South America, and the failed conquest of Florida led by James Oglethorpe, British naval and mercantile power grew apace on the seas, augmented by privateering, which American colonials actively engaged in against Spanish trade and colonies. (So much Spanish currency entered the British colonies that it became a major means of exchange, often used for calculating the value of local currencies, and eventually providing the model for the later United States currency.) The Anglo-Spanish War gave way in 1744 to the outbreak of yet another war between France and England: King George's War (1744–1748; the war was termed in Europe as the War of the Austrian Succession). This war provided new opportunities for colonial Americans to profit from imperial rivalries. Colonists from every port outfitted ships to go against French and Spanish shipping and colonies in the West Indies and elsewhere. Many fortunes were made by ship owners, while young men found profitable, if dangerous, employment, and the colonial economy benefited from the influx of valuable commodities like sugar and coffee. The negative impact of the war was great—war and privateering meant death, and widows left with hungry children: colonial port towns experienced growing poverty and the need to care for large numbers of the infirm and the indigent.

The human costs of war were rarely considered. Instead, imperial governments viewed war as an opportunity for expansion, conquest, and profits. Colonial men enlisted to earn bounties and salary, but it was not unusual for governments to save money by enlisting personnel whose pay came from whatever booty they could obtain. Money was not the sole motivator, although the most important; men enlisted for the adventure and the chance to earn glory against the Catholic enemy. Some New England sons obtained that goal in King George's War.

After several French assaults upon Acadia spread terror through New England, the English responded with a massive assault against the great bastion of Louisbourg, which guarded the mouth of the St. Lawrence. Its conquest in 1744 set off celebrations throughout the English colonies, and seemed to hearken the beginning of the end of French power in America. The French failed in a disastrous attempt to retake Louisbourg, but guerilla raids along the northern frontier held the English at bay. Employing all available men in these forays, the French did not have enough labor to harvest their crops, which led to famine in Canada. Colonial losses for France were countered by great success in continental Europe, so that when peace was made in the Treaty of Aix-la-Chapelle in 1748, the English returned Louisbourg, and the French returned Madras (now renamed Chennai), India, to the English. Stunned English colonists resented that their blood had been spilt for naught and that they ranked so low in imperial priorities. But a few English and French imperialists had come to realize the military and economic importance of mainland North America to the health of their empires—and that health depended not only on greater concern and oversight of colonial affairs, but in improving relations with native peoples who were perceived as holding the balance of power.

## The Ohio Country: Meeting Place of Cultures

In the Ohio Country—the great region extending west from the Alleghenies to the Mississippi, and south from the Great Lakes to the Wabash and Tennessee Rivers, there was great movement of native peoples from one place to the next from the middle of the 17th century to the middle of the 18th century. This migration arose from Iroquois attacks in the east that forced Algonquins and others to the north and west. Many established or joined settlements near newly built French trading posts in Illinois and the Great Lakes. These posts, at places like St. Louis and Green Bay, became surrounded by towns of Indians of a great variety of ethnicities, who found strength in numbers, French alliance, and the availability of supplies, including guns. The key French post of Detroit, established in the early 18th century, attracted over 6,000 Indians of diverse groups—making it a larger community than all but the largest European colonial settlements. Some Indian confederacies, like the Miamis, refused to relocate to these posts, and the French accommodated them by building at places of the Indians' choosing, such as Chicago and on various rivers in modern-day Indiana and Ohio. The power of the Iroquois had forced Indians north of the Ohio to accommodate to one another and with the French, who, in turn, relied on their Indian allies.

The areas around many French posts grew so crowded that shortages of resources led to dispersal and removal again. By the 1730s and 1740s, Indians began returning to many tributaries of the Ohio River, some abandoned over 50 years before as nearly indefensible. Re-settlement signified a reduced threat of warfare in the region. Since much of the Ohio Country had been depopulated for a half-century, game had replenished in the region. From the east, Indians of the Susquehanna Valley, particularly the Shawnee and Delaware, facing pressure from the Iroquois and the Pennsylvania government to accept Iroquois dominance, migrated west to the Shawnees' former lands—and to enjoy the once again rich hunting areas. A persistent source of alienation for the Delaware had been the fraudulent "Walking Purchase Deed," whereby they had been forced by Pennsylvania and the Iroquois to cede much of their land to Pennsylvania in 1737. The Delaware chafed under their tributary status to the Iroquois, who spoke for them (or tried to speak for them) in diplomatic relations, particularly with the European powers. Both the Iroquois and Pennsylvania made repeated attempts to convince the emigrants to return but to no avail. Both feared these Indians allying with the French.

Iroquois power was in decline, and French and British traders competed for trade in the west, but not by warfare. Representing the shift was the creation around 1730 by Shawnee migrants of the great trading community of Logstown about 18 miles south of modern-day Pittsburgh. Logstown, like so many other locales of Indian settlement in the Ohio Country was multi-ethnic, with both traders and residents coming and going. At Logstown could be found Shawnees, Delawares, Mingoes, Wyandots, Ottawas, Iroquois, and numerous others. Because of its commercial importance, location, and diverse population, Logstown became the site of numerous diplomatic meetings among Indians, French, and British with interests in the Ohio Country.

Indian peoples enjoyed a great deal of autonomy in their Ohio Country communities, which they joined and abandoned as they pleased. European governments grew frustrated conducting diplomacy with towns and groups, because of their shifting make-up and mobility. Leadership in these communities altered frequently and in new ways. As great numbers of Indians engaged in hunting and the trade of pelts for European goods, new avenues of status opened through the accumulation of material wealth. Older patterns of authority, particularly those denoted by age and tribal traditions, were challenged by young men who asserted themselves through successful hunting and trading in the market economy. Families that made marriage alliances with substantial French and British traders often gained status and power from their access to economic and diplomatic networks. European governments tried to create their own lines of authority in Indian communities by designating individuals as "medal chiefs." They gave these chiefs presents to distribute to followers, to buttress their status in the community. But there were no guarantees that Indians would heed the medal chiefs' authority, and in fact, further decentralization occurred as disgruntled Indians resentful of the medal chiefs went their own way.

Fluidity in social and ethnic relations thus characterized the Ohio Country. The native inhabitants traded with both French and English. The English offered better prices for furs, but trade with the French provided an important counter to English and Iroquois pretensions of dominance. For several decades, the peoples of the region enjoyed relative peace and prosperity. Unable to easily move their pelts to market, English, French, and Iroquois traders traveled to diverse Indian communities. The value of furs exported from Pennsylvania grew dramatically, tripling from 1741 to 1751. The trade, however, had only limited value for the French and English. A glut of furs exported from Canada depressed the French market—beaver pelts rotted in French warehouses before they could be processed into hats. The Ohio Valley pelts were much inferior to those from Canada—the furs were neither as thick nor well dressed. Many Europeans could not make the fur trade pay, but still it inspired the adventurous—and a few did make great fortunes. The fur trade stood as a symbol of America as Eden—a land of untapped wealth and resources—the most visible of which were the pelts of beavers and other animals. A few European traders of charisma and vision traveled to colonial and imperial cities with tales of riches to be made. They attracted investors and government support. The lands to the west of the Appalachian Mountains thus entered European consciousness as the next great area for settlement and imperial expansion. Even if the fur trade's profits were hardly worth government investment, in terms of maintaining good relations with the western Indians, France and England both believed they had to expend resources in the Ohio Country to keep their rival at bay. The decades of relative peace west of the mountains, from the end of the Iroquois Wars at the onset of the 18th century to the early 1750s, were about to end.

## The Ohio Country: The French and Indian War

The initial outburst of hostilities that enveloped England and France into the first "world war," the Seven Years' War, occurred in the Ohio Country where the two great powers' interests came into direct conflict. France and Britain both perceived possession of the Ohio Country as key to their North American empires. France sought to connect Canada to Louisiana by construction of forts in the Great Lakes and Ohio Country. They built forts in western Pennsylvania at Presque Isle, Le Boeuf, and Venango to control not only the fur trade, but the important portage route that connects Lake Erie to the "Three Rivers," at modern-day Pittsburgh, where the Monongahela and Allegheny Rivers create the Ohio River. About 1,000 miles to the southwest, the Ohio River empties into the Mississippi, permitting the movement of people and goods all the way from the mouth of the St. Lawrence Seaway in the north Atlantic to New Orleans on the Gulf of Mexico. In other words, possession of the Three Rivers would allow France to link Canada and Louisiana, and to seemingly secure control over the North American continent west of the Appalachians to the Mississippi Valley—which would hem in the British along the Atlantic Coast.

Many English colonists desired to settle the Ohio Country, which reputedly possessed rich agricultural lands, perhaps the best on the continent. Virginia claimed that Ohio fell into the land granted by the king in its original charter. Subsequently, the Ohio Company, a group of Virginia investors, received a grant to the land from the King of England under condition that they construct a fort and plant a settlement in the Ohio Country. As prelude, the Virginia governor sent troops under 21-year-old George Washington to scout French movements in the region and warn them to leave. Washington found the French much further along in fort construction than expected. The French rejected the Virginians' demand to abandon Ohio. When the Virginia government refused to take further action, the governor received funds from the Ohio Company to build a fort. He sent troops with Washington as second-in-command. On the march, Washington learned that overwhelming French troops had dismantled an English stockade, forcing the men to return to Virginia, and had begun the construction of Fort Duquesne (Pennsylvania). Under instructions, Washington proceeded. Joined by allied Indians, he attacked a French party, killing its leader, Joseph Coulon de Villiers de Jumonville. The French claimed Washington had assaulted a diplomatic embassy on its way to Virginia, and that the emissary had been shot while reading his message to Washington. Whatever the truth of the matter, the powder keg had been lit, and the struggle for Ohio snowballed into a battle for control of the continent east of the Mississippi River.

Washington only temporarily secured the English position by building Fort Necessity (Pennsylvania). The French attacked the fort and Washington surrendered. He was permitted, along with his men, to return to Virginia. The British countered by sending General Edward Braddock with thousands of regular and colonial troops. He began building a long road to move cannon across the Appalachians with the goal of taking the Ohio Country. Before Braddock could complete the road, the French and their native allies won an overwhelming victory over his army: the French lost 39 men to their opponents' 800. The defeated British fled to Philadelphia; their general was killed, though his unofficial advisor George Washington survived.

Fear spread through Anglo-America as the power of the French appeared unstoppable, especially as many native peoples allied with the French against the land-hungry English colonists. The English did enjoy success in Nova Scotia in 1755, when they captured Fort Beauséjour, which yielded 1,000 prisoners. They then deported 6,000 French Acadian settlers who refused to swear allegiance to Britain. Transferred to the southern colonies, where they received poor treatment by governments and people, many Acadians made their way on their own to French Louisiana where they gave root to Cajun culture.

Native allies of the French assaulted the Anglo frontier through 1756, with much success in Virginia and Pennsylvania. In Pennsylvania, hard hit by native and French advances, most of the Quakers resigned from the government. As pacifists, they could not undertake the military measures necessary to protect settlements. The disputes between natives and Pennsylvania colonists, which extended well beyond the imperial conflict, arose from encroachment on native land and trade abuses. Quaker resignations from the assembly meant that the most important Pennsylvania group to have worked to maintain peace and justice with the natives, and had done so with varying degrees of success since the colony's founding, no longer held political power to continue their policies.

## THE SEVEN YEARS' WAR: FROM COLONIAL TO GLOBAL TO COLONIAL CONFLICT

The French and Indian War (1754–1761) or Seven Years' War (1756–1763) outstripped the earlier imperial conflicts between France and England in terms of scope and global importance. The major powers contended for dominance at sea—in the Atlantic and Indian Oceans, as well as the Mediterranean Sea—and in places as far-flung as India, Africa, Europe, West Indies, and North America. The consequences for North America above Mexico were momentous. The Seven Years' War led to the loss of France's North American empire. Moreover, the war was the watershed event in American Indian history east of the Mississippi River—the war's outcome paved the way for Anglo-American dominance of the trans-Appalachian region and the ultimate removal of most Indians to the west.

Although the dispute over the Ohio Country lit the powder keg that began the war and much of the war's focus and fighting occurred in North America, there were larger global issues that created this conflict, which continued on and off into the 19th century. England and France were engaged in an economic, diplomatic, and military competition to control trade and spread their imperial power around the world. France held an advantageous position on the European continent because of its powerful armies. British strength lay at sea. But by the 1750s, a French ship-building program pushed France to near equality. The North American frontier between France and Britain formed the eye of the storm.

## William Pitt and British Victory

King George II officially declared war against France in 1756. British efforts to reorganize the military did not pay dividends as the tide of French victories continued. The French commander in New France, Lord Montcalm, captured Fort William Henry (New York), an episode immortalized in James Fennimore Cooper's *Last of the Mohicans*. The British lost 4,000 troops that year and made few gains. King George was forced to raise William Pitt, a man he despised, to Prime Minister. Pitt was an efficient and able military organizer who brought new energy and vision to war planning. While others focused upon British defeats, not just in North America, but at Minorca in the Mediterranean and at Calcutta (now renamed Kolkata) in India, Pitt perceived both British strengths and French weaknesses. Pitt realized that the French could not conquer the English colonies and that frontier losses were not irreversible. Moreover, he recognized there was much to be gained by a wholesale assault on French North America—the capture of an empire and the elimination of a constant threat and drain on the British treasury.

Pitt poured spectacular amounts of money into the war effort, borrowing unprecedented sums, reputedly in the neighborhood of £100,000. Since Britain required much of its army to serve in Europe and the Caribbean, he recruited many colonial troops. Ordinarily, Americans contributed to British war efforts in America through grants or gifts from their colonial legislatures. These were often considered insufficient, and the Americans held reputation in Britain as misers. Pitt promised the colonial governments that he would repay them for loans: suddenly Americans found money in their purses for the war effort. They rapidly raised troops and supplies. Pitt also sent thousands of regular troops to American shores who required food, wagons, and other supplies. Money flowed into the colonial economy to feed and supply the armies, spurring a period of prosperity, furthered by American privateering against French ships in the West Indies. To paraphrase one historian, the wheels of war ground slowly in America but profitably.

Despite Pitt's efforts, in 1758 the French withstood British advances in New York. Far outnumbered by the British, less than 4,000 French and allied Indians under Montcalm turned back 15,000 British at Fort Carillon (later renamed Ft. Ticonderoga, New York) on Lake Champlain. In Pennsylvania, John Forbes began a slow trek across the mountains to again try to remove the French from Ohio by capturing Fort Duquesne. The French decimated an advance party of 270 Scots Highlanders, but the British held off a French attack at Fort Ligonier (Pennsylvania), though they lost all their cattle and packhorses. Nevertheless, Forbes pushed on, and by the end of the year captured Duquesne and began a new edifice, Fort Pitt, at the site of Three Rivers and the future city of Pittsburg.

To the east, the British enjoyed even greater success. Land and naval forces captured Louisbourg, giving them effective control of the mouth of the St. Lawrence.

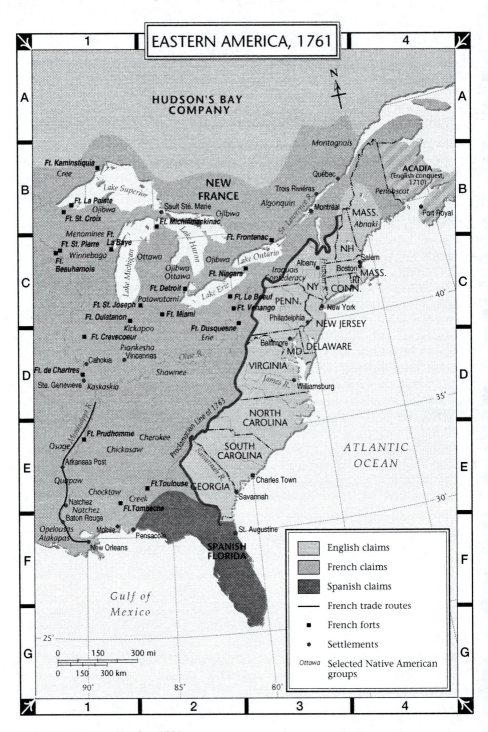

**Map 12.1 Eastern America, 1761**

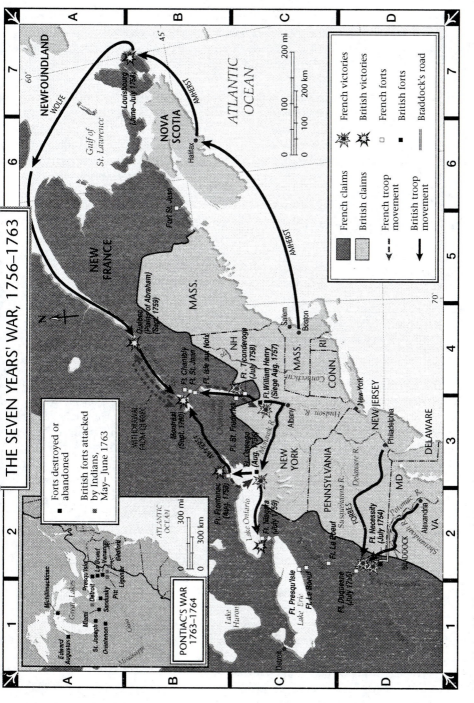

THE SEVEN YEARS' WAR, 1756–1763

■ Forts destroyed or abandoned

✳ British forts attacked by Indians, May–June 1763

PONTIAC'S WAR 1763–1764

NEWFOUNDLAND

WOLFE

Gulf of St. Lawrence

Louisbourg (June–July 1758)

AMHERST

NOVA SCOTIA

Halifax

Fort St. Jean

NEW FRANCE

AMHERST

ATLANTIC OCEAN

MASS.

Québec (Plains of Abraham) (Sept. 1759)

WITHDRAWAL FROM QUÉBEC

Ft. Chambly
Ft. St. Jean

Ft. Isle aux Noix

NH

Ft. Ticonderoga (July 1758)

Ft. William Henry (Siege Aug. 1757)

Montréal (Sept. 1760)

MASS.

CONN

RI

Ft. St. Frédéric

Ft. Oswego (Aug. 1756)

Albany

New York

NEW YORK

Ft. Frontenac (Aug. 1758)

Ft. Niagara (July 1759)

Lake Ontario

Mohawk R.

Hudson R.

NEW JERSEY

Philadelphia

PENNSYLVANIA

Delaware R.

Susquehanna R.

DELAWARE

MD

FORBES

Ft. Le Boeuf

Ft. Presqu'Isle

Lake Erie

Ft. Duquesne (July 1758)

Ft. Necessity (July 1754)

Alexandria VA

Potomac R.

Shenandoah R.

BRADDOCK

Salem

Boston

Connecticut R.

ATLANTIC OCEAN

0    100    200 mi
0    100    200 km

Michilimackinac
Edward Augustus
St. Joseph
Ouiatenon
Miami
Sandusky
Pitt
Ligonier
Venango
Le Boeuf
Presqu'isle
Bedford
Detroit
Great Lakes
Lake Huron
Lake Erie
Detroit
Ohio R.
Mississippi R.

0    300 mi
0    300 km

**French victories**
**British victories**
□ French forts
■ British forts
━ Braddock's road

French claims
British claims
French troop movement
British troop movement

N

45°

60°

70°

**Map 12.2  The Seven Years' War, 1756–1763**

Pitt then raised his successful generals at Louisbourg, Jeffrey Amherst and James Wolfe, to command the war effort. He directed them to push on to the heart of French power in America—Quebec and the Great Lakes. In 1759, Amherst aimed at Quebec from the west and swept the French from their New York forts. Wolfe led his troops upriver from the east all the way to Quebec, where they momentarily stalled beneath the high cliffs of the city that commanded the St. Lawrence River.

Following the advice of subordinates, Wolfe's men rowed past the city, then daringly ascended the cliffs to the Plains of Abraham. The totally surprised Montcalm, instead of waiting inside his fortress for reinforcements, sallied out to meet the British. The previously undefeated Montcalm lost his life, as did Wolfe, in a battle often described as one of the most important ever fought in North America. The British prevailed and so lay the seeds for France's loss of its North American empire. The race was on to see whose navy would arrive first at the St. Lawrence and secure the all-important river—for the St. Lawrence was the only way the French could re-supply their inland empire. The British made it first. French forts fell throughout the Great Lakes or surrendered. The French made one final effort to retake Quebec but lost to the British at Montreal (1760).

## The Cherokee and British in the Seven Years' War

In the South, a major war between the Cherokee and British grew out of the Anglo-French dispute, but largely owed to unrelated frontier violence and the breakdown of diplomacy. The Cherokee had agreed to help protect Virginia from Indians allied with the French. In 1759, they fought for the colony, but received poor treatment from those they protected, who could not be bothered to provide them with food on their way home. After some Cherokee took horses and food from settlers, the latter killed several and the Cherokee responded in kind. Cherokee leaders sent a delegation to Charles Town, South Carolina, to negotiate differences, but Governor William Henry Lyttleton seized them as hostages and confined them at Fort Prince George, where they later were put to death. The Cherokee attacked the fort, and British General Jeffrey Amherst sent 1,600 men to Cherokee country where they burned two Lower Cherokee towns. The Indians successfully counter-attacked, but the British burned another town. The Overhill Cherokee then forced the surrender of Fort Loudoun (in modern-day Tennessee). After giving the soldiers leave to march home, the Cherokee attacked them, later claiming the soldiers had not turned over ammunition in the fort according to the terms of the agreement. Twenty-four officers were killed—the exact number of Cherokee hostages who earlier had been murdered at Fort Prince George. Other British soldier captives either joined the Cherokee or were ransomed or killed. One of those spared, John Stuart, later played a pre-eminent role in English–Indian relations as Britain's Superintendent of Indian Affairs to the Southern Indians. He had learned during his captivity the necessity of maintaining "order and regularity" on the frontier—a view accepted by many Indians but few colonials.

The need for trade goods led the Cherokee to seek peace. They returned over 100 prisoners, but Lt. Governor James Grant of South Carolina refused to negotiate and led nearly 2,500 men into Cherokee country where they destroyed 15 towns. Future Revolutionary War hero Francis Marion observed of the carnage: I "saw everywhere around the footsteps of little Indian children, where they had lately played under the shade of rustling corn. When we are gone, thought I, they will return . . . with tearful eyes, will mark the ghastly ruin where they had so often played. 'Who did this?' they will ask their mothers and the reply will be, 'The White people did it—the Christians did it." Grant's army destroyed over 15,000 acres of crops. Five thousand Cherokee fled to the Appalachians, where they faced starvation. The Cherokee sued for peace, which was concluded in 1761.

## The Treaty of Paris and Pontiac's War

The Seven Years' War proved an utter disaster for France. British military forces prevailed by land and sea outside of Europe. They seized from France Martinique, Guadaloupe, St. Lucia, Dominica, St Vincent, as well as other islands in the West Indies, and took French ports in Africa. From the Spanish, they captured Cuba and the Philippines. At the Treaty of Paris (1763), France officially ceded its American empire east of the Mississippi (except for New Orleans' environs) and all of the Atlantic islands off the Canadian coast save for two. Martinique and several other islands in the West Indies were returned to France, in exchange for several trading posts in India. The French also abandoned all claims to Bengal, India. France restored Minorca in the Mediterranean and abandoned gains it had made in Europe at Hanover. Britain traded Cuba back to Spain in exchange for Spanish Florida and also returned the Philippines to Spain. Spain, which had entered the war late on the side of France, received as compensation from its French ally, New Orleans and the Louisiana territory.

In North America, little thought was given to the native peoples who inhabited the lands ceded by France to Britain. The Europeans claimed sovereignty over lands that Indians had never ceded and that Europeans had never controlled. In practical terms, Europeans understood that Indians owned these lands and that the Europeans did not possess the military power to enforce their paper claims against the rightful owners. But Britain believed it had the right to assert sovereignty, when it could, unencumbered by any other European power.

Many native peoples east of the Mississippi looked aghast at the French defeat. In most places, the French presence had involved occupation of trading posts and few claims to land, since the French mostly pursued trade, not planting. In contrast, the British colonists were a teeming people, constantly seeking new terrain for cultivation, bolstered by a high birthrate and the influx of emigrants. Thus, Indians observed with dismay the British army occupying French forts in the Great Lakes region, western Pennsylvania, New York, and elsewhere. An Ottawa Indian, Pontiac, probably born in modern-day Ohio, a renowned orator, soldier, and religious leader, was influenced by a Delaware mystic known as the "Prophet" to resist British encroachments. The Prophet had a spiritual experience with the "Master of Life," which directed him to promote the unity of Indians against whites. The Prophet called for a return to ancient ways and the rejection of European culture and technology. Traveling from one group of Indians to the next, he implored Indians to follow a restored life of virtue, end their disputes with one another, and unite together.

Inspired by the Prophet's message, after a prolonged period of meditation seeking spiritual guidance, Pontiac organized a meeting in Ohio of Great Lakes Indians. This council met for weeks. They decided to heed the Prophet's words, though they determined that not all whites were to be blamed for their problems—French colonials were not at fault—the enemy was the British and those Indians who supported them. The Council dispersed to convince their peoples to undertake war with Britain, each group given a task in the forthcoming enterprise.

The main focus of Pontiac and his followers was to capture Fort Pontchartrain de Detroit, though they intended to take numerous smaller posts as well. Pontiac himself led the assault against Detroit, a protracted siege that began in May 1763. Elsewhere, in May and June, the allies quickly took forts Sandusky (Ohio), Ouiatenon (Indiana), Michilimchinac (Michigan), Venango (Pennsylvania), Le Boeuf (Pennsylvania), St. Joseph (Michigan), and Presqu'ile (Pennsylvania). They also had success against British forces intending to re-supply Detroit. They had removed the British from every post west of Fort Pitt except Detroit.

The commander of British troops in America, Jeffrey Amherst, sent a force of regulars under Henry Bouquet from Fort Niagara (New York) to secure Fort Pitt, which had refused surrender demands from Delaware and other Indians. Amherst instructed Bouquet that when he arrived, he should offer the Indians a gift of blankets infected with small pox. He wrote: "You will be well to try to inoculate the Indians by means of Blankets, as well as every other method, that can serve to extirpate this execrable race." Simeon Ecuyer, the commander of Ft. Pitt, procured infected blankets and handkerchiefs from the fort's small pox hospital, gave them to two Delaware leaders who were captives, and then released them to spread the infection among their people. Many Delaware soon succumbed to small pox, though whether these very blankets caused the illness is unknown.

Bouquet's forces were met by Indian troops at the Battle of Bushy Run, to prevent British reinforcement of Ft. Pitt. For two days in August, Delawares, Mingoes, Wyandots, and Shawnees tried to stop the advance by circling the British, but they were unaware that two companies remained concealed outside the circle that then broke the Indians' lines. Dissent among Indian forces, and the failure of Pontiac to take Detroit, led to the breakup of the alliance and to various groups making separate peace with the British. Pontiac made peace in October.

## Indian Lands and the Proclamation Act

The British government, in great debt from the expense of the Seven Years' War, and seeking ways to limit expenditures, had been formulating a plan to prevent Indian hostilities since these led to costly spending on large numbers of troops in the west. In early October 1763, the king issued a Royal Proclamation guaranteeing Indians their lands, including their hunting grounds. It recognized that Indians possessed lands that had never been ceded to or purchased by Britain. The "Proclamation Line" drew a boundary along the Appalachians from New York to Florida that barred British colonists from crossing the line to the west. (The Proclamation also recognized that many Indians possessed lands east of the Appalachians.) These lands could not be procured from Indians by colonists or colonial governments, but only by the British government. Although formulated independently of Pontiac's War, the Proclamation Act had the effect of appeasing many Indians concerned about colonial expansion. But it became a sore point to thousands of colonists, who could not fathom why, after the defeat and removal of the French from North America, they should be denied the rich lands of the Ohio Country.

The British government had not issued the Proclamation Act out of any love for Indians. They still desired land cessions, but on their own, not colonials', terms. With emigrants pouring into the colonies, and joining land-hungry settlers moving south and west, the backcountries of the southern colonies from Maryland to Georgia filled with people. To obtain more land east of the Appalachian Mountains, the king's Indian Superintendent of Indian Affairs, John Stuart, called for a meeting with the Choctaw, Cherokee, Creek, Chickasaw, and Catawba at Augusta, Georgia, in August 1763. This congress was to settle differences and end hostilities between the southern Indians and colonists, which included many skirmishes and raids. In exchange for a liberal disbursement of presents, the Indians made land cessions, but relations soon soured when colonists settled lands that had not been ceded.

Recognizing the great military power of the Creek, Cherokee, Choctaw, and others, British political leaders accepted the futility of attempting to gain future concessions through force of arms. But with growing native dependency on European manufactures—guns, alcohol, textiles, and metal goods—the British could threaten to close off trade. Previously, Indians could turn to the French for trade goods when relations soured with the British, and many Indians, as a matter of policy, had played the French and British against one another to buttress their own power. But with the French removed from North America, and the Spanish in Louisiana too weak and distant to fill the gap left by the French, the native position was greatly undermined. Native military power remained strong in the coming decades, but the population growth of land-hungry Europeans in America led to westward expansion and the Indians' ultimate loss of the lands guaranteed to them by the Proclamation Act.

## Conclusion

From the 1740s through the early 1760s, colonists engaged in severe warfare abroad and in North America, which also enveloped American Indians. Armed force was the solution employed by colonials and their mother countries as they sought new lands for expansion, the elimination of enemies, attainment of personal and national glory, and monopolistic control over trade and trade routes. In North America, French settlements and trading posts had spread considerably in the Great Lakes region, and south through the Illinois country and Louisiana. But immigration to French colonies paled in comparison with the stupendous growth of the British colonies, which attracted hundreds of thousands of Europeans seeking free land. This forced the French into alliance with numerous Indian peoples, who perceived the British and Iroquois as the greatest threats to their interests. The construction of French forts in the Ohio Country not only threatened Virginia colonials' aspirations to settle west of the Appalachians, but seemed to portend a unification of western Indians against the British. The eruption of hostilities into the French and Indian War, and its enlargement into the Seven Years' War, spread this colonial conflict in North America to the West Indies, Europe, Africa, India, and the Philippines. With British victory in 1763, the map of North America was greatly redrawn. Britain took control over Canada from France and replaced Spain in Florida; Spain received French Louisiana. The Spanish held on to their Southwest colonies, whose distance from other European colonies gave them a measure of security. Britain claimed sovereignty over all the lands east of the Mississippi River save for the environs of New Orleans.

British colonials basked in victory. They had helped defeat the French, which ostensibly opened the western lands to new settlements. Then, to their dismay, they learned that Britain would not allow colonials to reap what they had sown: the Proclamation Line closed the west to colonial expansion. And this was but one of a series of measures designed to strengthen imperial control over the colonies. Nonetheless, most British colonials were confident in their future and their position in the British Empire. Many American Indians did not share this confidence in the future. They immediately perceived the consequences of French defeat. Pontiac and his supporters had attacked Britain's western forts in an attempt to hold back colonial expansion. Although some respite was provided by the Proclamation Line, the native position was undermined by the absence of France to check British pretensions. Indian military power remained formidable, but the French could no longer serve as alternative trading partners to the British, who could impede the flow of trade goods to wrest concessions from Indian peoples. Traders operating out of the Louisiana territory and West Florida did provide an alternative source of goods for several decades, which helped many southern Indians retain their lands, but Indians to the north were left in a more precarious position. They had grown dependent on European manufactures, such as textiles, iron implements, guns, and gunpowder,

and had no alternative to British suppliers. In an ironic shift, however, many northern Indians soon looked to the British government to maintain their interests, particularly against colonials seeking their land. For the British, reorganization of empire held benefits for Indians, who now treated with imperial agents to represent their interests against land-hungry colonists. (This tie remained significant for over a half-century as northern Indians received support from the British government through the War of 1812.) In 1763, at the conclusion of the Seven Years' War, most Indians in North America above Mexico retained their land and sovereignty, particularly west of the Appalachians and in Canada. The threat for America's indigenous peoples lay in the Trans-Appalachian West: the biggest challenge of the next half-century was holding at bay the European peoples determined to settle native lands.

For Britain, the great victory over the French had come at great cost. The nation was saddled with an enormous war debt and assumed new expenses administering the colonies won from France and Spain. Flushed with victory, but in need of money, many British politicians turned their gaze to North America and pondered different ways to rein in their colonials, whom they believed enormously benefited from the empire without contributing much to its support. Intending to extract obedience to imperial law and help shouldering the costs of maintaining the empire, the British government instituted a new activist program of regulation and taxation that alienated many mainland colonists. Britain and its colonies thus exuded confidence in the present and the future, even as alienation marked growing discontent between them.

# DOCUMENTS

## 12.1. The Marquis De Duquesne on the Prospects for War Between France and Britain

*After Washington's "assassination" of Jumonville, France and Britain steadily moved towards war. As Canada's Governor Duquesne reported to his superiors in France, the British rapidly constructed forts, attempted to shore up Indian alliances, and prepared for aggressive actions against Canada. The French, of course, pursued parallel arrangements against the British. This was a dance; Duquesne makes clear that he is not intending to provoke outright hostilities—the costs of war, such as sending troops to Canada was an immense expense. If France could achieve its ends in North America without war, it would do so—especially as they had many advantages over Britain in the interior continent, particularly through alliances with Indians. But war would come: the British were sending to America a large force of regulars to wrest control of the Ohio Country. How did Duquesne view the ability of the British colonies to act independently of Great Britain?*

### M. Duquesne, Governor-General of Canada, to M. de Machault, Minister of the Marine and Colonies

**Quebec, 28th October, 1754.**

My Lord,

I have received the letter you did me the honor to write me on the 19th of August last, which has reached me on the 22nd instant, wherein you are pleased to inform me of the views the King of England has manifested up to the present time, for the maintenance of peace, and that you presume he has not authorized the movements on the River Oyo [Ohio].

Without referring you, my Lord, to all that I have had the honor to submit to you in my last despatches, I have to observe to you, in addition, that it is not possible that the King of Great Britain has not consented to and even ordered all the movements which the English are making on this Continent, and the consequences thereof appear to me very just.

1st The Governors of New England, besides being independent one of the other, cannot levy troops without an order of the King of Great Britain, and you will have observed by Mr Washington's Journal that all the Provinces have furnished a quota to his detachment. I know, moreover, that the Quakers, who never make war, have also furnished their contingent.

2nd Sieur Drouillon, an officer who was with Sieur de Jumonville's detachment, has been taken by this same Mr Washington as a prisoner of war, as you will also see by his Journal.

3rd The irruption made by Mr Shirley, Governor of Boston, who has marched with a body of troops of 700 men to seize the upper part of the River Narantchouac where he has had a fort built, without waiting for the determination of the boundaries, as I have had the honor to inform you.

*(Continued)*

4th The Governor of Halifax has proclaimed throughout Acadia that every Acadian who will be taken with arms in his hands against them, shall be hanged.

5th The solemn congress held at Orange [Albany, New York] in the month of July by seven Governors, to persuade the [Iroquois] Nations they had invited thither to attack us.

After the assassination of M. de Jumonville and the above consequent proofs, do you believe, my Lord, that I am authorized to anticipate a rupture on the part of the English? but it is easy to perceive, that before arriving at that point, they wish to gain over our domiciliated Indians, since they employ all sorts of artifices to corrupt them, and do not disdain even the most unworthy means to effect their object.

On the other hand, I remark that the English, who have observed my cautious conduct, take advantage of it to encroach on our lands; and I will confess to you, my Lord, that my position, as critical as it is disagreeable, in consequence of the prudence I have to observe, so as not to occasion a rupture, induces them to make attempts to push on to the neighborhood of Quebec.

You will see, my Lord, by the reports I have already submitted, how cautious I have been in my conduct, and I defy the English to complain that I have given the least interruption to the good understanding which is so strongly recommended to me, but it is evident that the Governors of New England have not the same orders, or do not execute them, inasmuch as they have violated the most sacred laws, and think only of usurpations.

As for the expense, which concerns me, I am unceasingly occupied in diminishing it, but troops cannot be moved here without great cost.

I am with the most profound respect,

My Lord,

Your most humble and
Most obedient servant,
Duquesne.

Source: *Documents Relative to the Colonial History of the State of New York*. Vol. 10. Edited by E. B. O'Callaghan (1858), 264–265.

## 12.2. The Meeting of the Governors of the Southern Colonies with the Southern Indians in 1763

*In 1763, with the Seven Years' War over, Britain's Superintendent of Indian Affairs, John Stuart, and the governors of the southern colonies called for a congress to meet at Augusta, Georgia, to settle outstanding differences with the major southern Indian confederacies. With the French removed from Louisiana, British power in the region was greatly increased—the southern Indians had no real alternative to obtain trade goods. Unlike in the north, there was no forging of Indian interests against the British as occurred in Pontiac's War, but many of the southern Indian confederacies retained great military power. Although the British called for the southern Indians to bury their differences, in fact, they were pleased at the hostilities between groups that prevented unity of interests. The proceedings of the congress, the following excerpt, were published in South Carolina as a way to publicize to colonists and the mother country that the colonial governments had the wherewithal to control Indian peoples and maintain peace. It also laid the groundwork for future conferences, whereby the British sought land concessions from the Indians. What was the importance of trade and traders to both the British and the Chickasaw leader who spoke at the conference?*

The Southern Congress, at Augusta, in 1763.

Total number of Indians about seven hundred.

Interpreters—James Colbert, for the Chicasahs and Chactahs

John Butler, James Beamer, John Watts, for the Cherokees.

Stephen Forrest, John Proctor, for the Creeks.

And they being sworn,

Col. Ayers, the Catawba chief, was allowed to interpret for his nation.

The conference was opened by governor Wright, in consequence of its being held in his own province. He observed to the Indians, that the day was fair, and hoped that the talks would not prove otherwise; that the several governors had pitched upon capt. Stuart to deliver their sentiments; that they were agreed upon the declaration to be made to the Indians; and desired them to pay attention to what Mr. Stuart uttered, as they were the words of all the governors. And each respective governor, for himself, desired the Indians to look upon what Mr. Stuart said, as said by the respective governor himself. Mr. Stuart accordingly begun as follows:

"Friends and brothers,

We are come here in the name, and by the command of the great King George, who, under God, the master and giver of breath, is your and our common father and protector.

The talk you are now to hear, is from the great king, and ordered to be delivered to you by four governors of different provinces, and the superintendent, who is equally connected with all; for this reason, he is pitched upon to be our mouth.

Our words, our hearts, our intentions are the same; as our respective provinces join together, so are our interests inseparable.

No conference was ever intended to be more general, none more friendly.

This is not a partial meeting of one nation of Indians, with one governor; but the great king's good disposition towards his red children, is to be communicated to you, in the presence of one another.

His goodness is as extensive as the dominions he possesses; at a time when he has nothing to apprehend from any enemies, he opens his arms to receive his red children, and he does it the rather at this junction, as he knows the insinuations of falshoods, which have been formerly circulated among you, by the perfidious and cruel French.

We desire you to recollect, in how many instances they have misled

*(Continued)*

and deceived you; you remember their lies, and have been the dupes of their promises.

They are never easy, unless engaged in mischief themselves, or when engaging others; incapable of supplying your wants, they endeavor to detach you, from your best and only friends the English.

The great king, who wishes to extend the commerce of his subject, to live in peace and friendship, and relieve the distress of all mankind, bore with uncommon patience, the repeated insults and excessive cruelties, which the French alone could perpetrate, to cruelty they added treachery and perfidy: fair speeches were in their mouths, but mischief in their hearts; and when they did not act openly themselves, they decided to instigate the red people to outrages, which could only end in separating them from the white people, with whom they ought, for the advantage of both, to be united.

At length, when the great king saw his moderation disregarded, his children plundered and destroyed, and that the French were resolved to contend with him for superiority, that one country in short, could not hold them both: he then exerted himself like a man; and, in a short time, defeated and humbled that perfidious enemy, and also the Spaniards, who, by the fatal and mischievous practices of the French, had been involved in the quarrel.

The king has now given peace to both nations; and to prevent the revival of such disturbances and troubles, by repetitions of such dangerous proceedings; and for this purpose only, he insisted, in the treaty of peace, that

the French and Spaniards should be removed beyond the river Mississippi, that the Indians and white people may, hereafter, live in peace and brotherly friendship together: It will be your faults, if this does not happen, for we are authorized by the great king, to give you the most substantial proofs of out good intentions, and desire to live like brothers with you.

If you bring the same friendly disposition, what can you desire more, than a repetition of the assurances already given to you, by the king's orders, with regard to your lands; which we now from our hearts confirm.

Do we not act like friends and brothers, when we declare, that all past offences shall be buried in oblivion and forgiveness; and this we do, because we are persuaded, that the French imposed on your credulity, and deceived you.

Do you wish for anything more, than to be plentifully supplied with goods, by the white people, who alone can supply you, this we promise you, but it must also depend on yourselves, for those nations where traders reside, must provide for their security, or no man will stay with them.

Besides this, we engage as far as we can for ourselves, and those under our control, to manifest an attention to your interests, and a readiness to do you justice upon all occasions.

Lastly, we promise you faithfully and solemnly, that those forts now ceded to us by the French, shall be employed for your protection, assistance, and convenience; and for the better carrying on trade with you, by which we all shall be benefitted.

Consider now like wife men, whether this is the language of ill designing people, whether there is any occasion at this time, to make you such friendly assurances, unless it was our intention to keep our words.

The white people value themselves on speaking truth; but to give still greater weight to what we say, the great king has thought proper, as we observed before, that his four governors and the superintendent, from a great distance, should utter the same words, at the same time: and to remove every umbrage or jealousy, that you should all hear them, in presence of one another, and bear testimony for one another, in case we should ever act contrary to our declarations.

Given at Augusta in the province of Georgia, 5th of November 1763.

JAMES WRIGHT,
THOMAS BOONE,
ARTHUR DOBBS,
FRANCIS FAUQUIER,
JOHN STUART.

★★★★★

The Talks of the Chicasah, Upper and Lower Creek, Chactah, Cherokee, and Catawba Indians, to their excellencies.

James Wright, Esq; governor of Georgia,

Arthur Dobbs, Esq; governor of North Carolina,

Thomas Boone, Esq; governor of South-Carolina,

The hon. Francis Fauquier, Esq; lieut. Governor of Virginia, And

John Stuart, Esq; agent and superintendent of Southern Indian affairs.

At fort Augusta, monday the 7th and tuesday the 8th of November, 1763.

James Colbert, interpreter for the Chicasah;

Piamatah, a Chicasah leader, delivered himself to the following effect: "That he had been here a long time, and would give his talk first, and then give leave to the Creeks; that the day was at length come on which he hoped to see his dearly beloved brother of Charles Town, and also the other governors; and now the day is come he will give his talk. That he is come to return thanks for the services already done them; and says, if it had not been for the assistance of their excellencies, he should not have been here at this time: He was the man that sent express, when in want of things, and is ready to give any proofs of his attachment to the English; you must not look on him as on other Indian nations, for he is true and truly; he and his, are few, but faithful: That he has no fault to find, as none as been found with them; that we have of late heard of no mischief being done by Chicasahs; that he looked on the white people and them as one; that they are as good friends as if they had sucked one breast. Although his skin is not white, his heart is so, and as much so as any white man. He has now done on that subject, and will proceed to something else.

"He wants not to imitate other Indians nations, and declares he cannot do without the white people, and that he believes it is the same case with all the red people: He cannot find out the reason why other people are not as he is, he leaves it to the governors to find it; yet he will give his sentiments, viz. He and every one with him are of opinion, that so many white men being among the Indians, as traders, is the occasion thereof, and

*(Continued)*

he thinks in time it may be his case to act like other red people; the great numbers of traders create disturbances between the red and the white people; he has a very great regard for the white people, but they have not for one another. This is from his heart, and he hopes to be believed; the young people may become outrageous, and mischief be done, because the traders will not stay in one place, and before he can interpose, harm may happen; he hopes not to be doubted as to the truth, he therefore desires, that the headmen may be asked, and they will confirm what he says."

Source: *Journal of the Congress of the Four Southern Governors with the Five Nations . . . at Augusta,* 1763 (1764), 23–26.

## Bibliography

Anderson, Fred. *A People's Army: Massachusetts Soldiers and Society in the Seven Years' War* (1984).

Anderson, Fred. *Crucible of War: The Seven Years' War and the Fate of Empire in British North America, 1754–1766* (2000).

Anderson, Fred, and Andrew Cayton. *The Dominion of War: Empire and Liberty in North America, 1500–2000* (2004).

Anderson, William L., ed. *Cherokee Removal: Before and After* (1991).

Calloway, Colin G. *The Scratch of a Pen: 1763 and the Transformation of North America* (2006).

De Vorsey, Louis. *The Indian Boundary in the Southern Colonies, 1763–1775* (1966).

Dixon, David. *Never Come to Peace Again: Pontiac's Uprising and the Fate of the British Empire in North America* (2005).

Dowd, Gregory E. *War under Heaven: Pontiac, the Indian Nations, and the British Empire* (2002).

Faragher, John Mack. *A Great and Noble Scheme: The Tragic Story of the Expulsion of the French Acadians from their American Homeland* (2005).

Flexner, James T. *George Washington: the Forge of Experience, 1732–1775* (1965).

Gallay, Alan, ed. *The Colonial Wars of North America, 1512–1763: An Encyclopedia* (1996).

Gipson, Lawrence Henry. *The British Empire Before the American Revolution.* 15 vols. (1936–1970).

Hatley, M. Thomas. *The Dividing Paths: Cherokees and South Carolinians Through the Era of Revolution* (1993).

Jennings, Francis. *Empire of Fortune: Crowns, Colonies, and Tribes in the Seven Years War in America* (1988).

Leach, Douglas Edward. *Roots of Conflict: British Armed Forces and Colonial Americans, 1677–1763* (1986).

Mercantini, Jonathan. *Who Should Rule at Home?: The Evolution of South Carolina Political Culture, 1748–1766* (2006).

Merrell, James H. *Into the American Woods: Negotiators on the Pennsylvania Frontier* (1999).

Merritt, Jane T. *At the Crossroads: Indians and Empires on a Mid-Atlantic Frontier, 1700–1763* (2003).

Murphy, Eldersveld Lucy. *A Gathering of Rivers: Indians, Metis, and Mining in the Western Great Lakes, 1737–1832* (2000).

Richter, Daniel K. *Facing East from Indian Country: A Native History of Early America* (2001).

Shy, John. *Toward Lexington: The Role of the British Army in the Coming of the American Revolution* (1965).

Steele, Ian K. *Betrayals: Fort William Henry and the "Massacre"* (1990).

White, Richard. *The Middle Ground: Indians, Empires and Republics in the Great Lakes Region, 1650–1815* (1991).

# 13

# Politics and Politicization in Early America, 1761–1774

## INTRODUCTION

In 1763, the first British empire reached its zenith. Canada and Florida had been added to the American colonies, which now appeared entirely secure from other European powers. The British Navy had crippled the French and was dominant at sea. British colonists shared in the glory and looked forward to a golden age of prosperity that would allow them to take advantage of enviable economic prospects for growth and expansion. Colonists like George Washington, Patrick Henry, and Benjamin Franklin hoped to obtain riches from the empire's westward expansion: all three speculated in western lands, and Washington made a fortune doing so. Immigrants from Europe flocked to the colonies seeking land, leading the British government to conduct an investigation on why people were departing the British Isles and its potential impact on the mother country. Members of the British government privately undertook huge speculative land schemes, most notably in Florida, for which they recruited settlers from Sardinia and Greece—these schemes ended disastrously, most of the settlers dying from disease and malnutrition, as little thought had been given to their welfare. Expansion boded ill for native peoples, who faced Europeans pouring through the gaps in the Appalachian Mountains, in disregard of the Proclamation Act of 1763.

After the Seven Years' War, politics emerged at the forefront of colonial life because of political changes prompted by the British government. Americans were well prepared to respond to the mother country's new political program because of the long-standing tradition of political participation within the colonies, which had given colonists experience governing their own affairs. Although colonists in Spanish and Portuguese colonies possessed significant political power in their communities by electing local officials to city and town governments, only in the British empire did elected assemblies exist as part of the governance for entire colonies. When Britain's Parliament embarked on a plan to more actively direct its colonies, and to raise revenue through taxation of colonists, the American assemblies maneuvered to protect their role in governance.

Institutions, like assemblies, have rules, traditions, and privileges that govern their operation, but their character and success depends on the people who work for them. The assemblies' elected officials not only possessed ideas on how their institutions should function, but had to respond to the opinions of those they served, the populace, both the electorate and the population at-large. Outside the walls of the colonial assemblies, American colonials, both those enfranchised and those denied a voice through suffrage, pressured their political leaders at home and abroad to fulfill their own political directives. The political activism of both common people and assemblies in the 1760s shocked not only the mother country, but many colonists, particularly elites, who perceived a grave threat to governance and the proper ordering of society.

The euphoria of victory over France thus disappeared in a battle of wills between the mother country and its mainland colonists. The dispute was brought to a head in Parliament's enactment of a series of acts designed to raise revenue from the colonists. American refusal to accept these taxes, their lack of deference and subservience to Parliament, and their destruction of property and intimidation of public officials as a method of protest alarmed and annoyed the mother country. These actions confirmed the British conception of the colonists as unruly, self-interested children who required a strong hand and occasional punishment. Americans had developed their own conceptions of rights and privileges in the empire that were at stark loggerheads with assertions emanating from Great Britain. Colonists made their stand on constitutional principles, which Britain often dismissed as ill-founded and self-serving. The inability of successive imperial administrations to understand the American situation, politically and economically, led to repeated missteps by second-rate politicians who unnecessarily provoked American hostility that led to outright rebellion.

## COLONIAL GOVERNMENT AND POLITICS

British colonial governments existed by rights of charters granted by the monarchs of Great Britain. The colonial governments created laws to govern colonial life—defining crimes and their punishment, promoting economic development, raising taxes to support themselves, and legislating religious affairs. Colonial governments' power and role was limited by their charters, imperial laws, and monarchical directives, as well as the mother country's appointment of imperial officials, including governors in the royal colonies. Before the 1760s, disputes over governance between Britain and its colonies, though existent, were rarely bitter or sustained. The political system had developed in such a way that colonial governments largely controlled local political affairs, with the mother country looking the other way at non-compliance with its agendas, or acceding to colonial wishes.

Colonial assemblies were divided into two houses: a lower and an upper house. Lower house members were selected by those qualified to vote: adult male colonists who fulfilled their colony's property requirements. Most upper house members were appointed by the king or proprietor, from recommendations made by the governor among the local elite. Some colonies tended towards oligarchy rule as small groups of families dominated both the lower and the upper houses from one generation to the next—in effect, fathers passed their seats to their sons, particularly in Massachusetts, New York, Virginia, and South Carolina.

## The Assemblies and Their Governors

Although modeled on the House of Commons in the British Parliament, the colonial lower houses assumed more rights than the Commons possessed. The colonial lower houses steadily assumed the exclusive power to initiate tax legislation, and held more power than the Commons enjoyed in England in matters of distributing patronage, determining how appropriations would be spent, and controlling governors' salaries. Unlike in Britain, all lower house members in America represented a specific geographic district, and were much more attuned to public opinion than members of Parliament. They also possessed greater knowledge of colonial affairs than most colonial governors, who usually were outsiders appointed by the king or the colony's proprietors in England. Governors came and went, many accepting their positions in hopes of increasing their personal estates in service to those who appointed them. They often bucked heads with the lower houses, and it was not unusual for the legislatures to win these battles, sometimes by obtaining the governor's recall.

Unlike in England where seats in the House of Lords were filled by nobility, the colonial upper houses were comprised of commoners, albeit economic elites. The upper houses generally were comprised of 10 to 12 men, who frequently worked with the lower house assemblymen, with whom they shared family and economic ties, to pass legislation. Upper houses also sat as executive councils to advise the governor in administrative matters, which increased their political power. Since property requirements for election to the lower houses were usually higher than for voting, the well-to-do tended to monopolize seats in that body as well.

Governors possessed veto power over legislation, which could not be overridden by the assemblies, but that power was checked by the latter in a variety of ways. In some colonies, the legislatures refused to pay salaries to non-cooperative governors, and then lobbied the king or proprietors to remove governors with whom they could not get along. Governors received instructions from the Board of Trade or the colony's proprietors as to what they should accomplish during their tenure, which often conflicted with the interests of colonial legislators; they were caught between a rock and a hard place in trying to negotiate imperial and local concerns.

## Ruling Colonies from Great Britain

The king also possessed a veto over colonial legislation, and had one year to exercise it before a colonial bill became permanent law. The king vetoed about 5% of colonial bills in the 18th century. The veto was usually used on legislation that countered Parliament's Navigation Laws, illegally authorized issuance of paper money, or attempted to limit religious rights—the king would not allow colonists to be denied religious privileges enjoyed in the mother country.

Since the empire had so many colonies, in the late 17th century, England created a Board of Trade to oversee colonial affairs, particularly in economic matters. The Board recommended policies to king and Parliament, and received agents from the colonies who lobbied for local interests. The most famous agent was Ben Franklin, who served Pennsylvania, Massachusetts, and Georgia.

Within the empire, the king bore responsibility for protecting the colonies and its trade routes, through his command of the army and navy. Parliament defined the colonies' economies through Navigation Laws. These laws proscribed what colonists could or could not produce and export, where they could trade and under what conditions, and offered bounties to colonists for items the empire needed that could not always be profitably cultivated or manufactured. Overall, the colonies economically benefited from membership in the empire. Bounties on naval stores and indigo propped up these important industries, while imperial protection from foreign competition and pirates greatly lowered costs for producers. Britain benefited from the raw materials received from colonists, from the taxes garnered on particular colonial products that had to be shipped to England before re-export to world markets, and from the colonists' purchase of manufactured goods produced in the mother country.

Before the Seven Years' War, the mother country interfered little with colonial life and economy. Britain paid scant attention to rampant colonial smuggling and legislative intransigence against governors and the Board of Trade. Britain was too preoccupied with affairs at home and in Europe to pay much notice to the American mainland. As long as Americans purchased British goods, and supplied tobacco, wheat, iron, naval stores, and other valued items in exchange, there was little reason to tinker with the imperial system. Historians label this "Salutary Neglect"—a British neglect of colonial affairs that allowed colonial governments (and local elites) to shape their societies to their own liking. Enjoying a large degree of self-governance and economic prosperity, free Americans were proud and patriotic members of the British empire. They modeled themselves, their societies, their polities, and their culture on the mother country. They viewed their king as a benevolent father who protected and nurtured them, and his empire as the most forward-looking, economically successful, and politically advanced. American colonists were especially proud to enjoy a degree of political liberties and rights unknown in most places outside the British empire. The defeat of the French in the Seven Years' War harkened to an even more glorious future. With the French removed from Canada, colonists believed there were few obstacles to expansion—the Indian peoples would be removed in time. But French removal meant something else: the mainland colonies no longer needed the mother country to protect them to the same extent. In effect, the mother country had lost one of its basic functions in the imperial system. It also began to dawn on some colonists that their economies had evolved to where they might not need to be so dependent on imports of manufactured goods from Great Britain. The American economy could compete rather than complement the British economy. These realizations would have been of no immediate consequence if Britain had not put an end to Salutary Neglect—for Americans basked in their membership in the empire. But, indeed, Salutary Neglect came to an abrupt end towards the close of the Seven Years' War.

## The End of Salutary Neglect

The Seven Years' War had shifted attention in Britain to the mainland colonies. A new generation of more active British officers of empire and members of Parliament wished to bring the colonies into conformity with imperial laws. Many had been disturbed by colonists' behavior during the war. After the British Navy had bottled the French Navy into its home ports, Americans enthusiastically smuggled goods to the French West Indies. Moreover, in British eyes, Americans had contributed to the war effort in a half-hearted fashion. Colonial legislatures had not been forthcoming with funds and assistance (until promised reimbursement), and provincial troops infamously departed or threatened to depart in the middle of campaigns because their terms of service expired. In the wartime experience, familiarity bred contempt. Americans chafed under rules providing that the lowest ranking British regular army officer outranked all colonial provincial officers. And in the combining of armies in the middle of the war, Americans were aghast at the draconian punishments given by regular army officers to disobedient soldiers and deserters. British officers viewed American soldiers as incompetent and disrespectful of authority. Officers made constant complaints to their superiors in London about American lack of help in the war effort. British soldiers returned home with reports of colonists' miserliness, cowardice, and lack of patriotism towards the empire. It also rankled people in the mother country that colonials, their social inferiors, bragged that the center of empire would shift across the Atlantic as American wealth and population grew. As far as many in Britain were concerned, the colonists had grown too big for their britches, and Americans' blatant disregard of imperial law and authority evinced a basic lack of respect that demanded response. Even before the war ended, many in the imperial government believed that changes had to be made to bring the Americans into line—they must be taught respect for the mother country, and reminded of their subservience and place within the empire.

The desire to reorganize the empire and make Americans heel overlapped with a determination to find new sources of income to relieve Britain's great war debt and growing imperial costs. Britain had to find funds for manning frontier forts and to administer the new colonies of East and West Florida and Canada. American wealth was considered an untapped source, though imperial officers were unaware that the end of the war brought a recession, as British funds no longer flowed into the colonies to support the war effort. In Britain, taxation had reached very high levels, and it made sense to draw on the Americans for relief, at least to help pay the colonies' administrative costs. Furthermore, to cut smuggling and make governors beholden to the mother country, the government wished to raise an income from Americans to put into a fund to pay the salaries of judges and governors. Americans already paid these salaries, but British deliverance of the funds would make imperial officers beholden to them rather than colonial legislatures.

Before the war ended, the British government attempted to enforce the Navigation Acts with writs of assistance. These blank search warrants were issued to naval captains to search ships presumed to be engaged in smuggling. Previously, naval captains had to go ashore to obtain search warrants from a judge, which allowed the alleged perpetrators opportunity to escape or dispose of contraband. The government also decided to move smuggling cases to British courts, as colonial courts ordinarily would not prosecute American smugglers. American opposition arose in Boston where merchants hired the lawyer James Otis to represent their interests. Otis argued that the writs were unconstitutional—only a judge could issue a search warrant, and then only for a specific place—and that removal of smuggling cases to Britain would prove a hardship on the accused, who would have to travel across the ocean to defend themselves. There they would receive an unconstitutional trial, since they had not been tried by their peers—members of their own community on the same social level. The British viewed American arguments, then and later, as disingenuous attempts to avoid the law for the sake of self-interest. In the event, few writs were issued, but the arguments had stirred Bostonians, such as John Adams and Samuel Adams, to keeping an eye peeled for any other attempts by the mother country to infringe on colonists' rights.

In 1764, Parliament enacted the Sugar Act as part of its program to eliminate American smuggling with the French islands and to ensure that colonials would buy sugar and molasses only from British islands. The powerful sugar lobby instigated this legislation to replace the Molasses Act of 1733, a measure that failed from lack of enforcement. Americans smuggled with the French islands to obtain sugar because the British islands did not produce enough to support the American rum industry, which was especially important in New England. The British government inspired naval captains to pursue smugglers with the promise that crews would receive half the value of seized cargoes and ships. Some Americans argued that a tax on sugar and molasses was legal if the income was only a by-product of regulation—no one denied Parliament's right to control and regulate trade—but that a tax could not be enacted for the purpose of raising revenue. It was an Englishman's right, Americans believed, to pay taxes assented to only by his *own* legislature. The British asserted that colonial legislatures existed as a privilege and not a right and that Parliament could tax Americans because each member of Parliament represented everyone in the empire—a concept of "virtual representation" not accepted by Americans.

A Currency Act also passed Parliament in 1764. British merchants had tired of American attempts to pay debts with their own local currencies. The act restricted colonies from issuing paper money, a measure that hit hard those engaged in commerce because of the shortage of specie in the colonies, compounded by British law barring hard money from leaving the mother country for the colonies. British administrators seem never to have understood the negative impact of the scarcity of money in America, nor would they take into consideration the economic recession that occurred at the end of the war.

Some Americans believed a conspiracy to impoverish them was afoot. The Sugar Act had actually lowered the tax on molasses: Were Americans being seduced into accepting the tax by making it minimal? If they complied with the tax, would Britain raise new taxes on the premise that Americans already had accepted the Sugar Act? Opposition to the Sugar and Currency Acts took the form of petitions from colonial legislatures, pamphlets, and the efforts of lobbying by agents in Britain. Most Americans, however, were unconcerned with the Sugar and Currency Acts, for their impact was mostly felt by merchants and rum producers. The paranoia of the bills' opponents, however, was well placed—Britain indeed planned to expand the tax program. The Grenville Administration was searching for revenue to support troops to guard the American frontier, and to protect Canada from its French population and a feared French attempt to retake it. In the fall of 1764, Grenville pushed through Parliament a Stamp Tax, which received royal approval in March 1765, to go into effect on November 1. By this tax Americans would have to purchase a stamp for all written documents, including legal papers, pamphlets, and newspapers. Grenville made a huge mistake by allowing the Americans so much time to consider the tax before it went into effect. Instead, Americans had time to stew and plan their opposition.

## THE STAMP ACT AND POLITICIZATION OF AMERICAN COLONIALS

This was the beginning of a great era for politicization in the British American colonies and western Europe. Previously, most commoners could only assert their political will directly through crowd activities like rioting and rebellion, often employed as a response to single issues that adversely affected them—such as food shortages, military conscription, new religious policies, and onerous tax burdens. In 18th-century political culture, elites expected the lower orders to defer to their judgment in political matters. In the English hierarchical world, the ideal of "deference" provided that those above ruled those below in society and within the family. Those above were presumed to have larger interests, and thus possessed a broader vision entitling them to make decisions for their social inferiors. In exchange for deference, those above were expected to defend the interests of inferiors and exercise authority in a benevolent manner. Hierarchy by blood, gender, and class was viewed by elites as God-ordained and natural—its absence would lead to disorder and anarchy. The general view of hierarchy was that all owed obedience to God, then to the king, nobility, and so on down the social order, which placed servants and slaves at the bottom. Likewise, fathers held authority and expected obedience within their families, and through voting represented the interests of wives and children. Political participation depended on property ownership, which gave "independence" to voters. Working for someone else disqualified an individual from voting in most places, since it was believed that the employer could control his worker's vote. Voting was *viva voce*, by voice. The secret ballot was considered unmanly—a man must have enough property, in terms of real estate or tax payments, to be beholden to no man. Thus, servants, slaves, tenant farmers, and most day laborers were denied suffrage.

Common people held their own political ideology, usually referred to as the "moral economy." This provided that deference would be paid to social and economic superiors, but could be withdrawn if rulers did not act in the interest of the community. The overthrow and beheading of King Charles II in the English Civil War (1639–1649) stood as a precedent for the overthrow of future kings, as was the later forced removal of his son James II in the Glorious Revolution (1688–1691). Getting rid of the monarch (and killing him) were actions not to be taken lightly and widely feared as dangerous to the natural ordering of society—but they became as much a part of English political history and memory as any other events, traditions, or policies. The English people might speak of the Magna Charta, the Constitution, balanced government, Parliament, and the rights of Englishmen as basic to their political development—but the "legal" removal of two monarchs also shaped political culture in the 17th and

18th centuries—the country and the political system had survived the overthrow of the king; it had protected the rights of Englishmen and the Magna Charta, restored balanced government, and maintained the constitution. England's two 17th-century revolutions insured the power of Parliament in relation to the monarch and set the English political system apart from most others in its limits on executive power.

This history was as vibrant in the American colonies as in the mother country, as the political activities of Americans reflected those that took place in England. Food rioting, property destruction, and parades were political expressions practiced by common people in England and the colonies. These occurred when common people believed that their superiors had disregarded their obligations. For instance, the cost of bread was regulated by a "just price"—since bread was the staff of life and a major source of calories for many people in Europe and the American colonies. When in 1710, and again in 1713, Andrew Belcher and other merchants bought up wheat in the New England countryside and shipped it to the West Indies, where they could get a better price, Bostonians rioted.

Politicization in the mid-18th century—the process by which British people at home and in the colonies became ever more politically aware and active—was prompted by the growth of the print industry. It became cheaper to publish newspapers. This fostered the spread of political information and ideas to ever larger numbers of people, while providing a venue for those wishing to express their political thoughts to a wide audience. Both pamphlets and broadsides (large notices attached to buildings) became popular means to address local and imperial concerns, allowing non-elites to reach beyond their neighborhoods to society at large and ending the near monopolization of elites over literary and political culture. Newspapers brought information from abroad to the colonies, and made colonists more knowledgeable of events in other colonies. They offered a new way to challenge local power structures. In a famous 1734 case, New York's Governor, William Cosby, arrested John Peter Zenger for publishing scurrilous attacks against him in the New York *Weekly Journal*, throwing him in prison for nine months. Eventually Zenger was brought to trial and the jury rendered a verdict of not-guilty: truth was a defense against libel. Newspapers retained their status, and built upon it, as watchdogs of government policy. Public print culture thus provided Americans with timely and inexpensive ways for discussing and disseminating information regarding Britain's attempt to tax Americans and reorganize the empire. The press helped create a highly charged atmosphere, particularly in coverage of the Stamp Act, as printers objected to taxation of their newspapers and other publications. Politicized Americans recognized the value of the press, and purchased printing machines to start their own newspapers, or bought previously existing papers, in order to have the means to transmit their views to a wide audience. American society was transforming from a predominantly oral to both an oral and written culture.

## The People Assert Themselves: Opposition to the Stamp Act

Newspapers, pamphlets, and broadsides were widely used to spur popular opposition to Grenville's Stamp Act. Colonial legislatures responded by not only drawing up petitions protesting the inability of colonists to pay the tax, but disavowing Parliament's right to raise a revenue from American subjects, since colonists had no representation in that body. Only Rhode Island's legislature sanctioned outright resistance to the measure.

Many colonists disregarded their legislature's conservative reaction to the Stamp Act and took extra-legal measures to prevent enforcement.

In Boston, even before the Stamp Act went into effect, nine men, mostly artisans and shopkeepers, formed an organization called the Loyal Nine, which later expanded and evolved into the Sons of Liberty. One of its members, Benjamin Edes, printed the Boston *Gazette*, which gave them a newspaper for disseminating their views. In the summer of 1765, the *Gazette* put forth a steady stream of propaganda against the Stamp Act, and apparently inspired the shoemaker Ebenezer McIntosh to organize his fellow South Bostonians to oppose the measure.

On August 14, Boston townspeople created an effigy of Andrew Oliver, reputedly the crown appointee as Stamp Distributor for Massachusetts. They hung the effigy on a tree on Newberry Street. The governor and council wished to ignore the public display, but Lieutenant Governor Thomas Hutchinson, who was also the colony's chief justice and Oliver's brother-in-law, ordered the sheriff to remove the effigy. The sheriff reported that he and his men could not do so without endangering their lives. As the council considered their options, a crowd marched around the Town House with the effigy thumbing their noses at government authority.

The crowd then marched to Kilby Street, where Oliver had recently erected a building to divide into shops. Bostonians thought the building would house the stamps for distribution in the colony. Under McIntosh's lead, they destroyed Oliver's building in five minutes. They then moved to Oliver's house, ceremoniously beheaded and fired his effigy, and stoned his home. The mob dispersed, but later in the day some returned to the house, destroying what they could, including the furniture. Governor Barnard ordered the colonel of the militia to raise his troops, but the colonel noted that the drummers who sounded the call would be attacked, and anyway, they probably were at Oliver's house contributing to the destruction. Barnard fled to the safety of Castle William in Boston Harbor, but the less timid Hutchinson enlisted the sheriff to join him at Oliver's house. When they attempted to disperse the crowd, they were pelted with stones and fled.

The next day a number of townsmen informed Oliver that he must resign his office. Oliver replied that he had nothing to resign as he had not received official notice of his appointment as Stamp Distributor, but he promised to resign as soon as the papers arrived. Hutchinson then became the focus of hostility by Stamp Act opponents, as the newspapers alleged he had played a role in encouraging Parliament to pass the act.

Two weeks later, the crowd again undertook property destruction. Dividing into two, one group damaged the home and office of William Story for allegedly criticizing Boston merchants in letters to London. The second group destroyed the home of Benjamin Hallowell, the Comptroller of Customs. The two groups then united for an onslaught on the house of Thomas Hutchinson. They not only leveled the house, wrecked the furniture, and stole the princely sum of £900 as well as the silverware; they cut down the trees in a final act of disdain for the lieutenant governor and British authority. The governor ordered the sheriff to seize McIntosh, but a deal was brokered that if the crowd refrained from further destruction—rumor arose that the Customs House would be next—then no one would be arrested. In fact, no one was prosecuted for all the property destruction in Boston, though for the most part it ended.

The town quieted down until November. The stamps had arrived in September, but no official was brave enough to open the chest that presumably contained them, as if not seeing the stamps meant they might not have to enforce the act. When the Stamp Act went into effect in November, Bostonians had two options—ignore it or refuse to conduct any business that required stamps. No ships legally could leave Boston without the stamps, and courts could not operate without them. The Sons of Liberty entreated the government to proceed as if the Stamp Act had never been passed—to disregard an act of Parliament. As in other colonial ports, ships sat in harbor awaiting governors' decisions. Colonists everywhere strongly urged their governors to let the ships leave and to open the courts. In mid-December, 2,000 Bostonians met to force Andrew Oliver's public resignation as Stamp Distributor. They then succeeded at forcing open the Customs House to release clearance papers for the ships and convinced Governor Barnard to open the courts.

If Boston had been alone in its defiance, the British government would have crushed the resistance. But in all the colonies that eventually revolted in 1776, except Georgia, the populace prevented the Stamp Act from going into effect. Stamp distributors were forced to publicly resign their offices, courts opened, and ships cleared without the stamps. Those who did not publicly resign were punished. Zachariah Hood of Maryland, for instance, chose to flee the colony rather than resign, but New Yorkers captured him and made him renounce his commission. The stamp distributor appointed to Georgia arrived in the colony totally unaware of the angry colonists awaiting him. After disembarking from his ship, he disappeared never to be heard from again.

## The Stamp Act: Outcomes and Consequences

Britain was stunned by the nature of opposition to the Stamp Act, particularly the property destruction and intimidation of public officials, but also by the seeming unanimity of colonial elites. Parliament held hearings to investigate and called Ben Franklin, the resident agent in London for three colonies, to explain colonial behavior and objections. Franklin, too, had been caught unaware by the strong reaction against the tax, having earlier secured a stamp distributor position for a friend. Better informed, he recognized the huge gap between the views of Parliament and colonists on Parliament's power to tax Americans. Knowing Parliament could not accept the colonial position, he explained that Americans only objected to direct, internal taxes, like a stamp tax, and not external taxes (on imported or exported goods), though Americans had not made that distinction. Meanwhile, British merchants lobbied Parliament to repeal the tax, as its damage to business relations and American affections were not worth the sums the Stamp Act was intended to raise. In 1766, Parliament agreed to repeal, but also passed a Declaratory Act that asserted its right to legislate for the colonies in "all cases whatsoever." In other words, Parliament agreed that the Stamp Act was impolitic, but asserted its right to pass this act, or any other, as the supreme legislature for the empire. Most Americans celebrated their victory over the Stamp Act and ignored Parliament's stark statement of power.

A few Americans paid close attention to the Declaratory Act. They became watchdogs over parliamentary measures to reorganize the empire. Some of these men joined the Sons of Liberty, secret groups that worked behind the scenes to coordinate opposition to future measures. Their membership included not just elites, but "common men," those who worked with their hands; the populace, particularly urbanites, was more apt to follow one of their own than the wealthy. Some Sons of Liberty from different colonies had met at the Stamp Act Congress in New York, an intercolonial meeting called to discuss how to oppose the Stamp Act. After returning home, they maintained their ties, sharing propaganda and political strategies from one colony to the next. In the coming years, as the dispute with the mother country re-emerged, they played a pivotal role in organizing opposition to parliamentary assertions of power. The Sons of Liberty held town meetings, forced citizens to publicly proclaim where they stood on issues of American rights, created committees of correspondence to coordinate inter-colonial activities, and eventually led the way in not just fomenting resistance, but forming new governments to replace those that fell. As Russian Revolutionary Vladimir Lenin later observed, for a revolution to succeed, it requires a small cadre of individuals to work behind the scenes—planning, orchestrating, administrating—the Sons of Liberty filled that role. No one in 1765 could foresee that a revolution was on the horizon, for most Americans the dispute with Great Britain had ended with repeal of the Stamp Act. But the Sons of Liberty kept their eyes on events, and the Stamp Act pushed to the forefront several later revolutionary leaders. In Virginia, Patrick Henry gained acclaim as a firebrand for his opposition to the Stamp Act, with his radical proclamation against parliamentary taxation, "Give me liberty, or give me death!" South Carolina merchant Christopher Gadsden enjoyed a spectacular rise in public favor by his battling for colonial rights. And in Massachusetts, Samuel Adams, a brewer and tax collector, cultivated public opinion in taverns and the press, to emerge as the most powerful and important individual organizing opposition to British authority in the coming decade. All three of these men would not only be leaders of the opposition movement to British attempts to tax Americans and assert their authority over the colonies, but also would hold key positions of power when revolution finally came.

## The Townshend Acts

After the repeal of the Stamp Act, William Pitt was asked by the king to form a new ministry. Pitt was a great friend to the Americans, having ardently spoken against the Stamp Act in Parliament, which led to the erection of statues of Pitt in several American communities. The king had not recalled Pitt because of American esteem for him; he appeared to be the only one who could put together an effective government. Unfortunately, Pitt fell ill with gout, underwent convalescence in the country, and refused to discuss political business. Into the breach stepped his minister of the Exchequer Charles Townshend, who faced the same ostensibly unsolved problem of the last administration: the need for tax revenue. There was great clamor in Britain to reduce the land tax, which had been raised during the Seven Years' War. Townshend proposed a tax on Americans to replace revenue lost by lowering Britain's land tax. The new tax, Townshend argued in Parliament, Americans would accept. Instead of a direct tax like the Stamp Tax, Parliament would place a duty on goods imported into the colonies from Britain—surely Americans would not argue that Parliament could not tax trade.

The Townshend Acts (1767) taxed paint, tea, glass, lead, and paper. The government estimated the duties would bring in £40,000 per year—hardly enough to offset the £500,000 loss per year from the lowering of the land tax, and a paltry amount to raise American ire over—but it received strong support in Parliament because symbolically it represented American help for Britain's economic woes. Nevertheless, the final bill provided that none of the projected revenue would return to Britain—it would be used for administering the colonies. The Acts proved an incredible blunder by convincing colonists that Parliament had designed a program to reduce them to "slavery." Americans believed, and constantly stated, that to deprive a man of his property without his consent made him a slave. In a society based on slave labor, it was easy for free people to envision what they could become.

The Townshend Acts appeared especially sinister to Americans because the revenue would be devoted to the salaries of colonial governors and judges. At first glance, a colonist might think that since the revenue stayed in the colonies they should not object—the revenue would not provide a new burden since these salaries were already paid by colonial legislatures. To the contrary, Americans immediately perceived their rights as being trampled. Governors and judges would be beholden to Britain for their salaries, not to colonial legislatures. If there was any doubt that the Townshend Acts were intended to reduce colonists' control over their governments, Parliament's simultaneous suspension of the New York legislature left no doubt. The legislature had refused to comply with the annual Mutiny Act, which required colonists to supply British troops stationed among them. New York was the headquarters for the army in America and its legislature protested that the Act placed an unfair burden on them. They repeated the assertion that Britain could not tax colonists. Parliament suspended the legislature hoping to both assert its powers and isolate the New Yorkers. The assembly voted £1,500 for the support of the troops just before the suspension went into effect, averting the crisis—but Parliament's heavy-handedness alienated Americans rather than reduce them to cowering obedience. Many colonists were convinced that Parliament had no respect for their rights as Englishmen—that all their legislatures were subject to parliamentary whim.

## The Circular Letters and Non-Importation

In 1768, the Massachusetts legislature produced a circular letter written by Samuel Adams that affirmed Parliament as the supreme legislature for the empire, while iterating that this sovereignty did not include the right to tax Americans. The letter also affirmed the impracticality of extending parliamentary representation to Americans—that body was too distant from the colonies, which were better served by their own legislatures. The Massachusetts letter, and another by Virginia approving of its propriety, were sent to the other colonial legislatures to forge a united front. With Townshend's death, the British cabinet intended to placate the colonies, but the new secretary of state for the colonies, Lord Hillsborough, given the power to end the matter, took it upon himself to take a hard stance. He threatened to dissolve the Massachusetts legislature if it did not withdraw the circular letter. Again, Americans were told that the British government did not consider their possession of legislatures a "right," but merely a privilege. Instead of isolating Massachusetts, Hillsborough united Americans to oppose a tyranny that threatened all. By a vote of 92 to 17, the Massachusetts legislature refused to withdraw the letter—the 17 who voted nay were denounced as traitors throughout the colonies. Engraver Paul Revere published a popular cartoon depicting the 17 on the road to hell.

To pressure Parliament to repeal the duties, Americans resorted to non-importation: a boycott of British goods. This had the practical purpose of pressuring British merchants to lobby on their behalf, while showing the government the value of American consumers to the British economy. Americans, and particularly Virginians, overspent on British luxuries, many falling into deep debt and losing their estates—they now had the opportunity to reduce spending relieved from the social pressures of keeping up with their neighbors. Women played the key role in the boycott. As the major purchasers of imported goods from colonial shops, they were called upon to do without, and to do what they could in the household to produce formerly imported items, particularly clothing. It became a mark of virtue for colonists to wear homespun and to not attire themselves in the ornate fripperies and fashions of Europe. Women responded that men, too, should do without luxuries, such as imported wine and rum manufactured from West Indian sugar. Unwilling to do without alcohol, there was rapid development of American distillation of homegrown corn into whiskey, which became an important commodity in the American economy for over a century.

American artisans welcomed non-importation, proclaiming their own goods as equal to British goods. Colonists, in effect, were announcing that their societies had sufficiently developed economically as to no longer warrant dependence on Britain. This challenged the basic tenet of mercantilism—that colonies produced raw materials for the mother country, which turned them into finished goods, thus providing a captive marketplace for British manufactures. Americans were overwhelmingly an agriculture people, but the widely proclaimed threat that they could become producers of finished goods raised fear and hostility in Britain: the government compromised. It agreed to repeal all the Townshend Duties but one: they retained the tax on tea as evidence that they had not given up the *right* to tax Americans. On the other hand, the British cabinet announced that no further attempt would be made to tax Americans—the British ministry had tired of American grievances, were frightened by colonial unity, and still hoped to exert greater control over the colonies by eliminating smuggling—new customs houses were built in the colonies and vice-admiralty courts erected to prosecute smugglers.

To many Americans, the dispute with Great Britain was finally over, perhaps never to be renewed. The government dropped its threat to dissolve the Massachusetts legislature for not withdrawing the circular letter. Despite the pleas of colonial artisans to retain non-importation until the tax on tea was repealed, the boycott fell apart. Most Americans continued to drink tea. Most of it was smuggled, but in Boston, where the British cracked down on smuggling, the people drank taxed tea. John Hancock's ships alone brought in 45,000 pounds of dutied tea in 1771 and 1772. Ironically, most modern Americans believe that the American Revolution occurred because colonists stood on principles of "No taxation without representation." But after 1767, the British government enacted no new taxes on Americans.

## From the Boston Massacre to the Boston Tea Party

Celebration of the impending repeal of the Townshend Acts was dampened by the Boston Massacre (March 5, 1770). In Boston, there had been much resentment over the stationing of troops in the town. During their off-hours, many soldiers supplemented their income by performing odd jobs at less than standard wages, taking away employment from the working poor. Resentments boiled over when an interracial gathering of young men and boys wielding clubs threatened the troops. The troops opened fire killing five—the first to fall was a free black named Crispus Attucks.

The Boston Massacre riled the populace against the stationing of troops among civilians. The opposition movement argued that the troops were in Boston to force

Americans to accept British taxes. But elimination of most of the Townshend Duties made this argument ring hollow. Only Boston and New York had large numbers of troops, and many Americans wondered whether the incorrigible Bostonians required more law and order. Though colonists did not support the shooting of civilians, they could rationalize that Bostonians' behavior provoked the attack.

Despite the Boston Massacre, the opposition movement almost entirely disintegrated. Prosperity's return and no further attempts by Parliament to tax Americans or reorganize the empire seemingly ended the dispute with Great Britain. After three years of harmony, it seemed to most Americans in 1773 that the dispute with Parliament was a thing of the distant past. But fear of British attempts to enforce second-class citizenship upon the colonists simmered beneath the surface. And, in fact, the British government and much of the citizenry still harbored notions that Americans, indeed, were inferiors owing obedience and subservience. These attitudes colored the perceptions of yet another British administration out-of-touch with its colonists. Insouciance towards American opinions, ignorance of American affairs, and preoccupation with non-American matters led to missteps by a new British administration.

The revival of the opposition movement to Parliament in 1773 involved no new tax—British ministers knew enough not to travel that treacherous road. But the imperial government again blundered by setting in motion a series of events that led Americans to believe a conspiracy afoot to deprive them of their rights as Englishmen.

England's greatest company, the East India Company (EIC), held a monopoly over trade with India, where it exercised political power in the name of the British government. The EIC was a cash cow for the government, providing revenues of £400,000 per year. But the company was woefully mismanaged—its coffers fleeced by officials and overpayments to shareholders. Its stock dropped precipitously and the company faced bankruptcy, which meant the government would lose a major source of revenue. Millions of pounds of company tea sat in British warehouses. The Townshend duty on tea had not been repealed, and though some Americans purchased East India tea, most purchased Dutch tea smuggled into the colonies. The EIC hoped to tap the American market to help solve its problems.

Lord North devised a plan to save the company. Despite EIC urgings, he refused to eliminate or even lower the 3 pence per pound tax on tea. But in the Tea Act of 1773, he provided the company a government loan of £1,420,000, relief from the £400,000 yearly tax to the government, and freedom to ship tea to the American colonies directly from India, saving not just transport costs, but cutting out the British merchant middlemen. This, he believed, would lower the cost of tea so much that it would undersell smuggled Dutch tea and Americans would choose drinking dutied tea over the principle of not paying the parliamentary tax.

British attempts to eliminate American smuggling had largely failed outside of Boston. The EIC threatened the economic self-interests of American merchant smugglers in the other port towns. This threat was compounded by the company's decision to place all its tea with a select group of merchants, who would monopolize distribution. Many colonial merchants feared this was just the tip of the iceberg—that Britain would arrange monopolization of other imports by favored merchants. Americans thought that Britain was attempting to control the colonies through monopolies. Rather than impoverish them through taxes, they would seize control over the local economy. But fear of new taxes remained: many believed that Britain made the tea inexpensive so that Americans would be unable to resist its purchase—once they did so, Britain would levy new taxes and say that Americans had accepted the principle of the tea tax, so why not others. This fear was founded on tea being such a popular beverage in the colonies, particularly among women—an estimated 1 million Americans (out of a population of 2.15 million) drank tea twice daily.

In the colonies, the merchants consigned the tea by the EIC resigned their commissions, not wishing to face the hostile crowds that had forced the stamp distributors to resign during the Stamp Act crisis. The landing of tea in Boston proved a great embarrassment to the opposition. American colonists had been berating the Bostonians for drinking duties tea, and then for allowing the EIC ships to land. Dressed as Indians, 150 Bostonians boarded the three EIC ships holding £10,000 worth of tea in Boston Harbor. With hundreds of onlookers making sure that no one stopped them, and with the assistance of the ships' sailors, the chests of tea were broken open and the contents tossed in the water—the famed Boston Tea Party.

## Intolerable Acts

After the Boston Tea Party, the British government believed they had to invoke some sort of punishment to restore law and order in the colonies—the fate of the empire was at stake. The resident agent for Massachusetts, Ben Franklin, was called before Parliament and personally attacked by a ministry intent on venting its spleen against American pretension at standing on principles and foregoing obedience. Franklin, who did not answer any of the charges, never forgave the government for the humiliation: he became an inveterate enemy of the empire to which he had once been so patriotic.

American assertions of rights fell on deaf ears. Many British considered criminal colonial denial of parliamentary authority. The imperial government's attorney general and solicitor general both determined that the destruction of the tea was an act of treason, but the evidence was too scanty to bring individual perpetrators to trial. The ministry then offered Parliament opportunity to pass judgment on the Boston Tea Party—to allow Parliament to evince its authority as the legislative body for the entire empire. Under the ministry's prodding, Parliament passed a series of bills collectively known to Americans as the Intolerable Acts or the Coercive Acts. These were designed to obtain reimbursement for the destroyed tea, limit local government power in Massachusetts, and provide evidence of Parliament's uncontestable right to legislate for the colonies.

The Boston Port Bill closed Boston to all shipping (save for food and fuel) until the city compensated the EIC for the destroyed tea. The Massachusetts Government Act effectively revoked the colony's charter—an unprecedented act in the empire—reducing colonial control over many colony-wide and local officials, increasing the powers of the governor, and prohibiting town meetings without the king's permission. A related bill provided that if a royal official was charged with a capital offense, his trial would be removed to another colony or to England. The Quartering Act of 1765 was then revised to allow the housing of soldiers in private domiciles. Finally, the Quebec Act, which had nothing to do with the others, was defined by Americans as another Intolerable Act. Enacted to placate Canada's French colonists, it permitted the use of French civil law and the practice of Catholicism in Canada. It also extended Quebec's boundary in the Ohio Country to the Ohio River. To American colonists full of hatred towards French Catholics, it was "intolerable" that they should be allowed to practice their religion and enjoy their preferred legal system. Moreover, the Ohio Country, which had been preserved for American Indians against British colonists' wishes, would be under Quebec's control if the Proclamation Act of 1763 was repealed.

The British Ministry and Parliament again had miscalculated. The inability to punish the actual perpetrators of the Boston Tea Party and instead punish an entire city raised questions of British justice and fairness. Nonetheless, if Parliament had just punished Boston, it might have succeeded in isolating the city and displaying its authority against criminal activity. The revocation of Massachusetts charter rights, however, boosted sympathy for Boston not only in the Massachusetts countryside but in other colonies. It was unjust to punish an entire colony for the actions of one city, and raised fears that no colony's charter rights, or any other rights, were safe from a Parliament that believed it could do as it may.

## Conclusion

The dispute between the colonies and the mother country was a political one. Colonists and the British government (with strong popular support) held divergent conceptions of the nature of the empire, and the respective political roles and powers of colonial governments and Parliament. This divergence became important in the 1760s only because the mother country was intent on wielding greater control over its colonies. Discontented with their colonists' contribution to the war effort against France, Americans' ubiquitous smuggling with French colonies (especially egregious during war time), and the seeming ungratefulness to the mother country for the prosperity they enjoyed and the great expense extended by Britain on defeating France, British officers of the empire looked to colonials for help to alleviate the financial strain of the Seven Years' War.

The British viewed American complaints about the reorganization and taxation as self-interested and spurious. American arguments that parliamentary taxation amounted to their enslavement were mocked in Britain. In numerous pamphlets, British imperialists pointed out American hypocrisy: how could

colonists' "principles" be taken seriously when *they* were the true slaveholders denying liberty to their fellow humans. Slaveholding provided evidence to Britons of colonists' baseness, the inferiority of colonial society and institutions, and the superiority of the mother country, which presumably had prohibited slavery in Britain. These imperialists overlooked the continued existence of slavery in the mother country, Britain's great profits from the slave trade, and that Britain enormously benefited from slavery in the colonies. Americans like Ben Franklin penned pamphlets to counter British arguments, but these had little influence on British public opinion. Nonetheless, the dispute with Great Britain led both the colonies and the mother country, for the first time, to give widespread attention to the morality of slavery.

Yet the dispute would have withered (for how long no one can say) if not for frequent turnovers in parliamentary leadership that led to new administrations in London with short memories. A series of second-rate ministers rekindled American protests by failing to understand the American situation. After these ministries bungled colonial policies and raised colonial ire, they blamed the American response on a few New England rabble-rousers. The ministers were correct in identifying the existence of a small group of men determined to resist both parliamentary taxation measures and assertions of parliamentary power against their own colonial assemblies. But they miscalculated the extent of popular support and the depth of convictions Americans held concerning their rights as Englishmen and the rights of their own legislative assemblies.

After the failed Townshend Acts, there were no new attempts to tax Americans, but the British government's granting a monopoly to the EIC to supply tea to the colonies had the unforeseen consequences of convincing Americans they were being tricked into accepting the principle of parliamentary taxation. The subsequent destruction of tea in Boston harbor led Parliament to assert its supremacy by reorganizing the Massachusetts government, closing Boston's port until the city paid for the tea, outlawing public meetings, and other "intolerable" acts that led many Americans to believe that Britain was intent on reducing them to slavery. Instead of isolating Massachusetts and winning colonial obedience, these measures rallied support from other colonies and stiffened resolve. A situation was created where neither side could back down. The British were sure that colonials wished to rule the mother country: the assertion of colonial rights (rather than privileges) made little sense to the British imperial mind. Nor could Americans retreat from their position. Their charter rights could not be abrogated: Britain could not arbitrarily eliminate, reduce, or change colonial governments or deny individuals their rights as Englishmen.

# DOCUMENTS

## 13.1. John Peter Zenger's Trial for Libel

*John Peter Zenger was a German newspaper printer arrested and tried for libel for publishing articles that criticized the governor of New York, William Cosby, and the New York government in 1734. The crux of the government's case against Zenger was that truth was no defense for libel, if anything, it made the libel worse in bringing the government and its officers into disrepute. Zenger's lawyers were disbarred to prevent them from conducting Zenger's defense, so Ben Franklin and others in Philadelphia convinced Andrew Hamilton to go to New York and take up the case. The justices did not allow Hamilton to discuss the truth or falsehood of the charges, but Hamilton persisted in arguing that truth did matter. The jury found for the defense, establishing an important precedent for future publications critical of government. According to Hamilton, what actions can a free people take against an unjust governor? (Archaic f modernized to s.)*

Mr. Hamilton, May it please your Honour; I am concerned in this cause on the Part of Mr. Zenger the Defendant. The Information against my Client was sent me, a few Days before I left Home, with some Instructions to let me know how far I might rely upon the Truth of those Parts of the Papers

*(Continued)*

set forth in the Information and which are said to be libelous. And tho' I am perfectly of the Opinion with the Gentleman who has just now spoke, on the same Side with me, as to the common Course of Proceedings, I mean in putting Mr. Attorney upon proving, that my Client printed and published those Papers mentioned in the Information; yet I cannot think it proper for me (Without doing Violence to my own Principles) to deny the Publication of a Complaint, which I think is the Right of every free-born Subject to make, when the matters so published can be supported with Truth; and therefore I'll save Mr. Attorney the trouble of Examining his Witnesses to that Point; and I do (for my Client) confess, that he both printed and published the two News Papers set forth in the Information, and I hope in so doing he has committed no Crime.

Mr. Attorney, Then if Your Honour pleases, since Mr. Hamilton has confessed the Fact, I think our witnesses may be discharged; we have no further Occasion for them.

Mr. Hamilton, If you brought them here, only to prove the Printing and Publishing of these News Papers, we have acknowledged that, and shall abide by it. . . .

Mr. Chief Justice. Well Mr. Attorney, will you proceed?

Mr. Attorney, Indeed Sir, as Mr. Hamilton has confessed the Printing and Publishing these Libels, I think the jury must find a Verdict for the King; for supporting they were true, the Law says that they are not the less libellous for that; nay indeed the Law says, their being true is an Aggravation of the Crime.

Mr. Hamilton, Not so neither, Mr. Attorney, there are two Words to

that Bargain. I hope it is not our bare Printing and Publishing a Paper, that will make it a Libel: You will have something more to do, before you make my Client a Libeller; for the Words themselves must be libelous, that is, false, scandalous and seditious, or else we are not guilty.

★★★★★

Mr. Hamilton. May is please Your Honour; I agree with Mr. Attorney, that Government is a sacred Thing, but I differ very widely from him when we would insinuate, that the just Complaints of a number of Men, who suffer under a bad Administration, is libeling that administration. Had I believed that to be Law, I should not have given the Court the trouble of hearing any Thing that I could say in this Cause.

★★★★★

Mr. Hamilton. May it please your Honour; I cannot agree with Mr. Attorney; for tho' I freely acknowledge, that there are such Things as Libels, yet I must insist at the same Time, that what my Client is charged with, is not a Libel; and I observed just now, that Mr. Attorney is defining a Libel, made use of the words, scandalous, seditious, and ted to disquiet the people; but (whether with Design or not I will not say) he omitted the word false.

Mr. Attorney, I think I did not omit the Word false: But it has been said already, that it may be a Libel, notwithstanding it may be true.

Mr. Hamilton. In this I must still differ with Mr. Attorney; for I depend upon it, we are to be tried upon this Information now before the Court and jury, and to which we have pleaded Not Guilty, and by it we are charged with printing and publishing a certain false, malicious, seditious and scandalous Libel. This word false must have some meaning, or else how came it there? . . . if he can prove the facts charged upon us, to be false, I'll own them to be scandalous, seditious, and Libel. So the Work seems now to be pretty much shortned, and Mr. Attorney has now only to prove the word false, in order to make us Guilty.

Mr. Attorney, we have nothing to prove; you have confessed the printing and publishing. . . .

★★★★★

Mr. Hamilton . . . May it please Your Honour, I was saying, That notwithstanding all the Duty and Reverence claimed by Mr. Attorney to Men in Authority, they are not exempt from observing the Rules of common Justice, either in their private or publik Capacities; the Law of our Mother Country know no Exemption. It is true, Men in Power are harder to come at for wrongs they do, either to a private Person, or to the publick, especially a Governour in the Plantations, where they insist upon an Exemption from answering Complaints of any Kind in their own Government. . . . Our constitution has (blessed be God) given us an Opportunity, if not to have such Wrongs redressed, yet by our Prudence and resolution we may in a great Measure prevent the committing of such Wrongs, by making a Governour sensible that it is his Interest to be just to those under his Care; for such is that Sense that Men in general (I mean Freemen) have of common Justice, that when they come to know, that a chief Magistrate abuses the Power with which he is trusted, for the good of the People, and is attempting to turn that very Power against the Innocent, whether of high or low Degree, I say Mankind in general seldom fail to interpose, and as far as they can, prevent the Destruction of their fellow Subjects. And has it often been seen (and I hope it will always be seen) that when the Representatives of a free People are by just Representations or Remonstrations, made sensible of the Sufferings of their Fellow-subjects, by the Abuse of Power in the Hands of a Governour, they have declared (and loudly too) that they were not obliged by any Law to support a Governor who goes about to destroy a Province or Colony, or their Privileges, which by his Majesty he was appointed, and by the Law he is bound to protect and encourage. . . . But to conclude; the Question before the Court and you, Gentlemen of the Jury, is not of small nor private Concern, it is not the Cause of a poor Printer, nor of New-York alone, which you are now trying: No! It may in its Consequence affect every Freeman that lives under British Government on the Main of America. It is the best Cause; It is the Cause of Liberty; and I make no doubt but your upright Conduct, this Day, will not only entitle you to the Love and esteem of your Fellow-citizens; but every Man, who prefers Freedom to a Life of Slavery, will bliss and honour You, as Men who have baffled the Attempts of Tyranny; and by an impartial and uncorrupt Verdict, have laid a noble Foundation for lecturing to ourselves, our Posterity, and our Neighbors, That, to which Nature and the Laws of our Country have given us a Right,—The Liberty—both of exposing and opposing arbitrary Power

*(Continued)*

(in these parts of the World, at least) by speaking and writing Truth.

The Jury withdrew, and in a small Time returned, and being asked by the Clerk, Whether they were agreed of their Verdict, and whether John Peter Zenger was guilty of printing and publishing the Libel in the Information mentioned? They answered by Thomas Hunt, their Foreman, Not Guilty. Upon which there were three Huzzas in the Hall which was crowded with People, and the next Day I was discharged from my Imprisonment.

Source: *A Briefe Narrative of the Case and Tryal of John Peter Zenger, Printer of the New York Weekly Journal* (1736), 12, 13, 15, 20–21, 29, 30.

## 13.2. A New Yorker Fears the Leveling Unleashed by Opposition to the Stamp Act

*The assault on property by Stamp Act rioters frightened many who believed the social order undermined by all extra-legal activity, and that the dispute against Great Britain threatened to unleash the common people's leveling tendencies. Certainly, in parts of New York and the Jersies, disgruntled leasers of land used the occasion of the Stamp Act riots to assert the legitimacy of their own land claims by ejecting tenants of those they believed illegally held their land. These long-standing land disputes took precedence over the dispute with Great Britain in many communities. The self-described Sons of Liberty, who condemned the ejectors' behavior in the following broadsheet, claimed the ejectors disregarded the law to pursue their ends; the ejectors argued elsewhere that their oppressors controlled the courts, unfairly dismissed their legal claims, and did not possess legitimate authority over them—just as Britain had no legal authority to tax them. How did the author of this tract's understanding of liberty differ from those he condemned? When was it legitimate to take extra-legal action against a government? (Archaic f modernized to s.)*

I congratulate my Countrymen on the near and certain Prospect of the Repeal of the Stamp-Act, and hope that the Disquiets which that occasioned, will now subside; and I am sure every Person who shewed his Firmness in Opposition to it, from the true Principles of Liberty and Patriotism, will do the same in maintaining the public Tranquility, and supporting the Law: But there are a set of desperate Men who have pretended to join the Sons of Liberty, from very different Motives: These dread nothing so much as the Restoration of Peace and the good Order; and the Law which is the grand Security of every Thing valuable in social Life, is the peculiar Object of their Detestation. Hence it is, that these Enemies to Society, in a Corner of *Dutchess* County, and in the contiguous Parts of *West-Chester*, have largely erected Courts, chosen Colonels and Captains, and set up a new Government, the Principles of which are a Discharge from the Payment of all Debts and Rents, but such as the principal Director of the Mob shall Order; and they have also resolved, that no Person shall live amongst them but those who acknowledge the Supremacy of this Mob. In Pursuance of these Principles, they have lately, in a Riotous Manner, attended with many

Circumstances of Cruelty, turned two Persons out of their Dwelling-Houses and Farms, and put others who had not the least Pretensions to them is Possession, meerly because the former would not consent to hold under them ....

And because some of these Rioters were brought to Town on the Chief Justice's Warrant, and for Want of Bail committed: They threaten (to such a Height is there Insolence arrived) to come to *New York*, with several Thousands, and break open our Gaol; but this is not all, they have ventured to send a Message to Colonel *Philips*, ordering him to pay a very large Sum of Money to Mr. *Dickman*, for his Bridge; and to what Lengths they will proceed, if not restrained by the due Execution of the Law, no Man can tell.

To give some Colour to these Insults on the Government, they pretend that they are oppressed by their Landlords, but when they come to Particulars, all they can alledge, is that their Leases are not such as they would chuse, tho' they thought themselves very happy when they received them: They do not complain that I can hear, of any Breach of Promise or Contract: but forsooth [in truth], the Leases are for Years or Lives, and they would chuse them for ever; the Leases require a Rent, and they would chuse to pay no Rent, or only such as their riotous Leader will permit the Landlord to take; and yet these very Leases are such as their Landlords have generously given to them: If they dislike them why did they take them? ...

But Liberty is the Word, and Liberty as they conceive it, is an Exemption from the payment of Debts and Rents, and a Discharge from the Obligation of all Contracts: How is this delightful Sound perverted to the worst of Purposes; Men that have a Mind to free themselves from the Restraints which Honour, Conscience, Gratitude, Religion, and the wholesome Laws of their Country lay on them, cry out Liberty! But the true Lovers of it will hold in the utmost Detestation every such Profaner of that sacred Name.

The Liberty, the true Sons of Liberty in *New York* contend for, is that the Laws by which their Property, their Religion, and every Thing they hold dear in Life are secured, may have their free Course. If any has a Complaint against another, the Law is open, let them implead [sue] one another: This the Sons of Liberty in *New York*, have ever contended for, and it is not their Fault that the Civil as well as criminal Law, has not been executed in all its Parts: But they are not for sending Persons to the remotest and most uncultivated Parts of *Dutchess* or *West-Chester*, to beg humbly for Justice, from the desperate Head of a Pack of Rioters; the very Principles of whole Government is founded in Injustice. No, for the Good of Mankind and the Peace of Society, makes it absolutely necessary that such Persons should be obliged to submit to civil Government, and every Son, every Friend of Liberty, will exert himself for that Purpose.

What shall the true Sons of Liberty, who warm with the Love of their Country, contended zealously for the Laws and Constitution of their Ancestors suffer themselves to be disgraces by the Junction of Dastards [malicious cowards] who trample on all Law, Justice and good Government! Forbid it Honour! Forbid it Shame!

*(Continued)*

> He that is willing to be tried by the Laws of his Country, we will support, and Law, Constitutional Law, we have contended for, and will ever maintain.
>
> A Son of Liberty

Source: "I congratulate my Countrymen . . ." by a Son of Liberty. Broadsheet of 1765. From Evans, *Early American Imprints*, Series I, no. 41592.

## Bibliography

Ammerman, David. *In the Common Cause: American Response to the Coercive Acts of 1774* (1974).

Bailyn, Bernard. *The Ideological Origins of the American Revolution* (1967).

Bailyn, Bernard. *Voyagers to the West: A Passage in the Peopling of America on the Eve of the Revolution* (1986).

Becker, Carl. *The History of Political Parties in the Province of New York, 1760–1776* (1909).

Blanco, Richard, ed. *The American Revolution: An Encyclopedia* (1993).

Breen, T. H. *The Marketplace of Revolution: How Consumer Culture Shaped American Independence* (2004).

Breen, T. H. *Tobacco Culture: The Mentality of the Great Tidewater Planters on the Eve of Revolution* (1985).

Countryman, Edward. *A People in Revolution: The American Revolution and Political Society in New York, 1760–1790* (1981).

Douglass, Elisha P. *Rebels and Democrats: The Struggle for Equal Political Rights and Majority Rule During the American Revolution* (1955).

Gross, Robert. *The Minutemen and Their World* (1976).

Hoerder, Dirk. *Crowd Action in Revolutionary Massachusetts, 1765–1780* (1970).

Holton, Woody. *Forced Founders: Indians, Debtors, and Slaves and the Making of the American Revolution in Virginia* (1999).

Kammen, Michael. *Rope of Sand: The Colonial Agents, British Politics, and the American Revolution* (1968).

Knollenberg, Bernhard. *Origins of the American Revolution, 1759–1766* (1961).

Maier, Pauline. *From Resistance to Revolution: Colonial Radicals and the Development of American Opposition to Britain, 1765–1776* (1973).

Middlekauff, Robert. *The Glorious Cause: The American Revolution, 1763–1789* (1982).

Miller, John C. *Origins of the American Revolution* (1943).

Morgan, Edmund S., and Helen M. Morgan. *The Stamp Act Crisis: Prologue to Revolution* (1953).

Nash, Gary B. *The Urban Crucible: Social Change, Political Consciousness, and the Origins of the American Revolution* (1979).

Pencak, William. *War, Politics, and Revolution in Provincial Massachusetts* (1981).

Waldstricher, David. *Runaway America: Benjamin Franklin, Slavery, and the American Revolution* (2004).

Waters, John J. *The Otis Family, in Provincial and Revolutionary Massachusetts* (1968).

Young, Alfred, ed. *The American Revolution: Explorations in the History of American Radicalism* (1976).

# 14

# From Colonists to Revolutionaries, 1775–1776

**The First Continental Congress**
Lexington and Concord: The Onset of War
Lord Dunmore's War
Bunker Hill and British Strategy

**Towards Independence**
Tom Paine's *Common Sense*
Declaring Independence
Who Should Rule at Home?
Revolutionary Sentiment
Republicanism

## INTRODUCTION

Colonial governments had long held control over their own affairs and their members could not fathom ceding or losing that power to the British government, let alone other colonies. Yet to counter the Intolerable Acts, Americans would have to put aside their prejudices against colonists from other colonies and work together. This was made easier by the decade of publications since the Stamp Act, in pamphlets and newspapers, in which arguments were honed on colonial rights. Although all those engaged in public discourse did not agree, certainly there was recognition that the colonies shared a similar situation in their relationship to the mother country: the political importance and power of their respective governments was threatened by the actions taken against Massachusetts.

While Americans considered Parliament's reaction to the Boston Tea Party as intolerable, the British considered colonies uniting together as equally intolerable, and they considered

Massachusetts' refusal to pay for the tea and to accede to parliamentary demands as fostering a rebellion that must be nipped in the bud before spreading to other colonies. The British response to domestic rebellions and uprisings in Ireland involved the use of brute force: the government instructed General Gage to use his troops to bring order to Massachusetts. But the use of troops only led to open rebellion by American colonists and war spread through the mainland colonies. In the coming conflict, the imperial government directed the military to punish the American rebels with an iron fist. But the commanders of British forces realized that such a policy would be folly. For a variety of reasons, the generals needed to crush the rebellion with a restrained use of force. They experimented with different strategies to raise manpower, including arming slaves and organizing Loyalists. They developed strategies that acceded to government purposes, but only on the surface. Ultimately, there was little coordination between British government expectations and the military's actual conduct of the war. This was a far different situation than in the Seven Years' War, for waging war on one's own people created enormous complexities and difficulties.

Even when the American Continental Congress declared independence of Great Britain, the British militarily could not prosecute their war effort with any more vigor— they had to find a way to return *their* disobedient colonists to the fold without permanently alienating them. But the Americans' waging of war was also constrained. Limited supplies, untrained soldiers, and ill-advised or unformed strategies limited military effectiveness. The survival of the Continental Army was necessary for the attainment of independence, but just what independence would mean, the character and nature of the new states, societies, and nation was up for grabs. Individuals and groups held varying and conflicting views on the organization and power of governments, and defining who could participate in politics and wield political power. Competing ideologies shaped the course of the rebellion against Great Britain, but they also shaped the new American nation in both its formation and its evolution through the centuries.

## THE FIRST CONTINENTAL CONGRESS

After the enactment of the Intolerable Acts, the call went out throughout the American colonies for an intercolonial meeting to forge a united front. The Connecticut and Rhode Island legislatures selected delegates to attend such a meeting. When other colonies' governors prorogued their legislatures to prevent them from sending representatives, alternative measures were taken. In some colonies, illicit legislatures were created to select delegates, while other colonies and locales held conventions to elect representatives. The resulting intercolonial assembly was called the Continental Congress, which met in Philadelphia beginning in September 1774.

This Congress possessed an extraordinary array of men of talent—many dynamic individuals schooled in local politics, who for a decade had been honing arguments on colonial rights and Americans' place in the empire. Some excelled with the written word, having published pamphlets, essays, and newspaper articles stating the American case. Others, like Patrick Henry and Richard Henry Lee of Virginia, were electrifying speakers who could articulate these ideas orally for popular audiences. The delegates' letters and recollections display an unusual degree of respect for one another, and a keen sense of the important public charge upon them: to define the American position and prescribe a course of action. Agreement, however, was hard to come by. The most likely course of action was to use non-importation and non-exportation to pressure Parliament. But the Virginians and South Carolinians stood opposed—at least for the moment—they wanted to first get their crops to market. Some delegates, led by Joseph Galloway of Pennsylvania, wished to create a permanent intercolonial legislature—that Britain would recognize as legitimate—as a permanent solution to the imperial problems that beset the empire. This legislature would have the right, in effect, to veto any laws that Parliament passed regarding the colonies. The plan was defeated by a vote of six colonies to five—too many delegates feared creating a centralized authority in the colonies that could become as corrupt, as many believed, as Parliament. What Congress did do was issue a Declaration of Rights affirming that their charter rights could not be abrogated. It also provided for future bans on imports and exports if grievances were not redressed—the Congress, however, had no power to enforce these measures. The delegates went home in late October 1774 having done their duty.

## Lexington and Concord: The Onset of War

In Massachusetts, the governor, General Thomas Gage, sent numerous letters to Britain pleading for more troops to enforce the Intolerable Acts, particularly the Boston Port Bill. The ministry refused to send the troops but agreed to send some generals to assist him. Gage was ordered to arrest leaders of an illegally called Provincial Congress in Massachusetts, prevent the smuggling of weapons into the colony, and repress the "rabble"—the British government did not see that the general populace, not just a small group of troublemakers, were preparing to defend the colony against British military measures. The ministry expected Gage to use what troops he had to nip colonial rebelliousness in the bud.

Gage decided to seize military stores in the Massachusetts countryside. He sent a force of 400 on April 19, 1775, to Concord with more to follow. Learning of their plans, Paul Revere and William Dawes rode to warn of the troops' impeding march. Drums were sounded to wake the people—a sign to grab their arms to meet the invaders. At Lexington, the Americans and British fired on one another—the "shot heard round the world"—the volley lasted but a minute or two; eight Americans were killed and ten wounded. Only one British soldier was lightly wounded. The British proceeded to Concord, where many militia from the surrounding countryside had gathered.

The British searched Concord houses for powder, shot, and muskets, while the militia continued to gather. After the Americans began firing on the troops, the regulars retreated along the road to Boston. Americans peppered the troops with shot from the woods. The routed British fled to Lexington, reinforced there by fresh troops. The battle then became its most intense. All told, there were slightly fewer than 100 American casualties, the British lost around 270. War between Britain and her colonies had begun, but despite the modern popular perception that it was largely fought as it was in this first battle, with American militia hiding behind trees and rocks, and British redcoats facing them in formation, in fact, American regulars would largely fight in the future as the British did in organized troop movements.

The Continental Congress reconvened in Philadelphia, adding several august members: Thomas Jefferson, Benjamin Franklin, John Hancock, and James Wilson, to name a few. George Washington donned his military uniform at the Congress—perhaps to provide a reminder of what the Congress then faced: war. But was there a war? It still was unclear to most Americans if the events at Lexington and Concord would spiral into greater violence or lead to new negotiations. Some delegates hoped the colonies would break with Great Britain, but there remained strong sentiment reflected in public opinion for reconciliation. In many ways, all the Congress could do was to react to events as they unfolded. Without legal authorization, Ethan Allen and Benedict Arnold seized Fort Ticonderoga in New York. Not only had they taken a British fort, but New England men had done it in New York without sanction from the New Yorkers. Congress did not know how to respond—what powers did it possess?

When New Yorkers expected the arrival of British troops in New York City, they asked Congress for advice. Congress instructed the New Yorkers to take up a defensive position and fight only if British troops fought with them. But by June 1775, the Congress became more aggressive and sanctioned an invasion (that failed) of Canada. Having yet to declare independence—it would be more than a year before they did so—the Congress authorized the raising of troops and securing of supplies *in case* they were necessary. George Washington was selected to command the army.

## Lord Dunmore's War

Worried about where to procure manpower to repress rebellion, British leaders in both the colonies and the mother country considered employing American slaves. Lord Dunmore, governor of Virginia, had considered the possibility of arming slaves several years before Lexington and Concord. With so few Loyalists or British regulars available in Virginia to uphold the government after the outbreak of war, he took the bold step of offering freedom to slaves of rebel masters. General Gage applauded the measure and considered doing the same in Massachusetts, while in Parliament the arming of slaves received consideration before rejection by a vote of almost three to one.

The parliamentary vote did not deter Dunmore. In November 1775, he began active recruitment of slaves; many flocked to the British standard as soon as rumors arose of the offer of freedom. Prominent Virginians like Landon Carter could not understand why his slaves fled to the British. He thought of himself as a benevolent master who took care of his slaves. In his diary, Carter alternately berated the runaways, believed they had been led astray by troublemakers, hoped they would meet a terrible end, or return asking for forgiveness. The slaves' drive for freedom so preoccupied Carter that he dreamed of their fate, as did his daughter. In the end, he learned nothing of what happened to them and satisfied himself that he was a good master by listing all the things he had done for them.

The rebellion, indeed, became a war about freedom even before independence had been declared, as thousands of African Americans throughout the colonies used the conflict as an opportunity to escape the shackles of slavery. The inconsistency of the rebels' position—that they were the ones fighting for freedom, while denying Africans *their* freedom—was not lost on either the American or the British populace. Famed author of an English dictionary, Samuel Johnson, wryly observed, "How is it that we hear the loudest *yelps* for liberty among the drivers of negroes?"

Dunmore rapidly organized the runaways into an "Ethiopian regiment" of 600, about evenly divided between blacks and loyal whites. Despite defeat by Virginia militia at the Battle of Great Bridge, African American recruits from Maryland, Virginia, and North Carolina continued to flock to British camps in hopes of freedom.

Rebel masters tried to dissuade their slaves from leaving, calling the British offer of freedom a ruse, informing their slaves that the British intended to enslave them in the West Indies. Masters' pleas were to little avail. Wherever British patrol boats appeared along Virginia rivers, slaves departed the plantations for freedom. At Washington's Mount Vernon plantation, 17 slaves accepted the offer of freedom and left with the British. Almost three dozen deserted Robert Carter's estate as soon as a British boat appeared. Learning of Dunmore's ex-slave army, African Americans, many of whom had lived freely for more that a generation in the largely inaccessible Great Dismal Swamp that straddled the North Carolina–Virginia border, emerged to strike a blow for freedom alongside those who had only recently achieved their freedom. But Dunmore did not have the manpower to maintain the British position in Virginia. In August 1776, he took most of his freedmen with him when he left Virginia for the new British headquarters in New York (see next chapter).

There is little doubt that the mass flight to freedom was a seminal moment in Virginia history. Previously, when slaves ran away, masters attributed the slaves' motives to personal reasons: unhappiness over punishment, the desire to locate a relative, or to obtain relief from work. But these slaves were reacting to the promise of freedom. They desired to possess what their masters cried for in the dispute with Great Britain. For many masters, it forced them to reconsider the institution of slavery, as well as the character of their slaves as humans who might possess the same natural rights that they claimed. By Revolution's end, slaveowners, particularly in Virginia and Maryland, actively discussed the prospects of emancipation. Many individuals actually freed their bondpeople. Robert Carter, for instance, who lost over 30 slaves to Lord Dunmore, later emancipated around 500 slaves. All told, the number of free African Americans rose from under 10,000 in the 1760s to over 200,000 by 1810, with the bulk located in Virginia and Maryland.

## Bunker Hill and British Strategy

After Lexington and Concord, the king and his ministers were determined to employ even greater coercion to force the colonists to heel—both ministers who opposed force, Lord North and the Earl of Dartmouth, were removed from the cabinet. Instead of negotiating an end to the conflict, the king sent three major generals, William Howe, Henry Clinton, and John Burgoyne, to support Gage. All three would play significant roles in Britain's military fortunes. Their charge was to end the dispute quickly with a show of British invincibility in the face of disobedient colonists.

To restore control over Boston, General Howe was ordered to attack the colonial position at Breeds Hill on June 17. The resulting battle, known as Bunker Hill, was a disaster for the British. They won the hill but lost 1,000 men. As one British officer observed, "a few such Victories would Ruin the Army."

Bunker Hill ended the first stage of the conflict. The British learned that Americans could fight, and would fight, and more force would be needed to restore the colonies to obedience. Two thousand soldiers were immediately dispatched to the colonies with the promise of 20,000 more to come. But these new men had to be strategically used and placed. The British needed a quick end to the conflict and could not afford a costly war. The government and much of the British populace wanted to punish the Americans for their rebelliousness, and compel them to accept the mother country's supremacy, but no one wanted to raise taxes to do so. Britain's great debt from the Seven Years' War had not gone away, and the government had to keep constant vigil against France, who might use Britain's "distraction" with its colonies to push its own interests in Europe, the West Indies, and elsewhere. Funding thousands of troops 3,000 miles away was expensive, and the British generals understood that they could not afford to lose too many—they might not be replaced.

Despite the limitations on British resources, the rebel colonists faced their own immense problems. They had to form, organize, supply, and feed an army. Few colonists had military experience. The generals and the Congress were unsure as to what strategy to take against the British.

Working in the mother country's favor was General Howe, who replaced Gage as commander of British forces in America. The brother of Lord Richard Howe, who commanded the navy, their relationship could facilitate the two branches coordinating operations more effectively than was often the case. Both men were in agreement that a peace should be negotiated with the Americans as soon as possible. In fact, Lord Howe had assumed his position on condition that he could negotiate with the colonists. The Howes could grant peace if the colonies accepted parliamentary supremacy. Whereas the British ministry intended to discuss peace only after conquest, the Howes foresaw that if they prosecuted the war with too much vigor, then peace would be impossible to attain.

The strategy agreed upon by the government and the generals was to abandon Boston and occupy New York, while using a naval blockade to close off trade. A blockade would hinder colonial movement of troops and shut off American shipping, preventing the import of weaponry and the export of crops. Abandoning Boston meant exiting the center of colonial discontent, while New York held greater strategic value and was less of a hot bed of insurgency. New York was more centrally located, possessed an excellent harbor, and could eventually become home for the British fleet in American waters. As things stood, the British had no place between Halifax, Canada, and St. Augustine, Florida, to re-supply their ships and do yearly repairs, which hindered emplacement of an effective blockade.

New York had another strategic advantage. The British envisioned New York City as the best place from which to regain military control over its colonies. From New York, they could easily move into Philadelphia and south to Virginia. But more importantly, the ministry wished to isolate New England. Once they conquered New York City, they intended to send troops up the Hudson River, which would meet with troops moving south from Canada. This would create a cordon cutting off New England from the other colonies.

General Howe marshaled his forces for an all-out assault against New York. He expected to destroy Washington's army and thus convince Americans of the futility of rebellion. In the summer of 1776, Howe landed his formidable army on Long Island, New York. His opponent Washington intended to protect New York at all cost. Howe easily pushed the rebels to the western tip of Long Island. He might have—could have—crushed the Americans with an all-out assault—10,000 American troops were trapped—with one aggressive push he could ruin the American ability to wage a conventional war by eliminating the largest part of their army. Instead, Howe chose to siege the American position. This way he would lose few troops—Howe believed it enough to display British military superiority to bring the rebellion to an end. Under cover of darkness, and in fog, the American troops escaped their position by crossing to Manhattan in small boats.

Despite the escape, the British knew they could take Manhattan. From Brooklyn Heights, they could bomb the rebels into submission, which Lord Howe could also do with his navy. But, instead, at a leisurely pace, the British moved into Manhattan. This would allow him to avoid the kind of violence and destruction that might so alienate the Americans that they would never accept restoration to the empire. Instead of destroying the rebel army, Howe allowed it to flee to the north end of Manhattan. Washington then made his biggest blunder of the war—he refused to abandon Fort Washington. Critics claimed he was too vain to let go of a fort named for him. The British bombed the fort and 3,000 Americans surrendered; British losses were about a tenth of that number. Despite this great victory, the British allowed the bulk of Washington's forces to flee once again.

## TOWARDS INDEPENDENCE

Despite the rebels' military setbacks, more and more Americans saw the efficacy of separation from Great Britain. Britain's use of armies to force American acquiescence to their will alienated colonists. Waging war against one's "children" pulled the rug from beneath the more moderate elements in colonial society, particularly from the representatives in the Continental Congress.

Declaring independence from Great Britain would be a revolutionary act, although overthrowing an imperial power was not new. The Netherlands, for instance, had obtained their independence from Spain in the 17th century. (The Dutch polity provided something of a model for the Americans as they considered the character of their new governments.) What was unusual in the American situation was that the rebellion occurred outside of Europe and was generated from the mother country's colonists, not from conquered peoples. The American rebellion provided an inspiration and a model for future colonies and peoples, whether colonists, indigenous, or slaves to overthrow imperial powers.

The overthrow of British rule forced Americans to establish new governments. English governmental forms, which Americans knew best, provided them the forms to follow, but they also drew on their understanding of Greece, Rome, and the Dutch Republic. Just as importantly, Americans were steeped in English political discourse, much of it dating from the 17th century, particularly from the Glorious Revolution (1689–1691). This "republican" discourse infused American debates over the purpose and role of government, and the placement of limitations on the powers of rulers. But it was not the only political ideology then current in revolutionary America. Various strains of leveling and egalitarianism could be found in both countryside and towns, some of this the American inheritance of the English Civil War. Americans contested not only whether they should be free of British rule, but "who" would be entitled to rule in Britain's place, and what powers they would possess. The overthrow of British authority led many Americans to challenge numerous lines of authority—slaves against masters, children against parents, poor against rich, and so on. This revolutionary sentiment of leveling could be seen in new forms of fashion, styles of language, and familiarity between people of different status. The break with Great Britain provided opportunities for Americans to attack many lines of authority, while fortifying a determination to prevent future tyrannies.

## Tom Paine's *Common Sense*

Tom Paine had arrived in Philadelphia at the end of November 1774. The one-time staymaker and excise collector in Britain had dabbled lightly in politics having penned a pamphlet calling for a pay raise for excise men. Higher salaries for tax collectors was unlikely to receive support from the populace, Parliament ignored the request, and Paine lost his job. With a letter of reference from Ben Franklin, Paine sought his fortune in America.

In Philadelphia, Paine rubbed shoulders with the city's politicized artisans, as well as members of the Continental Congress. He also befriended the physician Benjamin Rush, who had recently published an attack on the institution of slavery. Living in the center of the political whirlwind that engulfed the colonies' dispute with Great Britain, and as editor of the *Pennsylvania Magazine*, Paine's sharp mind digested political tracts and arguments, preparing the way for his own unique contribution: *Common Sense*.

Under the prodding of Rush, Paine considered the colonies' position at war with the mother country, but not having declared independence. Yet if the possibility of independence was foremost in his and his allies' minds, Paine started his lengthy pamphlet *Common Sense* with an extended attack on hereditary monarchy, while promoting the idea of the republic. Paine altered the political discussion by combining the political grievances of the colonies with the promise of a glorious future in an American republic. Earlier writers had discussed the benefits and virtues of a republic, but Paine presented the first sustained argument instructing Americans that they could create a republic for themselves.

Paine ridiculed humanity permitting itself to be ruled by hereditary monarchs. The virtue of blood was denounced in tracing the lineage of English kings to William the Conqueror: "a French bastard landing with an armed banditti and establishing himself king of England against the consent of the natives." Paine completely condemned the unwritten English constitution, praised by those in the mother country and in the colonies as providing the world's best form of government. He proclaimed it inherently corrupt by virtue of its empowerment of both the monarch and the aristocracy. It was time for Americans to declare their independence and create a new form of government, a republic free of the irrational binders of the past.

Paine's argument succeeded because of his gift for language. He wrote in plain English, eschewing the Latin and Greek phrases that ordinarily buttressed political tracts by confirming the writer's learning. Instead he alluded to biblical teachings, emphasized the colonists' innocence and freedom from the corruptions of the Old World, and offered a millennial belief that the world's future depended on the New World. Meant to appeal to the common man whose future was at stake, Paine spoke to them in a way that could leave no doubt that he and they shared the same interests. With cogent and sharp sentences, he galvanized readers to see the folly of the ties to Great Britain. He referred to the king as the "royal brute of England." Yet, "Even brutes do not devour their young, nor savages make war upon their own families." The colonies had no choice but to dissolve the ties and declare their independence. He beckoned his readers to look into the future. Once they accomplished this inexorable end, "We have it in our power to begin the world over again." The new nation could then become "an asylum for mankind."

*Common Sense* was a spectacular success. At least 100,000 copies in 25 editions were published in its first year. It reached an astounding number of people, for whom the question was no longer should Americans declare their independence, but their obligation to do so for themselves and for the world's oppressed millions.

## Declaring Independence

With the British campaign to conquer New York, sentiment in the colonies to remain in the empire greatly declined. By the spring of 1776, proponents of independence in Congress, led by John Adams and Samuel Adams of Massachusetts and Richard Henry Lee of Virginia, began making preparations to that end. They considered the powers necessary for a new nation to negotiate with foreign powers, further measures to support a national army and develop a national currency, and how to go about securing a political break with Great Britain.

To achieve independence, it was necessary for the colonies to authorize their congressional delegates to approve it. By March, most colonies had illicitly established provincial governments. Rhode Island declared its own independences from Great Britain in May. Those colonists who supported reconciliation had little hope to hold back the tide for independence, especially after news arrived in the colonies that the king was sending an army of German mercenaries to America.

On June 7, the Congress listened to Richard Henry Lee's motion declaring independence. Moderates won a postponement until July, arguing that many inhabitants of the Middle Colonies were not yet ready to take the plunge. In the meantime, a committee was formed to pen a formal declaration, with Thomas Jefferson taking on most of the work. On July 4, the Declaration of Independence was approved by all the state delegations except New York, whose state convention shortly thereafter ratified the measure.

Jefferson's original draft was greatly altered by the Congress. His placing of blame on the British people was largely excised to emphasize the shortcomings of the king and Parliament. Also removed was putting the responsibility on the king for the institution of slavery in the colonies, and for promoting slave violence (by Dunmore's recruitment of slaves), though the king was blamed for having "excited domestic insurrections amongst us."

On the other hand, Jefferson's assertion that "all men are created equal" and "are endowed by their Creator with unalienable Rights" was retained. How contemporary Americans reacted to this affirmation is unknown, but in the future this became the most memorable and influential part of the document, providing a creed for the new nation. Most of the document catalogued the reasons Americans felt compelled to declare their independence of Great Britain. It recounted the wrongs committed by the king, American refusal to accept his continued tyrannical rule, and their right to become a free and independent people. The declaration neither insured independence nor defined the form of the new nation. First, the British had to be convinced to accept it. That involved the new United States winning the war.

## Who Should Rule at Home?

The dispute between the colonies and the mother country, historian Carl Becker once noted, was not just over home rule but who should rule at home. In other words, the Revolution instituted a break with Great Britain and presented the opportunity for Americans to alter how power was exercised and by whom in the United States. Many Americans were unhappy with elite rule, particularly the discontented underclasses in urban areas, as well as the rising middle class who wished a share in political power that would reflect their economic and social status and represent their goals. Most Americans opposed consolidating political powers in the hands of the few; multiple office-holding under the British was an especial grievance. Many hoped to create a more equitable society by enlarging the franchise and limiting the opportunities of the few to control government and invoke tyranny.

Americans did not stand united, even within the patriot movement. Members of the merchant and professional classes, who opposed parliamentary power and chafed under imperial economic restrictions, feared the underclasses—the working poor who might turn their hostilities against Britain into attacks on the large property-holders. Once independence was declared, many became Loyalists—they abhorred the social disorder they expected would accompany independence. Others who remained Patriots did all they could to prevent a true revolution from occurring: they desired no radical alteration in the political, social, and economic order.

The urban areas were not only the crucibles for agitation against parliamentary measures, but among the foremost to call for democratization of society. The seaport towns, especially in the north, had experienced growing poverty, some of it caused by the creation of widows and orphans from the Seven Years' War—many urbanites proposed radical solutions to political and economic problems. Discontent with the political order, however, was not just confined to urban areas. The backcountry of many colonies, which experienced great population growth from the 1740s through the 1770s, was marked by resentment of coastal elites. Their resentments were not necessarily focused on the British government, but upon the rebel leadership: the great planters, merchants, lawyers, landlords, and the colonial legislatures and county courts the elite controlled. Many common people looked to the king as their protector against the corrupt landlords, merchants, and officeholders.

In South Carolina, many in the backcountry still held resentment against the lowcountry patriots whom they opposed a few years earlier during the Regulator Movement. The same was true but to an even greater extent in North Carolina, where the end of the Regulator Movement had brought little healing to the backcountry farmers, and patriot leaders were viewed as their oppressors. In New Jersey, New York, and the disputed land that later became Vermont, tenants frequently rioted against landlords, destroyed fencing and houses, and broke into jails to release their comrades in disputes over rents and multiple overlapping grants to land. These disturbances lasted for years, the parties often formed into committees and paramilitary organizations, exacerbated in some areas by tribalism. People of Dutch and German descent opposed those of English descent. In the area east of the Hudson River, New Yorkers faced off against New Englanders to control the land. There was a definite class element to the disputes. Whether in the Carolinas or New Jersey, people of modest means united against the wealthy. The tendency of many common people, probably the bulk of people in the colonies outside New England, was to side initially with the king against the opposition leadership. This proved to be one of the greatest challenges for the rebels: How to enlist the common people to their cause.

In the early stages of the war, the Patriots took a pro-active view to promote their position. In North Carolina, they sent two ministers popular with backcountry people to obtain support. In urban areas, the leadership went to businesses, and sometimes house-to-house, to put people on record over where they stood in the dispute with

Great Britain. Those who refused to signify their support for an opposition measure were publicly declaimed and excoriated, their names put on lists declaring them ene- mies of the community, their businesses subject to boycott. But the British, too, alien- ated the common people. Lord Dunmore's recruitment of slaves in Virginia pushed many Loyalists and neutrals to support the Patriots. British recruitment of native war- riors alienated many whites, particularly in Georgia, South Carolina, New York, and Pennsylvania.

The patriot leadership, to a large degree, did not desire a social and political revolution, but they needed the support of the mass of free people. The leadership offered to broaden political power in many of the new states, but commoners demanded more than many were willing to concede. In Pennsylvania, radicals proposed that militia service should qualify men for voting—effectively doing away with the property qualifi- cations for suffrage. They seized control of the state and created a radical constitution— a one-house legislature shorn of the checks and balances of the state's elite in an upper house or governorship. Vermont and Georgia followed suit with their own radical constitutions creating unicameral governments.

## Revolutionary Sentiment

Language—both oral and written—altered during the course of the Revolution. Common folks began addressing their social betters in familiar terms, a leveling tendency that alarmed the "better sort" that the entire social hierarchy was crumbling. A few patriot leaders, like Patrick Henry, became very influential and immensely popular by delivering speeches in the fiery manner of the evangelical preachers by appealing to people's hearts. The Declaration of Independence, *Commons Sense*, and a steady stream of propaganda put forth from the pen of Thomas Paine in the employ of the Continental Congress inspired Americans not only to maintain their patriotism, but to consider themselves as important members of the body politic. With shortages of imports and the need to devote resources to the war effort, many Americans turned the simplicity of commoners into a virtue. Ornate clothing and hairstyles of the elite came under attack: the wealthy should not make materialistic displays in the midst of deprivation. "Virtue" should be exemplified by wearing homespun clothes or deer- skins, or like Patrick Henry, to adorn oneself in basic black. European high fashion in men was attacked as effeminacy, though women, too, were castigated for not adorning themselves simply.

There was resistance to the new conventions. Many men who aspired to high social status refused to do without their wigs, and many females rejected the accusations of depravity reflected in their adornment. They countered that Americans should don the latest European fashions as evidence that a polite society could be created in the American wilderness equal to any European nation. When French allies entered the new states in large numbers, Americans became less critical of these styles, many of which the French generated, but there remained a strong element of opposition to displays of status as representing the corruptness of the Old World. After the war, there would even be riots destroying luxury goods that arrived in American ports from Europe.

Among urbanites, particularly merchants, but also many southern planters, another sentiment gaining currency was to replace the layers of trade restrictions that characterized Old World commerce with free trade. Americans, with their long history of smuggling, had always chafed under mercantile restrictions. Elite Americans welcomed the publication in Britain of Adam Smith's *Wealth of Nations*, which promoted the benefits and moral virtues of free trade. Smith argued for not only the economic benefits, but that removal of trade barriers would reduce conflict between nations, doubling its appeal to idealistic Americans hoping to create a peaceful new world *and* earn profits. American craftsmen believed that ending mercantile restrictions on manufacturing would help them sell their wares at home and abroad.

## Republicanism

Revolutionary sentiment was clearly connected to political ideology, referred to in the 18th century as political economy, as Americans did not separate economic policy from politics. The most important strain of political economy shaping revolutionary leaders, as well as many of the "middling sort," as the small property-holders were often called, was republicanism. This collection of ideas carried to the colonies from England in the late 17th century included a strong suspicion of government, particularly of government corruption, and the necessity of "virtuous" men, the landed property-holders, remaining vigilant in defense of liberty against tyranny. At its root, republicanism was an agrarian ideology hostile to cities, which were viewed as breeders of vice, the unfortunate residents not owning their own land and thus presumably possessing no stake in society. Early republicans affirmed farming as the most noble of occupations. Working one's own land was deemed inherently virtuous, providing the economic independence that allowed a man to become a full citizen beholden to no one for his subsistence. Agrarians viewed urbanites, particularly the mass of laborers, as possessing no real independence because they worked for others. They also suspiciously viewed merchants and lawyers as non-producers who made their living off of the labor of others. Ironically, most planters did not view themselves in the same light, despite their economic well-being owing to the labor of their slaves.

Urban artisans developed their own brand of republicanism. They retained from the agrarians suspicion of government and emphasis on the necessity of a virtuous citizenry to guard against tyranny. But they emphasized their own accrual of virtue by working with their hands. The urban artisans stressed egalitarianism among the "producing classes"—those who worked—against both the rich and, sometimes, the poor. The artisans rejected the deferential politics of the past—why should the rich rule when they did so for their own benefit and not for the good of the community.

Although the number of urban artisans was quite small given the overwhelmingly rural nature of American society, their location in cities gave them influence beyond their numbers. In Philadelphia, New York, Boston, and elsewhere, they led the call for creation of a more egalitarian society, politically and socially. In this they were joined by many of the small farmers, who also rejected deference and demanded a greater voice in political affairs. Together these "common men" gained control of several state governments, and had enough influence to shape all the new state constitutions to limit government power and usually to provide a greater voice for the small property-holders. For the most part, the poor remained disenfranchised, as property requirements were retained for political participation in government, though Pennsylvania extended the vote to any white male taxpayer aged 21 and over. Some radicals called for giving the vote to all white males, even servants, but this failed. Many elites opposed the "leveling" tendencies of the small property-holders. They struggled, sometimes successfully, to keep political power in the hands of the wealthy (and would push their agenda hard after the Revolution). But the old concept of deference was steadily eroding, replaced by an assertive egalitarianism that emphasized equality among all those who owned property. Strong rumblings also could be heard for equality regardless of possession of property.

## Conclusion

The battles of Lexington and Concord, and then Bunker Hill, displayed the lethal force Britain had chosen to use to force American acceptance of parliamentary supremacy. British public opinion strongly supported these efforts to reduce "inferior" colonists to subservience. The successful conquest of New York evinced British military capabilities, but expansion of the war effort made it easier for American radicals to convince moderates to support declaring independence. Tom Paine's *Common Sense* articulated for Americans a set of ideas that ridiculed the colonies' connection to Great Britain—what parent wages war on his or her children—while making independence seem logical and necessary, not just for Americans but for the future of the world. The Declaration of Independence ratified the separation from Great Britain and offered the American colonists' rationale to the world—the colonists had been wronged by their king and entitled to form a new nation. The process of creating a nation was a work in progress. The Continental Congress bore responsibility for the war effort. Each state was equally represented in Congress. This new government was defined by the Articles of Confederation, a document ratified by all the states by 1781, which defined the nature of the alliance among the states in the new United States and the power wielded by the Continental Congress. As with the congress, state governments operated even before independence was declared. Each state then produced its own constitution to define government in its domain. Thus, the rebellious colonists had quickly provided the political infrastructure to operate as independent units. All these constitutions and governments underwent much revision in the following decades, a result of both practical and ideological concerns. For Americans were not unified in their political views and interests.

Large numbers of Americans retained strong loyalty to Great Britain, while a significant portion of the population had no strong feelings for either Loyalists or Patriots, and in fact possessed or developed hostility to both. This middle ground would grow in the course of the war. Within the Patriot ranks (as among the vast numbers of Loyalists and neutrals), there were ideological differences that went beyond the question of independence from Great Britain. Patriots held wide differences of opinion on what the character of the new nation should be in terms of government structure and responsibilities, the qualifications for political participation, and the nature of social relations, rights, and privileges. In 1776, these variances of opinion were of secondary importance to the inability of the rebels to show that they could secure their independence against British military might.

# DOCUMENTS

## 14.1. A British View of American Colonists' Assertions of Rights

*Josiah Tucker was one of many in Great Britain to pen a pamphlet ridiculing the American colonists in their claims of political sovereignty. Tucker saw great hypocrisy in colonial assertions of natural rights, while these same colonists denied these same rights to their slaves, defrauded American Indians of their land and the products of their labors, and their attempt to lure French Canadians to join them despite their previous condemnation of the British allowing the free practice of Catholicism in Canada. How did Tucker view the "tyranny" of Great Britain towards the colonies? Did his view of the situation in Canada imply that he saw all colonists as taking advantage of the benevolence of the mother country until they too would rebel?*

*To the Plenipotentiaries of the several Republics of* New-Hampshire, Massachusetts-Bay, Rhode-Island, and Providence Plantations, Connecticut, New-York, New-Jersey, Pennsylvania, Newcastle, Kent and Sussex on Delaware, Maryland, Virginia, North-Carolina and South-Carolina, deputed to meet and fit in general Congress in the City of Philadelphia,

Gentlemen,

The public Character, with which you are now invested, attracts the Attention of Mankind, as well in *Great-Britain*, as in *America*.

Most People here in *Britain* thought that you would not so soon have thrown off the Mark, and set up for Independence. And very many there were, who either could not, or would not see, that you intended it at all. Nay, even since the breaking up of your Congress, it has been solemnly declared, and that in Parliament, that you entertained no such design. Now, to convince such as these of their Mistake, would have been a tedious affair, and have cost the Author of this Tract a good deal of Trouble, in the Way of Reasoning and Argumentation. But you have done it effectually at once:

And for the future it is impossible to misapprehend your Meaning. You have now plainly and flatly told us, without any Coloring or disguise, that you renounce all Subjection, whatever to the Legislature of the Parent-State; and that you will not acknowledge that she has any other Authority or jurisdiction over you;—*but what you yourselves shall please to give her.* This is speaking plainly and to the Purpose; And so far you have acted a fair and consistent Part.

But, Gentlemen, are you and you constituents, (for I here include you all) equally consistent and uniform in other Parts of your Conduct? And can it be affirmed, that you are as strenuous Advocates of Liberty in other Cases, as you are in this? You bravely declare, "That by the immutable Laws of Nature, you are entitled to Life, Liberty, and Property."—Certainly you are: And the Reason you give is not a bad one, when *soberly* understood, viz. "Because you have never ceded to any Sovereign Power whatever, a Right to dispose of either without your Consent." Permit me therefore to ask, Why are not the poor Negroes, and the poor *Indians* entitled to the like Rights and Benefits? And how comes it to pass, that these immutable, Laws of Nature are become so very mutable, and so very insignificant in respect to them? They probably never ceded to any Power,—most certainly they never ceded to you, : Right of disposing of their lives, Liberties, and Properties, just as you please. And yet what horrid Cruelties do you daily practice on the bodies of poor Negroes; over who, you can have no Claim, according to your own Principles? What shameful Robberies and Usurpations are you daily guilty of in respect to the poor *Indians*, the only true and rightful Proprietors of the Country which you inhabit? These Things, Gentlemen, ought not to be: For whilst you, and your Constituents, are chargeable with so much *real* Tyranny, Injustice, and Oppression; you declaim with a very ill Grace against the imaginary Tyranny, and the pretended oppression of the Mother Country. I am not unacquainted with your Manner or carrying on your . . . Trade with the *Indians*, any more than with your treatment of your unhappy Slaves the blacks. I could also give some Specimens of your *equitable Mode* of measuring, and making purchases of Lands from the Natives;—even when you condescend to the Formality and Farce of making a Purchase from them;—Also how you contrive to thin the Numbers of these unhappy Tribes by Means of your grand Engines of Death, Rum, and the Small-Pox; And then how you drive the miserable Survivors away, and seize their Lands. But I forbear:—For my Design is not to rouse the Indignation of my Countrymen to go to War with you,—but to throw you entirely off: Which perhaps may prove the greater Punishment of the two. . . .

But in order to strengthen you Cause, and increase your Numbers, you wish to draw the large and extensive Province of *Canada*, into your general Association. You needed not to have given yourselves all the Trouble. *Canada*, when it has grown rich by our Means, and our Capitals, will assuredly set up for independence, as you have done. And in a few Years, we shall have the same Scenes of Malevolence and Ingratitude displayed there, which you are pleased to exhibit in your Provinces. . . .

You think it an object worthy of you pious Endeavour to seduce her from her Allegiance. In order thereunto, after you had painted the Popish Religion in the blackest Colors in your Address to the Inhabitants of *Great-Britain* . . . you suddenly change your Notes, and in your Address to the Inhabitants of the Province of *Quebec* you are pleased to compliment them in the following fulsome Strain. "We are too well acquainted with the *Liberty of Sentiment distinguishing your Nation,* to imagine, *that Difference of Religion,* will prejudice you against an hearty Amity with us. You know that transcendent Nature of Freedom elevates those who unite in her Cause above all such low-minded Infirmities. The *Swiss* Cantons furnish a memorable Proof of this Truth. Their Union is composed of Roman-Catholic and Protestant States, *living in the utmost Concord and Peace one with another,* and thereby enabled, ever since they bravely vindicated their Freedoms, to defy and defeat every Tyrant that has invaded them."

---

Source: Josiah Tucker, *The Respective Pleas and Arguments of the Mother Country and of the Colonies* . . . (1775).

*(Continued)*

## 14.2. Lord Dunmore's Proclamation

*Governor of Virginia, Lord Dunmore, took the extraordinary measure of raising troops from the slaves of rebels to fight the American Rebellion. The following is a copy of his public proclamation to that effect. What will happen to those white men who refuse to join his forces?*

By His Excellency the Right Honorable John Earl of Dunmore, His Majesty's Lieutenant and Governor General of the Colony and Dominion of Virginia, and Vice Admiral of the same.

A proclamation.

As I have ever entertained Hopes that an Accommodation might have taken Place between Great-Britain and this colony, without being compelled by my Duty to this most disagreeable but now absolutely necessary Step, rendered so by a Body of armed Men unlawfully assembled, bring on His Majesty's [Tenders], and the formation of an Army, and that Army now on their March to attack His Majesty's troops and destroy the well disposed Subjects of this Colony. To defeat such unreasonable Purposes, and that all such Traitors, and their Abetters, may be brought to Justice, and that the Peace, and good Order of this Colony may be again restored, which the ordinary Course of the Civil Law is unable to effect; I have thought fit to issue this my Proclamation, hereby declaring, that until the aforefaid good Purposes can be obtained, I do in Virtue of the Power and Authority to me given, by His Majesty, determine to execute Martial Law, and cause the same to be executed throughout this Colony: and to the end that Peace and good Order

may the sooner be [effected], I do require every Person capable of bearing Arms, to [resort] to His Majesty's standard, or be looked upon as Traitors to His Majesty's Crown and Government, and thereby become liable to the Penalty the Law inflicts upon such Offences; such as forfeiture of Life, confiscation of Lands, &c. &c. And I do hereby further declare all indentured Servants, Negroes, or others, (appertaining to Rebels,) free that are able and willing to bear Arms, they joining His Majesty's Troops as soon as may be, for the more speedily reducing this Colony to a proper Sense of their Duty, to His Majesty's Leige Subjects, to retain their [Quitrents], or any other Taxes due or that may become due, in their own Custody, till such Time as Peace may be again restored to this at present most unhappy Country, or demanded of them for their former salutary Purposes, by Officers properly authorised to receive the same.

Given under my Hand on board the ship William, off Norpole, the 7th Day of November, in the sixteenth Year of His Majesty's Reign.

Dunmore.

(God save the King.)

_____

Source: John Murray, Earl of Dunmore, *A Proclamation* (1775).

## 14.3. Thomas Paine Appeals to Americans to Overthrow the Shackles of Monarchy

*Thomas Paine's Common Sense, written to convince Americans to declare their independence of Great Britain, pithily denounced the monarch of the mother country, in particular, and monarchy in general, as a corrupt form of government that had no place in the New World. Paine believed independence a necessary prelude not just to ridding the colonists of the present connection to Great Britain, but to creating a glorious future built on reason and common sense. Thus, he ridicules the British monarch in both his right to rule and his actual practice. What reasons did Paine provide for throwing off kingship? What should replace the king in America?*

Perhaps the sentiments contained in the following pages, are not *yet* sufficiently fashionable to procure them general favor; a long habit of not thinking a thing *wrong*, gives it a superficial appearance of being *right*, and raises at first a formidable outcry in defense of custom. But the tumult soon subsides. Time makes more converts than reason. . . .

The cause of America is in a great measure the cause of all mankind. Many circumstances hath, and will arise, which are not local, but universal, and though which the principles of all Lovers of mankind are affected, and in the Event of which, their Affections are interested. The laying a Country desolate with Fire and Sword, declaring War against the natural rights of all Mankind, and extirpating the Defenders thereof from the Face of the Earth, is the Concern of every Man to whom Nature hath given the Power of feeling; of which Class, regardless of Party Censure is the

AUTHOR.

I know it is difficult to get over local or long standing prejudices, yet if we will suffer ourselves to examine the component parts of the English constitution, we shall find them to be the base remains of two ancient tyrannies, compounded with some new republican materials.

> *First.*—The remains monarchial tyranny in the persons of the peers.

> *Secondly.*—The remains of aristocratical tyranny in the persons of the peers.

> *Thirdly.*—The new republican materials in the persons of the commons, on whose virtue depends the freedom of England.

The two first, by being hereditary, are independent of the people; wherefore in a constitutional sense they contribute nothing towards the freedom of the state.

To say that the constitution of England is a *union* of three powers reciprocally *checking* each other, is farcical, either the words have no meaning, or they are flat contradictions.

To say that the commons is a check upon the king, presupposes two things:

> *First.*—That the king is not to be trusted without being looked after, or in other words, that a thirst for absolute power is the natural disease of monarchy.

> *Secondly.*—That the commons, by being appointed for that purpose, are either wiser or more worthy of confidence than a crown.

But as the constitution which gives the commons a power to check the king by withholding the supplies, gives afterwards the king a power to check the commons, by empowering him to reject their other bills; it again supposes that the king is wiser than

*(Continued)*

those whom it has already supposed to be wiser than him. A mere absurdity!

There is something exceedingly ridiculous in the composition of monarchy; it first excludes a man from the means of information, yet empowers him to act in cases where the highest judgment is required. The state of a king requires him to know it thoroughly; wherefore the different parts, by unnaturally opposing and destroying each other, prove the whole character to be absurd and useless. . . .

England, since the conquest, hath known some *few* good monarchs, but groaned beneath a much larger number of bad ones; yet no man in his senses can say that their claim under William the Conqueror is very honorable one. A French bastard with an armed banditti, and establishing himself king of England against the consent of the natives, is in plain terms a very paltry rascally original.—It certainly hath no divinity in it. However, it is needless to spend much time in exposing the folly of hereditary right; if there are any so weak to believe it, let them promiscuously worship the ass and lion, and welcome. I shall neither copy their humility nor disturb their devotion. . . .

Small islands not capable of protecting themselves, are proper objects for kingdoms to take under their care; but there is something very absurd, in supposing a continent to be perpetually governed by an island. In no instance hath nature made the satellite larger than its primary planet, and as England and America, with respect to each other, reverses the common order of nature, it is evident they belong to different systems; England to Europe, America to itself.

But where, says some, is the King of America? I'll tell you. Friend, he reigns above, and doth not make havoc of mankind like the Royal Brute of Britain. Yet that we may not appear defective even in earthly honors, let a day be solemnly set apart for proclaiming the character; let it be brought forth placed on the divine law, the word of God; let a crown be placed thereon, by which the word may know, that so far we approve of monarchy, that in America THE LAW IS KING. For as in absolute governments the King is law, so in free countries the law ought to be King; and there ought to be no other. But lest any ill use should afterwards arise, let the crown at the conclusion of the ceremony, be demolished, and scattered among the people whose right it is.

A government of our own is our natural right: And when a man seriously reflects on the precariousness of human affairs, he will become convinced, that it is infinitely wiser and safer, to form a constitution of our own in a cool and deliberate manner, while we have it in our power, than to trust such an interesting event to time and chance.

Source: Tom Paine, *Common Sense* (1775).

# Bibliography

Berkin, Carol. *Revolutionary Mothers: Women in the Struggle for America's Independence* (2005).

Blanco, Richard, ed. *The American Revolution: An Encyclopedia* (1993).

Brown, Christopher Leslie. *Moral Capital: Foundations of British Abolitionism* (2006).

Calhoon, Robert M. *The Loyalists in Revolutionary America, 1760–1781* (1973).

Carp, E. Wayne. *To Starve the Army at Pleasure: Continental Army Administration and American Political Culture, 1775–1783 (1984).*

Ferling, John. *A Leap in the Dark: The Struggle to Create the American Republic* (2003).

Fischer, David Hackett. *Paul Revere's Ride* (1994).

Foner, Eric. *Tom Paine and Revolutionary America* (1976).

Greene, Jack P. *The Quest for Power: The Lower Houses of Assembly in the Southern Royal Colonies, 1689–1776* (1963).

Gruber, Ira D. *The Howe Brothers and the American Revolution* (1972).

Higginbotham, Don. *George Washington and the American Military Tradition* (1985).

Middlekauff, Robert. *The Glorious Cause: The American Revolution, 1763–1789* (1982).

Quarles, Benjamin. *The Negro in the American Revolution* (1961).

Rakove, Jack. *The Beginnings of National Politics: An Interpretive History of the Continental Congress* (1979).

Wood, Gordon S. *The Creation of the American Republic, 1776–1787* (1969).

# 15

# A Revolution and a Civil War, 1776–1783

## INTRODUCTION

In 1776, the most immediate concern for Washington and the Rebel cause was finding a way to defeat British arms. To secure pubic support, maintain soldier morale, and have any hope for receiving foreign recognition and aid, the Continental Army had to show that it possessed some chance of success. And it had yet to do so. British arms appeared invincible. Even if they could prove their mettle, the task before them would remain daunting. One battle victory would not win the war. The Rebels had to supply and train an army, and find a way to defeat an enemy that possessed numerous advantages: skilled generals, great naval superiority, an organized army, the ability to hire mercenaries, and plenty of armaments. For the Rebels, conducting a guerilla-style war, where soldiers lived off the land and were politicized to fight, was not an option. General Charles Lee had recommended this to the Continental Congress, but Washington insisted on meeting the British on their terms. He would construct an army to fight in a traditional European style. Soldiers should fight because they feared the consequences of not following their officers' orders. Politicizing the "rabble" was considered dangerous. Moreover, success of arms in a traditional manner, Washington believed, would earn respect for the American cause in Europe. Rebellion of colonists from their mother country was a radical enough measure in the eyes of European governments without compounding it further by political and social radicalism among the people. The tension of defining what the Revolution meant to Americans proceeded through the course of war and after.

The Rebels had not only to contend with divisions among their supporters, but to find ways to enlarge their support by swaying neutrals to their side, countering the opposition of large numbers of people loyal to the king, and contending with American Indians who might support the British. Also, despite the influx of foreign aid in the form of supplies, money, men, and naval support, the conflict evolved into a lengthy war of attrition in which neither side was capable of obtaining the upper hand. With American and British armies locked in a near stalemate focused on a few geographic areas, a vicious civil war ensued between Patriot and Loyalist militias characterized by atrocities. Civilians lost their homes and lives as armed bands took advantage of the lack of law and order. Indians fell victim to settlers and soldiers intent on using the war and its chaos to kill them and take their land. On the other hand, thousands of African Americans used these same circumstances to flee their masters—some obtained freedom, while others became war booty put to work as laborers or given to soldiers as rewards for military service.

In effect, the war *did* politicize American society. Common people demanded a host of political reforms. Not only did African Americans expect that the creed of "all men are created equal" applied to them, but many white folks argued for the elimination of all social distinctions. Women saw the potential for change in their lives as a result of the Revolution, though men resisted as best they could (and successfully) prevented alteration of the legal system to recognize women's rights. The war led to immediate radical changes in the political realm, as the initial state constitutions severely limited government power, and the Articles of Confederation government—the Continental Congress—could exercise but little authority over the states. Some celebrated the limitations on government power as the price for maintaining the peoples' liberties, while others believed that the people enjoyed too much liberty, and that more powerful governments were needed to secure social order and promote economic development. All these struggles unleashed by the forces of revolution would be contested in the years following the defeat of Great Britain in the forging of the new nation.

## PARRYING THE BRITISH OFFENSIVE

Despite the fact that the Continental Congress had declared the colonies' independence, the assertion seemed ill-founded. British military success proceeded unimpeded through the fall of 1776. General Howe became more ambitious in pursuit of the Continental Army. He sent General Charles Cornwallis to harry Washington's retreat through New Jersey. The pursuing Redcoats defeated the Rebels in each battle. The Continental Army was on the verge of falling apart. By December, the Americans were poised to flee into Pennsylvania. To the east, General Clinton had taken much of Rhode Island. The only American success lay at sea where privateers fared well capturing British merchant ships and re-opened trade with the West Indies, from which they obtained huge stores of gunpowder; the British blockade had failed. Nevertheless, American defeat on land lay in everyone's minds. The Howes made overtures of peace to the Americans.

The Continental Army was indeed disintegrating. Many troops' enlistment ended on December 1. More would expire with the new year. Few could be expected to re-enlist, and it was unlikely that new men would sign on. Washington rued, "a noble cause lost." Thomas Paine, enlisted to write propaganda to promote morale, famously affirmed that "These are the times that try men's souls." But words had little meaning when the army knew only defeat. Under the urging of junior offices, Washington agreed to attempt an offensive action before the troops' enlistments expired. On Christmas Eve, he led his small army across the Delaware River and surprised the British garrison of German mercenaries at Trenton, New Jersey. It was an overwhelming victory: 1,200 of 1,400 men at the outpost were killed or captured. Cornwallis then pursued Washington, but the Americans won a second victory at Princeton.

Both sides recognized the significance of these victories. American morale was boosted and the army could again enlist troops. Howe's strategy for peace, to show that American arms could not defeat British arms, was destroyed. The hope for a quick crushing of the rebellion had itself been crushed. The British would have to increase their efforts.

More troops were on the way to America, and the British held high hopes of enlisting large numbers of Loyalists and Indians to fight the Rebels. The Rebels, on the other hand, looked to counter the impending British offensive. They needed to secure military stores and foreign recognition and aid. They also needed to neutralize Loyalist forces and try to prevent Indians from allying with Britain. The war was becoming ever more complicated, and would continue in this fashion for a long time.

## From Trenton to Philadelphia

Washington learned a valuable lesson from the 1776 campaign—to never again risk his army as he had done in New York. His generalship would be characterized by parrying British moves, when possible assaulting smaller contingents of British forces, and most importantly, keeping the army together if for no other reason than as a symbol of an American independence that the British could not eliminate.

The British, rather than the Continental Army, were in the position to be pro-active, to assert themselves to defeat the Rebels and restore the authority of the king and Parliament. But the home government would not allow enough ships to effectively blockade the American coast: fear of France entering the war on the Rebel side kept much of the Navy home to protect Britain. Defeat at Trenton did not deter the British government from pursuing its plans to isolate New England. General Burgoyne, who had returned to England, was given an army to take to Canada. He was ordered to march from there into New York and connect with Howe's forces who would move north. Together their armies were to form a chain to separate New England from the colonies to the south.

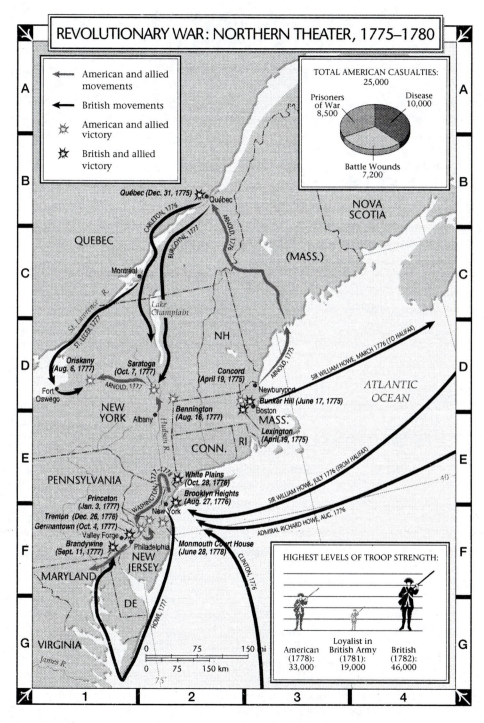

Map 15.1 Revolutionary War: Northern Theater, 1775–1780

But Howe had different ideas. Looking to restore his reputation after Trenton, he determined to capture the Rebel capital at Philadelphia. After chasing Washington around New Jersey, Howe returned to New York for ships to take his army to Philadelphia. The British defeated Washington at the Battle of Brandywine, ensuring their conquest of Philadelphia, but this success was offset by a disaster of mammoth proportions. In September 1777, Burgoyne's army was captured at Saratoga, New York, by Rebel troops led by Horatio Gates. American victory brought France into the war as an ally. France provided the Americans with desperately needed economic aid, soldiers, and naval help. France intended to facilitate the splintering of Britain's empire, as Britain had done to France in the Seven Years' War.

Since the end of the Seven Years' War, France had rebuilt its fleet, and in 1778, it had no enemy on the continent of Europe: it could focus its efforts on Britain. Britain, on the other hand, abandoned the successful strategy of the previous war of blockading French ships into its home ports and instead took a defensive posture to protect itself. The British considered granting the Americans their independence to focus on France, perhaps take the valuable French sugar islands in the Caribbean as compensation for the loss of the mainland colonies: the French islands were far more important sugar producers than the British islands. But the British government could not let the colonies go. The king would not allow it, and the war was too popular at home—the government might fall if it lost its colonies. The British were prepared to offer the Americans every concession, including renouncing Parliamentary supremacy in the colonies, if the Americans would remain in the empire. But it was too late for that.

## Foreign Aid

Foreign assistance was crucial to the Patriots. Even before the French officially had allied with the rebellious colonies, they secretly provided enough aid to outfit 20,000 soldiers. This aid included gifts, loans, and agreements to purchase American crops. By 1777, nearly all American artillery and small arms, as well as uniforms and tents, were supplied by France. American privateers sold their prizes in France, and France provided the new nation both soldiers and naval assistance. The Spanish (1779) and Dutch (1780) also entered the war as French allies against Britain, their governments and private bankers providing loans to the United States, while their pursuit of military aims against Britain in other parts of the world forced the British to divert precious resources elsewhere. The Spanish had great success against the British in the American South along the Gulf of Mexico and in the Mississippi Valley. And their naval aid was substantial later at both Yorktown and in threatening Britain itself. Dutch aid was less direct, and largely resulted in Dutch imperial losses to the British, but served as a valuable diversion of British resources.

Many individual foreigners also contributed to the American cause. Prussian Baron Frederick von Steuben served in the Continental Army as a general and held great responsibility for training the soldiers, helping to keep the army together at Valley Forge. The youthful and idealistic Frenchman Marquis de Lafayette became an aide to Washington and commanded troops in battle. Lafayette's wartime service made him one of the foremost heroes in the United States for decades after the war. The bold cavalry leader Count Casimir Pulaski from Poland was granted a commission as brigadier general, and performed excellent service with a "legion" composed mostly of

European officers. He died in a failed Franco-American assault to retake Savannah, Georgia, in 1779. Another Pole, Thaddeus Kosciuszko, served as a colonel of engineers and was responsible for many important fortifications, including at West Point, Philadelphia, and elsewhere. He rose to the rank of Brigadier General.

## Valley Forge

In the winter of 1777–1778, the main encampment of the Continental Army was at Valley Forge, Pennsylvania. Morale was low with the British having captured the Rebel capital at Philadelphia 20 miles away. Although the winter was not especially severe, the lack of clothing and food brought the army to the brink of destruction. Around 2,000 soldiers fell ill and died. In comparison, the winter was far more severe two years later at the main encampment at Morristown, New Jersey, but only 83 died then. Conditions were more deplorable at Valley Forge because the army had yet to figure out the logistics of wartime encampment, illustrating the difficulties Americans faced in fighting a war with limited knowledge of how to do so.

The army's inefficient quartermaster department failed to obtain supplies and move them to where they were needed. Not enough wagons and drivers had been procured. Shortages were compounded by poorly constructed shelters, the officers not knowing how to discipline the men to build according to Washington's instructions. The soldiers practiced poor hygiene, relieving themselves and disposing of refuse too close to living quarters. The appointment of Nathanael Greene as quartermaster general led to much-needed reforms. He and General Anthony Wayne eventually procured supplies for Valley Forge, while order was brought to the troops and the encampment through the efforts of von Steuben, who drilled both the troops and their officers. Hospitals were also established. Despite the great losses at Valley Forge, the army that emerged was much better organized, supplied, and disciplined with the ill and injured receiving improved care, providing the new nation with its greatest symbolic asset through the rest of the war: an army in the field that the British had not destroyed.

## American Indians and the American Revolution

American Indians were caught between a rock and a hard place in the American Revolution. Most decided to remain neutral, but the British and the Patriots both pressed Indians for active assistance and alliance. The war proved particularly brutal in "Indian Country."

In the decade before the Revolution, from the Great Lakes to Georgia, European settlers had forced their way onto Indian lands. The Proclamation Act (1763) had prohibited settlement west of the Appalachians, so the British government compelled Indians to cede lands in the east, to placate colonists' desires. With the French removed from the continent, Indians could no longer play the French and British against one another, allowing the British to threaten closing off trade to obtain cessions. Georgia Governor James Wright made the Indians' weakened position explicit in his "bargaining" with the Creek in 1773. If they would not cede land, he informed the Creek, "the trade with you will be stopped from all parts . . . And what can you do? Can you make guns, gunpowder, bullets, glasses, paint and clothing etc.? You know you cannot make these things . . . how will your women and children get supplied with clothes, beads, glasses, scissors and all other things they now use and cannot do without?"

In addition to lands ceded by treaty, large tracts were illegally sold to settlers, sometimes by Indians who had no legal claim to the lands. Frequently, settlers just took Indian land and hoped to construct a legal claim at a later time. Despite the Proclamation Act, settlers poured through the gaps in the Appalachian Mountains, particularly into Kentucky, western Pennsylvania, and Tennessee. The inability of the British government to protect Indian land rights alienated many who otherwise would have supported the British against the rebellious colonists. As the exasperated Mohegan Christian minister Samuel Occam pleaded to Rebels seeking native support in 1775, "let the poor Indians alone, what have they to do with your quarrels."

The war raged widely in Indian country, from the Ohio Country west to the Mississippi Valley, and from Canada south to the Gulf of Mexico. As in the earlier Cherokee War (1759–1761), the Americans focused on the destruction of corn to reduce the Cherokee to famine. In one campaign in 1779, 11 Cherokee towns were destroyed, as well as 20,000 bushels of corn. The soldiers also took substantial amount of plunder valued at over £25,000. The process was repeated against other Cherokee in the coming years, with cold-blooded killing of women and children. Indian polities divided one town against another, and one clan against another, in making the difficult choices about which side to support, and what form support should take. The Iroquois fell into a devastating civil war. Oneida and Cayuga, and Oneida and Mohawk fought one another, as did Tuscarora against Seneca, and so on. Years later, aged Seneca chief Blacksnake recalled of one battle, "There I have Seen the most Dead Bodies . . . I never Did see and never will again."

The Delaware in Pennsylvania and the Ohio Country used the war, and their support of the Americans, as a means to break from their subservience to the Iroquois. The consequences were terrible. The Americans inexplicably failed to provide the Delaware with promised goods for waging war against the United States' enemies, nor would they restrain militia and settlers who constantly sought Indian land and deaths. Militia and settlers attacked faithful Delaware allies and massacred neutral Delaware living in Christian villages with Moravian missionaries. In 1782, the Pennsylvania militia entered the town of Gnadenhütten and cold-bloodedly killed approximately 90 Delawares. Massacres of other Delaware villages followed.

As with the Delawares who were allied or neutral in the Revolution, American forces attacked Shawnees, even under a flag of truce, though these Indians favored the Americans over the British. Disregarding the policies of the Continental Congress and their own states, frontiersmen attacked other Indian allies and neutrals to the detriment of the Rebel cause. For many of these frontierspeople, the war with Britain took a backseat to their desires to kill Indians and take Indian land. Racist settlers frequently were less interested in protecting their settlements and more interested in burning Indian villages, no matter the latter's political affiliation. But even those who commanded American military forces followed policies of scorch and burn, murdering women and children, and collecting scalps on the general principle that the only good Indian was a dead Indian. George Rogers Clark, who commanded the most active units of American troops in the west, and who fought from the Appalachians to the Mississippi Valley, operated under the assumption that his troops must "excel" Indians in "barbarity": it "is the only way to make war upon Indians and gain a name among them." Clark's ruthless barbarism did indeed become legendary on the frontier.

Throwing off the yoke of British imperial control unleashed whites' hostilities upon Indians. Wishing to be in complete control of their political destinies and the lands they claimed for their own, backcountry Patriots wasted no time in attempting to eliminate the peoples who ostensibly stood in the way of their mastery of the lands east of the Mississippi. With a growing population, and few to no checks on their activities, Euro-American settlers acted with impunity. The disruptions of the Revolution had reduced native access to the accoutrements of war, to which the settlers had greater access: they took advantage of this situation immediately. As Americans struck for freedom against British imperialism, they instituted their own imperialism, one where the genocidal policies of settlers against Indians would go unchecked and unpunished by the American government.

## Loyalism

General Howe resigned, succeeded by General Clinton, and the British abandoned Philadelphia for New York in 1778. For the next few years, Britain had no clear strategy for ending the war. Troops were occasionally sent on small forays, and often enjoyed success, but there was no overall plan for returning the Rebels to the fold. One problem was the lack of troops, which Britain tried to overcome with enlistment of Loyalists. But Loyalist recruitment was greatly mismanaged by the government. In the early years of the war, thousands of loyal Americans offered to serve. Many had no choice, as they had been run from their homes by Rebels and needed employment. The Loyalists were fed many promises—of bounties, land grants, and commissions in the British army—but these often went unfulfilled, making recruitment after 1778 more difficult. Nevertheless, nearly 50,000 Loyalists served in the war. Many other Loyalists served in semi-official capacities, much as many Rebels did, particularly in backcountry areas where there were few regulars. Some Loyalist units enjoyed great success, but compared to what the British government expected of them—they hoped they would provide a major fighting force to save the government the expense of sending regulars to America—the Loyalists proved a great disappointment, which was largely owing to the home government's ignorance of how to best recruit and use these troops.

Loyalists came from all classes. Many opposed the Revolution because they feared social anarchy, believed the British government the best known to man, and could not forego loyalty to their king. Others viewed the Rebel leadership as mostly concerned with their own political power, possessing few cares for the good of society. Many Scots, German, and Dutch colonists were Loyalists because the British empire had treated them well in America, and they could see no reason to support the rebellion. Notable Loyalists included William Franklin, Ben Franklin's son, who had been governor of New Jersey and during the war headed the organization, The Board of Associated Loyalists. Joseph Galloway of Pennsylvania had been a leading pamphleteer and member of the Continental Congress in 1774, but became a Loyalist in December 1776. Two other American-born Loyalists of note were the former governors of Massachusetts and Georgia, Thomas Hutchinson and James Wright, the latter of whom returned as governor when Britain re-conquered Georgia at the end of 1778.

During and after the war, thousands of Loyalists fled the United States. Many moved to Canada, some to the West Indies, and others to England, where they filed claims for compensation for their losses. Thousands of other Loyalists remained in the United States (or returned to it). Rebel governments frequently confiscated Loyalist estates, but their property generally did not go to the poor but to wealthy Rebels who could purchase the estates from the state governments.

## A WAR OF ATTRITION

When the British removed from Philadelphia, they concentrated their army in New York. Washington dug in his troops to keep their eyes on the British and harass them when they could. To a large extent, after 1778, the war was a matter of seeing which side could outlast the other. The states had great difficulty obtaining supplies from its citizens, and often had to impress wagons and foodstuffs. Inflation was rampant, there was a shortage of hard money, and both the state militias and the Continental Army were frequently desperately short of clothing and shoes—it was not unusual for soldiers to wear only a wrap around their waist. French supplies, money, and men allowed the Patriots to hold on, but the Americans also needed the French Navy to have any chance of decisively defeating the British. For three years in a row, from 1778 to 1780, poor weather conditions and bad luck prevented the French from bringing their navy into position to significantly help the Americans turn the tide of war.

British objectives against the Americans after 1778 were modest, as they could not do anything in North America that would risk either losing the West Indies to the French or allowing France and Spain to attempt an assault on Britain. The British successfully conquered Georgia and restored royal government. They hoped to use Georgia as an example of the re-assimilation of a rebellious colony into the empire. But they did not effectively hold the Georgia backcountry, and a brutal civil war left civilians without law and order, as roving bands of Loyalist and Rebel militias plundered the countryside. The French navy unsuccessfully tried to retake the colony but failed.

The Revolution had become a war of attrition. Unable or unwilling to undertake major offensive actions that might turn the tide in their favor, and fearful of the consequences of failure, the British and Continental armies each hoped the other would lose their will and retire. British commanding General Clinton pinned his hopes on the lack of supplies and economic doldrums inducing the Americans to sue for peace. The British government repeatedly demanded more from Clinton, but not until the spring of 1780 would he make his move.

### The Southern Campaign: From Charleston to Yorktown

Periodically, the British had considered expanding their efforts in the South, particularly after the capture of Savannah and the reinstitution of royal government in late 1778. Early in the war, the British had also tested the waters with a foray into South Carolina. Although successful, they abandoned this initial effort. They also periodically struck Virginia, but again made no sustained effort at conquest. Clinton resisted expanding operations because the British government refused to provide adequate troops and he did not want to weaken his New York base. Finally, in 1780, he led a force of 8,000 by sea in an assault on Charleston, South Carolina. Instead of abandoning the city, General Benjamin Lincoln determined to stand and fight—almost his entire

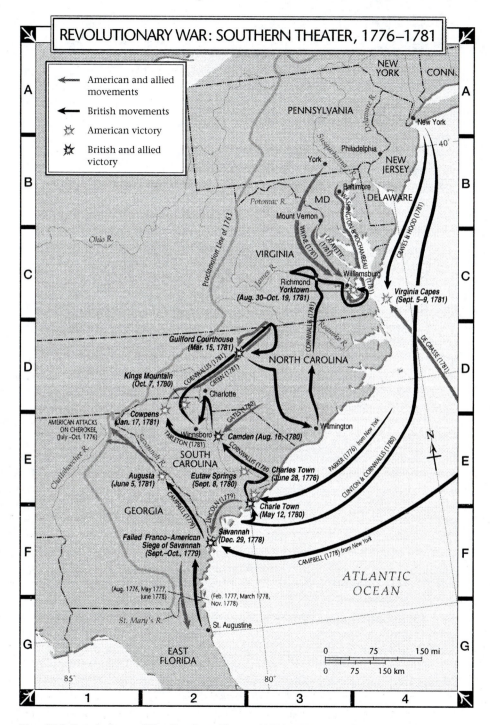

# REVOLUTIONARY WAR: SOUTHERN THEATER, 1776–1781

American and allied movements

British movements

☆ American victory

✺ British and allied victory

**Map 15.2 Revolutionary War: Southern Theater, 1776–1781**

army was captured. The Americans lost between 5,000 and 6,000 men, and great stores of supplies. This was the high-water mark of British military success.

More British victories lay on the horizon, but in these lay the seeds of a final defeat. After Charleston, Clinton returned to New York and left General Cornwallis in command. Cornwallis provided the British government what it wanted—someone who would aggressively fight the Americans and not ask for more troops. Cornwallis pursued the Rebels through the Carolinas. The British won at the Battle of Camden in South Carolina and then lost at King's Mountain. Clinton intended a war that would subdue the Americans from their secure bases at New York and Charleston, steadily gaining land and recruiting Loyalists to make up for the lack of British troops by holding conquered areas and protecting supply lines. Conquest of the Chesapeake could then provide a base in the middle. But Cornwallis did not take the time to secure areas in the Carolinas or recruit enough Loyalists. And he made the cardinal mistake of moving away from the Atlantic Coast and the ships that supplied his army. He also divided his men into detachments to pursue the Americans, rather than maintain an overwhelming force. After General Nathanael Greene defeated Cornwallis at the Battle of Cowpens, Cornwallis refused to retreat. He recklessly pursued American forces through North Carolina—Greene refused to stop and face the British, who were further and further from their supply lines. Forced to search for supplies, Cornwallis finally retreated—Greene promptly turned his army around and pursued the British. Cornwallis won a brilliant victory at Guilford Court House, but as one historian noted, it "left him no better off than before, except that he had fewer mouths to feed." In desperate need of supplies, Cornwallis should have returned to Charleston, but instead headed north to the Chesapeake, shifting the focus of the war to Virginia, and risking contact with greater numbers of Rebel soldiers.

Perhaps Cornwallis's move could have led to a British victory. The American cause was running out of steam. Three years of French help had not led to victory. American civilians were exhausted trying to maintain themselves and supply the troops. The inability of the British or Americans to control much of the countryside led to unimpeded plundering and violence by roaming bands of marauders. Most people's main concern lay in preserving their lives and property. Both Rebels and Loyalists confiscated property, evicted their enemies from their homes, and ruthlessly pursued war aims by lining their own pockets. Well-meaning leaders were hard pressed to subdue what had become a brutal civil war marked by atrocities on both sides. When regular armies or state militias came through an area they demanded oaths of allegiance from the populace, and it was not unusual for people to sign four or five of these alternatively to each side. The war, indeed, was one of intimidation and terror.

The pessimistic Washington in 1781 asserted, "We are at the end of our tether . . . now or never our deliverance must come." Deliverance was at hand. Cornwallis led his men to Yorktown, Virginia. But instead of securing his new base, he went off raiding through the countryside. Washington saw his chance. He and the French would lead armies from the north to Virginia. Meanwhile, the French would bring their entire navy from the West Indies to close off Yorktown. The British never suspected that the French would leave their valuable sugar islands defenseless—their own navy could easily have taken the jewels of the French empire. The British also did not believe that Washington would leave his supply lines—for the British controlled the Chesapeake coast and Washington could not be re-supplied. Thus, the British did not worry about the Continental Army. Meanwhile, the French added into the mix another fleet from Rhode Island and the Spanish sent ships as well. They would have overwhelming numbers in Virginia waters.

Inexplicably, as the trap closed around Cornwallis, he refused to flee. Perhaps he hoped that Clinton would send reinforcements and a fleet to save him. In the fall of 1781, the trap snapped shut. The French fleet bottled the British in by sea, while the French and American armies shut off all avenues of escape by land. On October 17, ironically, the fourth anniversary of the American capture of Burgoyne's army in New York, Cornwallis surrendered his army to Washington.

## After Yorktown: Securing the Backcountry and Taking Care of the Soldiers

Few Americans thought the war was nearing an end. For many Americans, the ideals of Revolution and Loyalism had less meaning in the midst of the lack of law and order, and the shortages of goods and provisions. Subject to continued pillaging and the cycles of violence between Loyalists and Patriots, many Americans desired above all else security for themselves and their property. As the war wound down, the Rebels learned to be more lenient and reduced punishments of the disaffected: the Loyalists and the large number of people who supported neither side energetically and could be labeled as neutrals. General Nathaniel Greene played a key role in the South in winning support for the Patriots by forcing civil authorities to stop punishing the Loyalists and neutrals. Moreover, he accomplished what the British and state governments had failed to do: bring law and order to the backcountry. Previously, American and British forces moved into an area demanding allegiance and punishing opponents. Then the other side would come through and do the same. Greene determined that when the Americans came through an area, there would be no punishments, and they would *stay* and secure the area. This way the people would see that the Americans were the legitimate authority and that people could trust that they would not be abandoned to the other side or to the plunderers. Americans had become so hostile to both sides' political autocracy—the intimidation, confiscations, plundering, and privileged interests—that simple security and minimizing government and military interference with civilian lives could carry the day. As American leadership steadily learned, public opinion was critical to military and political success.

More and more territory became secure under the new American government, but threats within the Continental Army shook the government to its core. The country's economy remained in chaos, the government unable to adequately support the troops and to fulfill promises made to the soldiers. The most immediate problem lay in the discontent of army officers and regulars, though the two considered their grievances separately. Both had not been paid for months. In 1780, the officers had been promised that at war's end they would get half-pay pensions for life. They had served for years during which their personal affairs had suffered. A meeting of officers in Newburgh, New York, drew up a petition to Congress. It would be "honorable and just," they affirmed, for Congress to recommit itself to the promised compensation for their sacrifices for the nation. The petition also added a stern warning—refusal by Congress would have "fatal effects."

Many in Congress were understandably alarmed. The common perception was that the officers would demand, if not take the initiative and create, a more powerful government, one that would take care of their needs—perhaps through a coup d'etat establish a military government. Two and a half months later, the petition was followed by the Newburgh Address, which condemned Washington for not taking up their cause. It also promised a mutiny—if the war continued, the officers would go home, and if peace was made, they would refuse to leave. Washington ordered the officers together for a meeting. In a great performance, he reminded them of the mutual sacrifices they all had made in the common cause, and he promised to make every effort to convince the slow-moving Congress to redress their grievances. The cabal was defused. Congress committed itself to pensions and back pay.

Even more than the officers, the common soldiers had long-standing complaints with their service. One source of grievance was the officers themselves; soldiers and officers viewed each other along a cultural and class divide. Many soldiers resented the officers' imperiousness and disdain for them. The officers perceived themselves as gentlemen, the lower-ranking ones taking from their superiors cues of haughtiness towards the rank and file. Soldiers believed that their officers had no concern for their welfare; the resulting hostility led to violence, sometimes ending in death. Mutinies were not infrequent, though generally of short duration. The soldiers laid the blame for their mistreatment not just at the feet of their officers, but at Congress and the public. Shortages of food and clothing, which had led to much suffering, were usually attributed to civilians' refusal to adequately support the military, and Congress's weakness and incompetence in seeing to the soldiers' needs.

Although there were several smaller mutinies, significant ones in 1780 resulted from the lack of supplies and pay: the Massachusetts Line at West Point, New York; the Connecticut Line at Morristown, New Jersey; and the New York Line at Fort Schuyler, New York. Another source of grievance arose from many troops believing their enlistments had expired. In 1777, soldiers had signed up for three years or "the duration of the war," the latter meaning their enlistments would end if the war ended in less than three years. General Washington wished to disregard the agreement and keep the soldiers in their ranks until the war ended, though it had gone beyond the three years. A compromise was reached, whereby the soldiers received a $100 bounty, but would have to remain in arms until the war actually ended. Still, it is notable that Washington and other generals believed that the common soldiers were patriotic to the cause and continued their long service out of a sense of duty to their country and fellow soldiers. In fact, the soldiers were the most nationalistic element in the new nation, as their wartime experience in arms alongside men from other states gave them stronger ties to the concept of one nation than the civilians whose identity was more bound to their states. Devotion to the cause they had long served overcame their hostilities to their officers and their treatment by Congress and civilians to keep them in the army.

As rumors arose of impending peace, however, soldiers again threatened their officers and displayed displeasure at their treatment. Fearing mutiny, Washington authorized furloughs for most of the soldiers—he would send them home before things got out of hand. The soldiers needed their pay to get home, but instead of money received certificates for later redemption. Without actual money, most exchanged their certificates to speculators for small bits of money so they could travel home. Some of those who had not taken furloughs marched around the Philadelphia

State House to intimidate Congress. When a second contingent arrived, the congress-men fled Philadelphia, making three successive moves to avoid hostilities. After the war, officers, but few soldiers, received proper compensation for their wartime service. Rubbing salt in the wound, over the following decades, a mythology developed in American society that the militias had done most of the fighting and the Continental soldiers' contribution had been relatively insignificant. Not until most of the soldiers were dead did the soldiers begin to receive credit for their contributions and pensions for those disabled.

## Treaty of Paris

The British were ready to conclude a peace with the Americans by June 1782. Ben Franklin, soon joined by John Adams and John Jay, conducted most of the negotia-tions in Paris. The process was complicated by the United States' alliance with France, Spain, and the Netherlands, and the fact that Britain's war with the Americans was only one aspect of their larger war with the European powers. Questions of boundaries in North America further complicated the peace process, as well as advantages and com-pensations that both sides wished to attain. Britain was willing to assent to American independence, but hoped to restore close commercial ties, threatened by the new nation's link with France.

The Americans desired all land south of Canada east to the Mississippi River and insisted on fishing rights off Newfoundland—the world's greatest fisheries. The British insisted on the Americans compensating Loyalists for their losses. France desired a quick peace with Britain, so that it could focus attention on a dispute between Russia and the Ottoman Empire in Eastern Europe. Also at stake for the European powers were their possessions in Africa, Europe, the Mediterranean, the West Indies, and India, for islands and outposts had changed hands during the war, and might still do so as the war continued. Spain was preparing for an assault to retake Gibraltar and desired Britain to restore Minorca.

The American allies' position declined when a French fleet under Admiral de Grasse, who earlier had played the critical role in bottling up the British at Yorktown, was defeated in the West Indies, and the admiral taken prisoner. The Spanish also failed in their assault on Gibraltar. All the parties were then ready for peace. Spain received from Britain West Florida, which it had taken during the war, and East Florida in exchange for the Bahamas, which had been captured from the British. France returned to Britain islands it had captured in the Caribbean in exchange for St. Lucia, which the British had captured. France also kept Tobago, which it had taken. The Americans received all land between Canada and Florida east of the Mississippi River, but no rights to resume trade with the British West Indies. The inability of Britain and the United States to determine borders between Canada and the United States remained a sore spot between the two countries until settlement in 1841. The Americans also promised that Congress would "earnestly recommend" to the "States to provide for the Restitution of all Estates, Rights & Properties which have been confis-cated belonging to real British subjects" who had "not borne Arms against the said United States. . . ." The failure of the Loyalists to obtain compensation under the treaty, and the unfulfilled stipulation that British creditors could collect prewar debts from Americans, remained a bone of contention for many years. Failed American

**Map 15.3  Territorial Claims in Eastern America After the Treaty of Paris**

compliance led Britain to refuse to evacuate nine forts on American soil until ratification of the Jay Treaty in 1794.

By the Treaty of Paris in 1783, the United States had its independence recognized by Britain and the war came to an end. The seeming disaster faced by Britain proved no disaster. The United States remained Britain's best trading partner, and no feared close economic alliance between the new nation and France occurred. France was left in the worst position. While the British economy and military power recovered quickly after the war, France was saddled with an enormous debt that played no small role in contributing to the outbreak of the French Revolution. The Spanish thought they had benefited from the war, but Florida and Louisiana were insecure against the United States, which, when powerful enough, would pressure Spain from its possessions.

The United States had won the war. But the government was bankrupt, the economy in disarray, and the European powers uninterested in making commercial treaties on American terms—free trade between nations. The United States found it difficult to find trading partners to purchase her commodities. The military was extremely weak, and without funds could not restore its power. In great debt to Europeans and its own citizens, no one wished to extend more credit to the United States, though France provided some funds when the treaty was made.

## WAR'S LEGACIES

The end of the war brought great rejoicing—the former colonists had defeated the most powerful nation in western Europe. But a host of problems remained. Most pressing: the economy was in a shambles. Both the Articles of Confederation and state governments held great debt to their citizens, and to foreign governments and private interests. The debt to foreigners was critical: unless the United States made payments, they would be unable to borrow more. Moreover, there was no stable currency. Inflation had rendered the continental dollar nearly worthless. Americans needed foreign currency, which could be obtained through foreign trade, but Britain refused to purchase American crops and would not allow American trade with the British West Indies. Britain was willing to sell to the United States, but not to purchase anything. The Americans sought to make trade treaties with the nations of western Europe, including Britain, but found these nations unwilling or unable to oblige. The Continental Congress proved inadequate for solving the economic woes. Indicative of its weakness was the inability to raise tax revenues, which any single state could block by veto. Americans saw little need to support the Continental Congress, whose main task of conducting the war had ended. Americans viewed their state governments as more important in their lives, and they sought to restrict those governments' powers as well.

Americans were proud of their accomplishment at achieving independence, and patriotic to their new nation, but for most free people their concept of the nation was an alliance of states without a strong national authority. Most Americans lived on small farms, were locally oriented, and saw little need for powerful state governments, let alone a national government. The problems of currency and state and national debts had little meaning to those engaged in barter. Smaller, but influential groups of people had other ideas and concerns. The tobacco planters of the Chesapeake, the rice planters of South Carolina and Georgia, the northern merchants, and many urban artisans came to believe that a powerful national government was needed to promote economic development. The latter ultimately succeeded in 1787 by the ratification of a constitution that created a new form of government, but the tensions between national authority, state power, and individual and community autonomy persisted and remain one of the defining features of American society.

Another important legacy of the Revolution was continual debate over the concepts of freedom and equality, and the rights of citizenship. Freedom was deemed a "natural right" possessed by individuals, but which individuals were entitled to freedom, and what rights and privileges would they possess? Did the Declaration of Independence dictum "all men are created equal" apply only to men? Why were there exceptions in society? African American males were denied freedom, equality, and citizenship because of their skin color. White men without sufficient property were denied full political rights. What rights, privileges, and freedoms did women possess in the new society? Most free white males would not consider granting full equality to women, who not only were barred from political participation but were denied equality before the law. More free white males were willing to consider liberating Africans from the bondage of slavery (albeit not with the granting of full equality) than allowing female equality. On the other hand, few white Americans, male or female, considered American Indians as potential citizens. Indians possessed natural rights, and obviously lived as free people, but generally they were deemed as savages incapable of becoming citizens and must be excluded from society.

## Native America: The War Continues

Indian allies had provided Britain much military aid during the war. With British defeat, these allies were abandoned. The British and Americans gave Indians nary a thought at the peace talks. Indians soon learned that, for the most part, it did not matter whether they had allied with or against the United States, or remained neutral. At the Treaty of Paris, Britain ceded Indian lands to the United States though these lands were not theirs to cede. The United States made few distinctions between Indians who had supported them and those who had not. The end of the Revolution thus did not end the war in Indian country as American settlers were intent on Indian lands. Some Indians migrated north to Canada, but most remained hoping to keep the settlers at bay. Violence increased as American settlers wished to kill and remove Indians in their way. The federal government, needing money, sold Indian lands to prospective settlers. Native military power, however, remained formidable. In the Ohio Valley, scene of so much settler–native violence during the Revolution, Indians defeated American armies in 1790 and 1791. But the writing was on the wall. There were just too many Euro-American migrants. This, and the rebirth of American military power, would lead to the forced removal of Indian peoples of the Old Northwest from their lands. Indians below Tennessee had more military power and less pressure from settlers—they retained most of their lands into the early 19th century, when the economic success of cotton led to settler expansion and federal government acquiescence in "Indian Removal" from southern lands east of the Mississippi River.

Some Euro-Americans held out hope that Indians could be converted to Christianity, would adopt European gender roles, become instilled with western notions of individual property rights (and thus give up communal ownership of land), and in effect transform into white people. Most Indians refused, but even those who adopted to varying degrees—and some did most everything asked of them—were denied their land rights and forced to move to new lands distant from their homes. Even those Europeans who accepted that Indians possessed "natural rights," often thought they must possess them elsewhere. Whites believed they were entitled to Indian lands because they would make better use of them than Indians, who were considered savage, archaic peoples who would disappear in the face of a superior civilization. The pathway was set for Indian dispossession of land and removal at the end of the Revolution and over the following half-century. The states and federal government were often at odds over Indian policy. The federal government considered Indians as separate peoples who must enter into treaties with the United States. On the other hand, some individual states viewed Indians within their borders as subject peoples who possessed no treaty rights and could be evicted from their lands. In the end, the forces desiring Indian removal were so great that even Supreme Court decisions in favor of Indian rights were ignored, and most of the Indian population east of the Mississippi River were forced to remove to Oklahoma and elsewhere in the west.

## A War of Liberation: African Americans in the American Revolution

Thousands of African Americans used the upheaval of the Revolutionary War to claim their freedom. In South Carolina and Georgia, where the British had much military success, patriot masters had great difficulty keeping their slaves. Thousands fled to British lines or hid out in marshes and swamps. New York, Florida, South Carolina, and other colonies' white Loyalists enlisted African Americans in their ranks. At no point, however, did the British issue an offer of freedom for *all* slaves; they were intent on freeing only slaves of Rebel masters. Both sides also used slaves captured from the opposition as rewards for their soldiers. Captured slaves and those who freed themselves often wound up as working side-by-side digging roads and performing other manual labor in support of the troops. Nevertheless, many freedmen became soldiers fighting for the British; African American women, too, were offered their freedom when they reached British lines.

The Rebels used slaves captured from the British as rewards for recruits. The patriot governments in Virginia and North Carolina, for instance, promised white recruits free land and a slave upon completion of military service. The Rebels also utilized African American soldiers. The New England states early on recruited free blacks for military service. Washington opposed the use of black troops, but desperate for soldiers, especially as the war dragged on and it proved difficult to recruit whites, he acceded to the Continental Congress authorization of $400 compensation to masters who allowed their slaves to serve. Recruits would receive freedom upon completion of their enlistment. The most notable proposal, put forth by John Laurens, son of Henry Laurens (one of the largest slaveholders in South Carolina and president of the Continental Congress), was a "general emancipation" of southern slaves who would serve in the Continental Army. Responding to a low ebb in Rebel fortunes—the disaster of Valley Forge—and a strong hostility to slavery, John had urged his father to convince Congress of both the military necessity and the moral imperative of ending slavery for those who would risk their lives for the country's and their own freedom. In the spring of 1779, Congress approved the plan as a recommendation to South Carolina and Georgia, where the British were having military success. Some northern congressmen applauded the plan as an important step that would lead to broader measures of emancipation. The South Carolina Rebel government, however, overwhelmingly rejected it by a vote of about 100 to 12. Nonetheless, northern states continued to enlist free blacks and slaves who received freedom for their service—so many that perhaps 10% of the Continental Army at the end of the war was composed of African Americans.

When the war came to a close, the British army evacuated 5,000 to 6,000 ex-slaves from New York, many of them previously having been evacuated from South Carolina and Georgia. Those two states lost about 15,000 slaves in all during the war. Some had been removed to St. Augustine by Loyalist owners, and then to the West Indies when Britain ceded Florida to Spain. The British army also recruited many slaves into "Black Corps," which saw long-term service in the West Indies. Over 3,000 free blacks, most of whom were ex-slaves, were transported to Nova Scotia, Canada. Many of these later were re-transported to West Africa, particularly to Sierra Leone, a colony established by Britain for ex-slaves.

One of the most powerful consequences of the American Revolution lay in its spreading of anti-slavery sentiment in both Britain and the United States. Many of the northern states soon ended slavery, or passed laws of gradual emancipation providing for the institution's ultimate demise. Widespread debate ensued in American society on both the character of peoples of African descent and whether the new nation could truly possess freedom if much of the population remained as slaves. In Britain, the loss of the colonies led to much soul-searching on the nature of empire and society, with the result of the formation of the first anti-slavery societies—a significant and devoted group of abolitionists steadily pressed for the ending of the international slave trade and of slavery, ultimately having great impact on both in the western world.

## War's Legacy for Women

A little over three months before the Continental Congress had issued the Declaration of Independence, Abigail Adams wrote to her husband who was then in Philadelphia attending the Continental Congress. Aware that John was of the party pushing for Congress to declare American independence, Abigail penned a scolding and sarcastic letter urging her husband to "Remember the Ladies," when the Congress formed a "Code of Laws" for the new nation. She desired Congress to "not put such unlimited power into the hands of the Husbands." Echoing Thomas Paine's views in *Common Sense* that all kings would be tyrants, she chided her husband, "Remember all Men would be tyrants if they could. If particular care and attention is not paid to the Ladies we are determined to foment a Rebellion, and will not hold ourselves bound by any laws in which we have no voice, or Representation."

John responded to his wife's missive with humor that reflected the common fear that the war with Britain, already underway, had loosened the bonds of deference from social inferiors to their superiors. "Children and Apprentices," John rued, had grown "disobedient. Indians slighted their guardians and Negroes grew insolent to their Masters. But your Letter was the first Intimation that another Tribe more numerous and powerful than all the rest was grown discontented.—This is rather too Coarse a Compliment but you are so saucy, I wont blot it out." John then dismissed his wife's charge: "We know better than to repeal our Masculine systems," asserting that "in Practice" men are the true "subjects" of women.

Abigail Adams knew that the Continental Congress would pass no laws in favor of women—but the thought, as her letter shows, was not inconsiderable. Over a century earlier in Maryland, Margaret Brent had demanded the right to vote from the legislature, declaring that she met the suffrage requirements through property-ownership. Her demand was rejected. Shortly after the Revolution, New Jersey women cast ballots as the state constitution had not explicitly excluded them. The all-male legislature quickly banned them through explicit legislation.

Tom Paine spoke out for women's political rights (as he also did for the abolition of slavery). Most men, however, were unwilling to consider women's political rights, let alone other rights. Wives were civilly dead, and their husbands represented their interests before the law. Husbands legally possessed all family property except what was protected for women by dower rights. The legal system entirely favored men over women—few men were willing to cede their privileged position in society and the family. Men rationalized that women could not vote because they were like children and slaves living in economic dependence on their master. But women like Margaret Brent did possess a substantial estate and thus economic "independence." Having no logical reason to ban the independent woman from suffrage, men fell back on arguments of females' inherent inferiority.

The American Revolution brought no legal or political changes to women, yet more subtle alterations ultimately had great impact on their lives. The Revolution gave birth to the idea of republican motherhood. As potential repositories of virtue, women were given the responsibility of holding their husbands to the virtues of the good citizen, and of raising their children to a citizenship necessary for maintaining the republic in future generations. To be republican mothers, women had to be educated. In the 1780s and 1790s, education for girls expanded, particularly through public education; the subject matter expanded as well. Previously, much of the focus in female education lay in the ornamental arts of music, French, reading, and needlework—females were educated to entertain men, to become an ornament for their husbands. After the Revolution, the curriculum expanded considerably to include writing, history, rhetoric, science, geography, and grammar. This prepared the way for a new profession opening for females: teaching, which allowed single women to earn income and economic independence. Moreover, this new generation of educated females would become writers, engaging in missionary work, and ultimately leading the way in the social reform movements of the early 19th century, such as temperance and abolition, and paving the way for the first women's rights movement. Republican motherhood, and its necessary adjunct of education, allowed females to escape the constrictions of colonial women in terms of employment and social and political aspirations.

## Conclusion

The victory over Britain held enormous consequences in world history. American colonists overthrowing an imperial power inspired others throughout the globe in the coming centuries. Creating a republic as the product of Revolution—the people eliminating archaic, foreign, and privileged forms of government—meant that national liberation movements could result in societies based on the concept of self-determination. Moreover, the creed of "All men are created equal," and in possession of "certain unalienable rights," including "life, liberty and the pursuit of happiness," justified the overthrow of tyrannical forms of government.

Most male Euro-Americans considered equality to apply only to themselves, and many elites resisted extending suffrage to those without property—democratization was a slow process. It took decades for equality to be applied politically to all white males, much longer to non-whites, and even longer to women. Yet the thrust for equality and self-determination quickly spread to France and Saint Domingue in more radical forms than in the United States. In France, the monarchy was overthrown in the French Revolution. France outlawed slavery and instituted a radical re-ordering of society. The French colony of Saint Domingue eliminated slavery, and the ex-slaves then overthrew French colonialism and created the republic of Haiti. The "Reign of Terror" in France alienated many in America from the French Revolution, and also confirmed the belief in many Americans that unchecked liberty was dangerous and tyrannical. "Liberty and order" were emphasized by these elements of American society in the coming years. The Haitian Republic, too, was rejected by many

Americans. The United States government refused to recognize Haiti because of its abolishment of slavery and the assumption of political power by ex-slaves. American slaveholders' desire to retain slavery in their republic radically limited the application of the natural rights philosophy in the new United States, though its ideals ultimately, though slowly, were embraced in the new nation.

At the end of the war, the impulse of the large property-holding classes north and south was to restrain the leveling democratic tendencies of the poor—but the creed of equality steadily eroded resistance. The new state governments reflected the leveling tendencies of the Revolution. The state constitutions provided for weak governments to prevent tyranny of the citizenry. Josiah Quincy of Massachusetts aptly summed up the general view of the age-old quandary of trying to balance the people's freedom with the government's role of maintaining order: it was "much easier to restrain liberty from running into licentiousness than power from swelling into tyranny and oppression." Tyranny was generally associated with the executive—despite the fact that before 1776 Americans had looked at Parliament—a legislative body—as their oppressor. Thus most of the former powers of the executive in the colonial governments shifted to the legislatures in the state governments: the power to raise arms and declare war, coin money, establish courts, and make appointments. Americans had won their independence, but the contest over defining the forms and meaning of the new nation remained. Nonetheless, with some issues there was no going back. Religious toleration was evolving into a concept of religious freedom, which became a cornerstone of American society to be upheld by government. And there was a widespread belief that what-ever form government actually took that the consent of the governed was necessary for society's stability and prosperity.

# DOCUMENTS

## 15.1. Abigail and John Adams on Women in the New Nation

*Abigail and John Adams maintained a regular correspondence while John was a delegate to the Continental Congress in Philadelphia and Abigail remained in Massachusetts. John kept Abigail informed of affairs, particularly the movement towards independence and the fortunes of war. In a letter that much surprised her husband, Abigail urged her husband to "remember the ladies," when independence was declared and new laws would be formed. If nothing else, this letter provides evidence that American women considered that with independence the new nation would start with a blank slate and could address and improve women's position in society. John's response is equally enlightening. His condescending attempt at humor dismisses Abigail's request, but also highlights how the Revolution had provided license to many dependents, including children, slaves, and Indians to become "turbulent" and "insolent." How does Abigail Adams's understanding of tyranny compare to Tom Paine's (see document at end of chapter 14)? How would Josiah Tucker (see document in chapter 14) view John Adams's letter to his wife?*

**Abigail to John Adams,**

**Braintree, 31 March, 1776**

I wish you would ever write me a Letter half as long as I write you; and tell me if you may where your Fleet are gone; What sort of Defence Virginia can make against our common Enemy? Whether it is so situated as to make an able Defence; Are not the Gentery Lords and the common people vassals, are they not like the uncivilized Natives Brittain represents us to be? I hope their Riffel Men who have shewen themselves very savage and even Blood thirsty; are not a specimen of the Generality of the people. I am willing to allow the Colony great merrit for having produced a Washington but they have been shamefully duped by a Dunmore.

I have sometimes been ready to think that the passion for Liberty cannot be Eaquelly Strong in the Breasts of those who have been accustomed to deprive their fellow Creatures of theirs. Of this I am certain that it is not founded upon that generous and christian principal of doing to others as we would that others should do unto us.

Do not you want to see Boston; I am fearfull of the small pox, or I should have been in before this time. I got Mr. Crane to go to our House and see what state it was in. I find it has been occupied by one of the Doctors of a Regiment, very dirty, but no other damage has been done to it. The few things which were left in it are all gone. Cranch has the key which he never deliverd up. I have wrote to him for it and am determined to get it

*(Continued)*

cleand as soon as possible and shut it up. I look upon it a new acquisition of property, a property which one month ago I did not value at a single Shilling, and could with pleasure have seen it in flames. . . .

I long to hear that you have declared an independancy-and by the way in the new Code of Laws which I suppose it will be necessary for you to make I desire you would Remember the Ladies, and be more generous and favourable to them than your ancestors. Do not put such unlimited power into the hands of the Husbands. Remember all Men would be tyrants if they could. If perticuliar care and attention is not paid to the Laidies we are determined to foment a Rebelion, and will not hold ourselves bound by any Laws in which we have no voice, or Representation.

That your Sex are Naturally Tyrannical is a Truth so thoroughly established as to admit of no dispute, but such of you as wish to be happy willingly give up the harsh title of Master for the more tender and endearing one of Friend. Why then, not put it out of the power of the vicious and the Lawless to use us with cruelty and indignity with impunity. Men of Sense in all Ages abhor those customs which treat us only as the vassals of your Sex. Regard us then as Beings placed by providence under your protection and in immitation of the Supreem Being make use of that power only for our happiness.

### John Adams to Abigail Adams

**14 Apr. 1776**

You ask where the Fleet is. The inclosed Papers will inform you. You ask what Sort of Defence Virginia can make. I believe they will make an able Defence. Their Militia and minute Men have been some time employed in training them selves, and they have Nine Battalions of regulars as they call them, maintained among them, under good Officers, at the Continental Expence. They have set up a Number of Manufactories of Fire Arms, which are busily employed. They are tolerably supplied with Powder, and are successful] and assiduous, in making Salt Petre. Their neighboring Sister or rather Daughter Colony of North Carolina, which is a warlike Colony, and has several Battalions at the Continental Expence, as well as a pretty good Militia, are ready to assist them, and they are in very good Spirits, and seem determined to make a brave Resistance.-The Gentry are very rich, and the common People very poor. This Inequality of Property, gives an Aristocratical Turn to all their Proceedings, and occasions a strong Aversion in their Patricians, to Common Sense. But the Spirit of these Barons, is coming down, and it must submit. . . .

As to your extraordinary Code of Laws, I cannot but laugh. We have been told that our Struggle has loosened the bands of Government every where. That Children and Apprentices were disobedient-that schools and Colledges were grown turbulent—that Indians slighted their Guardians and Negroes grew insolent to their Masters. But your Letter was the first Intimation that another Tribe more numerous and powerfull than all the rest were grown discontented —This is rather too coarse a Compliment but you are so saucy, I wont blot it out,

Depend upon it, We know better than to repeal our Masculine systems. Altho they are in full Force, you know they are little more than Theory. We dare not exert our Power in its full Latitude. We are obliged to go fair, and softly, and in Practice you know We are the subjects, We have only the Name of Masters, and rather than give up this, which would compleatly subject Us to the Despotism of the Peticoat, I hope General Washington, and all our brave Heroes would fight. I am sure every good Politician would plot, as long as he would against Despotism, Empire, Monarchy, Aristocracy, Oligarchy, or Ochlocracy.—A fine Story indeed. 1 begin to think the Ministry as deep as they are wicked. After stirring up Tories, Landjobbers, Trimmers, Bigots, Canadians, Indians, Negroes, Hanoverians, Hessians, Russians, Irish Roman Catholics, Scotch Renegades, at last they have stimulated the to demand new Privileges and threaten to rebell.

---

Source: Charles Francis Adams, *Familiar Letters of John Adams and His Wife Abigail Adams, During the Revolution: With a Memoir of Mrs. Adams* (1876), 148–150, 153–155.

## 15.2. A Continental Army Soldier Explains Why the Soldiers Mutinied

*Joseph Plumb Martin was a Connecticut soldier in the Continental Army through most of the American Revolution. Long after the war ended, he penned the most detailed and valuable account of the common soldiers' military service in the war. The following excerpt provides his eyewitness report on the Connecticut Line Mutiny of 1780, one of several mutinies in 1780 and 1781 by soldiers facing starvation in the army. What did Martin think of the officers? How did the officers try to break up the mutinies? (Spelling and punctuation are modernized.)*

We left Westfield about the 25th of May and went to Basking Ridge to our old winter cantonments. We did not reoccupy the huts which we built, but some others that the troops had left, upon what account I have forgotten. Here the monster Hunger still attended us. He was not to be shaken off by any efforts we could use, for here was the old story of starving, as rife as ever. We had entertained some hopes that when we had left the lines and joined the main army, we should fare a little better, but we found that there was no betterment in the case. For several days after we rejoined the army, we got a little musty bread and a little beef about every other day, but this lasted only a short time and then we got nothing at all. The men were now exasperated beyond endurance; they could not stand it any longer; they saw no other alternative but to starve to death, or break up the army, give all up, and go home. This was a hard matter for the soldiers to think upon. They were truly patriotic; they loved their country, and they had already suffered everything short of death in its cause; and now, after such extreme hardships to give up all was too much, but to starve to death was too much also.

*(Continued)*

What was to be done? Here was the army starved and naked, and there their country sitting still and expecting the army to do notable things while fainting from sheer starvation. All things considered, the army was not to be blamed. Reader, suffer what we did and you will say so too.

We had borne as long as human nature could endure, and to bear longer we considered folly. Accordingly, one pleasant day the men spent the most of their time upon the parade growling like soreheaded dogs. At evening roll call they began to show their dissatisfaction by snapping at the officers and acting contrary to their orders. After their dismissal from the parade, the officers went as usual to their quarters, except the adjutant, who happened to remain, giving details for next day's duty to the orderly sergeants, or some other business, when the men (none of whom had left the parade) began to make him sensible that they had something in train. He said something that did not altogether accord with the soldiers' ideas of propriety, one of the men retorted; the adjutant called him a mutinous rascal, or some such epithet, and then left the parade. This man, then stamping the butt of his musket upon the ground, as much as to say, I am in a passion, called out, "Who will parade with me?" The whole regiment immediately fell in and formed.

We had made no plans for our future operations, but while we were consulting how to proceed, the 4th Regiment, which lay on our left, formed and came and paraded with us. We now concluded to go in a body to the other two regiments that belonged to our brigade and induce them to join with us. These regiments lay 40 or 50 rods in front of us, with a brook and bushes between. We did not wish to have anyone in particular to command, lest he might be singled out for a court martial . . . we therefore gave directions to the drummers to give certain signals on the drums; at the first signal we shouldered our arms, at the second we faced, at the third we began our march to join with the other two regiments, and went off with music playing.

By this time our officers had obtained knowledge of our military maneuvering, and some of them had run across the brook by a nearer way than we had taken (it being now quite dark) and informed the officers of those regiments of our approach and supposed intentions. The officers ordered their men to parade as quick as possible *without* arms. When that was done, they stationed a camp guard, that happened to be near at hand, between the men and their huts, which prevented them from entering and taking their arms, which they were very anxious to do. Colonel Meigs' of the 6th Regiment exerted himself to prevent his men from obtaining their arms until he received a severe wound in his side by a bayonet in the scuffle, which cooled his courage at the time. He said he had always considered himself the soldier's friend and thought the soldiers regarded him as such, but had reason now to conclude he might be mistaken. Colonel Meigs was truly an excellent man and a brave officer. The man, whoever he was that wounded him, doubtless had no particular grudge against him; it was dark and the wound was given, it is probable, altogether unintentionally.

When we found the officers had been too crafty for us, we returned with grumbling instead of music, the officers following in the rear growling in concert. One of the men in the rear calling out, "Halt in front," the officers seized upon him like wolves on a sheep and dragged him out of the ranks, intending to make an example of him for being a "mutinous rascal"; but the bayonets of the men pointing at their breasts, as thick as hatchel' teeth, compelled them quickly to relinquish their hold of him. We marched back to our own parade and then formed again. The officers now began to coax us to disperse to our quarters, but that had no more effect upon us than their threats. One of them slipped away into the bushes, and after a short time returned, counterfeiting to have come directly from headquarters. Said he, "There is good news for you, boys, there has just arrived a large drove of cattle for the army." But this piece of finesse would not avail. All the answer he received for his labor was, "Go and butcher them," or some such slight expression.

The lieutenant colonel of the 4th Regiment now came on to the parade. He could persuade *his* men, he said, to go peaceably to their quarters. After a good deal of palaver he ordered them to shoulder their arms, but the men taking no notice of him or his order he fell into a violent passion, threatening them with the bitterest punishmen0t if they did not immediately obey his orders. After spending a whole quiver of the arrows of his rhetoric, he again ordered them to shoulder their arms, but he met with the same success that he did at the first trial. He therefore gave up the contest as hopeless and left us

and walked off to his quarters, chewing the cud of resentment all the way, and how much longer I neither knew nor cared. The rest of the officers, after they found that they were likely to meet with no better success than the colonel, walked off likewise to their huts.

While we were under arms, the Pennsylvania troops, who lay not far from us, were ordered under arms and marched off their parades upon, as they were told, a secret expedition. They had surrounded us, unknown to either us or themselves (except the officers) . . . they inquired of some of the stragglers, what was going on among the Yankees? Being informed that they had mutinied on account of the scarcity of provisions, "Let us join them," said they, "let us join the Yankees; they are good fellows, and have no notion of lying here like fools and starving." Their officers needed no further hinting; the troops were quickly ordered back to their quarters from fear that they would join in the same song with the Yankees. We knew nothing of all this for some time afterwards.

After our officers had left us to our own option, we dispersed to our huts and laid by our arms of our own accord, but the worm of hunger gnawing so keen kept us from being entirely quiet. We therefore still kept upon the parade in groups, venting our spleen at our country and government, then at our officers, and then at ourselves for our imbecility in staying there and starving in detail for an ungrateful people who did not care what became of us, so they could enjoy themselves while we were keeping a cruel enemy from them.

*(Continued)*

While we were thus venting our gall against we knew not who, Colonel Stewart of the Pennsylvania line, with two or three other officers of that line, came to us and questioned us respecting our unsoldierlike conduct (as he termed it). We told him he needed not to be informed of the cause of our present conduct, but that we had borne till we considered further forbearance pusillanimity; that the times, instead of mending, were growing worse; and finally that we were determined not to bear or forbear much longer. We were unwilling to desert the cause of our country, when in distress; that we knew her cause involved our own; but what signified our perishing in the act of saving her, when that very act would inevitably destroy us, and she must finally perish with us.

"Why do you not go to your officers," said he, "and complain in a regular manner?" We told him we had repeatedly complained to them, but they would not hear us. "Your officers," said he, "are gentlemen; they *will* attend to you. I know them; they cannot refuse to hear you. But," said he, "your officers suffer as much as you do. We all suffer. The officers have no money to purchase supplies with any more than the private men have, and if there is nothing in the public store we must fare as hard as you. I have no other resources than you have to depend upon; I had not a sixpence to purchase a partridge that was offered me the other day. Besides," said he, "you know not how much you injure your own characters by such conduct. You Connecticut troops have won immortal honor to yourselves the winter past by your perseverance, patience, and bravery, and now you are shaking it off at your heels. But I will go and see your officers, and talk with them myself." He went, but what the result was I never knew. This Colonel Stewart was an excellent officer, much beloved and respected by the troops of the line he belonged to. He possessed great personal beauty; the Philadelphia ladies styled him *the Irish Beauty.*

Source: Joseph Plumb Martin, *Narrative of Some of the Adventures, Dangers and Sufferings of a Revolutionary Soldier . . . 1830.* Taken from *Ordinary Courage: The Revolutionary War Adventures of Joseph Plumb Martin,* edited by James Kirby Martin (1993).

# Bibliography

Calhoon, Robert M. *The Loyalists in Revolutionary America, 1760–1781* (1973).

Calloway, Colin G. *The American Revolution in Indian Country: Crisis and Diversity in Native American Communities* (1995).

Dull, Jonathan R. *A Diplomatic History of the American Revolution* (1985).

Egerton, Douglas R. *Death or Liberty: African Americans and the American Revolution* (2008).

Frey, Sylvia R. *Water from the Rock: Black Resistance in a Revolutionary Age* (1991).

Griffin, Patrick. *American Leviathan: Empire, Nation and Revolutionary Frontier* (2006).

Hall, Leslie. *Land and Allegiance in Revolutionary Georgia* (2001).

Hoffman, Ronald, Thad. W. Tate, and Peter J. Albert, eds. *An Uncivil War: The Southern Backcountry During the American Revolution* (1985)

Mayer, Holly A. *Belonging to the Army: Camp Followers and Community During the American Revolution* (1996).

Morris, Richard B. *The Peacemakers: The Great Powers and American Independence* (1965).

Neimeyer, Charles P. *America Goes to War: A Social History of the Continental Army* (1996).

Norton, Mary Beth. *Liberty's Daughters: The Revolutionary Experience of American Women, 1750–1800* (1980).

Royster, Charles. *A Revolutionary People at War: The Continental Army and American Character, 1775–1783* (1979).

Skemp, Sheila. *Benjamin and William Franklin: Father and Son, Patriot and Loyalist* (1994).

Wilcox, William B. *Portrait of a General: Sir Henry Clinton in the War of Independence* (1964).

Young, Alfred, ed. *Beyond the American Revolution: Explorations in the History of American Radicalism* (1993).

Young, Alfred. *Masquerade: The Life and Times of Deborah Sampson, Continental Soldier* (2004).

# INDEX